Flashing Back: Coming of Age in the American 1960s

A Memoir of My Somewhat Misspent Youth

W. Eugene Johnson

COPYRIGHT

Copyright © 2019 W. Eugene Johnson
Front and Back Cover Design & Original Art © W. Eugene Johnson
Cover Photo Credit: Maria Billitier Kingston
All Rights Reserved.

ISBN:9781981032075

This is a work of creative non-fiction. While situations depicted are real, some names have been changed for reasons of privacy.

With the exception of short quotes used in critical reviews, no part of this book may be reproduced in any manner, stored in any retrieval system, electronic, digital, mechanical, photocopying, recording in any form without the prior written permission of the author.

Portions of this work have previously appeared in print:

Texas Panhandle Encounter was published in the 1988 edition of *Frameworks*, the literary magazine for the University of Pittsburgh, Bradford, PA, campus earning a first prize for fiction.

Rock 'n Roll Is Here to Stay is excerpted from a 1995 issue of The Highland Gazette magazine.

Buddy was originally published in a 2006 special section of *The Bradford Era* on the Vietnam Moving wall coming to Smethport, PA.

That Day originally appeared in *The Bradford Era* on the 50th anniversary of John Kennedy's assassination.

Portions of *Guitar Obsession* are excerpted from *The Highland Gazette* magazine.

FAIR USE

While this is a work of creative non-fiction, it is also a first-hand social history of a particular demographic at a unique time in the American 20th century and, as such, serves an instructional purpose suitable for American Studies. In order to adequately portray the spirit of the American 1960s counterculture, articles, excerpts, clippings and scans from underground newspapers and comix have been included that portray the attitudes, passions, ideals and aesthetics of the 60s generation as well as illustrating the social effects resulting from the interaction of the freak media, the counterculture, and society at large.

"Fair Use" rule applies to excerpts taken from the following defunct periodicals sourced from https://voices.revealdigital.com/:

San Francisco Good Times © The Trystero Company. Archives and Special Collections of the Thomas J. Dodd Research Center, University of Connecticut.

Vietnam GI © Vietnam GI Committee. Archives and Special Collections of the Thomas J. Dodd Research Center, University of Connecticut.

The Old Mole published by Old Mole chapter of the Students for a Democratic Society, Cambridge, MA, no visible copyright. University of Michigan.

The Berkeley Tribe © Red Mountain Tribe, Berkeley, CA. Berkeley Historical Society and Michigan State University.

The Berkeley Barb © Berkeley Barb. Berkeley Historical Society, UC San Diego Library, The Long Haul, Berkeley California, Free Speech Movement Archives, Michigan State University.

Illustrations from these Underground Comix appear here under the Fair Use rule. These are sourced and scanned from the author's private collections.

"Zap #4," Apex Novelties, 1970: cover illustration by Victor Moscoso;

"Mickey Mouse Meets the Air Pirates #1" by Dan O'Neil, Hell Comics

"Doings of Dealer McDope" drawn by Dave Sheridan, *Mother's Oats Comix* 1969 Rip Off Press.

Artwork for Scoop Nisker's bootleg album cover, Greg Irons 1970.

CONTENTS

Copyright -- ii
Contents -- iv
Acknowledgements --- x
Dedication -- xi
For Buddy --- xii
Words to Live By --- xiii
Author's Note --- xiv
The Old Curmudgeon's Sage Advice ----------------------------------- xv
Prologue --- 17
Chapter 1: Freaking Out -- 23
Chapter 2: Life on Route 6 --- 28
    Family --- 29
    School Daze --- 41
    The Polio Epidemic --- 46
    Rock n' Roll is Here to Stay ------------------------------------- 47
    My Little Sister -- 49
Chapter 3: Losing My Mind To Save My Soul ----------------------- 51
    The Mystery/Misery of Religion ------------------------------- 51
    Sister Mary Mindfuck -- 59
    Altar Service --- 66
    Spanking the Monkey -- 69
    Immaculate Deception --- 74
    Thou Shalt Not Have an Unauthorized Orgasm! ------------ 76
    Cocksucking in the Sacristy ------------------------------------- 78
Chapter 4: Academic Discipline -- 81
Chapter 5: The Kennedy Years --- 89
    A Shiny Brand New Decade ------------------------------------ 89
    The Missile Gap --- 92
    And Thus He Prophesied -- 93
    Missile Crisis -- 96
    Mr. DuSchnozzle -- 97
Chapter 6: *That* Day -- 103
Chapter 7: Beatlemania Onward -------------------------------------- 108
    Drum Line -- 109
    Honky-Tonkin' --- 110
    Oh My God! I Broke Her! -------------------------------------- 111
    The Star Spangled Lie & The Class of 1965 ---------------- 112
    Near Death Experience --- 113
Chapter 8: Like a Bug on a Windshield ------------------------------ 115
    Can't Hack the Math -- 115
    Beer Bust 101 -- 116

Chapter 9: The Endless Boogie – Part 1 ---------------------------------- 119
    The Bradford Crew -- 120
    While Sgt. Pepper Played ------------------------------- 122
    Back to the Hallowed Halls of Academia --------------- 123
    My Pad -- 124
    Rock and Roll All Night --------------------------------- 125
    Marissa --- 128
    I'm Living in a Whorehouse? --------------------------- 130
Chapter 10: Buddy -- 133
    Classmate, Friend, & Madman Extraordinaire! ------- 133
    AWOL --- 135
    The Bad News -- 137
    Sgt. Campbell -- 143
    Buddy Looks Back at Us -------------------------------- 146
    Fondly Remembered ------------------------------------- 149
Chapter 11: The Endless Boogie - Part 2 --------------------------- 152
    Athsmador Abuse -- 152
    The Oracle -- 154
    The Spring Frolic --- 154
    Neal Gets Busted --- 156
Chapter 12: They Want Us to do *What?* ----------------------- 159
    All Hell Breaks Loose ----------------------------------- 163
    After Action Report ------------------------------------- 164
    The Trimester Ends ------------------------------------- 165
Chapter 13: Boston -- 169
    The Scene -- 169
    The Mayor of Shepherd Avenue ------------------------ 170
    Smoke-in on the Boston Common! --------------------- 171
    Both Doors Flew Back! --------------------------------- 176
    Dropping Acid --- 178
    14 Shepherd Ave. --------------------------------------- 179
    Take two, You'll Get Off For Sure! -------------------- 182
    Tripping with Trotsky ---------------------------------- 182
    Partying With The Huns -------------------------------- 187
    The Boston Tea Party ---------------------------------- 187
    Led Zeppelin --- 188
    Runaways -- 190
    Edgar's Hearse -- 192
    Kenny Baird --- 193
    Partying with the Disciples ---------------------------- 194
Chapter 14: Crisis of Conscience -------------------------------- 197
    The War -- 197

Westmoreland's Incompetence --------------------------- 199
Blood and Politics ------------------------------------- 199
The War Church --- 202
Me and My Uncle -- 204
The Boston Draft Resistance Group ---------------------- 207
Road Trip! --- 212
Seeing The Shrink -------------------------------------- 217
Time is Running Out ------------------------------------ 219
Their Game. Their Rules. I win. Fuck 'em! ------------ 221

Chapter 15: George Wallace Must Die! ---------------------------- 230
Drug-Addled Psycho-mutants ----------------------------- 230
Chemically Enhanced Lunacy ----------------------------- 233
A Rolling Clusterfuck ---------------------------------- 235
What Kind of Dope Was Artie Doing? ------------------- 238

Chapter 16: Fall & Winter 1968-69 ------------------------------- 239
Santa's Hippie Helpers --------------------------------- 239
Acid in the Alleghenies -------------------------------- 241
We All Live in a Yellow Submarine --------------------- 244

Chapter 17: The Heroin Plague ---------------------------------- 247
Follen Street -- 247
Smack City --- 249
The Shit Rolls Downhill -------------------------------- 251
Marijuana by Mail -------------------------------------- 251
Needle Freakz -- 251
Cozmic Dave -- 255
Cocaine Blues -- 256
Dirty Deals Done Cheap --------------------------------- 257
Who's That Narking at my Door? ----------------------- 259
Connie --- 263

Chapter 18: Getting Our Kicks On Route 66 ---------------------- 266
Time to Go --- 266
Texas Panhandle Encounter ------------------------------ 268
Santa Fe --- 271
Bad Weed & Paranoia ------------------------------------ 272
Where'd Joe go? -- 276

Chapter 19: The Left Coast ------------------------------------- 280
Arrival -- 280
The Haight-Ashbury Switchboard ------------------------- 281
Survival --- 281
J.C. Burkhouse --- 283
Stephen Gaskin and The Monday Night Class --------- 285
Heroin Karma --- 290
Faye --- 294
The Captain -- 295

  3,4,5-trimethoxyphenethylamine ------------------------ 296
  Stanyan Street --- 298
  Michael Ferguson --------------------------------------- 303
  Tommy and George ------------------------------------ 305
  Operation Intercept ------------------------------------ 306
  The Holy Man Jam ------------------------------------- 309
Chapter 20: The Music -- 310
  Rock n' Roll Comes of Age ------------------------- 310
  The Fillmore West ------------------------------------- 315
  The Altamont Free Concert -------------------------- 317
  Meeting Led Zeppelin -------------------------------- 321
  Guitar Players I Have Known ----------------------- 323
  Radio Ray -- 324
  Albert Shuffle --- 324
  Guitar Curtis -- 325
  Virgil --- 326
  Lefty Lewie -- 328
  Homecoming -- 329
  Jacob's Ladder --- 330
Chapter 21: The Emergence of Freak Media ----------------------- 332
  KSAN -- 336
  Moratoriums -- 337
  Earwitness to the Birth of Topless Radio --------- 339
  The Straight Dope on Street Dope ---------------- 340
  Underground Newspapers --------------------------- 342
  Mellow Yellow --- 344
  The Empire Strikes Back ---------------------------- 347
  The San Francisco Good Times ------------------- 349
  Underground Comix ---------------------------------- 352
  Sketches From My Past ------------------------------ 358
Chapter 22: Nixon's Theater of Blood ------------------------------ 366
  Kent State, Jackson State & South Carolina State ---- 366
  Hell and Revolution ----------------------------------- 370
  The [Bullshit!] War on Drugs ----------------------- 372
  The Park Station Bombing --------------------------- 373
  The Marin County Civic Center Shootout -------- 375
  The Weathermen --------------------------------------- 375
  The Symbionese Liberation Army ----------------- 376
  Revolutionary Violence of the Era ---------------- 376
Chapter 23: Life in the City -- 378
  Whole Lotta Shakin' Goin' On! -------------------- 378
  Programming and Systems Institute -------------- 379

The Mission District --- 381
The R. L. Polk Company -- 383
What Goes Around Will Bite You In The Ass --------- 385
Boegershausen Hardware -------------------------------------- 386
The Clientele --- 389
Walter Johnson --- 391
Customer Relations 101 -- 392
Russian Naval Officer's Club --------------------------------- 394
Naked Hippie Chicks! -- 395
Norm -- 396
Is Irving There? -- 397
The "Oak Street Sniper" & My '42 Dodge ------------- 398
Corner Groceries --- 401
Watergate --- 403
Matrimonial Bli$$ -- 406

Chapter 24: Transcendental Medication ------------------------------- 410
Why Drugs? --- 411
Entheogens --- 414
Reefer Madness -- 418
LSD --- 422
Tripping -- 425
Seeing Sounds, Hearing Colors --------------------------- 429
Acid Telepathy -- 429
Communion --- 431
The Nature of It All --- 432
Psychedelic Drugs FAQ -- 435
A Window On The Universe ---------------------------------- 441

Chapter 25: Aftermath --- 443
San Francisco -- 443
Anita --- 444
Mock Riot Retrospective --------------------------------------- 445
Reflecting on Marissa --- 447
Family --- 447
Becoming a Recovering Catholic -------------------------- 452
Bill Wassam -- 455
Draft Dodging Son-of-a-Bitch -------------------------------- 457
MacNamara --- 458
The Myopia of the Peace Movement ---------------------- 459
Gray Areas -- 460
Honoring the Dead --- 461
Too Tall Paul --- 462
World View -- 465

Finis --- 467
About the Author --- 468

Photo of the author by Maria Billitier Kingston, fall 1968

ACKNOWLEDGEMENTS

I owe a debt to the late Linda Leshinski Underhill, my writing instructor at the University of Pittsburgh, Bradford Campus who told me "Writing is the most difficult of all the arts because you have to create an entire universe out of black marks on paper." True that. I also want to thank the late author, David McCain, for the advice and encouragement he gave in his creative non-fiction writing workshop in 1990. I could not have completed this work without it. I send a big "thank you" to those who have helped me with this endeavor: my wife for having married someone as insane as myself and tolerated me for over four decades, Maria Billitier Kingston for a lifetime of friendship and decades of encouragement, harassment, and support regarding this book, as well as the photo that appears on the cover; Brent Vossler, Dennis Maynard, Chris Murray, Josephine Feit, Katy Mayo Nichols, Dan Nichols, Chuck Daniels, Dave Lamborn, Lew Doss, John Burns, D. T. Lowery, David Sherman, Caren Wallerstein Belby, Eric Hurwitz, Don Thomas, Andrew Spore, Georg Lindy, Ron Lattin, Terry Palmer, Harold Anglovich, Ross Porter, Mark Caminite and all the others I have pestered about long forgotten stuff over the decades it took me to write this.

Jeannie Loudon and David O'Brien played a very important part in my life back in the day. We have long since lost touch. I wish I knew where they are today.

I wish I could thank these dear friends who have passed on who were a part of this back in the day and are part of this work: Anita Polishuk, Robyn Doss, Bill Wassam, Mike Quirk, Neal Ochs and Jay Peterio.

The biggest thanks goes to the U.S. Central Intelligence Agency for purchasing the entire world's supply of LSD in 1951–ten pounds–and subsequently unleashing it on America. At 100 μg (that's 100 *millionths of a gram!*) a dose...that's...45,400,000 doses; *enough trips to open the world's largest travel agency!* Without it this book would have never been possible. Or necessary!

DEDICATION

For Baby-Boomers, the American 1960s were like a long tunnel we all had to enter. Not everyone came out the other end. I dedicate this work to the memory of nineteen young men from McKean County, Pennsylvania who lost their young lives in the savage waste and slaughter of Vietnam.

FOR BUDDY

My beloved friend,
It has been twenty years
Since I received the sad news
That, while saving the lives of others,
You lost your own in Vietnam
Never has a week gone by
And, many times, not a day has passed
When I have not thought of you
And our friendship.
I sought out your name
Chiseled into the black granite wall,
Touched it with my hands,
Viewed it through my tears.
Though the years may pass
I shall never forget you
And our bond.

– © W. Eugene Johnson 1/25/88

WORDS TO LIVE BY

"Speak your mind. Even if you are a minority of one, the truth is still the truth." – Mahatma Gandhi

"Never attribute to malice that which can be properly ascribed to incompetence." – Napoleon

"Those who can make you believe absurdities can make you commit atrocities." –Voltaire

"Seek always the path of least destruction." – Buddhist aphorism

"Life got a lot better after I figured that karma shit out!" – Randy Lee Miles

"Make the most of the Indian Hemp Seed and sow it everywhere." – George Washington

AUTHOR'S NOTE

I write in a candid (that means "profane") conversational style, I may dangle a participle or split an infinitive here and there. Sentence fragments. I concur with the late Saint George of Carlin there are no "bad" words, certainly no obscene ones.[1] Words are black marks on paper, nothing more. It is the ideas they represent that give them power making them loved and making them feared.

This raw language in my book contains pejoratives of various sorts. I present them without asterisks and always attribute them to others, they are never my own. I will not self-censor or sugar-coat the truth, however "offensive" it may be. Complaints will be ignored.

This book serves as my personal memoir as well as a historical, first-hand account of a unique period in 20th Century American culture. In an effort to capture the *zeitgeist* I have included articles, clippings and scans from underground publications of the day, claiming "Fair Use" under U.S. Copyright Law. They effectively illustrate the attitudes and mores of the 1960s counterculture as well as forming a content review of the publications involved.

While some of these are directly addressed in the text, many are presented without comment just to illustrate the spirit of the times and the mores of the counterculture.

This work contains accounts of illegal activities and risky behavior. This is a memoir, not an instruction manual. For Chrissakes, be sensible.

---

[1] Not that obscenities do not exist. As of 2019, examples of obscenities would be endless wars of choice – not necessity – waged for financial gain. Add to that the kidnapping, maltreatment and abuse – including deaths - of children in U.S. Government run concentration camps. Those are red-white-and-blue obscenities directly in opposition to the principles upon which this nation was founded.

THE OLD CURMUDGEON'S SAGE ADVICE

The Merriam-Webster Dictionary defines curmudgeon as:

1. (archaic) miser and
2. a crusty, ill-tempered, and usually old, man.

Having passed the age of seventy, I am now endowed with Full Curmudgeonhood and accordingly entitled to all rights, privileges, and rewards pertaining thereto. I have license to expound at length on anything I wish while being as cynical, profane and politically incorrect as I please without giving a rat's ass what anyone else may think. You have been warned.

I have seen some shit happen and been involved in some shit happening. These observations form "The Old Curmudgeon's Sage Advice." What started out as an exercise in cynical smartassery ended up revealing some stunning truths.

1. You never know when or with whom you will fall in love. Period.
2. You may not recognize person or event upon which the entire course of your life pivots until decades after the fact, if ever.
3. Shit happens. You have to deal with it even if it's not your shit. Hell no, it's not fair! Don't feel special, it happens to everybody.
4. Learn the difference between belief and knowledge. *Beliefs* are information. You can change beliefs like you change your socks, there is no consequence. *Knowledge* has consequence. It is ex-

periential. Once something is *known*, it cannot be *un*-known. *Knowledge* changes your life forever.

5. Happiness and friendships are fleeting. Appreciate it when you are blessed with them. Let others enjoy theirs.

6. *Always* question authority. Do not let career parasites – preachers, bankers and politicians – rob you of your free will, your money, your rights, or *your life!*

7. Truth and spirit are free and non-exclusive, gained only through active pursuit. Critical thinking is essential. Trust your inner voice.[1] If sounds like bullshit, it probably is.

8. Life is about choices. Moral choices require courage. Be compassionate and seek the path of least destruction. What you don't do is as important as what you do. Karma is unerring and relentless.

9. You are unique. You need nobody's permission or approval to be who and how you are. It's OK to love yourself for that. It helps you understand and be compassionate with others.

10. We all have a certain number of assholes we have to deal with before we die. It's nothing personal, that's just the way it is. Each one brings you closer to fulfilling your lifetime quota. Yes, it's a challenge!

11. It doesn't cost anything to be nice to others.

12. VOTE!

---

[1] That's the one that, when you ignore it, you always end up losing money or getting arrested. Conscience.

PROLOGUE

This work is about my experiences and my feelings while coming of age in a most passionate and turbulent time. It is also about the Baby Boomers, the Vietnam generation, and the events, attitudes (and chemicals!) that shaped our collective worldview.

I refer to this work as "A Memoir My Somewhat Misspent Youth," but not because I have regrets about what I did. The institutionally approved method of living your life, as we were taught, was to believe *everything* puked at you by established authority figures. Make up your mind what you want to do with your life by the age of eighteen, but *only* if it follows the program society has laid out for you. Your guidance counselor will help you find your proper pigeon-hole. Never deviate. Questioning authority is intellectual disobedience and will turn you into a communist. Thinking for yourself is unnecessary. Get a haircut.

I "misspent" my youth by living my life as it happened, letting it take me where it would, learning about the world and learning about myself. It has been a Zen journey full of wonder, chaos, heartbreak, happiness, and an incredible array of amazing people from whom I learned so much. I danced the kozmic boogie!

Born in 1947 in rural Pennsylvania, I am part of the of the postwar baby boom, the fruit of the exuberance of the generation that saw the largest armed conflict in history. At 72 million, we were the pig in the python, a swollen population demographic, a bumper crop of future consumers conceived in the optimism of a booming postwar economy.

We grew up with Howdy Doody, the Mickey Mouse Club, Gunsmoke, Elvis, Buddy Holly, Little Richard, Dylan, and the Beatles. We partied like there was no tomorrow with no thought of getting old. Born into the Cold War, we were the Generation of the Bomb. We learned to duck and cover in first grade. It seemed far more likely that we would be vaporized in a global orgasm of thermonuclear stupidity than die of old age.

About as spoiled as a generation could get, we were indulged by our parents who had endured The Depression. They wanted us to have what they never did.

Coming of age in the 1960s, we were blindsided by a massive cultural upheaval. The smoldering social injustices of institutionalized racism burst into flames and cities burned. One by one, assassins murdered our heroes, leaders to whom we looked, individuals with charisma and vision who could make a positive difference in the world, those who held out the prospect of hope for a generation rapidly becoming lost.

The Vietnam War polarized America. You either embraced the war or despised it. There was no middle ground. To some, Vietnam was America's effort to save a fledgling democracy – and the world – from the insidious spread of international communism. To others, Vietnam was a fraud perpetrated upon the American people by the military/industrial complex to generate billions of dollars in war profits with zero regard for anything else. Dead boys in uniform not old enough to need to shave every day paid the butcher's bill. The spirit of the time demanded that you make a choice. You *became* that choice with a passion born of righteous conviction.

The war consumed hundreds of billions of dollars, more than fifty-eight thousand American lives and millions of Asian lives. It rent the social and political fabric of our nation. Drugs, revolutionary violence and associated lunacy consumed many others.

We found ourselves caught in a maelstrom of social and political social chaos. There were two diametrically opposed psycho-social forces at work: the Vietnam War and LSD. Absolutes disappeared. There was no clear cut right or wrong. No one could give satisfactory answers, not our government, not our teachers, not our churches, none of them. We had to find our own way.

Psychedelic consciousness developed as an alternative to the mainstream of American culture. The established order was sending its young men off to bleed and die in a foreign jungle war without giving any coherent reasons, except star-spangled bullshit. Vietnam became a modern day Moloch, a man-made idol born of the avarice of rich men, the denizens of corporate board rooms, a God of Commerce devouring America's children in its fiery belly by the tens of thousands. Parents willingly made the sacrifice.

Getting high was a revolutionary act because it threw aside the red-white-and-blue-whistle-Yankee-doodle-flag-waving-bullet-head-gung-ho-mom-dad-buddy-and-sis-motherhood-and-apple-pie frame of mind. It freed you to look at things from a different point of view. To *dare* to *think differently*, to embrace alternative values, to experiment in consciousness, yes, *this* was *revolution!* And it, too, became an excess and generated casualties.

Our parents couldn't understand us. The political system disenfranchised us. What we were told was morality we saw as hypocrisy. We acted on the dictates of conscience. It was all we had. It was all we needed.

The early 1960s were full of optimism: JFK, the Peace Corps, and the feeling that America was on the right track to ultimate greatness. The late 60s turned into a gonzo-acid-tripping-110-decibel-full-tilt-boogie-psychedelic-rock &-roll odyssey, an amalgam of war, peace, politics, drugs, birth, death, revolution, and mysticism, all recombining and bursting forth in a kaleidoscopic myriad of cultural mutations. Anything seemed possible. Nothing was off limits. Every day was a new social experiment. Every act went against accepted conventions. Every day and in every way it was flat-out "Fuck the system!"

It was a time of music and peace, of death and violence, of fear and love, a time to turn inward, a time to run free, a time to feel passion in everything. It was the age of the guitar as loud as God's own voice pounding out the rhythm, the wail and scream, the psychedelic dreams, the electric rage of a generation convinced it was going to perish by thermonuclear obliteration.

It was a time of Timothy Leary, Abbie Hoffman, John Lennon, Stokely Carmichael, Huey P. Newton, and H. Rap Brown. It was the era of Watts, Laos, Vietnam, Haight-Ashbury, Columbia, Khe Sanh, Hue, Kent State, My Lai. It was the age of JFK, LBJ, FBI, CIA, MIA, KIA, POW, VC, LSD, STP, DMT, DMZ, CORE, SDS, SNCC. It was the season of grass, acid, Zen, Aum, Hare Krishna, tantra, karma, dharma, nirvana. It was a time of politics: Republican, Democrat, Peace and Freedom, Radical, Panthers, La Raza.

We saw teenage jungle warriors, boy soldiers with sucking chest wounds, and the body count on the six o'clock news, our schoolmates coming home in flag draped (reusable) aluminum coffins.

It was a reckless time, undisciplined and so very passionate with the zeal born of the righteousness of the young. We were idealistic, and– almost hopelessly–naïve.

Music was a massive social conspiracy, a secret language, a hidden means of communication that was entirely out in the open, indecipherable by the unhip.

We smoked dope, danced and made love to the music of the Beatles, the Rolling Stones, the Grateful Dead, the Doors, the Jefferson Airplane, Crosby Stills & Nash, Janis Joplin, Jimi Hendrix and countless others.

Dance halls were cathedrals of psychedelic consciousness, music was communion: a rollicking Zen boogie, 12-bar satori with a walking bass line, rhythmic nirvana, disembodied consciousness without ego, no boundary between self, music, or anything else. Oneness.

We congratulated ourselves for the way we came together in love and peace at Woodstock. The Age of Aquarius seemed, indeed, at hand. And then we saw our own society reflected right back at us in ourselves with death and violence at Altamont.

We witnessed the effects of the CIA spit-roast raping America, boning her from one end by buying up the world's supply of LSD and unleashing it on the world and plowing her from the other end with cheap and deadly heroin from Southeast Asia's Golden Triangle.[1]

It was as easy to score smack[2] as it was to breathe. People injected death as if they were shooting up God.

A generation was being devoured piecemeal by a war, survivors wandering aimlessly through America, shell shocked by upheaval in a society gone mad with violence, racism, fear, drugs and madness.

It is as if our entire generation was shoved by the forces of history into the long dark tunnel that was the 1960s. Many never made it through. But if and when you *did* come out the other end, by God, you knew you had *lived* through something, you were a witness to forces of history.

A generation adrift on a sea of alienation, we were mystics, radicals, revolutionaries, assassins, smugglers, dopers, dealers, and assorted lunatics. We were pilgrims, Dante dosed on acid, Holden Caulfield ripped to the tits on heavy psychedelics, strangers in a *very* strange land.

---

[1] McCoy, Alfred W.' The CIA and the Politics of Heroin in Southeast Asia 1972
[2] Heroin

I felt the explosive shock wave of revolutionary violence. More than a half century on, I can still feel the loss of a friend in the charnel house of Vietnam. I saw friends return from war wounded in body and broken in spirit, haunted by and penalized for the rest of their lives because the service they so willingly gave to their country.

I found myself faced with having to make the choice of following basic principles of my upbringing or following my own conscience and risking estrangement to my family. I dropped acid, opposed the war, resisted the draft, smoked great weed and communed with my peers in the electric church of and rock n' roll.

When I remember the events I recount here, it seems like happened a million years ago. And then again, it seems like it was all just yesterday.

Some people think the 60s were all about sex, drugs, and rock n' roll. That is not true, it wasn't *all* about sex, drugs and rock n' roll. There was also war and politics. Oh, and miniskirts! The soundtrack was an incredible musical renaissance.

This book focuses the American Vietnam War era. It was for many an age of ethical challenges, of having to confront issues and situations for which we had no preparation.

This is how a country kid from a working class family growing up rural Pennsylvania, a wholesome Catholic altar boy, Boy Scout (and second prize winner of the 1960 American Legion Post #138 "Americanism Today and Tomorrow" essay contest!) went from rural Pennsylvania to the hippie ghettoes of Boston and ended up in San Francisco's Haight-Ashbury, a cynical dope smoking thoroughly psychedelicized LSD-soaked antiwar freak on a sojourn for truth, or at least some… understanding… Whatever it was, I was after it!

The human maturation process through adolescence to adulthood involves learning how to make choices. We were told about the choices available to us by our parents, teachers, religious leaders, guidance counselors and Sunday School teachers as to which paths we should, no, not should, we were *required,* take in life. Men could be anything. Women could be secretaries, nurses, teachers and housewives. And of course we believed it. After all, these people knew better than us, didn't they? And they deemed it proper. After all, they were *adults*. They knew because they *are* adults. *Adults know.* No way *they* would be feeding *us* a line of *shite*…right…?

The 60s were not a teenage fad. It was a daunting time often involving life and death decisions. The textbook answers we were brought up with on what constitutes freedom, spirit, and morality were inadequate.

For many, including me, the 60s were largely a search for spirit and truth. People being what they are, and with the help of powerful psychedelics drugs, some rather bizarre cultural mutations were produced in that search.

We remember the dope, the music, the camaraderie, and the good times. We can *never* forget the heartaches, the loss, the despair, the helplessness, the many thousands of us that, for whatever reasons, didn't survive. Those feelings come from the passion of that time, the forces of society, conscience, and consciousness that compelled us to make our choices. It was the most important time of our lives.

Each of us who went through the 60s has their own perspective. This is mine. I am no hero here, just a guy that stumbled through it. I saw stuff. I heard stuff. I did stuff. I met fantastic people from everywhere. I experienced life. It has been amazing. It has been heartbreaking It has been wonderful. And, God**damn**, the drugs were great! It's my story, and I somehow managed to still have enough functioning brain cells left to tell it! That in and of itself is remarkable.

WEJ

Hazel Hurst, PA

November 28, 2019

CHAPTER 1

FREAKING OUT

In 1968, I was the first visible hippie-freak-weirdo in Smethport, Pennsylvania, population about 1,300. According to my mother before she passed, my father used to catch a lot of shit for that. At 43, he was young to have a kid my age compared to his peers. I was older than their kids when I went weird. They would blather on within earshot of my father with "…my kids gonna do this and my kid's gonna do that and–"

At that point my father – never a man to suffer through anybody's bullshit – would interrupt with "Let me tell you something right now. You don't have the *faintest* goddamned idea *what* your kids are going to do! *None* at all." He spoke from experience.

Mom said, "They stopped giving your Dad a hard time about you when their kids turned out a lot worse!"

So they turned out *worse* than me! An interesting comment from my own mother. I didn't ask her how bad she thought I was! I know that's not what she meant, but I think it's quite amusing!

The counterculture that emerged in America in the mid-sixties was an amalgam of disaffected youth. The flower children of the Haight-Ashbury were the most visible part of it because of media exposure. They were not all of it. It was everywhere.

American youth in the 1960s were on a search for more than that which was presented to them by the establishment. Their parents grew up with the privations of the Great Depression, only to be presented with World War II.

Born into the booming postwar economy, the counterculture generation was raised in a culture of Madison Avenue materialism puked into the American consciousness by the newest communication miracle, television. While lip service was given to American freedoms, American society of the 1950s was, under the surface, a rigid, lockstep, gray flannel suit, broomstick-up-the-ass culture. Parents, teachers, and preachers told us what to believe and what – not how – to think. You by God got with the program or you were wrong, and probably a goddamned communist too!

Sen. Joseph McCarthy's anti-communist hysteria of the 1950s, infected the American psyche with his booze-fueled brand of frothing-at-the-mouth paranoid pseudo-patriotic bullshit. While American currency stated "In God we trust," the *de facto* national motto during the McCarthy era was "Better dead than red!" Civil Defense propaganda of the day gave us the message that atomic war with Russia was, not just possible, but inevitable. We were all going to be crispy fucking fried in a nuclear holocaust! Period. No doubt about it.

The emergence of rock n' roll as a pop music art form in the middle 1950s was the first crack in the American cultural monolith. Characterized by authorities as a godless communist conspiracy from hell, rock n' roll was in fact a capitalist's wet dream generating mountains of money. An emerging youth culture, something not seen before in America, coalesced around it.

This cultural schism was also reflected in movies like Marlon Brando's *"The Wild One"* and James Dean's *"Rebel Without a Cause."* Teenage rebels, "hoods" in the parlance of the time, wearing black leather jackets, jeans and engineer boots, sporting greased back pompadour haircuts, switchblades in their pockets, became the epitome of "cool."

The intellectual side of this movement, the beatniks, were precursors to the masses of alienated youth of the 1960s. They smoked pot, hung out in coffee shops, wrote poetry, listened to jazz and adopted the *patois* of urban black culture.

In the mid 60s the Beatles widened this cultural gap by making it acceptable – at least among the young – for men to have long hair. The appeal of their music spread worldwide because they had one of the best songwriting teams in history, John Lennon and Paul McCartney. The Beatles held the two top slots in the top ten for weeks at a time, sometimes the three and four top slots, and in April, 1964, they had *five* top slots!

Add to this John Kennedy's assassination and Lyndon Johnson's subsequent commitment of American ground troops to Vietnam. American soldiers started dying by the hundreds, then the thousands, then the tens of thousands. The generation designated to fight this war had no political representation since the voting age at the time was twenty-one. The assassinations of Robert Kennedy and Martin Luther King, Jr., helped fuel political alienation and a growing sense of despair among the baby boomers.

The CIA experimented with psychoactive drugs in the 1950s, having bought up the world's supply of LSD, ten pounds of it,[1] so the Soviets wouldn't get it. Unwittingly, their paranoia of the Soviets and resultant testing of LSD on human subjects brought the psychedelic experience into American society where it was taken up by artists, musicians and disaffected youth, giving rise to the counterculture.

LSD widened the crack in the American cultural monolith into a chasm. The generation gap appeared. "Don't trust anyone over thirty" became the watchword of the young. Psycho-socio cultural mutations heretofore unseen and unimagined started popping up. This was reflected in the music and alternative – called "underground" – publications of the day. Communes sprung up as young people searched for lifestyles based on values they viewed as missing in mainstream American society.

The advent of LSD and its visionary consciousness was the common experience that spawned the counterculture and bound it together. It gave young people the spiritual experience religious leaders promised but never delivered. Boomer's rejected the empty materialism of their parents' generation. Refusing to support a war against a tiny country that presented no threat whatsoever to America galvanized them into opposing it. The Baby Boomers sought contact with spirit, the essence of God that exists within us all.

Young people found out they had been lied to about marijuana. It was a harmless intoxicant and did not turn people into depraved murderers as depicted in the 1930s film *"Reefer madness."*. Smoking pot became a universal youthful conspiracy against The Man, that being any and all parents, teachers, preachers and, of course, cops! Kids always like to rebel. Smoking pot and finding it harmless proved to a generation that they were being lied to by their elders, giving them a common outlaw

---

[1]Gillespie, N. (2017). *How the CIA Turned Us onto LSD and Heroin: Secrets of America's War on Drugs. Reason. com*. Retrieved 7 March 2018, from https://reason. com/blog/2017/06/23/anthony-lappe-lsd-heroin

experience and widening what came to be known as the "generation gap." The generation gap widened into a chasm that became "fuck the system!"

Teachers, many being potheads themselves, saw seventh graders stoned during first period. While sharing a joint with a teacher back in the day, he told me about a police officer was invited to lecture a class on the dangers of drugs. The officer brought a single joint with him for the kids to pass around so they would recognize this deadly menace if and when they encountered it. He got three joints back!

Hair was the badge of membership. When longhairs encountered each other they knew each other to be kindred spirits with shared taste in weed, music, psychedelics, and opposition the war. On the road, it was easy to find a place to crash for the night among longhaired brethren. Thousands of youths hitchhiked millions of miles in search of whatever they were after. Everyone was pursuing, or trying to get away from, something.

Tens of thousands of teenagers left home fleeing abuse and other horrors, disappearing into this morass of homogenized youthful anarchy. Others fled warrants, the draft, the FBI, military authorities or private detectives.

While the media coined the term "hippie," we often referred to ourselves as "freaks." We appeared freaky to "straight" people, the non-freaks, so we owned it. Long hair, facial hair of all description, colorful clothing and outrageous costumes, beads and jewelry of all kinds, and of course, rock music, signaled our separation from the "plastic" culture, the mainstream culture, the culture of death that was sending American kids off to die in an endless war. Bob Dylan penned the line "I'm gonna grow my hair down to my feet so strange I'm gonna look like a walking mountain range."[2]

Another reason was the verb of "freak," in the sense of "freak out" which meant to get excited. To "freak" was to just let go, shed your inhibitions. A counterculture cliché was "freak freely," meaning be yourself with no limits, no guilt, no apology. There was "freak" in the sense of your "thing." "What's your freak, man?" meant "What are you into?" Underground cartoonist Gilbert Shelton developed his stoned comic book buffoons, "The Fabulous Furry Freak Brothers".

The counterculture – freak culture – was not all peace, pot, and pussy. Politically disenfranchised youth were drafted and shipped off to Vietnam leading some Boomers to adopt radical and revolutionary poli-

---

[2] From "I Shall Be Free Number 10" © Bob Dylan

tics. If the system was going to send them off to fight and die in an undeclared war against an enemy that posed no threat to America, then bring down the system.

The reaction was violence. Peaceful protests – such as the antiwar demonstrators at the 1968 Democratic national Convention in Chicago – became police riots, with citizens beaten bloody in the streets for exercising first amendment rights.[3] National Guard troops and police murdered students at Kent State University in Ohio, Jackson State College in Mississippi, and South Carolina State. The SDS (Students for a Democratic Society) became the Weather Underground committed to revolution and went around blowing things up in an effort to "bring the war back home." The SLA (Symbionese Liberation Army) kidnapped heiress Patty Hearst. Most of them died in a shootout in Los Angeles. And of course there was Charles Manson and his murderous cult of cutthroats.

The Black Panthers were not a part of the counterculture *per se*, they were a self-defense organization that formed in black communities throughout America in response to repression and violence against them by white police forces acting like occupying armies. White radicals and revolutionaries held solidarity with the Panthers.

Freak culture disappeared from the fore of American society after a few years. Some say the counterculture disappeared when it became the over-the-counter-culture, the triumph of materialism over spirit. The fact is, the Vietnam War, along with LSD the *raison d'ete* for the emergence of the counterculture, ended. Bits and pieces of freak culture live on integrated into the societal mainstream.

The truest adherents to the spirit that emerged during that chaotic time were Stephen Gaskin and the band of longhairs who founded The Farm commune in Summertown, Tennessee, the oldest commune in the U.S. It still exists today as a cooperative.

The American 1960s was the confluence of a number of social, political and spiritual factors and forces. There was a build-up to them and there is an aftermath left in their wake. This is my odyssey. The journey of a thousand miles begins with a single step. Here we go.

---

[3] The Walker Report, issued by the commission investigating the protests at the 1968 Democratic Party Convention, determined the violence to be a "police riot" directed at protesters.

CHAPTER 2

LIFE ON ROUTE 6

My birthplace is in the Allegheny Mountains of McKean County in northwestern Pennsylvania. I have spent fifty-nine of my now seventy-two years in these mountains. They are beyond beautiful; they are everywhere, they are everything, enfolding towns, villages and farms. Covered with hardwood forests, the creeks – rhymes with "sticks"– and rivers wend their way between them, the roads and highways snake their way over and around them. The seasons paint them. From the pure snowy barrenness of the winter, they turn to vibrant yellow-green hues of springtime, exploding into the lush, virid foliage of summer. Autumn infuses them with riotous tones of ocher, orange and red. Winter comes again and blankets them in white. The hills are always there, firm, secure, holding you as if cradled in the hands of God.

A summer storm is special: thunder reverberates, echoes rolling down the valleys and between the hills the way a child rolls a marble around in a box. A split second of nature's crashing fury becomes a long booming rumble forming a magnificent echoing rhythm diminishing with each repetition, lingering until the next.

I was an only child for my first nine years. The earliest place I remember is living with my parents and maternal grandmother in her old farmhouse, the Henry Wright house, on U.S. Route 6 about two miles west of the borough Smethport. The first sounds heard in the morning were the chirping birds and the syncopated chuffing of the engines from the powerhouses in the hills. In the early fifties, the oil industry was a strong economic force in the area, providing wealth for some and employment for many McKean County residents. Creaking rods radiated in all directions from these corrugated tin shanties rocking the pumping jacks to and fro, extracting the rich, dark, stinking crude oil from the earth. The cool morning mist often carried with it the smoky smell from the brick retorts of the chemical wood factory in Marvindale, six miles up the road cooked wood into charcoal. If you smelled it strongly in the morning, you knew it was going to rain.

The house itself had seven rooms on the first-floor and two rooms on the second, sided with asphalt shingles, the kind that looked like sandy colored bricks still seen on some aging structures today. An electric pump supplied us with water from a well. The pipes would sometimes freeze during the winter and my father would get out his big brass blowtorch, the kind that used white gas and roared when lit, and thaw them. A most impressive device to a small boy!

Hot water came from a large teakettle on the kitchen stove. A cast iron coal stove with isinglass windows provided us with heat, the coal scuttle always sitting next to it. I remember how much fun it was for a small mischievous boy to poke out the isinglass. Grandma was not delighted in the least! While we had hot and cold running water, the house had no sanitary plumbing, just a couple of commodes that held slop buckets which emptied daily into the privy that located behind the house.

FAMILY

My mother's side of the family can be traced to the Mayflower. We are descendants of John Billington who has the singular distinction of being the first Englishman hanged in America for murder!

Born in 1898, my maternal grandmother, Alwilda Fource Wright, was a hard working, patient, long suffering woman. In January of 1929 when my mother, the youngest of four children, was fifteen months old, my grandfather, Walter Leo Wright, went to the nearby hospital in Bradford, PA, with pneumonia. There was a mix up. My grandfather taken to surgery for an appendectomy and given ether. The ether killed him. He was forty. This left my grandmother to raise four children ranging from a year and a half to seven years through the coming depression.

Neither my aunt or my mother knew their father. "I think I remember him," my Aunt Jean told me, "I remember a man and being on a grassy knoll. I think that might have been my father. But…I really don't know. It's just a memory."

I asked her what she knew about the surgery, did they ever discover that they had the wrong person? Did they take his appendix out? What happened? "I don't know. We never talked about it…I wish I did know," was her reply.

Nowadays, a person suffering such a loss as the result of hospital incompetence would obtain a settlement and be set for life. "She was told," my aunt said, "probably by a lawyer working for the goddamned hospital, that if she tried to sue, the hospital would take the farm." My grandmother persevered, stoically bearing her burden, raising four children by herself during the depression.

Life during The Depression had its moments. Some years back I showed a photograph to my Uncle Don of him and his brother Bob as children standing on the running board of grandma's Model T at a family outing.

"That's the car I drove through the back of the barn," Uncle Don said with a grin, "Mum wasn't home, she had gone away for the day and I was going to put it in the barn for her, that's where she parked it. It was a Model T and you shifted gears with the floor pedals. Well, I put it into second instead of putting on the brake and drove it through the back of the barn! A neighbor came by and saw the predicament and helped me pull the boards off it so's I could drive it out. I wanted to surprise Mum. Well, she was surprised all right!"

Grandma's house had no electricity and wouldn't until the RES (Rural Electrification Agency, an FDR era program) installed it after the war. The house had free gas from a well near the house. In a winter during the worst of the depression the gas well gave out. Don and Bob would go across Marvin Creek to the Shawmut grade part way up the hill behind the house. There was a curve where the trains slowed. Bob and Don would hop onto a gondola, throw coal off, hop off and take it home.

During one of those Depression years Grandma worked out a deal with a farmer up the road. In exchange for milk for her family over the winter, Uncle Bob spent the following summer working for the farmer.

Grandma loved me dearly. I spent many evenings in her part of the house where she taught me all my prayers – there were many of those if you were Catholic – my ABC's, and how to count all the way to a hundred!

Grandma worked as a cook for the Digel family in their mansion at the intersection of Routes 6 and 59 in Smethport. They spent their summers at a cottage in the Thousand Islands in upstate New York. I would occasionally stay at the Digel house overnight with my grandmother while they were gone. We slept in beds on a screened-in porch in the cool of the summer evenings. I explored this house; it was as grand as grand could be. The dining room was long and elegant with a red oriental rug and huge crystal chandeliers. The library mantelpiece featured ornately carved cherubs and was decorated with game trophies of birds and fish. The woodwork on the main staircase, the one used by the family members, was ornately carved. This house was the epitome of the opulence, elegance, and craftsmanship of the turn of the 20th century.

In the days before television, radio provided our electronic entertainment. Many evenings I sat with Grandma in her parlor and listened to the radio shows. *Jack Benny* provided many laughs, Grandma just loved Rochester, the butler. *Our Miss Brooks* was funny, especially Dexter, what a dork! *The FBI*, *Gangbusters* and *Dick Tracy* provided crime drama and blazing machine guns. The *Lone Ranger* and *Gunsmoke* brought the old west into our house, with my imagination providing the images to go with the sounds from the radio. And there was the *Big John and Sparky* children's show with *The Teddy Bears' Picnic* theme music. This was the last gasp of the network radio shows, the Golden Age of Radio had passed, and was soon replaced by television.

My mother, Mary Katherine Wright, quit school in tenth grade to go to work in 1942. The depression was over, the war was on, and the family needed money. Working in Smethport at the Backus Company which made mica stampings used vacuum tubes. She and my father were married in 1947. Mom was pregnant and Grandma wouldn't let her marry my father until he converted to Catholicism. He did, and they were married in the rectory – no brides afflicted with the nine-month belly-swell in the church sanctuary, thank you – of St. Elizabeth's Church in Smethport August 9, 1947.

My mother was a very pretty woman, and remained so until she died suddenly in 1979. I remember watching her make cookies, performing her magic that turned those ingredients on the kitchen table into pure deliciousness. Chocolate chip cookies were my favorite, and are to this day. I could barely see over the table top, which had a white porcelain top, chipped to the black metal underneath on the edges of the blue border that went around it.

Her Sunbeam Mixmaster, the most amazing piece of technology I had ever seen, was such a fine machine! It had the big black dial on the back end with white lettering on it that she turned to select just the right speed, the grill on the front, and translucent white glass mixing bowls. I stood on a chair, clutching my ever-present teddy bear, and marvel at the beaters turning as the bowl revolved, watching the butter, flour, water, sugar and chocolate chips turning. Why, it was as neat as our brand new 1953 Chevrolet. Even neater, because I got to lick the dough off the beaters!

The thing I remember most about my mother was her love, the feeling that flowed warm, comforting, and unceasing from her to me. It wasn't anything in particular she said to me or what we talked about, the words weren't important, anyway. Mostly I chattered, she listened. But I remember that feeling. It is a feeling I miss.

On my father's side we were Swedes. My great-grandmother, who emigrated From Sweden in 1888, left us this marvelous one-page autobiography.

About Me by Anna Sophia Swanson Johnson

I came to this country when I was eleven. We came here the fourth of December got to Mt. Jewett about eight in the evening and there was very few houses there then. My father and two brothers had been here two years before we came.

There was Mother, three girls and three boys that came together. We were ten children in all at one time. My father was sick when we came and had been for some time and had not been able to work and he died the 10th of February. He was 42.

In two years my Mother married again and my Stepfather did not like a lot of kids to keep so he got my mother to go back to Sweden. I was fourteen then and his parents were rather well fixed and my Stepfather was the only child so he would get it all. So Mother went back and three of the youngest went along. And after they had been in Sweden, they had two more children, one boy and one girl that I have never seen. My Mother and Stepfather are still living. Mother is 87 or 88. They are not a bit well but they have everything they need and they now live with my half-brother and have for the last five years.

Since Mother went to Sweden I had to look out for myself. I had no place that I could call home. I was working in Hazel Hurst at that time and believe me the woman was everything but nice to me. But there was nothing to do but stand it. I was very little then but had to do all the work and wash and also eat what she gave me. Nobody will ever know all the nights I cried myself to sleep.

When I was eighteen I married. My man was fourteen years older but he was good to me. We had five children in over six years and I took care of them and everything else. Then he got sick from too much lifting in the saw mill and was not able to do anything for the last two years he lived and my oldest boy was crippled from Infantile Paralysis. He is the one at home now still a little lame, but not much.

My husband died when the oldest was ten years old and not a speck of insurance or anything and my baby girl was sick when he died and she died three months later. She would have been five years old that fall.

Since then I have worked like the dickens and taken care of my children with God's help and things could have been worse, I suppose, so I have no kick coming. God has been good to me and given me strength to work, so all is well.

My father, Kenneth Eugene Johnson, was a union carpenter as was my granddad, Walter Benard Johnson. Work in those years was plentiful most of the time.

Work or no, we always had meat on the table, some of it from my uncles' farms, some of it venison shot out of season with a .22. My dad and his friend Melvin would go out on the hill behind the house and shoot a deer and dress it out. When they brought it back to the house, they would butcher it. The only freezer most anyone had in those days was the little one in their fridge that only held a couple ice cube trays so the wives would cook and can the meat to preserve it.

One Saturday, my father and Melvin went out with their .22s to harvest some illegal venison. Approaching the creek, they saw a half-dozen or so deer on the opposite bank. My dad fired. He was sure he couldn't have missed, but neither man saw a deer fall. Melvin fired, dropping a deer. When they finished dressing out the fallen deer, my dad looked up and saw the first deer lying some distance away, dead. They dressed it out and brought both deer back to the house. The wives were more than a little upset at having to cook and can two deer at once! The venison was always good. A deer shot in or out of season was always valued and never, ever wasted.

An oil company road crossed Marvin Creek just beyond my grandmother's property line, went across Marvin Creek and up the hill crossing two railroad grades. The lower one had been the Shawmut grade, a standard gauge road carrying passengers and freight. The upper grade was a narrow gauge timber company road where Shay and Baldwin locomotives pulled flatcars of cut timber during the clear cut logging days. Both railroads had fallen into disuse, the tracks torn up and salvaged. The oil companies used these grades to access the hundreds of oil leases dotting the hills.

On some Saturday afternoons, Dad would take me into town. We would always go to the American Legion. It was dark and cool and smelled of stale liquor. I had my first Coca-Cola there. It fizzed in my mouth and drizzled out my nose as I sat on one of the tall stools at the bar. My father chuckled, "That's not how you're supposed to do it, Bub!" as he dabbed the cola off me with a bar rag!

I would drink my pop and watch my dad's glass of beer as he talked with his friends. Where did all those bubbles come from, anyway? They just seemed to come from nowhere and keep on going up and up and up...

Dad was a Machinist's Mate Second Class in the Navy and was in charge of a shop that repaired planes in San Diego during the war. He hated it "That's the goddamned Navy for you," he would say, "I'm a carpenter so they make me into a machinist. Of course, they also call for truck drivers and then give you a goddamned wheel barrow!" All of my dad's friends, the WWII vets, went to the Legion. They would treat me to sodas and games on the shuffleboard machine.

The cooler in the corner of the Legion held more flavors of pop than I ever knew existed! I could choose root beer, cherry, lemon lime, grape, black cherry, 7-Up, ginger ale or chocolate. One of Dad's buddies, "Sticky" Tarbox, showed me how to take the cork out of the bottle cap and push it into the back of the cap from inside my shirt and I could wear them like badges. He was a great guy, and what kid wouldn't like someone named "Sticky?"

Dad would also buy me Cracker Jacks and I would look for the toy inside. I didn't like the peanuts very much, but I loved the sticky sweet popcorn. A box was too big for me to finish by myself and I would take it home where it would sit around until it became a sticky, stale block and my mother would throw it out. There were other Saturday treats, such as the bags of potato chips and cheese corn. I would try vainly to open them by myself, but my father would always have to pull the top of the package apart with his strong hands. Saturdays were fun. To this day a whiff of stale liquor smell can transport me to those marvelous Saturday afternoons with my father at the Legion.

In 1953 we had a centennial celebration in Smethport. It was super, there was a parade every night for a whole week with marching bands, drum & bugle corps and fire engines! All the men became "Brothers of the Brush" and grew their whiskers. The women formed "The Sisters of the Swish" and wore hoop skirts! Sticky Tarbox was a ringer for Gabby Hayes and dressed up like him for the parades. A pageant was held on a stage erected at the football stadium. Mom wore her hoop skirt and danced the can-can. The Keystone Kops, one of whom was my dad, raided the can-can show!

Fall canning season was a great annual event. Jars were washed and counted, caps and rubber rings were bought, jars of pectin, bags of sugar and boxes of paraffin needed to make the jams and jellies. The kitchen became a sweltering place full of activity and wonderful smells with pressure cookers and canners steaming all day long and into the evening. Mom and Grandma worked for what seemed like weeks at a time putting up everything and anything that could be canned: pears, tomatoes, corn, beans–green and yellow–peaches and cherries. Some of what was canned came from our garden, but mostly we purchased produce from farmers' markets.

Jams and jellies were prepared, cooked and canned: grape, strawberry, blackberry, elderberry, currant, quince, and peach. Cutting apples into chunks, Grandma cooked them in to apple sauce and made her special dark brown apple butter. Large earthenware crocks were filled with brine for pickles. Narrow shelves along the sides of the dirt floor cellar bowed with the weight of this annual bounty.

Decades before cell phones, our telecommunications consisted of a party line, a concept now foreign to most living human beings! A party line was a single telephone line shared by a number of customers. Each customer had their own number and an accompanying distinctive ring. Telephone numbers did not seem to follow any discernable pattern. Numbers in town – Smethport – were short. Out of town they got longer. My aunt and uncle's number in town was "413." Our number three miles east of town was "6011R6" with our ring being six long rings. Our nearest neighbor's number was "6011J2" with six short rings. Any customer on that party line picking up their receiver could eavesdrop. This would infuriate my mother as she thought a neighbor about a mile up the road was always listening in.

Our telephone was an old "Eliot Ness" candlestick type with no dial. Twisted wires covered with fraying brown fabric connected it to an oak box on the wall. It had a crank on the right-hand side, and two bells on the front. Inside the box were the electronics and two large dry cell batteries, two-and-a-half inches in diameter and six inches tall. Red white and blue, they proclaimed "Eveready–The Battery With 9 Lives" with a cat jumping through the "9." Threaded brass posts with knurled nuts connected the wires.

While dial service was introduced in the 1920s, we did not have it.[12] To place a call, you picked up the receiver and listened. If the line was in use, you hung up…or eavesdropped! If the line was free, you replaced the receiver on the hook and cranked the handle on the box, picked the

---

[11] Smethport did not get dial tone rotary (DDS, Direct Dial Service) service until 1962.

receiver back up, and waited for Mabel Swanson to say "number, please."

Doctors made house calls in those days. Doctor Hockenberry (I liked calling him "Hoctor Dockenberry") used to call at our home. He was a marvelous man, in his fifties, salt and pepper wavy hair, and very distinguished looking. He really liked children. When I was four I had tonsillitis and Dr. Hockenberry made a house call. I watched as he opened his doctor bag.

He took out his stethoscope and listened to my chest. He took out a tongue depressor and had me say "aaahhh." Then he took out a hypodermic needle that looked like *HOLY SHIT! It's a foot long!* He affixed a spike to it that looked big enough to impale a child as small as myself! The red markings on the glass syringe looked like pure demonic evil against the white penicillin. *Red! The color of BLOOD! Oh no! Pain and torture! I'm outa here!*

I was off like a shot, my mother and grandmother in pursuit. After a short but frantic chase, I was pulled terrified from underneath my grandmother's bed and stuck with that fearsome instrument. Actually, it wasn't as bad as I had expected! I still do not like needles though.

I had my tonsils out shortly after that at the hospital in Kane, PA. My memory of this event is quite vivid. I remember being put on the gurney and wheeled into the OR. I was talking to the nurses. Then, they put the masks on their faces. *Uh oh!* I thought, but before panic could set in, the ether cone was over my face and that was it. All in all, it wasn't a bad experience, and the ice cream afterward was grand. A whiff of ether starter fluid brings me back to that experience.

U.S. Route 6, also called the Grand Army of the Republic Highway, was our connection with the world. It lay about twenty feet from our front porch. It took us where we wanted to go, and brought us a great many things. Trucks laden with large logs or a load of coal would rumble past. An endless stream of vehicles passed by day and night. The whole world seem to revolve around U.S. Route 6.

The mailman came down Route 6 every day and left mail in our mailbox. It was a strange contraption and did not carry the "Approved By the Postmaster General" stamp that other boxes did. I guess it was illegal, but the mailman didn't care. It did not open in the front like the "legal" boxes did, the whole top pivoted over to one side,. It made a peculiar creak when he opened it, a sound that I can still hear in my mind.

Depositing the mail, he closed it. The peculiar creak followed by the clank meant our mail had arrived! The child in me wondered what kind of criminals we were if we had an *illegal mailbox!*

The orange school bus, a rather short one with dark blue lettering designating it "No. 7," made its daily sojourns past our house. The great, sleek Greyhound buses with their cargo of passengers would fly past, leaving diesel smell behind them. One time when a bus went past I asked Grandma what that smell was. "Buses burn diesel fuel." she said. My child's mind held a mental image of people riding in the bus warming their hands by a diesel fuel fire in the aisle!

I remember the tramps who traveled Route 6. Today I guess we would call them homeless transients. Indeed, they were that. A source of endless fascination for me, they would be heading north toward Smethport, having gotten off a freight train about fourteen miles west near Mt. Jewett. Always alone, they would trudge past the house carrying a carpetbag or small, battered suitcase. If my mother saw one, she would hustle me inside the house and lock the door, peering through the living room curtains to see if he was gone. When Laddie, my collie, was off his chain, he saw to it that these transients did not tarry!

Their clothing seemed to be a shabby uniform in shades of gray. Frayed and tattered clothes that had once been fine, even elegant and worn with dignity, were patched and covered with the grime from their travels. They trod the highway in well worn work boots. Always seeming to have a three-day growth of beard, their grizzled visages spoke of tremendous personal woe.

I felt pity for these men, for they were out in the world without a roof over their heads. To a small boy like myself, it was inconceivable – and so terribly sad – that people would be adrift in the world with no place to stay, no place of permanence and security where you were assured of warmth, comfort, hot meals and the love of others.

A week never went by without one stopping to ask for food. My grandmother would always give them something. My mother never did if we were alone. If a tramp caught her unawares and got to the kitchen door, my mother would maintain that "we don't have a crust of bread in the house," even if there was a plate full of food in sight on the table. I would tell my mother that it wasn't right to say something that wasn't true. "Never mind!" she said.

About two miles west of Grandma's house was the County Home, also known as the "Poor Farm." It was an old folks' home and a farm maintained by the county. The residents grew their own crops and had a small herd of dairy cattle. My dad, if he was home, would sternly give the tramps directions to the County Home and tell him they could get a meal there.

"Kenny," my grandmother said once after my father had chased one down the road, "it won't hurt to give them something."

"*Bull*shit! They have this house marked, I know *damned* well they do! They stop here because it's an easy free meal. This house has a reputation for being a soft touch."

"They know where the county home is," he would say, "but they might have to work for their meal if they go there. They're just lazy, that's all! Goddamned lazy bums!"

Lazy. That's what they were, according to my father. Kenneth Eugene Johnson was just the opposite of a lazy man, working as many jobs as he needed to so we would have food on the table. He was always right and there was no arguing with him, his speech liberally sprinkled with the oaths used by men who worked hard for a living. The subtle inflections he gave to the epithet "goddamn" could impart seemingly infinite shades of meaning.

My father was a fiercely independent a man. A straight-A student, he left home at fourteen, taking a room at the Colonial Hotel in exchange for night clerking and stoking the coal furnace. His matter-of-fact explanation was that he didn't get on with his father. I have several of his school pictures. My favorite is one of him when he was about thirteen, his eyes having the same determined look that I saw so many times in my life before his death from alcoholism in 1993.

One evening when I was about five years old, my father was in the cellar butchering a deer. A tramp stopped by and asked for a meal and my grandmother agreed to feed him. When she turned from the door to go get the food, the man entered the house without first being invited to do so. Mom went to the cellar and told my Dad. He instructed her to let him know when the "guest" finished his meal. When the man finished his meal, my mother knocked on the cellar door. The man was sitting at the table in the kitchen wiping his face with a napkin when my father came into the kitchen, gore covered butcher knife in hand and blood up to his elbows! "Mister, you *got* your meal. Now you *get* the hell out of here and *don't* come back!" He gestured toward the door with the knife. "And don't you *ever* come inside a house again unless you're invited!"

The poor man at the table was aghast at my father's terrifying appearance and wasted no time grabbing his carpetbag, putting on his battered fedora and hauling ass out the door!

One evening around dusk, there came a knocking from the front porch. Dad went out and saw a man standing, not on the porch, but in front of it.

"Excuse me, Sir. Do you think you could spare a bite to eat, and could I possibly sleep in your barn tonight?"

"Well, I'll tell you what," my father replied coolly, "you're only a little way from the County Home. Just keep going down the road. You can get a meal there, and they'll have a cot for you to sleep on. And in the morning you can get cleaned up and get a breakfast before you leave."

The man thanked him and left. A short while later, Mom discovered she needed bread so she and Dad got in the car and headed to town. In the headlights of the car they saw the same man who had come to the porch walking toward the County Home using two canes. My father felt badly that he had sent him away.

"Do you think we should go back and offer him a ride?" Mom asked him.

"No, he'd probably refuse it. He's almost to the County Home, anyway."

The fact that this man, whom most would simply dismiss pejoratively as a "tramp," had his sense of dignity impressed my father. When Dad first saw him, the man was standing, bracing himself against the porch, his canes concealed. If he was going to accept charity, it was not going to be because someone pitied his lameness, but because he or she genuinely wanted to help him.

Not all who trod past on Route 6 were tramps. I remember one fellow, a Polish man known as "Willie the Peddler." Willie traveled everywhere on foot with a large bag over his shoulder in which he had an amazing array of goods. From Willie, you could buy blue jeans, handkerchiefs, doilies and a myriad of other useful items. When he stopped at a house, he would empty the entire contents of the enormous bag for you to see, and after you had made a purchase–as everyone would, they just couldn't stand to see him go through all that unpacking for nothing–he would pack it all back up and continue on his way.

For all his walking, Willie was a large man, and, as I remember him, the kind you could draw a picture of using nothing but circles.

"You know, it's amazing how fast that man could move," my father once recalled with a smile. "If the dog was loose when he came down the road, the dog would go after him. And there was no stopping the dog once he took off. Willie would make a dash across the road and cut up through the neighbor's property, and then go back down to the road with that big bag over his shoulder!"

I last remember seeing Willie one afternoon over sixty years ago. I have no idea whatever became of him. He is the only foot peddler I ever remember seeing, certainly the last one to ply his trade along Route 6.

On one occasion Route 6 brought drama past our house. We were all out on the front porch one evening when an unusual procession came past. The man in the lead was staggering and cursing. Following along a short distance behind him was a thin, plain looking brown-haired woman with a careworn expression wearing a cotton print dress, and a small boy about my own age. The man was about as abusive as a man in that condition could be. Reeling drunkenly, he would turn around and hurl insults and curses at his wife. his man's conduct displeased my father, who told him to "…just keep moving" in a firm voice. The man stood on the berm shouting insults. The boy hunkered back by his mother, who hugged him close. She wore a very distressed expression on her face, looking back and forth, first at her husband and then at us.

"Don't pay any attention to him," she said, "He's jes' drunk. He don't mean any harm."

The man turned to his wife. "God*damn*it, woman! *Shut* up!" he shouted, followed by a stream of abuse.

The boy and I looked at each other. I felt embarrassed for him and could feel his hot shame. That man, the reeling drunk, the loudmouthed fool, was his father, his daddy, the man to whom he should be able to look as an example. I felt uncomfortable, as if I were an intruding on something I was not meant to see, an accidental witness to their shame and humiliation.

After running through a litany of abuses toward his wife he turned his attention back to my father. "…I know what you are, you're nothin' but a goddamned communist. Yessir! A goddamned communist. And I'm gonna turn you in to the FBI."

He then took a pencil and paper out of his pocket, staggered over to the car and jotted down the license number, nearly falling down as he did so. He then put the pencil and paper in his pocket, hurled a few more epithets, and the sorry-looking procession proceeded on up the road.

FLASHING BACK– COMING OF AGE IN THE AMERICAN 1960s

SCHOOL DAZE

I started first grade in the fall of 1953, riding to school in the old orange school bus, "Keating Township No. 7." I carried my lunch in a black lunch pail like just like the one my dad carried, only smaller, "Gener[3] sized." Each township had its own elementary school. We lived in Keating Township, so I went to the East Smethport school, a rectangular buff colored brick building built by the WPA in 1935. It housed grades one through six. My mother had attended the same school when it was new.

Our first grade class had twelve members, Mrs. Ruth Keller was our teacher. First and second grades each having about a dozen students, were in the same room. The tall, multi-paned windows that took up most of the wall on the left side of the room still had the heavy air raid blackout curtains on them from World War II.

I remember our first reading lessons. Mrs. Keller took a red card, a yellow card, and a blue card and set them on the eraser ledge of the blackboard. She wrote out the names of the colors above them and we learned to read the words "red," "yellow," and "blue." The second week of reading lessons we learned a REALLY BIG word, it had NINE letters in it! "S-O-M-E-T-H-I-N-G!" Wow! We were taught to read phonetically. Our first readers were the Dick and Jane series.

With school came air raid drills. School children of previous generations went through air raid drills, too, but we were the first generation to grow up with the threat of the atomic bomb. There has never been a moment in our lives when the possibility of nuclear obliteration of human civilization has not been a fact.

Mrs. Keller told us what the siren warnings would be. The dreaded signal for a nuclear attack could be a series of short blasts on a horn or a long, rising and falling tone, a siren.

We were instructed to go into the hallway, sit with our backs to the wall, and put our heads between our knees. The reason for this was because the glass in the large classroom windows would become like flying razorblades from a blast wave. We were especially warned to cover our eyes because the bright flash of an atomic explosion would blind us.

This did seem a bit crazy to me, but I didn't say so. After all, this was our teacher telling us to do this, and teachers knew what was

---

[3] I gave myself this nickname when I was learning to talk. My parents were trying to get me to say "Eugene," All I could manage was something like "dee na" so they called me "Gener." This has stuck with me all my life. In the years I lived in San Francisco, if I answered the phone and someone asked for "Gener," I knew it was someone from Smethport.

best...didn't they? If Mrs. Keller said that sitting in the hallway with your head between your knees was the way to survive an atomic bomb attack, then it must be true.

All through this, I thought that the Russians must be very bad people, indeed, to contemplate dropping an atomic bomb near the East Smethport school even though we hadn't done anything to them. Well, they were communists, though. Exactly what that meant I wasn't sure, but from the way adults used the word, it carried the connotation of something terrible. From the way Mrs. Keller talked, I figured the Russians must have had the school bus garage on the other side of the school strategically targeted for nuclear obliteration.

Years later, while having a beer with my father in the Fulton House in Smethport, I read a yellowed poster hanging on the wall at one end of the bar proclaiming "Instructions to Patrons on Premises in Case of Nuclear Bomb Attack" and carried a Civil Defense logo. The instructions, the last one being "Then kiss your ass goodbye," made me recall these air raid drills.

Mrs. Keller encouraged good behavior by reading to us every day if the class behaved. I still remember her reading *Pinocchio* when we were in first grade and *Black Beauty* in second grade.

She was not above using threats. Several times during the school year when we were being unruly she would say "If you don't settle down this instant I will give all of you standard tests!" I had no idea what a "standard test" was, so my six-year-old mind goes *WHOA! STANDARD TESTS? Sounds pretty bad. Probably something like...an enema!* Worse than getting a shot! Mrs. Keller never made good on the threat. Standard tests were obviously something diabolically punitive and to be avoided at *all* costs.

Then one Friday in the beginning of May she announces, "OK, next week I'm going to give you your standard tests."

HOLY SHIT! STANDARD TESTS! And here we've been GOOD! And we're going to get them ANYWAY! I spent the whole weekend in a state of anxiety. Monday morning I was wound so tight my asshole felt like it had puckered right up inside me! Bravely I got onto old No. 7 that morning not knowing what fate was about to befall me. Like a condemned man going to the gallows, I walked through the double entrance doors and into the classroom. After the Pledge of Allegiance, Bible verse and prayer, Mrs. Keller got out a stack of booklets and passed them out. *Oh hell, THIS is all it is? Why didn't somebody tell me!* I got the highest score in the class. I did so in first, second, third and fourth grades. My grades went down every year from the fifth grade on through graduation.

Instruction to Patrons on Premises in Case of Nuclear Attack:

UPON THE FIRST WARNING:

1. Stay clear of all windows.
2. Keep hands free of glasses, bottles, cigarettes, etc.
3. Stand away from bar, tables and cash register.
4. Loosen necktie, unbutton coat and other restrictive clothing.
5. Remove glasses and empty pockets of sharp objects.
6. Immediately upon seeing the brilliant flash of nuclear blast, bend over and place your head firmly between your legs.
7. Then kiss your ass goodbye.

Popular spoof of a U.S. Department of Defense poster, © 1970 The Carnaby Mfg. Company, Milwaukee WS.
source: https://www.thirdmindbooks.com

Everyone has a teacher who stands out as an influence on their life. For me it was Mrs. Dorothy Feit. Third and fourth grade, like first and second grade, were in the same room. Mrs. Feit was near fifty, a large lady with a very forceful personality, and an excellent educator. She not only taught us from books, she had us practice skills that were necessary for everyday living, like how to tell time, how to introduce people to each other, how to give directions, and how to make change.

She would bring in a pair of old telephones and put them on our desks and we would have "phone calls" with each other in which we could exercise our telephone etiquette and develop communication skills. I hated that. I thought the greeting upon which she insisted we use was dumb. I don't know why, I just did. It went like "Hello, this is the Johnson residence, Eugene speaking."

That greeting shows how times have changed. In the age of stalkers and various other telephonic nuisances, you really don't want to identify yourself to just anyone who calls. In the 1950s, that was not an issue. But I thought it was still a dumb greeting! And I never identify myself to an unknown caller. She taught us values, too, *real* values. I remember the day she introduced us to the concept of democracy.

"Can anyone tell me what democracy is?"

Several of us attempted answers, all of them, including mine, being something to do with "...when you have a lot of Democrats in one place you have democracy..."

Knowing that we had not the foggiest idea what democracy was and were all paying close attention in order to find out, she revealed the answer.

"Abraham Lincoln said it best. Democracy is government of the people...by the people...and for the people." That was my introduction to our form of government.

She fired my ideals too, for she told us how people should act toward each other in a democratic society. And from her I learned that prejudice was evil, and that all people were supposed to be equal under our form of government.

And she told us about caprices that occurred even in our tolerant, democratic society. The McCarthy witch hunt was just winding down, and she related how many educators had their careers destroyed from associations they had with socialist organizations when they were college students during the depression.

And when fifth grade came, she was transferred to that grade to teach. Our class was bigger that year because the kids from nearby Farmers Valley School came to East Smethport School for the fifth and sixth grade. She was a marvelous woman, a teacher who possessed real wisdom and know how to act on it. The death of her son, and my very good friend, in Vietnam would later draw us closer together. She remained a friend of mine until she passed in 1984

I have been a musician for over sixty years having learned drums, guitar, harmonica, bass and fiddle. Music has been a motivating factor in my life. It is my art, my form of emotional expression.

I had no inkling I possessed any musical ability whatsoever until the fall of 1957 in fifth grade at the East Smethport school, a man came into our class and started talking to us about…of all things…his name.

"My name is Mr. Partchey," he said, "that's kind of an odd name, I know, it's not easy to find any other Partcheys in the phone book…I always look in phone books for it when I travel…" I wondered, *what is this guy up to?* He was there to offer us instrumental music instruction and told us about different instruments: the clarinet, saxophone, trumpet, trombone – some of the kids would ask if their mouth was the right shape to play these various instruments and open wide for him to see and evaluate–flute, and …drums! *Ohhh*…I thought to myself…*that's what I want! Drums, you can hit' em, and they're loud!*

"…now drums are a difficult instrument…" Mr. Partchey said, and he continued to talk about them, but I was *convinced* that was what I wanted. I thought about standing at the curb during the parades in Smethport and feeling those drums just *pound* me on the way past! As they approached I sometimes wondered if their sheer concussive force might overwhelm me. They enveloped me with their boom, rattle and crash as the band passed looking *so* fine in their splendid uniforms. And *I* could be a part of *that? Ohhhh YES!!!*

At my first lesson, Mr. Partchey brought me a pair of Ludwig & Leedy 3S sticks and my rubber topped practice pad! He showed me how to hold the sticks and demonstrated the "dadda-momma," a hand-to-hand double stroke roll, the sounds of the sticks on the practice pad seeming to say "dadda-momma dadda-momma." I took the sticks and, with his help, formed my hands into the proper grip. It seemed natural. And then I did it. I mean *did* it. I didn't *try* to do it, I didn't *attempt* to do it, I *did* it! First time!

Mr. Partchey had me do it a couple more times pursing his lips and cocking his head as he observed me, then said, "Well, Eugene, you do that quite well. Would you like your second lesson now? *Hey, I might get to be good at this,* I thought. "Uh...OK." And that, over sixty years ago, was the start of my relationship with music.

Mr. Partchey promoted me into the Junior Band after about three months of lessons. There were three of us with that level of proficiency who bused to the Smethport Borough school twice a week for band. The concert band was fun, but the marching band was what I *lived* for! Strapping on the field drum and pounding out a marching cadence was a most satisfying feeling. This was real power, not just being the center of attention from virtue of the fact that the drums were loud, but being the rhythmic motivation for the entire band. We practiced marching around and around the borough school.

"...always start on the left foot...watch your rank! Keep your file straight...halt, one, two! Two beats after the command! Remember that."

Cadence. Tempo. Three whistles, mark time. One short whistle, forward march. One long whistle, roll off. Two short whistles, halt.

The event we were preparing for was the Memorial Day Parade. And when the day came for the parade, I was sick and unable to march. It was devastating. I had gotten my first taste of the power of music, though. It was like a narcotic, and I was hooked!

I was born with musical ability and Mr. Partchey brought it out in me. I never knew I had any music in me until then. I never considered playing music, I didn't even think much about music. Sure, I noticed it, and I liked some of the rock n' roll I heard, and I *loved* a marching band, but I was always outside of music. Now I could be *in* it.

Charles Partchey was known by the older kids as "Prof" or "the Prof." It was a term that, while somewhat familiar – no one ever even *thought* of calling a teacher by a familiar name in those days – but it was said with respect. Most of us never used that name in his presence, but a few did call him that to his face and I don't ever recall him getting upset, I rather think he liked it.

THE POLIO EPIDEMIC

Infantile paralysis – polio – was the scourge of the 1950s. It was an invisible killer and left many paralyzed. Many kids had to live in these contraptions called "iron lungs" which kept them alive. We had no cases of it in the East Smethport School that I remember. However, there were polio cases in Smethport, and one second grade girl died from it.

We live in a world where vaccines have made fatal childhood illnesses pretty much a thing of the past. With polio there was a creeping fear that pervaded our reality. There was no clear cut way to fight polio, except for closing swimming pools and other places where children might congregate.

Science saved us! We were all so glad for the Salk vaccine when it came along. It consisted of a series of three shots administered in the Smethport Borough school library at no charge.[4] School buses would take us there and back.

You don't hear about iron lungs[5] anymore, nor do you see kids wearing the clunky-clanky leg braces that were all too common in the 1950s and 1960s. While cases of polio are very rare in the U.S. these days, polio survivors are subject to debilitating post-polio syndrome.

ROCK N' ROLL IS HERE TO STAY

Baby Boomers grew up with two dynamic forces that changed the world: the nuclear bomb and rock n' roll. It wasn't that way with our parents. The music of their youth, the World War II era, was big band music. When my dad was a kid, he played the clarinet and Benny Goodman was his musical hero. Rock n' roll came along in the middle fifties and that was, well, *different,* certainly *much* different from big band swing. And we witnessed it from the beginning.

Elvis rocked and rolled with *passion*, he was lean and mean and had the *fire* in his belly, man, he was getting down *with* it, daddy-o! He gyrated with that rockabilly hepcat rhythm, just *bustin'* with hillbilly soul, giving a voice to that pent up Caucasian frustration clogging our cultural arteries, the tension of the postwar generation wanting to have something of their *own* to dance to, a reason to *howl* on Saturday night. He gave the kids something to *stir* those adolescent hormones, the musical equivalent to the throbbing glass pack rumble of a souped-up V-8, stuff to make the girls scream – like they wouldn't scream again until Beatlemania – and they'd jump out of their seats, dance in the aisles and behave in a generally unruly manner that was just ...*shocking*... to parents, teachers,

---

[4] And nobody bitched about "socialized medicine." Polio has been nearly eliminated worldwide. In those days diseases were to be completely defeated.
[5] At the time of this writing, February 2018, there are only a handful of polio survivors who are still alive in iron lungs. They have been this way for over 60 years. Buncombe, A. (2017). *This man has been locked in this obsolete machine for almost 60 years. The Independent.* Retrieved 1 February 2018, from https://www. independent. co. uk/news/world/americas/polio-iron-lung-survivors-photos-lives-inside-ventilators-a8070881. html#gallery

preachers, principals and other authority figures of the 1950s mindset. Yeah. Elvis *did* all that for us.

Rock and roll was like popping the clutch on a '57 Chevy, burnin' rubber in a midnight drag for pink slips[6], *kickin'* with a backbeat that's an amalgam of jungle rhythm and hillbilly jive. It was primitive, burning with rhythmic fury, roaring like a moonshiner's hot-rod Ford on a dark night, full throttle down the hollow, straight pipes shooting flames, loud and downright *dangerous*, Dead Man's Curve at ninety on two wheels, bumper clickin' on the guardrail posts!

Instrumentally, it was a guy twangin' on an electric guitar, another guy on a big old upright "doghouse" upright bass and another banging on a drum set and the occasional piano. It was sparse. What rock n' roll didn't have in lush, full instrumentation it made up for in volume. And the drummer didn't stay in the background and sort of "suggest" the rhythm, he put it *right in your face!* While Frank and Bing crooned bee-yoo-tiful melodies with their bee-yoo-tiful voices, rock n' rollers railed shattered-lung ear-busting nonsense over the rest of the racket. It was just goddamned magnificent!

Rock n' roll was not, as parents, teachers and preachers warned, a communist conspiracy from hell sent to destroy the flag, Mom, apple pie, virginity, all appreciation of melody, harmony, and Western civilization in general. Quite the opposite, rock n' roll was the ultimate in the spirit of American capitalism, a star-spangled entrepreneurial orga$m making money faster than a dozen printing presses! The idea was to buy a guitar, have a hit record, make a ton of money, and drive a brand-new Cadillac convertible, preferably a pink one with a continental kit! It just doesn't *get* more American than that!

Rock n' roll celebrated the liberation of American youth from melodically beautiful, tonally rich and emotionally empty pop tunes that just could not *move* this generation. Cars had to be *faster*. Music had to be *louder*.

While this reflected the exuberance and recklessness one expects of youthful hormonal excess, it also spoke of the fear, rage and pain of the "duck and cover" generation desperately trying to cram a lifetime of kicks into whatever time was left before the menopausal old bastards who ran the world nuked civilization to glowing embers.

Raucous music and wild dancing as an outer expression for inner pain was a new thing for white folks, but was certainly not new at all to

---

[6]"Dragging for pink slips" was the ultimate hot-rod challenge. A "pink slip" was the hot rod vernacular for the car title, whether or not it was pink. In a drag race for pink slips, you bet your car's title. If you lost, you lost your car!

American blacks. The musical tradition immediately preceding rock n' roll that defined its musical content, sound and purpose was *rhythm and blues,* a term applied to post WWII black music. Previously called "race music" and marketed to black audiences, it was now electrified. White kids had discovered its energy and called it rock n' roll. Music would never be the same.

MY LITTLE SISTER

When I was in fourth grade my parents adopted my sister, Debra Lynn. They wanted to have more children. My mother was pregnant when I was about three years old. She took a spill and suffered a miscarriage with complications leaving her unable to have any more children. An opportunity to adopt a baby born out of wedlock to a cousin presented itself.

My mother and I went into town one day and she bought all kinds of baby things: diapers, bottles, blankets and the like. My aunt had just had a baby girl, so I thought all this stuff was a gift for my new cousin Kathy.

"Are you gettin' all this stuff for Kathy?" I asked.

"No."

"Well, who're you gettin' all this baby stuff for then?"

"You're going to get a baby sister?"

"Aw c'mon. You're gettin' this stuff for Kathy."

"No, I'm serious, you're getting a baby sister."

"I am? *Really?*" this was a real surprise. I had no clue about the facts of life, but Mom wasn't big like my aunt was before cousin Kathy came along.

"Yes. You are."

"Oh yeah? When?"

"Next week."

"Wow!"

I told everybody at school I was getting a baby sister next week. Of course they didn't believe me, especially the teachers. But they found out I was right, I got a baby sister! She arrived the next week, just like Mom said she would, my new sister, Debra Lynn, a little tyke in a bassinet. I was no longer an only child, I had a baby sister!

Mom told me one time, "Gener, now that you have a sister, we...well...there may not be as much as Christmas." If there was any less, I never noticed it. My parents, products of the Depression, did their level best to make sure we were inundated with stuff each Christmas. We always were.

Grandma sold the farm and we moved to a rented house in the borough of Smethport in 1958.

CHAPTER 3

LOSING MY MIND TO SAVE MY SOUL

> Author's Note: The Congregation for the Doctrine of the Faith (CDF), formerly known as the Office of the Inquisition) which oversees the teaching of the RCC's doctrines is either woefully obtuse or a genius level manipulator of psyches and corruptor of the human spirit. I'm going with the latter.

THE MYSTERY/MISERY OF RELIGION

I was born a Catholic. *Born* a Catholic? Well, since they sprinkled me with Holy Water when I was an infant – without my permission – thereby making me one, it's as close to being born into a particular religion as one can get.

My grandmother was responsible for my earliest religious education. When I was very small, I pointed to the crucifix on her bedroom wall and asked her what it was. "That's God's Son," she replied. I was simply astonished. I knew that God was this being to whom I said my "Now I lay me down to sleep" and my "God Blesses" every night. Grandma taught them to me and followed them up with the "Our Father," "Hail Mary," "Glory Be," even the "Apostles Creed" and the impossibly long "Confiteor" with its required breast beating.[1] But here was God's Son nailed to the cross and obviously in a position of considerable pain and distress.

---

[1] In the Confiteor the phrase, "through my fault, through my fault, through my most grievous fault," required the supplicant beat their breast with their right hand on each "through." This was my introduction to the unwritten but very real and psychologically brutal Catholic doctrine that everything is your fault. EVERYTHING. If your pet dies, it's your fault. If your cousin is killed in an automobile accident, it's your fault. If your sister marries outside of the church, that's your fault too! You didn't pray enough! Everything bad that happens to you is related to God expressing His divine displeasure at your sinful existence on earth, and the very real possibility that you will spend an eternity burning in hell. No parole, no release. Do not pass "Go." Do not collect $200. You're fucked, that's all. Fucked. Eternally so.

"Why…is he on there, Grandma?"

"They crucified him, they nailed him to the cross."

"They…killed him?"

"Yes, but he arose from the dead."

??? OK. If Grandma said it, it must be true. After all, grandmas don't say things that aren't true…do they?

Grandma was a devout Catholic, devout enough that all four of her own children left the church. And she was doing her best to make sure I was a devout Catholic too. My parents were not at all religious and never went to church. So, if my parents were not churchgoers, how did I end up on the clutches of the Papists?

My grandmother made certain she raised me in the church. This happened because my mom and dad and I were living with her in her farmhouse. While Grandma seemed like a very mild person in most aspects, she was steadfast in her Catholic faith.

Mom and Dad got together after he got out of the Navy after the war. Mom got pregnant, and Grandma wouldn't let them get married until Dad converted to Catholicism, which he evidently did just in time as I was born twenty-seven days after the nuptials. Now, I was premature and spent six weeks in an incubator. But, hey, not THAT premature! I think she cut the same deal with my parents after economic circumstances forced them to live with her, "If you're going to live here, I will raise Eugene in the faith." She did.

I went to church virtually every Sunday for nineteen years and did all the things I was supposed to do as a Catholic. As I recall my early Catholic years, I sometimes think I was not fully convinced that the church really knew what was up. But then again, I experienced incredible emotional turmoil related to those years. Besides, there just wasn't anything else in my life to explain "all that stuff," meaning the purpose of life, what really happens when you die, who or what is God, things like that. One thing ultimately became very clear: the whole Catholic ethos revolved around fear, guilt, and shame. Period. The Catholic Church in which I was raised was not a religion to be practiced, it was a religion to be mourned.

The prime requirement for being a Catholic was to be guilty of original sin. That was easy because it was automatic: if you were alive, you were guilty. Beyond that, if you wouldn't be good just because you loved God, then you would because you feared burning forever in hell. This fear also provided an incentive to support the church economically. In addition to the Ten Commandments, Catholics are also bound, under pain of mortal sin – and thus eternal damnation – to also abide by the Canon Laws of the church, one of which is that you had to contribute financially to the support of the church.

So, the doctrine of Original Sin imposes on the parents the moral obligation to have their children baptized so that they can be members of the church and, therefore, eligible for heaven. Not coincidentally, this also assured the church of a steady flow of new customers lining up for psychological manipulation and obligated under pain of eternal damnation to contribute financially to the church.[2]

There was little room for the goodness of Christ and His doctrine of love for one's own fellow men. That had damned little to do with it. Very damned little. Nothing, in fact. Christ was the Son of God, the Savior, the poor guy nailed to the cross, the grisly, gory, fucked up, festering, beat-all-to-hell, scabby death-fetish displayed so prominently in Catholic cathedrals, churches, chapels, publications and real estate. He also stared at you from pictures and statues with his torso ripped open, displaying his Sacred Heart, shown surrounded by glowing flames with a crown of thorns around it.[3] That was a rather grisly item, too.

Indoctrination into the teachings of the Catholic Church started in first grade. Its purpose was to gradually turn you into to a quivering mass of ignorance and fear. They were goddamned good at it.

We were in a rural parish and there was no parochial school.[4] Catechism classes were held once a week after school. We went to St. Elizabeth's[5] Roman Catholic Church in Smethport where The Nunz and a few lay teachers taught us about life, death, sin, grace, heaven, hell, limbo, purgatory, sanctifying grace and the sacraments. The Nunz explained how limbo was for pagans, those pesky perfidious[6] Jesus denying Jews, and babies who died without being baptized. Limbo was a kind of netherworld, a warehouse for the souls that, according to the Divine Checklist, couldn't get into heaven. According to The Nunz, limbo was neither pleasant nor unpleasant, it just *was*.

---

[2] As well as a steady supply of children for pedophile priests to bend over the kneelers.
[3] Actually, this is a depiction of the fourth chakra, the heart chakra, opened (on fire) by love. This is well known among yoga practitioners. Lost on the Catholic church, they do not understand their own symbolism.
[4] Which was good because if I had to put up with their shit five days a week for twelve years I would likely have turned into a serial axe murderer!
[5] Named for St. Elizabeth of Hungary, she was a martyr, they cut her breasts off.
[6] This phrase is from the Easter Week liturgy.

Protestants, on the other hand, willfully denied the One True Church[7] and went to hell along with all of those who did not die in a state of Sanctifying Grace. Simple, cut and dried.

It was innocuous at first. Catechism classes in the lower grades could be fun with Bible stories about the Old Testament and Jesus.

We saved our pennies and gave them to The Nunz so we could buy pagan babies. You see, those poor pagan slobs were so damned dumb that they would sell their own kids. So we bought them and saved their souls![8] Wasn't that mighty white of us?

The Church had answers for everything in the Baltimore Catechism.

Q. Who made you?

A. God made me.

Q. Why did God make you?

A. Because he loves me, and so I can serve him in this life and be with him in the next.

See? Nothing to it. If the answer wasn't in the Baltimore Catechism, well, it was a question that probably shouldn't be asked. And, of course, it was most certainly possible to lose one's immortal soul into everlasting damnation and eternal torment with nothing more than some ill-chosen thoughts. Yes, the devil wanted our souls badly, and he was not above planting sinful soul stealing thoughts in our heads.

The church ruled that the age of reason, the age by which a child can distinguish between good from evil and can make choices accordingly, occurs at the age of seven. That's what they tell you. Having attained the age of reason, a child can now be knowledgeable enough to commit mortal sins, sins so heinous that God would be justified in immediately striking them dead. But God, being such a nice guy, doesn't actually do that anymore. Instead, he puts the stain of a mortal sin on your soul. If you die with that stain on your soul, your sorry ass is forever roasted in the fiery pits of hell.

---

[7] One True Church, Holy Catholic Church, Holy Mother Church, same difference. The Nunz loved to use these flowery references to the RCC, as if it was going to make their toxic mythology more palatable to the ignorant masses – us!
[8] I related this to an online discussion group for those wanting to recover from the effects of an association with the Catholic Church, some years back. An ex-nun responded "When I was a nun in China we would sometimes pick up unwanted babies and bring them to the convent when our superiors were giving us a hard time. It made them mad as hell because there were more mouths to feed and more asses to wipe. We didn't care what the Mother Superior thought. We loved those sweet babies just the same. All of them."

Yes, seven-year-olds can be *that* wicked! Having been force-fed a couple years worth of the church's toxic mythology, the sacraments of Penance and the Holy Eucharist bind young people to the Church – like fucking invisible chains.

This is entirely by design. The office responsible for instruction of the faithful is he Congregation for the Doctrine of the Faith (CDF), formerly the Office of the Inquisition. There were several inquisitions dating back to 12th century France where the first one was formed as a tool of genocide with which to murder the heretical Cathars and Albigensians. They were successful. The last inquisition was renamed the Congregation for the Doctrine of the Faith in 1965.

Since it is no longer socially (or legally!) acceptable torture people and burn them at the stake for heresy, the next best thing is to totally mindfuck them as children so they become adults so terrified of going to hell that they blindly swallow all the shit they are force-fed by The Church.

So, attaining the age of reason meant a seven-year-old had to bear the moral weight of understanding God, Jesus, heaven, hell, sin, confession, forgiveness, the Ten Commandments, a shit ton of prayers, and more. Given the quantity of diverse information and the ability of a seven year old has for abstract thinking, errors reign supreme. The priority was avoiding hell. And it looked like it was awfully easy to get there!

We made our first Holy Communion – The Sacrament of The Holy Eucharist – in second grade. We were told we were going to "receive Christ." The Nunz made this mystical process perfectly…opaque. Sister Noreen was a very sweet older nun who, although completely clueless as to the nature of anything existing outside her life in the church, genuinely loved children and was enthusiastic about her teaching vocation. She explained to us, "Our Lord gave us a great gift to help us get to heaven, the Holy Eucharist. Now, many churches have communion, but the Holy Catholic Church is the only one with the Eucharist. This is because the Holy Catholic Church is the only church that comes to us directly from Jesus Christ, the Son of God. All the others were founded by men. And they re-enact the Eucharist instituted by Our Lord at the Last Supper as a *symbol*. In the Catholic Church, the priests have received the sacrament of Holy Orders and are empowered by God to perform the mass and actually *re-create* the sacrament of the last supper and transform the bread and wine into the actual body and blood of Christ. This is our sacrament of the Holy Eucharist."

A bewildered child wondered, "But, Sister, the bread and wine look the same, don't they?"

Seeing that her clever setup had worked, she would smile and reply, "I'm glad you asked that. That's because the process through which this miraculous change occurs is called "transubstantiation..."

Trans *what the...?*

"...and transubstantiation means that, even though the bread and wine still look like bread and wine, they are in fact transformed into the *actual flesh and blood of Christ*. Just think of it, boys and girls! Isn't that wonderful?"

She would smile and look around the room seeing stares reflecting various degrees of astonished perplexity. But there was no disbelief. You'd go to hell for that!

My childish imagination came up with some interesting if somewhat blasphemous questions and heretical thoughts about this sanctified gruesome obscenity passed off as being a divine gift from God which I kept to myself. Seriously, you can't tell kids shit like this without provoking their imaginations!

OK, if the bread and wine are changed into the actual body and blood of Christ, what part of the body were we eating? I mean, was it just...you know...generic body parts? Or was it specific ones? Will we be munching muscle? Or guts? Liver? Oh no, not liver, I hate liver! How about an eyeball? Or perhaps the Holy Sanctified Sphincter? Yuk!

Does the priest know what parts we were getting? Do some people get better parts than others?

But then Sister Noreen informed us "the body of Christ is complete in the any portion of host, from the whole thing to the smallest crumb."

The whole thing sounded pretty gruesome. Seriously, eating flesh, drinking blood. What kind of shit was this to be telling little kids?[9]

Communion turned out to be an empty experience, a bright and shining void of mumbled incantations and liturgical nonsense. The whole thing makes me think of cotton candy. It looks so big and takes up so much space, and when you put it in your mouth the substance melts away to nothing. The Holy Eucharist was form without substance. Well, no, there actually was substance – the goddamned dry wafer that stuck to the roof of my mouth.

---

[9] Killing Jesus, eating his flesh and drinking his blood, like many aspects of church dogma and practices, are the Catholic adaptation of the ancient Pagan principles of regicide and cannibalism. Frazer, James George, Sir, MacMillan 1978: "The Golden Bough," XXIV Killing the Divine King p. 308; LIX Killing the God in Mexico p. 680.

I was underwhelmed to say the least. I figured that if this is the kind of razzamatazz God liked, heaven might be a boring place. *Oops!* Got to be careful, careful, careful! Have to watch those *sinful* thoughts!

Fact be known, I thought heaven was entirely irrelevant to the whole matter. I was so absolutely fucking terrified of eternal damnation that the main thing was to avoid going to hell. Anyplace else was fine. If it was heaven, well, so much the better, just as long as it was not *hell!*

It occurred to me that, according to the dictates of the Holy Mother Church, many, if not most, people were going to hell. All my relatives except Grandma. My parents, for instance. They didn't go to church. That was a mortal sin which merited eternal damnation in hell. My aunt and uncles had left the church, so they were going to hell. My great aunt had been divorced at a young age and then remarried, so she was going to hell too. It seemed that everyone I knew, loved, and cared about, according to the wishes of a merciful and loving God as taught by his One True Church was going to hell.

This caused me an enormous amount of emotional distress. I prayed they would all return to the church so we could be together in heaven. I spoke to no one about it, it was all too terrible to speak openly about. I mean, the church, via its spiritual enforcers, The Nunz, explained it all and there was no escaping the finality of what the church said on death and hell. The thought of people I loved so very much spending eternity in torment severely fucked with me.

No matter how hard I prayed, the situation did not change. Did God, whom I was told loved me so very much, simply not care? Or were the fervent prayers of one small boy simply not enough to compensate for such massive amounts of sin generated by myself and these people, about whom I cared so very much? Was salvation even possible? Would I, despite my faith, eventually go this way too, ending up on the road to hell? Was heaven, in fact, completely unattainable?

Heretical thoughts that heaven, hell, transubstantiation and a whole lot of other stuff might actually sort of a cosmological wagonload of manure[10] would kind of flash through my mind from time to time, but I didn't dare dwell on them because I knew that shining light from the realms of Hell, that Most Evil of all Most Evils, Lucifer, was trying to get me to doubt the church, thus causing me to commit a mortal sin in thought and therefore be eligible for a permanent membership in hell if I

---

[10] If you have lived in farming country, you know what this is. If you haven't lived in farm country, this is exactly what it says. It is the fragrance of early spring as farmers spread it on their fields.

croaked before my next confession! Although the basic heretical suspicions were there, I bought it all. It was true. It had to be true. Nothing else could be true. After all, neither Grandma nor the church would tell me things that weren't true...would they?

I was in a state of terror which I kept entirely to myself, tucked away deep inside. It was a place into which I tried to not go. But going there was unavoidable. When I did go there, it provoked ghastly torments.

These thoughts, which started occurring to me at around the age of seven or eight, terrified me. This was the beginning of the deep-seated emotional chaos resulting from my Catholic indoctrination. This defined my relationship with the Roman Catholic Church. No matter where I went, no matter who I was with, no matter what I did, this dread was lurking in the shadows of my consciousness, haunting my daily existence until I severed my relationship with the church. I was clueless, brainwashed and ever so thoroughly mindfucked, *i.e.,* a *perfect* Catholic schoolboy.

It was SO hard to be good. Why, committing a mortal sin was as easy as breathing...or...and maybe especially...*thinking*. Any direct violation of the Ten Commandments was a mortal sin. So, if I did something disobedient, like not picking up my toys when Mom told me to, that was – to me – a direct violation of the Fourth Commandment, "Honor thy father and thy mother," and therefore a mortal sin. Not cleaning all the food off my plate at supper time despite my mother's orders to do so was direct disobedience and thus a mortal sin. It was so hard to be good! I was such a *bad* little boy!

Worse, I never loved God. I was told I was supposed to love God, but...I just ...didn't. And I knew that made me *bad!* Neither did I love Jesus. And that compounded my sin because that was the point of the whole friggin' deal to begin with! I didn't love God, I didn't love Jesus. I loved my mother and my father. I loved my grandma. I loved my dog. But I didn't love God and I didn't love Jesus. What an *wicked* little boy I was! God and Jesus loved me so much, after all, if it wasn't for them, I wouldn't have these people to love. Or my dog. And I *didn't love them.* I did not feel anything I could describe as "love" when I thought of God or Jesus. I felt was a selfish rotten little bag of shit! And I was going to go to hell for it.

THEY WERE INVISIBLE for fuck's sake!! How do you love something that is fucking INVISIBLE? Even if the invisible things were God and Jesus? God and Jesus were just as invisible as anything involving the Sacrament of Penance and the Holy Eucharist. Empty. Fucking *nothing* there. A perfect vacuum! As real as made-up fairytales or an invisible friend!

But still, God and Jesus loved me so much and, if I didn't love them back – and in the very specific ways prescribed by the church – God and Jesus were going to roast my sinful ass in the eternal torments of hell because of their divine justice and infinite mercy. In other words, they would send me to hell to suffer eternal torment...*because they loved me.*

Now, I can't be sure if anyone else was bothered by any of this. This was not a topic of discussion among us kids. You were to believe what you were taught and not under any circumstance question any of it! *Any* of it! And we didn't. Or I didn't. If anybody else did, they never talked about it to me. Religion was to be "taken on faith" and NOT discussed. Faith was blind belief without empirical knowledge. Believe what you are told or burn forever. Those are the choices. The ONLY choices.

"Take it on faith" means "believe it without requiring any observable facts whatsoever." This is the complete antithesis of reason and logic. It is medieval. And the church is/was medieval. We went to school to learn things based on facts. And in church we were taught that facts are entirely irrelevant to what we believe. Another wonderful religious dichotomy for Catholic grade-schoolers! Well, believing something does not make it true.

The extended logic of this is that God, all-powerful and all-knowing, creator of heaven and earth who blessed us with a marvelous intellect requires that we not exercise its use in order to attain heaven. And avoid hell. *What the bleeding fuck?*

Those sonsofbitches had devious ways of sneaking cognitive dissonance[11] into vulnerable psyches. If The Fucking Church says $2 + 2 = 5$, then $2 + 2 = 5$! Fuck what your math book says.

SISTER MARY MINDFUCK

Sister Mary William is a legend among St. Elizabeth's Baby Boomers. If you took all the stereotypes of aggressive, intimidating, piss-miserable psychotically religious (or religiously psychotic, I could never tell which), sexually unfulfilled, sadistic nuns and rolled them all into one, you'd have Sister Mary William of the Little Sisters of Our Lady of Perpetual Misery. She was a *capo regime* for Christ, The Terminator in a habit: big, mean, ugly tempered and dykey. Her heart – assuming she

---

[11] Holding two contradictory ideas as both being true.

actually had one – must have pumped green toxic sludge. While the Sunday sermons the congregation got from the priest were fairly bland, Sister Mary William had at least as much unhinged religious horseshit as a congregation of Pentecostal snake handlers!

She would use scare stories of eternal damnation to instill proper classroom behavior. The old bat was psychic, too. She could read minds. She knew when you had gum in your mouth even if you never chewed it. And if she caught you (with gum, talking, not paying attention), she would make it a very unpleasant experience with some form of verbal humiliation in front of the entire class. It's hard to misbehave when a massive woman towers over you in her habit and wimple threatening you with eternity in Satan's own toaster oven. Never mind that it wasn't up to her to administer divine judgment, she was so intimidating that it made no difference. At all. I seem to recall occasions when her eyes glowed red like fiery coals. Well…OK…maybe not…but…they certainly *could* have!

If the class would start to get a bit noisy, she would quiet things down with the solemn pronouncement, *"Be quiet!* There's going to be a revolution *and the streets are going to run red with blood!"* She alternated that prognostication with items like "The communists are going to take over. *You must be prepared to die for your faith!"* A rather chilling thought for an impressionable little kid to ponder.

Those communists were BAD news though! We knew that from public school the communists wanted to drop A-bombs on us. Sister Mary William's dire predictions fired my child's imagination. When the communists took over, what would they do? Would they take my parents and say they were going to shoot one of them and make me choose which one would live? They would undoubtedly torture my poor old grandmother because she was a good Catholic! Maybe they would make me watch while they tortured my dog! Oh *no! Those EVIL fucking communists!*

And what did being quiet have to do with it? If we were noisy, would we miss it? Was the revolution going to come because we were being noisy? Would that be God's punishment to us for being so disobedient to this overweight, overbearing, embodiment of sadistic malice in a penguin suit? So much for God's infinite fucking mercy!

She had some other nice things to lay on us too." You know, when you are disobedient to your parents, *it's just like you are driving the nails into Jesus' hands and feet again!"*

Whoa, wait just a goddamned minute here, didn't he rise up from the dead and ascendeth to heaven, where he sitteth at the right hand of

God? Or was he still hanging on the cross somewhere, suffering terribly because of the grave sins of prepubescent children who didn't pick up their toys when told to do so? Or was this some kind of a mystical thing that by misbehaving *now* we increased Jesus' suffering *then?*

Well, Jesus suffering fuck! *We can change the past by altering the way we behave in the present!* It's a Holy Catholic Time Warp! Was this a secret church doctrine? Did anyone tell Einstein about this? If Jesus is still hanging around suffering, then Einstein has to be out there somewhere in the Holy Catholic Time Warp too, even if he was one of those "perfidious Jews," excoriated as such in the Easter liturgy. I guess that makes it a Holy Ecumenical Time Warp, not just a Catholic one!

Of course, you would never dare question her on a point like that. She was just too intimidating, a one-nun embodiment of The Inquisition, the Last Judgment and Eternal Damnation!

Along about the fifth grade we got the lowdown on those other "Brand X" churches. Sister Mary William was good at putting history into the proper Catholic perspective. She instructed us to never go to other people's churches, unless, they were Catholic too.

"Do you know what the difference is between a Catholic Church and a Protestant Church?"

No answer. I read beyond my school level and knew it had something to do with an event called the Reformation, Martin Luther, and the Diet of Worms. I thought that's what the Pope made him eat for starting the reformation. If the Pope could make you eat worms and excommunicate you to hell, you shouldn't mess with him! I wasn't going to say anything, though.

"Has anyone here ever been in a Protestant church?"

No answer. I had been, but I sure as hell wasn't going to admit it to *her!*

"If you ever go in a Protestant Church, you will notice that there is a difference from a Catholic Church. Do you know what it is?" She paused and looked around, her mustache twitching a bit. I wondered why she didn't she shave it. I guessed nuns weren't allowed to shave. They weren't allowed to drive either.[12]

"The difference between the Catholic Church and Protestant Churches is that God is not present in the Protestant Churches." Pregnant pause. Her voice had an irritating nasal quality to it and her manner of

---

[12] A classmate told me "My mom used to drive the nuns to Olean, NY, for shopping [about 30 mi.] and made me go along. Sister Mary William made us pray all the way there and back! It was simply awful!"

speaking was clipped. "God is not there. The Catholic Church is the one and only true Church. The Protestant Churches are empty of God's presence."

Well, fuck me running, so *that* was it! And here I thought it had something to do with The Reformation. I guess you can't believe what you read after all. All that Reformation shit must have been written by a Protestant presently broiling in the eternal torments of hell!

But wait a minute… if God is omnipresent, He would have to be in those churches too…wouldn't He? I guess He made an exception for the Protestants. After all, they rejected His One True Church and were bound for hell anyway. Evidently God figured He couldn't be bothered with those Protestant fuckers.

Sister Mary William's innate meanness and insensitivity was boundless. In eighth grade the older brother of a boy in our class rode his bicycle – which he had been forbidden to ride by his parents – down the driveway beside their house concealed by an embankment and directly into the path of an oncoming car. It was shocking to me because, well, when you are thirteen, death is something that happens to old people, not kids! We had to go, as a class, to the funeral home and say the rosary by the coffin with the dead boy in it.

At a subsequent class, she remarked that "If John had not disobeyed his parents he'd still be alive."

Of course, it was true, but that comment simply was both unnecessary and mean. "I hope he died in a state of grace. Because if he didn't he's burning in hell…"

She let that sink in for a moment then continued "…and that's why it's important to be in a state of grace. You never know when you might die."

Had John committed a mortal sin? A mortal sin was a sin so bad that God would be justified in striking you dead on the spot. In order for a sin to be mortal it had to go directly against one of the ten commandments. There are three conditions for a sin to be mortal. First of all, you had to *know* it was wrong. Then you had to *want* to do it. Then you had to actually *do* it.

John had committed a deliberate act of disobedience to his parents. This was in direct opposition to the fourth commandment, "Honor thy father and thy mother." He *knew* disobedience was wrong. He had been told to not ride his bicycle. He obviously wanted to do it because he *did* it. That takes care of all three conditions. Yes, fourteen year old John was beyond all doubt burning in hell forever because he broke the Fourth

Commandment. He dishonored his parents by disobeying them. God was so displeased with this action that he took John's life.[13]

Then there was the case where the older sister of a classmate was going to marry out of the church, to the son of a Protestant minister, no less! She was bound for hell for sure! And Sister Mary William would tell – more like order – us to pray for her. But the wedding was going to go ahead.

About a week before the wedding she said to the boy who's sister it was, "Tom, I don't think you are praying hard enough!"

Yeah. Like his prayers would cause his sister to fall out of love! And, of course, it then becomes *his* fault that his sister is going to burn in hell forever because he didn't pray hard enough. But then, when you are a Catholic, *everything* is your fault! She believed all that shit and was using it to an abusive end.

"False religions," Sister Mary William expounded, "are religions of sin. Pagan religions always involve the mortal sins of human sacrifice and sex outside of marriage."

As my spiritual outlook has evolved over the decades, I have examined Catholicism from the standpoint of no longer being mired in it. At the core, Catholicism is about the divine offspring of a creator God, being crucified as a sacrifice to his father. The purpose behind this is that the son must die so the creator can forgive all of mankind for all the sins that have been sinned and all the sins that will be sinned. The death of this one individual will undo all the bad shit mankind has ever done or will do. This act is recreated - not reenacted in the Holy Sacrifice of the Mass where the faithful actually eat the crucified Son's flesh and drink his blood, albeit transubstantiated..

To satisfy the Father, the Son must be killed, his flesh eaten, his blood drunk. This is because of the original sin of mankind, committed by Adam and Eve in the garden of Eden, which is imprinted upon the soul of everyone ever born since then. The sacrifice of Christ on the cross is the only thing that can cause god the father to forgive the sins of mankind thereby letting all the souls since creation go to heaven. The good ones that is.

---

[13] Looking past Catholic doctrine at this event, this is an example of "instant karma." Instant karma occurs when one acts in a manner that is out of context with the situation. Tom didn't die because his action in disobeying his parents displeased God, he died because he rode his bicycle down a concealed driveway and directly into the path of an oncoming car. No less tragic, but certainly not an act of divine retribution.

What the ever loving fuck? THAT *IS* HUMAN SACRIFICE! It is spiritually perverse nonsense, a medieval superstition fabricated along with heaven and hell to keep an ignorant populace firmly under the church's control. Nobody can absolve anyone else of sins, and by "sins," what we are talking about is karma, the Law of Compensation. You and you alone are responsible for the shit you cause and for setting it right. Similarly, you are also responsible for the good you do.

I wonder if people would be so quick to believe this horseshit if, instead of an altar, the church had a propane grill in the sanctuary and the priest's holy vestment was a Grillmaster apron. And we could sip blood of Christ out of the skull of some slain heathen, In Jesus' Name Amen!

Sister Mary William instructed us in spiritual realities facing Catholics. If that reptilian fiend got any joy out of life, this would have been it.

"Hell is eternal. Hell is forever. Once you are in hell, you can never get out. It is indescribable eternal torment of the most horrible kind. It never stops. The flames hurt just as if you are alive, but they never consume the body. You can't die. You can't sleep. You can't escape it. Never. It just goes on forever. *But don't think about it. People have gone crazy from thinking about hell.*"

Thanks a lot, Sister. I mean, really, who wouldn't think about it after a build up like that?

Our parish priest, Father Joseph J. Grode, brought the olfactory aspect of eternal punishment into play.

"The stench in hell is unbelievable," he would say, shaking his head, "There are smells in Hell that are so terrible that…you just can't imagine it. Sure, there is pain, real pain to be sure, oh, but the stench…" Evidently he had had a vision. Vision? Hmmm, that's when you *see* something. Now if you smelled it instead of saw it, that would be… an…*olfaction*…or perhaps a good time to take a bath.

The only way you could avoid hell was to die in a state of grace. The good sisters of Our Lady of Perpetual Misery also explained grace to us in second grade.

"This is your soul," Sister Noreen would say, drawing an awkward oval on the nice clean blackboard.

"Do our souls really look like that, Sister?" one of the kids would say.

"No, your soul doesn't actually look like that, but I am drawing this as a way of showing you how grace works."

"But if a soul doesn't look like that then how can that show us what it looks like…?"

Sister continued with the lesson after establishing that our souls were not in fact chalk ovals, but were merely assumed to be so for the didactic purpose at hand.

"So, boys and girls, this represents your soul. And when you do something good, God will give you sanctifying grace…" and she would lay the chalk sideways on the board and rub it, filling the awkward oval, "and it when your soul is full of grace, it looks so bright and shiny to God, like this…"

Bright and shiny? She made a mess on the blackboard and it's supposed to be bright and shiny?

"…but when you commit a sin, God takes away that grace, and you soul is black and empty and ugly to God…" She erased the chalk from inside the oval.

Black? Empty? Ugly? It was just a mess of chalk dust. Before she started it was black and empty. Ugly? Well, it was not a very well drawn oval to begin with.

"…and if you should die with no grace on your soul, you cannot get into heaven, you would go to hell."

So, if you croaked short of having your soul properly chalked, you could make a perfect Act of Contrition. Reciting that particular prayer before you croaked if a priest wasn't handy to give you last rites. But, counting on that was taking a real big chance. Suppose you were knocked unconscious before you died or killed instantly and couldn't make that Act of Contrition? Better to play it safe.

Even the Act of Contrition was fraught with risk. Perfect, it had to be *perfect*. That means that you had to *really mean it*, not only say it because you didn't want to go to hell (which of course you didn't). If you screwed up and said "Oh my God, I am *hardly* sorry," instead of "Oh my God, I am *heartily* sorry," you were fucked, too. Going to hell. Eternal damnation. *Bad smells! OH NOOOOOOOO!!!*

To avoid that meant going to confession and communion regularly, thereby hedging that, should you die unexpectedly, you would be in a state of grace. To this end, The Nunz herded us *en masse* to 8:30 am Sunday services to make our communion together. We marched into the church by classes, boys first. We were told by The Nunz that this is because, in the eyes of the church, men are more important than women.

Women couldn't become priests, nor could they perform altar service as boys could.[14]

So much for the abstract thinking capabilities of seven year olds! And so much for the education of nuns. While Roman Catholic priests are well educated,[15] nuns are not. After all, they did the shit what was too mundane for the priests to handle, basic sort of "housekeeping" for the church, and housekeepers don't need to be educated. Just tell 'em what to do and they'll do it.

To us kids, these women mysteriously garbed in their dark and flowing habits towering over us with their wimples, were the true representatives of God on earth as were the priests. I mean, you'd have to be a representative of God to wear a penguin suit every day, wouldn't you? It's just too goddamned weird for normal people. There was some discussion' I think in second grade, as to whether nuns had feet or wheels. We thought perhaps being special representatives of God, they had wheels under their habits instead of feet.

Confirmation in ninth grade turned out to be yet another disappointing adventure in liturgical nothingness. Months of deathly boring studies – which included extra mind-numbing confirmation classes after the 8:30 mass each Sunday, cut into precious weekend goofing off time – and endless rehearsals of the ceremony culminated in the big day when an auxiliary bishop came to our church to confirm us.

"You are now adults in the Holy Catholic Church," the Bishop said after anointing me and about twenty other kids with holy oil and giving us all a slap on the cheek, "and you can now die for the Faith."

Gee, thanks a fucking heap, Your Eminence, that's not exactly what I had in mind to do this week!

ALTAR SERVICE

Father Grode came up to me after Catechism one day and put his arm around my shoulders and said,

"Well, Gino, how about it?"

Gino? WTF...? "Uh... how about what...Father?"

"Don't you think you'd like to become an altar boy?"

---

[14] In light of recent revelations of rampant sexual abuse of children by priests, perhaps the priests made this a "tradition" so as to assure a steady supply of altar boys to bend over the kneelers and ass rape.
[15] Many have a PhD in Philosophy by the time they are ordained.

Oh, shit hell fuck no I don't! Got to think fast! Well, the priest is God's representative on earth. So if the priest asks me something, it's like God asking me something. My mind raced. *Should I say no to God and therefore endanger the well-being of my eternal soul? No way! Oh fuck…there's no way out of this one…*

"Uh…yeah…I…uh…guess so…Father…" That was a definite lie.

Thus I was corralled into altar service. This was before the Vatican II reforms and the liturgy was still in Latin (*Ad Deum qui latificat, juventutem meum*[16]).

I will say that there is probably nothing that can compare with the mystery, majesty and grandeur of the mass in Latin, especially the midnight masses at Christmas and Easter. That's when they trotted out all the good stuff: incense, the choir sang the most beautiful hymns – The Litany of the Saints in Latin with its hypnotic *"ora pro nobis"*[17] refrain was my favorite – processions around the inside of the church; it was profound and magnificent. In retrospect, it was grand enough to make you really believe all that shit – which I did – or at least to entertain you if you didn't.

These elaborate rituals required about six weeks of preparations so as to avoid a liturgical train wreck. Special practice sessions were held on Sundays after the 8:30 mass. Now, Father Grode was a rather severe priest. I have always thought that he should have had a parish where the people would walk on their bare knees over shards of broken glass to kiss the feet of a statue of the Blessed Virgin Mary.

He was a miserably poor verbal communicator and insisted on perfection in the performance of the liturgy. What this amounted to is that he couldn't really effectively explain what we were to do, then he would get upset when we failed do it right. Those weeks of practice between the Sunday 8:30 and 10:30 masses for the midnight masses at Christmas and Easter were grueling experiences, with us doing the right thing with the censer at the wrong time, or handing him the wrong prayer card or having it turned the wrong way and on and on… He didn't play favorites, we all caught hell!

His sermons were the verbal equivalent of valium. He would stand at the pulpit, gaze across the congregation, then clear his throat. He had a unique way of doing that that was long and high pitched. Then he would start with "My dear people…" and drone on endlessly. Over the years we would hear the same clichéd sermons recycled.

---

[16] Latin, "To God, the joy of my youth." This was the first Latin response altar boys were taught.
[17] Latin, "Pray for us"

Father Grode had this passive-aggressive[18] thing he would do. He would adjust his glasses with his upraised middle finger! He'd be talking to me while telling me to go fuck myself! I saw him do this a number of times over the years.

After Father Grode had the sanctuary carpeted, we altar boys discovered a neat prank! In the pre-Vatican II church it was strictly forbidden for anyone other than the priest to touch a consecrated host, crumbs were not to be dropped on the floor. When the priest was distributing the communion wafers, an altar boy holds a solid gold paten, a disk about nine or so inches in diameter with a wooden handle, under the chin of the communicant so as to catch any stray transubstantiated Jesus pieces. We would surreptitiously scuff our shoes over the carpet as we moved, building up a static charge. By putting ones thumb on the metal ferrule of the paten' one could then "accidentally" touch the chin or gullet of the poor communicant with the paten and ZAP, they would get a static shock! Timing it to the moment when the wafer touched the tongue was ideal! Yessiree, at St. Lizzy's we knew how to put some serious *snap* into the Holy Eucharist!

There was an average of one funeral a week at St. Elizabeth's. We had two funeral teams of older altar boys, five in each. The teams would alternate in serving for the funerals. There were no Catholics working in the school office so they had no idea how many altar boys it took to serve at a funeral.

We worked out a system where both teams of altar boys would be excused. The ladies in the school office probably figured that with ten altar boys, a Catholic funeral was one hell of a send off! The New York State drinking age at the time was 18, usually if you could see over the bar many places would serve you. One team would do the funeral, the other would go to Olean, NY and have a couple beers – and chewing gum to cover the smell of beer on our breath – and be back in time to go back to the school with the other funeral team.

It worked fine until one day both teams showed up at the church at the same time as the priest, Father Weber, Father Grode's successor, who exclaimed "What the hell are *all* of you doing here…ooohh…I get it." He contacted the school authorities and got the situation straightened out. I suppose this was a preferable alternative to no altar boys showing up at the funeral at all!

---

[18] A big dog that puts his paws on your shoulder and licks your face while pissing on your leg is displaying passive-aggressive behavior.

After Father Grode, Father Weber was a breath of fresh air. He was younger than father Grode, drove a brand new Buick Rivera, not at all a perfectionist, and could be amazingly human at times. The funeral ceremony at that time started with the casket wheeled to just inside the church entrance. A procession of altar boys and the priest met the casket. Brent had the aspergillum[19] which he had failed to fill with holy water. Father Weber did the prayers and took the aspergillum from Brent. He shook it. Nothing came out. He shook it again. Same. He shook it a third time. No holy water. He passed it back to Brent and gave him a dirty look. The rest of us were trying to suppress giggles. When we all got back into the priest's sacristy, he took the sprinkler from Brent and threw it against the wall exclaiming, "*God damn it!* Can't you guys get *any*thing right?" At the next funeral the old aspergillum had been replaced by a new one that had to be dipped in a bucket of holy water. It was easy to tell if there was holy water in the bucket!

SPANKING THE MONKEY

Confession and communion were really no big deal, until puberty set in. Adolescent males are motivated solely by hormones. Masturbation was a mortal sin. According to the church it carried the same penalty as murder. Hormone related situations would occur, like popping a boner in church, especially just before communion. I mean, what kind of a sin is it to receive Jesus when you have a hard-on? That's got to earn you a special place in hell! Then there is the logistical issue. If you have you hands folded in front of you in prayer, you are standing there about to receive the Holy Eucharist with a tent in your trousers! And how do you get rid of it? Well…yeah…ok…I know… but you can't do *that* in *church!* Can you…? For sure, thinking of Sister Mary William naked would make anyone's stiffy wilt, but then you've committed another sin…and lost your eternal soul to Satan for thinking about one of the world's most unappealing female without her clothes.

Puberty just brought dilemma after dilemma. I learned about "solitary sinning."[20] Whacking my carrot became my daily addiction and the whole sin and guilt thing took on gi-fucking-*gantic* proportions. Many was the Saturday evening I went to the confessional to unburden myself from the weight of my heinous and perverted acts for the week. I had a crafty technique for dealing with those confessions.

---

[19] holy water sprinkler
[20] Here is an interesting self-fulfilling prophecy. The nuns would excoriate us about "solitary sinning." This was at least a year before I started masturbating and I had no idea what it meant. I eventually found out!

Catholic priests could only celebrate two masses a day. Since there were three masses each Sunday, an extra priest was required each Sunday. This was usually a Franciscan friar from nearby St. Bonaventure University who would come over on Saturday and help Father Grode with confessions on Saturday evening, stay in the rectory overnight, and celebrate the 10:30 mass on Sunday. The trick was to go to the confessional that had the visiting priest in it, that way my pattern of transgressions would not be detected and I got off easy with five Our Fathers and five Hail Marys and the slate was wiped clean for a new series of sins. Sometimes I still got stuck with Father Grode.

Crossing myself, I whispered "Bless me, Father, for I have sinned," through the screen in the darkness of the confessional, hoping he wouldn't know my voice. "It has been a week since my last confession and these are my sins."

I had an inventory all worked out in my head with the worst one slipped in real fast at the end. I always rehearsed it in my head before going into the confessional.

"Father…uh…I…uh… took the name of the Lord in vain…and I…uh… disobeyed my parents…twice… and…uh…I…uh…" <very fast in a low voice> "…touchedmyselfimpurelyfivetimes! <regular voice> I am sorry for these sins and all the sins of my past life."

Then came the lecture.

"You say you touched yourself impurely five times…"

Aw shit! It didn't work. I lied anyway. I said five times It was at least seven (or more!). I figured that the actual number of times I pumped my peter would be between me and Jesus.

"You've got to get hold of yourself."

Strange choice of words, being as that is exactly to what I was confessing.

"If you can't exercise some will power and get this tendency under some restraint, Satan will completely take control of your soul, and you'll have to get psychiatric help."

I guess this was the official Catholic version of "if you do it for a hundred days, you'll go crazy." Better than going blind, I guess…I already wore glasses…no hair on my palms…yet.

"…for your penance say ten Our Fathers, ten Hail Marys, a Glory Be and the Apostles' Creed."

Whew! At least it wasn't the whole fucking rosary! Being the only one at the communion rail saying a ton of penance while other people were whizzing in and out was about as embarrassing as shitting your pants in a crowded elevator.

Exiting the congressional, it was as if I could feel the stares of the old ladies waiting on their turn in the magic sin box in the pews and imagined them thinking, "He's got a bunch of penance to say, he must've been flogging it a lot this week!"

Had I been run over sometime before noon on one of those Sundays I would no doubt have gone right straight to heaven. I just couldn't keep my hands off my tuminescent teenage wand for very long, though. The devil was putting in heavy overtime trying to get possession of my soul. By early afternoon on Sunday, my hormones would have gotten the best of me and once again I committed yet another heinous act of self-pollution. My adolescent years became an emotional maelstrom dominated by my acts of masturbation, the attendant pleasure and release they brought, and my desire to be a good Catholic and serve my Lord and Savior, and the horrible amount of guilt and self-loathing I felt over my betrayal of faith to my Lord and Savior…by jerking off.

As if the regular amount of guilt heaped on week after week through the graciousness of Holy Mother Church wasn't enough, there were yearly weekend retreats. These were strictly for the teenagers, to "…bind us tighter to the faith."

Bull. Fucking. Shit. They were really weekend long flames-of-hell mindfuck sessions that centered around our adolescent hormonal urges. This was one of the best tools the church had for ensuring continuing attendance by youth: make 'em feel like perverted scum with guilt and shame for nothing more than being perfectly normal. Make them feel that they are without a doubt bound for eternal torment in hell, then they'll have to be "good Catholics" so they can get to heaven! That way they will fill the collection plate and, since the church does not permit birth control, the horny little shits will grow up and spawn crotch fruit of their own for the church to "bind" to the faith as well.

An outside priest, no doubt specially trained by the church in the use of mindfuck psyops on horny adolescents, was invited to come into the church and do a heavy number on us. There were separate sessions for the boys and the girls. Nearly sixty years later I remember his spiel.

"When I was a young man, there was a pond in the country, a restful place with trees around it, clear water and many fish and other creatures thriving in it," said the priest, a large coarse featured man in his fifties with a square face, and thick, dark rimmed glasses." I used to go there and spend pleasant afternoons fishing and enjoying God's gift of that very special place."

He was stocky, quite imposing in his black jacket and Roman collar, his voice resonant and commanding, even when he spoke softly. He had a ruddy complexion and a full head of wavy salt and pepper hair.

"Then I moved away from that area and was not able to go back there for a number of years." His eyes moved from person to person around the room. "I happened to return to that spot one day, and…it had changed."

"The water was no longer clear, it was murky and polluted, trash was strewn about the shore. The waters that had once teemed with God's creatures were devoid of life, dead fish were floating on the surface." His voice started to boom." What had once been pleasant, wonderful and beautiful had become corrupt, foul and ugly!"

His eyes, distorted through the thick lenses of his Buddy Holly type glasses, [21]met mine.

"Your eyes are like that pool!"

ME? What the fuck…?

"I can tell by your looking into your eyes about your self-pollution and moral corruption!"

Oh shit! He knows I'm the weeniewhacker! Masturbation, in the eyes of the church, was worse than turning the Virgin Mary out on a stroll and ass raping the Pope! An *unnatural*[22] act! And I figured I was about the *only* guy in the world low and sinful enough to commit repeated acts of self-pollution!

"Your eyes are the mirrors of your soul!" He paused and his eyes finally moved away from mine.

Whew! I was relieved.

"You boys, you have hurt our Savior so much with the things you do in private, the things that no one but Our Lord can see, the hidden things, your secret, shameful sins of lust."

There was that what-you-do-in-the-present-can-affect-the-past thing again, the Divine Physics of the Holy Ecumenical Time Warp. I must

---

[21] Think of the character Bubbles from the Canadian TV series "Trailer Park Boys."
[22] "If God had intended for us to not masturbate, he would have made our arms shorter," – George Carlin

admit, it was a surprise to me that the RCC had the corner on a principle of physics of which everyone else seemed to be ignorant. Wow! That must be what makes it the One True Church!!

By the time Sunday afternoon rolled around and that horseshit was over, I was so bound up with guilt and shame at having shat upon Jesus' face while he hung on the cross–that's what sinning amounts to–that I contemplated cutting my penis off so I could never stroke it again. I was glad to confess my lustful dick massaging. But I couldn't stop doing it. No way. IT FELT *TOO GOOD!* My self-esteem was zero. I was a bad, bad, bad person and there was just no way I could be good, at least according to the church's standards.

The church wasn't the only source of misinformation about masturbation. I was thirteen when I discovered it. In those days, people did not talk about such things. There was no sex ed curriculum in school. Information on sex was hard to come by. Being inquisitive, I would take my information wherever I found it. Among my grandmother's books was a large two-volume set proclaiming itself to be "The Household Physician, a 20th Century Medica" copyrighted 1905. Well now, with a title like that, it just *has* to be reliable. I thought perhaps I could find pictures of female genitalia in it. There were anatomical illustrations, but nothing prurient. Damn it! I found across the section on "Venereal or Sexual Diseases". That was scary and had some rather unappealing illustrations. Then something caught my eye, a section titled "Self Pollution – Masturbation." *Holy shit! I have a venereal disease? And I caught it from my own hand? Woe is me!* In my thirst for knowledge I devoured the information presented.

"There is probably no vice to which so any boys…are addicted and from which so many constitutions break down than self-pollution…there are few objects more pitiable to behold than a young man…his nervous system feeble, tremulous, and broken; his memory weakened and fading out; his eye unsteady and incapable of looking a friend in the face; his loins and back weakened giving him the feeble gait of old age; his once erect form cowed and bent; his high sense of manliness all oozed out of him; his mind taking up and dropping the simplest threads of thought, losing its way in the plainest paths of reflection starting back affrighted t the at the glimpses of chaotic insanity opening before him – turning here and there for relief, but finding little hope of recovery, except in marriage, and yet knowing himself to be unfitted to be the husband of an intelligent woman!"[23]

Thirteen years old and I had already ruined my life!

---

[23] The Household Physician Vol 1, Physicians Publishing Company Inc., 1905, p. 410-411

In the summer between ninth and tenth grade my descent into carnal depravity deepened. I became a jerk off buddy with a friend thus becoming, in my own poorly informed opinion, a <*gasp, shudder*> homosexual! Now I was completely worthless to God or anyone else. This could only be the ultimate in perversion.

We spent the summer of 1962 sleeping in tents in our backyards and engaged in mutual masturbation. I felt tremendous pleasure – and a ton of guilt. Confessing these confusing feelings did not result in anything called counseling or comfort from Father Grode, who interrogated me in salacious detail about these mutual jack-off episodes I had with my friend, following it with only reproach and fiery condemnation.

One of Sister Mary William's favorite aphorisms was "Nobody goes to hell alone, they always take someone with them." My JO bud was not a Catholic, so he was committing mortal sins along with me but didn't have the sacrament of confession, so he could not get forgiven and was going to hell for certain. I could at least go to confession and receive absolution from my acts of adolescent lust! It might require a couple millennia in purgatory, but it wasn't eternity in hell!

Decades later, I realized that my friend and I were satisfying our normal teenage curiosity. I also realized Father Grode was most likely beating the bishop under his cassock as I was confessing to jerking off with my friend.

I had no one to go to. I felt worthless, so ashamed, and so terribly alone.

IMMACULATE DECEPTION

> *"Mary, conceived without sinning, please help us to sin without conceiving." — Catholic School Girl Prayer*

Then there is the doctrine of the Immaculate Conception, as forcefully and repeatedly pounded into our skulls states that Mary was conceived without sin.[24] That means it wasn't a sin for her parents to have

---

[24] This is the most misunderstood doctrine in the church. Most people think The Immaculate Conception applies to the birth of Jesus. It does not, it applies to the birth of Mary. She was conceived without sin, meaning her parents did not "sin" when they conceived her. Jesus, (allegedly) the Son of God, was born of a virgin, There was certainly no "sin" there. But, as a vessel of perfection which was to incubate the Son of God, Mary had to be completely purified to satisfy the myth, so the church made up this ridiculous shit. I think punctuation plays a role in this misconception of the Immaculate Conception. Leave out the comma and "Mary, conceived without sin," becomes "Mary conceived without sin."

sexual relations so she could be conceived and thereby become the mother of God. Yeah, right. Now, you talk about angels dancing on the head of a pin, they are doing the twist, the mashed potatoes and a whirling fucking tarantella, too, with this one.

Let's see, if Mary's folks were married, then it wouldn't be a sin for them to conceive a child in the first place, would it? Hell no. But if Mary was singularly conceived without sin, that means it is a sin for anyone else to conceive a child no matter what the circumstances.

But The Nunz, who would never ever lie, told us that sex was a special reward God had reserved for those who were united in Holy Matrimony and that it was a terrible, terrible sin outside of Holy Matrimony. But then they turn around and lay this Immaculate Conception crap on the poor mindfucked kids and it is entirely contradictory…so everybody who fucks is a sinner, which is what the church wants because it keeps them in business. It's just the church tripping over its own dick…uh…dogma.[25] *In vitreo* fertilization and artificial insemination excepted, humans can't procreate if they don't fuck. So if all fucking is a sin then we are all sinners conceived in sin whether our parents were married in the eyes of the church or not! Contradictory messages and…oh just…what the divine fuck…?

Sister Mary William would get so worked up about sex. I'll bet she never had an orgasm in her life (just the thought of that is too hideous to contemplate!). When the subject would come up she would snarl about "…people and their *animal passions!!* And follow it up with "Almost everyone who goes to hell goes because of sex! Most people will go to hell." Not a very optimistic pronouncement.

And how about Jesus birth to a virgin? Yeah. Right. I don't know any virgins who have given birth. It brings to mind a joke, though

God wanted to take a vacation and he was talking it over with the Archangel Gabriel.

"Why don't you try Mercury?" says Gabriel.

"The last time I was there it was too hot," God replies, "it's just too uncomfortable."

"Well, what about Mars?"

"Oh, too bellicose and noisy," counters God, "just can't get a moments peace there."

---

[25] The nuns never could explain this in any kind of satisfactory manner. It remains a Catholic Conundrum to this day.

"Well," says Gabriel, genuinely trying to help, "how about earth? It's got a temperate climate and it's not too noisy."

"Oh no!" says God." The last time I went there I got this little Jewish girl in trouble and I haven't heard the end of it yet!"

THOU SHALT NOT HAVE AN UNAUTHORIZED ORGASM!

So, how did sex, the act of procreation, the ultimate expression of love, passion, and intimacy between two human beings, get to be a sin anyway? I have a theory. It started with the Council of Nicea in 325A. D. The Roman Empire was going to hell fast and the Emperor Constantine was trying to forestall the inevitable. He saw the need for a new religion. Oh, and forget that vision of the sword in the sky *"in hoc signo vinces"*[26] story, that's just a made-up story for the credulous.

Imagine, if you will, the Emperor Constantine is sitting around with all these church high up muckitymuck bishops – there wasn't a pope yet – and they were deciding what was to become Christianity. They threw out most of the gospels and otherwise purged, codified, and hammered the crap that remained into an orthodoxy. But they still have one problem: How do they keep the people under control? After all, if the people don't feel a need for the church, Constantine is fucked because the empire is falling apart, and the bishops fear the persecution may resume and Christians will once again be lion munchies.

Constantine: OK guys, this has been a pretty productive brainstorming session. You know how important this is. I need to keep the empire together because I got the goddamned Visigoths, Vandals and Celts banging on the front door right now, and the fucking Mongol Hordes are trying to get a piece of my action too. You guys got a pretty good thing here, all organized and everything. You got these gospels with all this good shit in them, and it's mystical enough to keep them confused at the same time, that's a nice touch. A class act, definitely better than Jupiter and all that old crap. I like this. But how are you going to get everyone to buy into it? You need an overwhelming compelling reason.

Bishop 1: "That's a damned good question. Let's see…how about something really terrible if they don't –"

Bishop 2: "Hey, I had this idea a while back about a thing called "hell." If you fuck up, you get sent to hell and burn forever. No reprieve,

---

[26] Latin, "In this sign you shall conquer."

no parole. You are fucked for all time. Unless of course you are a church member in good standing."

Constantine: "Hell…I like that…has a nice ring to it, only one syllable…but how are you gonna convince people…I mean really make 'em believe?"

Bishop 3: "I had this idea called 'sin.' You do something wrong and it's a 'sin.' Commit a sin, go to hell. Mandatory sentencing."

Constantine: "'Hell.' Hmmm…I like that… another one syllable word and easy to remember…So what's a "sin," I mean what do you have to do? Spit on the fucking sidewalk? I need ideas here, gentlemen! C'mon! It's getting late and I have a round of golf scheduled!"

Bishop 2: "It's gotta be something that people really have to do that we can tell them is a sin and that they will have to come to the church to work out the deal so they can avoid going to hell."

Bishop 1: "Well, there are three things people gotta do. Let's pick one of them."

Constantine: "What three things are you talking about?"

Bishop 1: "Well, your High Imperial Emperorship, they gotta eat, for one. And they gotta shit. And they gotta fuck."

Bishop 2: "For Chrissakes, you can't tell 'em eating is a sin! They'll goddamned well starve themselves to death and then we're all out of a job."

Bishop 3: "And shitting can't be a sin. If they try to avoid doing that, they'll explode!"

Bishop 2: "Well, that leaves fucking. They won't die if they don't do it, it'll just make 'em cranky. And when they *do* do it, they'll have to come to us to work it out so they can avoid hell…we can call it… 'absolution.'"

Constantine: "Abs-so-loo…?…well…that sounds rather technical…but I guess it'll work. You guys are really getting your act together, I'm seeing real team spirit here. You guys got the ideas, I got the marketing skills to roll this out all over the empire and beyond. This is happening!"

Bishop 1: "So OK, you like our ideas, but I'm not convinced about the marketing end of this. How are you gonna sell this crock of shit?"

Constantine: "Now what do you think I got that big fucking army for anyway?"

And that, ladies and gentlemen, is how sex became a sin...not! But it *could* have!

COCKSUCKING IN THE SACRISTY

When I was about thirteen I stopped by St Elizabeth's on a Saturday afternoon to get my cassock and surplice and take them home so Grandma could clean them. Entering the sacristy, I opened the sacristy door. As I did so I saw Father Grode, on his knees with his head in another priest's crotch performing oral sex. The other priest made eye contact with me for a brief moment. Being young and naïve, I did not understand the peculiar look on his face. Without looking up, Father Grode said in a stage whisper, *"GET OUT!!"* I did.

I figured he knew it was me and I would catch all holy hell from the next time I saw him. That day came and went with not a word being said. I hadn't done anything wrong, if anything I was a victim to what I witnessed. But that made no difference whatsoever in my mind. Nothing was ever said to me though. Not one word. I felt guilty about it, even though I had done nothing wrong. As I have stated, if you are a Catholic, *everything* is your fault, even another priest's cock in Father Grode's mouth.

Shocking doesn't even begin to characterize this incident. Here was the parish priest *with another priest's cock in his mouth!* He was a *cocksucker.* Now, we adolescent boys used the term "cocksucker" as a pejorative, as an insult, as in this exchange::

"Fuck you, you're a cocksucker!"

"Takes one to know one, peckerbreath!"

"Oh yeah? You got pubes stuck between your teeth!"

And so on...

It was a subject for busting on your buddies. But for somebody to actually *suck* a *cock?* Nobody actually *did* things like that...did they...? That's what guys *pissed* through! Yuk! Who would want somebody's pissy dick in their mouth anyway? GROSS! YUK!!

That memory was immediately repressed and stayed that way for forty years. I couldn't possibly tell anybody I saw our parish priest sucking a cock. Who would believe me? I couldn't process it, so I buried it.

But why in the sacristy of all places? The rectory was only a couple dozen steps away and offered complete privacy. Why were these two priests committing a sex act together in a place where someone could walk in, as I did? This questioned remains unanswered. Or, as the Nunz said about so many things, "It's a mystery boys and girls. Isn't that wonderful?"

I am not aware he ever touched any kids. However, as I think back, there were times when Father Grode had me stay after mass to play ping-pong with him in the church hall. As I recall those times, it seems that there was a certain awkwardness in Father Grode's manner that was strange, especially after what happened one Saturday when I was helping him with some things at the church.

Father Grode would pay us altar boys to help with minor maintenance tasks. I was wearing an old pair of pants where the stitching had come out of the gusset that covers the zipper. Father Grode went off on me, I mean he just **PEELED MY ASS** because my zipper was exposed, going on and on about how I could cause someone else to sin thus becoming an "occasion of sin"[27] and thereby causing someone else to lose their eternal soul which would of course cause me to lose my soul as well yadda yadda... I was pretty naïve, completely ignorant of sex, not even having yet discovered masturbation. I had no idea what he was going on about. Later I realized the reason he got so hot and bothered was because he got hot and bothered about seeing my zipper and it gave him a stiffy!

In my thoroughly mindfucked teen years I had actually considered mutilating myself so I could not masturbate any more. Sister Mary William was big on "If thine eye offends thee pluck it out, etc." The solution was obvious: no penis, no problem. That way Jesus would love me and I could go to heaven, albeit dickless. Fortunately I did not act on this. That became yet another failing, showing me that I did not have the courage to do what the Bible commanded.

The Roman Catholic path to heaven was no superhighway, it was a tightrope stretched over a fiery pit. Just one teeny-tiny little itty-bitty slip and you were going to roast forever hell! Because of God's love.

I now know that what was motivating me was normal adolescent urges. At the time I figured there were maybe three people on earth who masturbated, and I was one of them. Ditto adolescent bisexuality. I did not know as I do now it is quite prevalent among boys and is a part of normal adolescent development. At the time it was just another enormous moral failing on my part, rotten hell-bound shit bird that I was. I never discussed this with anyone. I couldn't. It was all just too horrible.

---

[27] An occasion of sin was a person, place or thing that was likely to tempt one into committing a serious transgression against the Ten Commandments or the Canon Laws of the Church.

By the time I graduated high school, I was a fucked up, sorry mess with very little self-esteem.[28] It was only my involvement with music that gave me something I could do that I made me feel good about myself. In that respect, music saved me because it gave me some self-esteem. It was my own accomplishment and no one could take it from me. And it was not a sin. Of course, John Lennon did say the Beatles were more popular than Jesus, and I think he was right, Jesus couldn't even play rhythm guitar!

In my freshman year at Lock Haven State College in 1965 I was starting to doubt the validity of Church doctrine, but not so much that I wouldn't drag myself out of bed, with a hangover many times, and go to Sunday mass to avoid committing–yet another–mortal sin. I had nothing with which to replace the Catholic horseshit I had been force-fed for so long. I was just so damned sick of the guilt-ridden dogma that I was considering the possibility that if eighteen years of devotion wasn't enough to get me into heaven, heaven wasn't worth it. This shit was making me crazy. I went to mass every Sunday for the first semester, then started going sporadically. I wanted to say "Fuck the church. Fuck the Pope. Fuck the guilt. Fuck the dogma. Fuck the bullshit." But I just didn't have the courage to do it, yet. I still, deep in my being, believed it. The church's noxious mythology had so very deeply infected my psyche.[29]

I have been a lapsed Catholic for over 50 years. Over the decades, several people have tried to tell me how the church has changed, and I should check it out with an eye toward returning to it. I am polite to them, saying I will take it under advisement.

Thinking that superficial changes are in any way a remedy for the church's toxic dogma is like saying bad mayonnaise ruined the pickle and shit sandwich. The church is not changing and will not change any more than priests will stop ass raping altar boys. Fortunately, it is currently imploding from sex scandals and financial corruption. Perhaps humanity will no longer be burdened with the existence of the Catholic Church in the near future.

---

[28] The Old Curmudgeon's Sage Advice No. 9
[29] The Old Curmudgeon's Sage Advice No. 6.

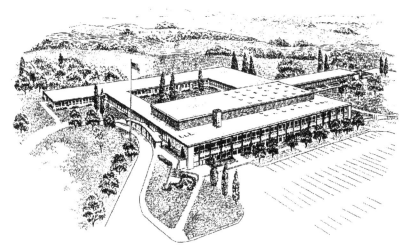

Architects rendering of our brand-new million dollar school which opened in September 1961

CHAPTER 4

ACADEMIC DISCIPLINE

Corporal punishment was inextricably bound to our public education. Any teacher – who was by law *in loco parentis*[1] – could slap the shit out of any student at any time for any reason without any – or very few – repercussions whatsoever, just as a parent could.

Additionally, if you got your ass kicked in school, your dad would find out about it and kick it again for you when you got home. Such was the social networking in rural communities long before Facebook!

Corporal punishment was viewed as acceptable and necessary to maintaining classroom order. The generally accepted method was for a teacher to take the first kid – always a guy and usually Barty Barton – who got out of line on the first day of school, put him up against the wall and give them something between a stern talking to and a high-volume ass-peeling in front of the class. Rinse and repeat. This was a time honored and highly effective method of setting boundaries of classroom behavior.

---

[1] Legal term, Latin, "In the place of the parent"

It's not like we were entirely undeserving. We were in fact obstreperous little bastards who viewed education as an adversarial process.

In seventh grade we were in gender segregated "guidance" classes. Our completely useless no, *less* than useless, Guidance Counselor, Mrs. Anderson, having us read books aloud on etiquette, would then rail at us about one goddamned thing or another. We truly just didn't give a shit. Mrs. A. wasn't scary at all. I swear, half the goddamned class period was Mrs. A bansheeing at us about our lack of basic civility, at least in her view. Oh Christ, she would rail and point her finger and screw up her face, giving you her silly-assed version of what she thought a "fuck you, you little smartass!" stare looked like. It was comical! I don't remember any specifics, it was the same litany of bullshit over and over and over. Mrs. A. had no children so she evidently had no idea that it is perfectly natural for 12 year-old boys to be undisciplined beasts!

In our junior year, my friend Mia and I had a friend who was talking suicide. We went to Mrs. A and told her our concerns. As I look back, it was as if you could see the fucking words float in one ear, through her empty head, and out the other ear. She thanked us in a somewhat condescending tone for being concerned about our friend and said she would take care of it. She called our friend in and "had a talk" with him. That was her cure for everything, a "talk." Three weeks later this same friend broke a beaker and intentionally cut himself with it in the chem lab. Mia and I went and got the school nurse. On the way back to the chem lab I said something about Mrs. A. being a useless bitch.

She said, "You shouldn't talk like that." It was the mildest rebuke I have ever received.

Mrs. A. brings to mind the phrase "useless as tits on a boar," so much so that it should have been a criminal act for her to be within a hundred yards of a school. During our (mis)guidance classes she used to blather on about the Ph.D. she was working on. It was evidently rejected, as she never got one and we heard no more about it. I guess her fellow academics thought she was clueless as well.

I made a mildly derogatory comment about her to my father when I was about fifteen. He replied, in a serious and deliberate manner, "Now Gener, you have to understand something here. She fills a necessary function. Mrs. Anderson is the living proof that someone can be educated and still not know their ass from a hole in the ground!"

Proof of her abject uselessness is that Pell Grants for college bound students became available in 1965, my graduation year. Mrs. A. never said anything to us college bound students about them. Not a word. Several students found out about them on their own and were able to apply for them. But Mrs. A? Not a word to us. It was her fucking *job* and she did *not* do it!

But she was very involved with *where* Smethport students attended college, to the point of interfering with their education. Ed wanted to go to college. Mrs. A. selected a school for him, Murray State in Kentucky, because "a student from Smethport had never attended there." Ed didn't want to go to Kentucky. Mrs. A did not help him any further. The POD[2] teacher helped him get into Slippery Rock State. All students matriculating to college were, to Mrs. A, only pins on a map. My father was right.[3]

Some of the women teachers were holy terrors with classroom discipline. Walking into a buzz saw was preferable to the irrational rage of a menopausal woman!

Our sixth grade teacher, Mrs. Lindquist, played favorites with the beatings she administered. I call them beatings because they were not simply a slap or paddling. Dave Lamborn sat in front of me. Several times she barely missed me as she rained blows on Dave's back. She just fucking *pounded* on him! It wasn't just a couple of slaps, she rained blows until her anger was spent, probably six, eight or ten of them. I never counted, I just stayed the hell out of the way of her flailing arm!

She also had it in for PJ Hergenrother who was a recipient of these fearsome and somewhat deranged attacks. This was particularly unfair as PJ was mentally challenged. As an infant he had surgery for a brain tumor. The operation that removed it left him acting what we called "retarded" in those days. But PJ was not intellectually deficient, he had communication issues and was socially awkward. Highly intelligent, every year he had the highest score in our class on the standardized science test. His brother told me how, after graduation, PJ enlisted in the Navy and was discharged after they determined his mental status. He was able to get GI benefits and disability. That was not the action of some who was intellectually deficient. He knew his life prospects were limited and he and took action accordingly. It was brilliant.

I still remember the hollow sound of Mrs. Lindquist's blows resonating in her victims' chest cavities. That is the *only* corporal punishment I witnessed in elementary school. It was scary as hell to see an adult lose it like that with students.

---

[2] "Problems of Democracy," senior level civics. Back in those bygone olden days they actually used to teach civics in schools so students could learn to be responsible citizens.
[3] Mad Magazine did a send up on guidance counselors, the climax of which was "Do remember the sinking feeling you got in the pit of your stomach the day your guidance counselor came up to you and said 'I think you've got what it take to become a guidance counselor,'?"

Miss Bell never had discipline issues. She was young, hot, stacked brunette with great legs, drove a '57 T-Bird, and had a marvelously trashy look about her in a Sophia Loren way that fired adolescent male fantasies! The boys paid too much attention to her mammalian protuberances (or her legs if she was sitting on her desk with her legs crossed) to be disruptive. Inattentive to her lessons, for certain, but not a bit disruptive!

Unique among the disciplinary styles was that of Miss Alma Johnson. She went to school with Moses, was rather imposing and quite stern. Oh, she had a sense of humor, quite subtle. Her discipline style was erudite sarcasm. If you got your ass peeled by Miss Johnson, you stayed quiet for one of two reasons: either you had no idea what the hell she just said to you and certainly were *not* going to ask her to repeat it, or you understood what she just said and were absolutely mortified by having it publicly applied to you! Miss Johnson did not do this gratuitously, you had to earn it. She was inerrant in this.

I never got crossways with Miss Johnson. She was an excellent teacher and was the first teacher to hint that I might have some writing ability. I wrote the first and only draft of an essay – no idea what it was about – in study hall the period before her English class and handed it in. It was a "Hail Mary" effort. When she handed it back with an "A," she complimented my writing ability. So I had a hint I could write, but the big lesson was do *something,* even in the face of an seemingly impossible deadline. There was the possibility that you might screw up and actually do it right!

Then there was Dorothy Bombard, referred to as "Dirty Dot" by students. She is the only teacher in my experience who had a disposition, exactly like a wolverine. Dirty Dot taught typing and business courses. I never had her for class but I was in her homeroom my senior year. She was a martinet, demanding absolute silence in the room even before first bell. Anyone breaking that silence would catch all hell! I'll say this, she played no favorites in this, everybody was fair game, from the class clown to the student council president.

Every Christmas there was a tree in the entranceway of the school. One year a beautifully wrapped package appeared under it with Mrs. Bombard's name on it. Oh, she was just so tickled about it, until she opened it and found it was filled with a fresh cowpie![4] To be fair to the old battle axe, I did hear a classmate speak well of her once, but this occurred well after graduation.

---

[4] The Old Curmudgeon's Sage Advice No. 8.

Mr. Vesper was a sweet guy and a great teacher. The only class I had him for was ninth grade general science. He had been the basketball coach at one time and could teach more in a class period than anyone else, even if he spent half the class discussing basketball! However, should you take advantage of his good nature you would be in for a rude awakening.

I was goofing off in a seventh grade study hall. Mr. Vesper told me to settle down a couple of times. Then he said, "EUGENE! Go to room 5 and get the paddle!"

Holy shit! The *PADDLE!* Like a condemned man walking to the gallows, I shuffled off to room 5 and knocked on the door. Mr. McBride opened it. I told him Mr. Vesper requested I bring him the paddle. Mr. McBride handed this fearsome instrument of retribution to me. I detected a slight smirk on his face, no doubt in reaction to my scared completely shitless expression.

Band-sawed from maple in the wood shop, the carefully shaped handle assured the executioner a firm grip, thus guaranteeing maximum buttock bruising impact and student discomfort. It was about two feet long, an inch thick and six inches wide. About a dozen ½ inch holes were drilled in it. This was allegedly to relieve air pressure from building up and cushioning the force of the blow. Some smartass had written "Board of Education" on it! Curiously, it was adorned with signatures, no doubt names of unfortunate miscreants who never survived adolescence having long ago been beaten to death with it for misbehaving in study hall!

Taking my time, I trundled back to Mr. Vesper's room and my certain doom. Confident I was about to draw my last breath, I entered the room, sauntered up to Mr. Vesper's desk and handed the instrument of my destruction to him. Laying the paddle on his desk he handed me a marker from his drawer. "Sign it!" he commanded. I complied. "OK," he said, "now your name is on the paddle. Only people whose names are on the paddle have it used on them. Make certain you are *not* one of them! Now return to your seat."

Well I'll be *damned!* He never intended to beat me with it! It was all a *con!* And it *worked!*

Mr. Vesper was one of the most beloved teachers Smethport ever had. And I never saw him strike a student, even Barty Barton, and *all* the teachers beat on him! Mr. Vesper certainly could put on an act though!

Emerson Havens taught my tenth grade World History class and was my home room teacher. One did *not* fuck with Mr. Havens either! I could see the door to Mr. Havens room from my seat in biology class across the hall. One morning I heard a hell of a commotion consisting of Mr. Havens' voice followed by thud, clatter and crash. The door opened and out limped my friend, Tom. The door closed and more noise ensued. The door opened again and out came Mr. Havens dragging Bobby, who had gone limp before Mr. Havens could bounce him off the wall.

We had two teachers students regarded as psychos, both WWII vets and football coaches. One was biology teacher, Neil Bailey who had a reputation for knocking the hell out of students. When some kid was due for an ass chewing, Mr. Bailey would take him into the hall, close the door, slam his victim against the lockers and yell at him while pounding on the lockers. To the rest of the students in the classroom it sounded like Mr. Bailey was beating this poor bastard to death! Then again it was not all that uncommon to see Mr. Bailey with some poor kid by the scruff of the neck walking him down to the office cuffing him repeatedly as they went, after having bounced him off a wall or six.

The other was Jim Donovan, football coach and health teacher. He and Bailey were both physically imposing men who deadpanned everything. If you made the mistake of thinking they were joking when they were not, you were in world of shit. Either one could pick a kid up one-handed and toss him across the room like a rag doll.

Jim Bennett was in the last seat in his row in our eleventh grade health class. His desk was slightly askew from the rest of the row. Donovan said, "Bennett, straighten out your desk."

Jim tried to move his desk but it was wedged by the desks in front and wouldn't budge.

"Didn't you hear me? I said *straighten that desk!"*

Once again Jim tried, but it won't move. He looks up at Donovan and says "But it—"

"I SAID STRAIGHTEN THAT DESK! *NOW!"*

With a mighty heave, Jim moves his desk back into alignment, pushing several desks in front of it several inches forward with a screech.

"OH, SO YOU WANT TO BE A *SMART GUY!"* Donovan snarled as he strode down the aisle to Jim's seat, and, grabbing Jim by the collar, tore him out of his seat and gave him a one-armed toss to the front of the room where he fell over the teacher's desk. Grabbing Jim again, Donovan then tossed him out the door with instructions to go to the office.

Every schoolroom has a sniveling, ass kissing snitch. You know. The one that ate paste and pencil erasers in first grade. We had one who was brown of the nose to the point that one day in sixth grade he raised his hand and said "Mrs. Lindquist, Teddy's chewing gum." Teddy would then have to spit his gum out, stand in the corner for the rest afternoon, and then beat The Snitch's ass after school. Being an evident masochist, The Snitch issued one invitation after another to break his balls. Even his jokes, corny beyond description and like The Snitch, were never funny and always annoying! I don't know how many times he got his ass beat on the way home front school, a one block journey for him.

Years later Teddy Hyde recollected, "My fondest memory of The Snitch is one day after school I was beating the shit out of him on the lawn in front of his house. His mother came out on the porch and said 'Now Teddy, you let The Snitch up and fight fair!' So I did. I let him up, then knocked him down and started beating the shit out of him again!"

After an eighth grade gym class, Dave Lamborn, Barry Wilson and Eric Donaldson held The Snitch fully clothed under a cold shower. Donovan heard the screeching and bitching and came in. The drenched Snitch gasped out the horrible truth between sobs. Donovan took the offenders to his upstairs office that overlooked the gym and beat the living bejesus out of them with his paddle. They were teary, red-faced and limping after that encounter. What they did was not nice at all, but there is a line between discipline and a beating. An appropriate punishment would have been standing the offenders under cold shower and soaking them. The Snitch is now a preacher, an accomplishment at the top of Maslov's hierarchy of How To Be A Pain In The Ass.

I don't think Bailey and Donovan were clinically crazy. They were both WWII vets. Donovan recounted being wounded in the hedgerow fighting in France. According to my longtime friend, Don Thomas, highly decorated U.S. Army Vietnam veteran and PTSD counselor, these two guys most likely had PTSD, which was not identified as such back in their day. From the way these guys could flip out in a nanosecond, Don thinks this may be the case. They were quite formidable.

Then there was George Larson. He was of a medium build, about 5'10," salt and pepper hair, glasses, no chin and an overall very mild demeanor. Like a shady *film noire* character, he always looked like he needed a shave. He taught eighth grade science. I was in his home room.

George used to say weird and/or outrageous stuff. My favorite: "If you're looking for sympathy, you can find it in the dictionary between shit and syphilis." Another was a rambling discourse on "chyme."[5]

---

[5] the semi fluid mass into which food is converted by gastric secretion and which passes from the stomach into the small intestine.

One morning there was the usual hijinks before first bell. Something pissed George off and he focused his anger on Chuck Daniels. "*DA-NIELS!*" George yelled. The boisterous room fell silent." *Get* up here!" He pointed to a spot at the head of the first row of desks. Chuck did as he was told while the rest of us scrambled into our seats. Shit was going to happen!

"Bend over. Palms on the desk." George's voice seemed calm, but had that little tremor in it that told you he was wound so tight he could pop an embolism. In other words, fucking crazy! Skinny, 13 year old Chuck bent over the desk. He was face-to-face with Beth Albright, whose desk it was. George proceeded to give Chuck what the British would call a "caning," striking Chuck repeatedly with a thin plastic dowel about 30" long. The blows fell on the backs of his legs between his buttocks and knees. I don't remember how many times George hit him, but I remember the demented look on his face. It was scary!

Long before it was over there was not a dry eye in the room. Each and every one of us shared Chuck's pain as we saw the agony in his face with each blow. Nobody ever talked about it. Nobody pissed George off in home room again either. The son-of-a-bitch might have been a bit crazy but he by God had earned some *respect!*

CHAPTER 5

THE KENNEDY YEARS

A SHINY BRAND NEW DECADE

In 1960 I turned thirteen joining the baby-boom teenagers. John Kennedy was elected president. JFK was more like a movie star than a president. Young, handsome and charming, his wit endeared him to us all. I watched the Nixon-Kennedy debates on TV. Kennedy was stunning in appearance and demeanor and contrasted starkly with shifty-eyed five o'clock shadow Nixon. There was no doubt in my mind JFK was the man for the time.

The local Baptist minister's son was a year older than me and considerably bigger. He could be a mean fucker and he delighted in bullying me the summer before Kennedy's election. My encounters with Billy usually consisted of him coming up behind me, grabbing me and twisting my right arm behind my back.

"Hey you little kyke, you know what's going to happen if Kennedy becomes president don't you? Everyone's gonna have to become a Catholic and worship the Pope! We'll all have to pay taxes to Rome!"

"Yeah. Right. Fuck you, Billy." Not exactly an original or snappy comeback, but, despite his pejorative name-calling, he didn't like cursing and I knew it.

"Don't talk that way, kyke." He twisted harder. "You little Pope lover. Kennedy'll make us all convert, won't he?" More arm twist. *Sono-*

fabitch! Ouch! This was hurting *seriously.* It was time to piss him off but good. Maybe I couldn't kick his ass but I could outrun him!

"Yeah, right. And after he does that he'll make us all line up and fuck your mother!" Now *that* one had some zing to it!

"Why you dirty little kyke –" He loosened his grip to smack me. I squirmed free and ran down the street, flipping him the bird shouting "Fuck you and your mom, Billy!"

As to the cursing, no one curses like a thirteen-year-old! It is a verbal art form boys start about the fourth grade and have perfected by junior high!

He never messed with me after JFK was elected. I silently gloated, though, thinking to myself, *ha ha asshole, Kennedy won and you still have the right to be a bullying Baptist bigot!*

A single television was set up on the stage in the gym on the day of Kennedy's inauguration. We had an assembly and watched and listened to him take the oath of office. JFK fired the ideals of our entire generation with "…ask not what your country can do for you, rather, ask what you can do for your country." It was a truly profound moment. Kennedy's election brought with it a feeling of confidence in America. I felt like he was my own personal friend.

The young have not yet had a chance to develop a sense of history. Looking back on my seven decades, I can still recall what a proud moment John Kennedy's election was for America, for all of us. We were the best! We had the strongest economy, exported our manufactured goods all over the world. We were One Nation Under God, the watchdog for the Free World. The rest of the world looked to us to keep the balance of power with the Soviet Union. America was already great, but with JFK, I felt America was headed toward a pinnacle of achievement in peace and democracy never before seen. It was not only obvious, it was inevitable. What could possibly thwart this new and obvious Manifest Destiny for America?

John Kennedy brought us his fireside chats on television, coming into our homes and talking to us like family. The pictures in the newspapers of the Oval Office showed JFK at his desk with the Kennedy children underfoot. He was one of us. I loved him. The whole world, or so it seemed to us, loved him. Little did we know what lay ahead.

The Kennedys were as close as America has ever come to having royalty. The press called the Kennedy presence in Washington "Camelot."

It was very different from the Eisenhower years. These were not old men who were in charge of our country now. They were young and dynamic, America wasn't going to stagnate, we were going *forward!*

John Kennedy meant much to me for other reasons. My parents were Democrats in a Republican county. My father talked about the "goddamned Republicans" and how they didn't care about the "little guys" who worked for wages and really made this country what it was.

"The Democrats," he would say, "aren't a hell of a lot better, but they're better for the working man than the goddamned Republicans."

When I was small, it took some corrections from my mother for me to understand that "goddamned" wasn't actually part of "Republicans."

In his later years my father was a Republican. I asked him why he became a Republican. His reply, "I figure I can do them more damage from the inside."

John Kennedy's election was also special because to me because I was Catholic. For a Catholic to run for president was a great event. In our history classes – they actually taught history in schools back then – we learned that a Catholic hadn't run for president since Al Smith was defeated in 1936. The Nunz had us say special prayers for JFK's election.

The Kennedy years were marked with an overall air of optimism. No, JFK wasn't perfect, but he had guts. The CIA fiasco at the Bay of Pigs took us all by surprise. Kennedy knew where the responsibility of his office lay and did not weasel out by lying to the nation on television or having convenient lapses in memory like other presidents we have seen since. It took a real man to own up to a disaster of this magnitude. JFK was just that, a real man with balls enough to take responsibility for what came his way.

The Peace Corps was John Kennedy's idea to export American know-how to countries that needed it. It was a way for Americans to share their good fortune with the developing nations of the world and help them to become self-sufficient. Our example of altruism could entice developing nations away from the pernicious influence of international communism. We would later learn this was all bullshit, and that the CIA had assets inside the Peace Corp. The CIA's intentions had nothing to do with peace and freedom and were never altruistic.

The Berlin wall went up and East-West cold war tensions mounted as U.S. and Russian tanks faced each other across the border checkpoints. A shooting war with the Russians seemed imminent. Kennedy went to Berlin and announced to the people, "Ich bin ein Berliner"[1] telling them he was one of them and America would not abandon them. I saw it in television. God, how the people in Berlin cheered for him! They loved him as we did. He made me feel proud of being an American.

The struggle for civil rights in the South allowed us to see racial hatred and the appalling fact of the brutality used against U.S. citizens by their own countrymen. This drama played out on our televisions as so many of the events of the 1960's would be. We saw vicious dogs and water cannon used against Negroes[2] who wanted an end to Jim Crow and institutional discrimination.

To assure the admission of a single black student at the University of Mississippi, James Meredith, JFK called out the National Guard. I expected no less of him. He was a real hero to me, a man who was bigger than life, a man of the people who cared about the least of us as much as he did his own family. This was a view many of us shared.

As the United States sought to contain international communism names like "Laos" and "Vietnam" became part of our classroom discussions. The U.S. sent military aid and advisors to South Vietnam to help their struggling democracy resist communist aggression from North Vietnam. Our Scholastic Magazines told us in 1963 – U.S. ground troops fighting in Vietnam was still two years off – that the U.S. Was spending a million dollars every ten minutes in Vietnam. This was infinitesimal compared to the final cost.

THE MISSILE GAP

Global thermonuclear world war took on a new and terrifying dimension. The media harangued at length about the "missile gap," that the Soviets had more missiles than we did. The network newscasts brought us the ominous news of the development of intercontinental ballistic missiles capable of delivering nuclear warheads over the north pole. In the days before military satellites, the "Distant Early Warning" system or "DEW Line" was our first line of defense. A circle of large radar domes set were up in the Arctic to warn us of a Russian nuclear attack.

I thought this absurd. The graphic behind Walter Cronkite plotted the soviet ICBM's making their deadly arcs over the north pole to wreak destruction upon America. My thinking was *if I'm gonna be nuked, it's*

---

1 The actual translation of JFK's remark is "I am a jelly doughnut" Close enough. The people of Berlin loved it!!
2 I use the terms "Negro,""colored," and "black." They are descriptive, accurate and in no way meant to be pejorative. They are terms I learned as being proper and respectful when I was growing up.

OK with me if it's a complete fucking surprise. I mean, who needs fifteen or twenty minutes of anxiety before being barbecued by an H-bomb?

I knew the answer was to enable a retaliatory strike. But I didn't care. It still seemed foolish. Hell, any damned fool could see there was no defense against nuclear madness once it started.

What principles were there worth immolating the civilization and accomplishments of mankind in a thermonuclear conflagration? Who would be the winner if the earth was turned into a glowing cinder spinning through space? Us? Them? Shit. Those questions were *never* asked. The answers were too terrible to contemplate. In the back of my mind, I expected to die in a thermonuclear conflagration that could happen at any moment.

I kept my opinions to myself, a habit I have since outgrown. It turned out that the missile gap was a fictitious claim designed to frighten a credulous population and funnel more money into the defense budget and thusly into the pockets of the Military-Industrial Complex.

Some of my teachers had political leanings so far to the right they made the John Birch Society look like mincing pinko pansies. My introduction to this type of political indoctrination came in my seventh grade general science class. During a lecture on brainwashing Mr. Bailey told us "…do you know what? The guys who were captured in Korea and went over to the communist side were guys who didn't play high school sports."

He looked around the class.

"That's true," he added.

Sports were a non-event in my life. I was not an athlete and didn't care one whit about athletics. Mr. Bailey's inference was subtle. One was or might become a communist because they didn't care about sports, the fact that Soviet bloc nations did extremely well in the Olympics notwithstanding. Christ!

AND THUS HE PROPHESIED

One of the advantages of having lived beyond the age of seventy is gaining some perspective on what you have witnessed and experienced. What was true over a half century ago is still true, but it can take on a different significance over time.

I have said many times that the reason I am so outspoken and hold radical views in my seventies is that no one did that for us when we were coming of age. The generation that was to lose tens of thousands of its members in the murderous meat grinder of Vietnam was not given a heads up about what was coming.

I was wrong. There was one teacher who did exactly that: Mr. Emerson Havens, our tenth grade world history teacher (and football coach!). He was an imposing man with receding red hair trimmed to a buzz cut. His ears stuck out, looking like they were glued onto a ball. Mr. Havens was a strict, no-bullshit guy. I didn't like him, I didn't dislike him. He thought I was a goldbrick. When he was giving us a look at our midterm grades–he called each one of us up to his desk individually–he said to me "Mr. Johnson, your intelligence is only exceeded by your laziness." This was the opinion of me held by several of my teachers.[3]

Despite his size, Mr. Havens did not have a booming voice. It was higher pitched than you would expect and he had a slight speech impediment. When we were studying Greece he called the Gulf of Corinth the "Gulf of Cornith." Mike Quirk, ever, um, helpful, corrected him.

"I think that is pronounced *Corinth*" to which Mr. Havens replied "You'll hear it a pronounced a number of ways," and proceeded with the lesson.

I thought it was an effective way of dealing with this shortcoming without calling more attention to it. His tone had the slightest tinge of *do NOT fuck with me!* in it. "You'll hear it a pronounced a number of ways" became a catch phrase!

"There will be no more wars like World War II," Mr. Havens said." With nuclear weapons, massed conventional conflict on that scale is pointless because a single nuclear bomb can destroy an entire army. The wars of the future will be brush fire wars. They will be little wars fought in small, seemingly unimportant, countries." His eyes were bright blue and penetrating, flashing with the fervor of his conviction as he spoke. "But they are important. Small wars are a way to relieve tensions between the U.S. and Russia. This will help prevent an all-out nuclear war."

"And there is another very good reason for these little wars." He paused. "We, the United States, are the most powerful nation in the free

---

[3] There were physiological reasons for my substandard academic performance that were not discovered until decades later, Lyme disease, which I contracted in the summer of 1955. No one knew about Lyme in those days. It was misdiagnosed as whooping cough and rheumatic fever and put me in the hospital for three weeks, I couldn't get out of bed. Then I was at home in bed for another three weeks in 1955-56. In adolescents, Lyme can cause - among many other things - dental problems and cognitive difficulties, such as memory issues and inability to grasp mathematical concepts. I was diagnosed in 2015.

world with the strongest economy and the highest standard of living.[4] The rest of the free world looks up to us." Mr. Haven's mouth would turn up on one side in a slight sneer – kind of like Elvis, but the comparison is beyond ludicrous – as he spoke. "It isn't as if there is a lot to be gained militarily in these conflicts. But we, as the leader of the free world, have to show the rest of the world what we are willing to sacrifice for freedom." He paused and looked about the room seeing that his point was made.

"That is why Korea was necessary," he continued, "that is why it was a success.[5] We had to show the world just what we would sacrifice to stand against communism."

He went on to explain at length that this was also the reason that Laos and Vietnam were becoming so important in Southeast Asia. They were the "dominoes." If one fell, the rest would topple in succession. Southeast Asia had to be kept free from communist domination at all costs. And there it was, the standard line which our generation was fed, revealed as prophecy by Emerson Havens.

Stopping communism. This was the *raison d'ete* for what was coming. And what was coming was a useless war fought with no strategy that would be a murder mill for the 60s generation. It was a big lie believed and promulgated by well-intentioned persons. America had not yet become so cynical that we would consider the Vietnam War as nothing more than a profit making venture for the military/industrial complex against which President Eisenhower had warned us in 1960.

Mr. Havens by God told us what was going to happen. He didn't guess, he didn't speculate, he didn't prognosticate. He *prophesied*. He stood in front of us and like a Biblical seer spoke the truth of what was to come. We had no idea of the import of what he was saying. But he said it.

I could understood the need to contain communism, but all I saw in this line of reasoning was the waste of human lives and attendant suffering. While the ground war in Vietnam was still two years in the future, Vietnam was already in our peripheral vision. *Scholastic Magazine* said it was consuming a million dollars every ten minutes – this was in 1963 – a mere drop in the bucket to the obscene amount of national treasure and number of American lives that were to go down the rat hole that was Vietnam.

---

[4] No longer the case.
[5] Korea? A success? Ending a war without a victory is not a success. The fighting stopped and an armistice was declared, but a state of war still exists nearly eighty years after the fact. This was the beginning of the era of endless wars without victory fought with no discernable strategy, save the desire to return to some status quo.

Many of the boys in that room would serve in Vietnam. One would die there. Others would return home wounded in body and mind and subjected to terrible diseases and psychological agony from their Vietnam service.

And Emerson Havens told us *exactly* how it was going down. Nobody else did. We didn't get it. It was mysterious, like a Nostradamus quatrain. That was then. Now it's all different.

But we had John Kennedy to lead us. We were confident he would make the right decisions.

MISSILE CRISIS

A spy plane flight over Cuba on October 15, 1962, revealed that the Soviet Union was building nuclear intermediate range ballistic missile bases in Cuba. Kennedy ordered a naval blockade, an act of war. For a time in October 1962, the world held its breath as the Russian warships steamed toward Cuba. It is a time forever etched on my psyche.

October 28th was the big day, the day Russian warships would meet the American blockade. We went to school that morning not knowing if all-out war would break out between the United States and the Soviet Union before the 3:15 bell. My stomach was queasy. We might all be incandescent gas by nightfall. It was not only just possible, but very likely, that we would be the witnesses to the end of human civilization that very afternoon.

The missile crisis was the only topic discussed in school that day. Our algebra II teacher, Mr. DuSchnozzle, used the entire class period to do nothing but stir the fear we all felt to a point approaching hysteria.

Mr. DuSchnozzle was a smarmy individual who perved on the girls. More than 50 years later, Gail Harmon recalls, "Mr. DuSchnozzle? Sure I remember him. Goddamned pervert! We girls had to make certain to keep our legs together and position ourselves so he couldn't look down our blouses when he walked around the classroom!"

"If war comes," Mr. DuSchnozzle told us at the high point of his lecture, "you're not only going to have to get used to seeing your classmates dead, the ones who might survive will have horrible burns."

Some of the girls in the class started to cry. Damn. What an asshole!

We were well aware of what might happen. He was taking advantage of the fact that we were all fearful of what the day might bring to inflict needless suffering on the more sensitive students. Weak men use peoples' fears to their own ends.[6]

The lyric to a Mad Magazine song parody kept repeating itself in my mind,

"Will you still find me attractive when I'm radioactive?"

The gallows humor of the atomic generation was no longer funny. Fear was in the air. It was palpable and had a life of its own, walking among us, chilling our souls.

That afternoon an announcement came over the PA system that the Soviet warships had turned away from the U.S. blockade. Cheers rang out! It was over, and I loved John Kennedy even more, for he had brought us through it. He had triumphed over Kruschev! Information released over the ensuing decades has shown us it was much more complicated than what it looked. The real reason for war being prevented may rest on the actions of a Soviet submarine officer whose boat was armed with nuclear tipped torpedoes that was, completely unknown to US intelligence, in the Caribbean at that time.[7] All we knew was that nuclear war had been averted and we were not going to die that day.

MR. DUSCHNOZZLE

There are teachers who stand out in one's life because they open vistas of education to you. Then there are the ones who stand out because they are complete assholes. Mr. DuSchnozzle was my tenth Grade Algebra II teacher who taught previously at a reform school where the kids were fearful of getting out of line. He could not command respect. At all. Respect was necessary to maintaining order in a classroom at Smethport in the 1960s. As I stated previously, the generally accepted method was for a teacher to take the first kid that got out of line on the first day of school and make an example of them. Mr. DuSchnozzle failed to do this.

He had one of the 10th grade home rooms (not mine). There is a legendary story about his home room. The lighting was the institutional lighting with a huge incandescent bulb – about 6 inches in diameter – painted silver part way up. The fixtures had concentric aluminum rings, the largest being about 3 feet in diameter.

---

[6] It works in politics too, as we see firsthand.
[7] Davis, N. (2017). Soviet submarine officer who averted nuclear war honoured with prize. The Guardian. Retrieved 20 February 2018, from
https://www. theguardian. com/science/2017/oct/27/vasili-arkhipov-soviet-submarine-captain-who-averted-nuclear-war-awarded-future-of-life-prize

In the usual pre-first bell mayhem before Mr. DuSchnozzle was in the room, a golf ball was playfully tossed around. Yes, stupid and foolish, it was fortunate no one was struck in the head. Someone – we are not certain who because Brent Vossler and Dan Nichols point fingers at each other each other to this day – tossed it and it lodged in the center fixture in the front of the room wedged between the bulb and the first concentric ring, out of reach and promptly forgotten.

Every boy has taken a golf ball apart at some time and knows underneath the rubber shell with the dimples in it are latex rubber bands tightly wrapped around a hard rubber core about a half-inch in diameter.

Before the Supreme Court's ban on school prayer, a teacher or a student – in Mr. DuSchnozzle's home room Mr. DuSchnozzle did it himself – would read a Bible verse and then lead the students in the Lord's Prayer before the first period bell. As Mr. DuSchnozzle was reading the morning devotions, the heat from the bulb – directly above where he was standing – caused the golf ball to become an IED. The rubber shell exploded and the layers of rubber bands underneath it snapping, becoming rubber shrapnel flying everywhere! Who expected that to happen? Naturally, the girls all shrieked. Mirthful chaos and general disorder ensued!

Upon restoring order, which took some time, Mr. DuSchnozzle – evidently thinking this spontaneous mayhem was the result of some foul and underhanded conspiracy – would not let anyone go to classes until the name of the culprit who had committed this heinous act of disorder and disrespect was revealed! No one ratted. Every student – boys, girls, nerds, and jocks – stayed in Mr. DuSchnozzle's home room for the entire day. Or maybe half of it, I don't remember which! Think that act epitomizes the *esprit de corps* of the Smethport Class of 1965.

A similar incident happened in my Algebra II class which Mr. DuSchnozzle taught. One of the students was Terry Tessena, Class of 1964, who had a deep voice who probably had to shave every day since he was 12, and who was physically imposing. Mr. DuSchnozzle was working a problem on the board with his back turned to the class and Terry passed the word around the class for everyone to look straight ahead no matter what happened. He had a big, nasty, wet, disgusting spitball, the kind made with that cheap lined paper from school-supplied tablets, about the size of a golf ball (there's the golf ball theme again!) and he threw it with incredible force and accuracy.

SPLAT!

It hit and stuck to the chalkboard just a couple inches to the right of Mr. DuSchnozzle's head looking for all the world like a disgusting blob of semi-congealed puke! Some of it got on Mr. DuSchnozzle's cheek. The circular radiating pattern it made was amazingly symmetrical, almost artistic!

Usually when something like this happened everyone would be looking at the perpetrator to see how badly he was going to get his ass kicked. Mr. DuSchnozzle turned around, his face crimson, eyes flashing with rage. Everyone was sitting silently with eyes straight ahead. This was open rebellion. You could almost smell the fear on Mr. DuSchnozzle. It happened again about a week later with a chalk dust filled eraser, same perpetrator.

Terry's role as the chief antagonist in Mr. DuSchnozzle's class was furthered one day when, at the end, of the period the room was littered with paper tossed about during class while Mr. DuSchnozzle had his back turned working problems on the blackboard. It really was a mess! A red faced DuSchnozzle barked at us that no one was to leave the room until the paper was picked up. No one lifted a finger. Just before the bell for the starting of the next class was to ring, Terry said "OK, let's go, pick it up." Everyone picked up paper near his or her seat and put it in the trash can when they filed past it out the door. It was clear to Mr. DuSchnozzle he was no way in charge. This was the Smethport's version of *"The Blackboard Jungle."*[8]

A couple days later Mr. DuSchnozzle came into class before the bell. Looking toward the back of the room he saw Terry Tessena, Dale Clutter and Jerry Fay flipping nickels.

"Tessena! Clutter! Fay! You three are expelled from this class! Go to the office. NOW!"

"But...Mr. DuSchnozzle, what did we *do*...? Asked Jerry.

DuSchnozzle thundered back *"You were GAMBLING!"*

Thus Mr. DuSchnozzle removed the immediate physical threat.

Mr. DuSchnozzle had a habit of starting shit with farm boys and got the crap kicked out of him at least three times – that I can recall, there may have been more – that year by high school sophomores.

Maybe he could pull the crap he did with the kids at George Junior Republic because juvenile inmates don't dare hit back. Not true in our part of the world. You would see him walking through the halls with red

---

[8]Directed by Richard Brooks. With Glenn Ford, Anne Francis, Louis Calhern, Margaret Hayes. A new English teacher at a violent, unruly inner-city school is determined to do his job, despite resistance from both students and faculty.
 https://www. imdb. com/title/tt0047885/ Based on the novel by Evan Hunter, this was the first film to have a rock and roll song on its soundtrack, "Rock Around the Clock" by Bill Haley and the Comets.

marks on his face wearing an "I'm so fucked" expression of abject humiliation. You knew someone was getting a two-week suspension for kicking his ass. I'm neither condoning nor advocating violence between students and teachers, that was just the way things were.

The most memorable ass kicking Mr. DuSchnozzle received was in the big study hall, Room 20, in the bowels of the school across from the boys' locker room. Brent Vossler (of the exploding golf ball and aspergillum incidents) asked to go to the library. Mr. DuSchnozzle refused the request. Brent put his head in his arms on his desk, closed his eyes to nap. Mr. DuSchnozzle came up behind him a gave him a sharp smack across the back of the head. Rudely interrupted from his reverie, Brent was on his feet and had Mr. DuSchnozzle in a full nelson in a split second. They were close to the wall and Mr. DuSchnozzle started to walk his feet up the wall while Brent had him restrained. Ed Maynard grabbed Brent from behind in an attempt to stop the altercation. Brent released Mr. DuSchnozzle, who fell to the floor, got up, turned around and pulled his fist back to punch Brent while Ed was holding him. Seeing that, Ed let Brent go and the scuffle continued. Brent got a two week suspension. Brent's father took that two weeks as vacation from his factory job (most of the farmer's had a regular job in addition to their farming) and made certain Brent spent every minute of it digging fence post holes!

Mr. DuSchnozzle and I did not get along. My father knew this and was aware of Mr. DuSchnozzle getting his ass kicked by students. Now, I was not a fighter and definitely not any kind of physical badass. I could scare nobody! Nevertheless, my father said to me, "Gener, 1 want you to understand this. No matter what happens, it is not your place to lay a hand on a teacher. Do you understand me?"

One day in class the guy in the seat behind me, Clarence Meritt, said some smartass thing and Mr. DuSchnozzle hoisted me out of my seat by the back of my collar and trotted me out into the hallway. I said, "Wait a minute, I didn't do anything, this time it wasn't me!" Mr. DuSchnozzle, still holding me by the back of my collar ignored my protestations and proceeded to smash my nose and forehead repeatedly into a locker, **bangety-bangety-fucking-bang!** After he finished I stood there rubbing my nose, looked him in the eye and said "This...is *not* over." He told me to go to the office. I went to the band room and fucked around for the rest of the class period. When I went back to Mr. DuSchnozzle's room to retrieve my books we exchanged heavy duty "fuck you" looks!

After supper that evening I told my father what had transpired. His facial expression was very serious. He said "C'mon" and got up from the kitchen table and started toward the door. My mother said "Now Kenny…" and was ignored.

When my father was young he was a scrapper. My mother, who had seen him fight before, was afraid he would beat Mr. DuSchnozzle to death. I had no idea what was going to transpire and followed my father out the door as instructed, figuring I was in some kind of trouble.[9]

We got in the car and went to Mr. DuSchnozzle's apartment on the third floor above Lindgren's Five and Dime on Main St. I was 5'10," 125-130 pounds soaking wet, not at all built like my father who was a large, muscular man. My father gave me that "what I am about is goddamned serious so pay attention!" look and instructed me in his "portent of doom" manner that usually preceded him kicking my ass.

"*You* keep your mouth *shut! Don't* say a *God*damned word. *Understand?*"

His threatening demeanor could be terrifying. Usually when he was this way around me, I was in some kind of trouble, and I did *not* want to set him off.

"Yessir!"

He knocked and Mr. DuSchnozzle answered the door, looking surprised to see us, especially my father's size. His expression was as if the grim reaper had come calling! He invited us in and we sat down. My father asked "Mr. DuSchnozzle, what happened today between you and my son, Eugene?

Mr. DuSchnozzle proceeded to stammer on, with the occasional splutter, in a voice tinged with panic about how I was not working hard enough, not working up to my potential, had a bad attitude, didn't try, sometimes disruptive, how other teachers agreed with all of this, yadda yadda yadda, mentioning absolutely nothing about the day's disciplinary incident. He finally finished and sat there wide-eyed looking like he didn't know whether to shit, go blind or wind his watch!

My father said in his slow, deliberate and ever-so-authoritative "portent-of-doom" voice, "I'm going to tell you something, Mr. DuSchnozzle. In the future, if you *ever* find it necessary to discipline a student, I strongly suggest you not use anything more than an open hand. The next parent that comes along might not be as…*nice*… as me. *Understand?*"

Mr. DuSchnozzle nodded his head and squeaked "…yes."

---

[9] Catholic guilt. Everything is always your fault.

It was SO fucking cool to see how someone *else* reacted to my father's threatening manner! And it was *this* smarmy piss brain. *YES!* Sometimes life is just so *God*damned sweet!

We left, driving back across town in silence. I figured I was going to catch all hell for the stuff Mr. DuSchnozzle said about me. My father never made reference to it. This was about a teacher laying his hands on me, his son, in an improper manner. He had my back. We had our differences over the years, but he was the most decent man I ever knew.

Mr. DuSchnozzle was gone the next year. Good fucking riddance.

CHAPTER 6

THAT DAY

Friday, November 22, 1963 started out as just another ordinary school day of high-spirited hallway camaraderie alternating with the boredom of classroom regimentation. I was sixteen, a junior. The thing we most looked forward to that Friday was Saturday. Before the final bell, it would become *that* day, that one single day in a lifetime, the one where something so crucial, so momentous, so violent, shocking and historic occurred that it stands apart from all other days, that day when everything changed forever.[1]

We began our fifth period gym class with the usual calisthenics. Danny Nichols slipped out into the hallway to get a drink from a fountain. Rushing back in, he resumed his pushups and exclaimed, "They've shot Kennedy!"

"Who?" came the incredulous group rejoinder.

"The *commies!*" he replied.

This pronouncement was met by hoots of disbelief and we resumed our calisthenics. The Cuban Missile crisis a year earlier was fresh in our memory. John Kennedy got us through it. If anyone shot him, it *must* have been the commies!

Derided by some, Danny was anxiously questioned by others. An unspeakable idea was forming in my mind. I dismissed it immediately as if it were an "impure thought," the kind that could lead to a mortal sin.

---

[1] The Old Curmudgeon's Sage Advice No. 2

For the rest of the period we half-heartedly played skins-and-shirts hoops, preoccupied with thoughts about JFK.

Rumors flew in the halls between classes. Kennedy was shot. Kennedy was dead. The Russians did it. Jackie had been shot too. We were going to war with Russia. Jackie was dead. Kennedy and Governor Connelly were both dead. The word "vibe" was not yet in the national lexicon, but the vibe in those halls was electric, apprehensive, edging toward panic. We were desperate for information.

I thought, hoped really, to myself that if the President really has been shot, he's probably just wounded. He'll be OK, JFK will be fine. Always.

Next period was American History with Mr. Gates. Joseph Gates was an intelligent and sensitive individual. A good-natured man and fine teacher, we used to take ruthless advantage of him calling it "taking the hinges off Mr. Gates." He wore rather thick glasses, so those of us who liked to mess around would sit at the back of the room where we could screw off without being clearly seen. Or so we thought! Mr. Gates would give us hell. We didn't care.

What good was history anyway? It was boring. Stuff that happened a long time ago. No good to us. Where was the *relevance?* On that afternoon, we found out. We *witnessed* history.

Eddie Anderson came into the room and announced "JFK's dead! The president is dead!"

"Now Eddie," said Mr. Gates, "you really shouldn't be circulating unsubstantiated rumors at a time like this."

Eddie replied, "No, it's true. I was just in the office and heard it on the radio!"

Our noisy discussion was interrupted by the principal's somber voice coming over the loudspeaker, his usual authoritarian tone missing.

"For those of you who have not heard…the President…is dead."

The room fell silent. Life was never the same for any of us after we heard those twelve words. I felt as if a hole had been ripped in my guts. Some of the girls quietly sobbed, dabbing their eyes with tissues, we boys silently looked at the floor so no one could see our eyes welling up, tears misting over the stark unreality of that afternoon. After what was I think the longest moment in my life, Mr. Gates led us in the Lord's Prayer violating the Supreme Court decision only months earlier forbidding prayer in school. [2] His voice cracked toward the end. He removed his glasses and dabbed tears from the corners of his eyes with a tissue. We all felt the same way.

Were we praying for John Kennedy? Were we praying for America? Or were we praying for ourselves, for some understanding of this unforeseen, unimagined and brutal event?

School was dismissed early. We filed out the doors in silence, a few hushed conversations here and there. Students boarding the buses were unusually subdued with none of the usual boisterousness of kids being liberated from classroom captivity. Stunned, we were like zombies walking around in a trance. That single, desperate act of murder changed our entire world.

Tears glistened on cheeks cooled by the autumn chill. The November grayness of the hills mirrored our inner feelings as we went home from school. John Kennedy was dead, taken from us by an assassin.

We loved JFK and his family. The Nunz told us to pray for JFK's election. We did and he was. He was young, engaging, and charmed the press. He challenged us to make America a better nation and the world a better place. We could identify with him. It was easy to think he was a personal friend.

Wrong. *Wrong!* Something was terribly, *horribly* wrong with America. But, how could that be? We, as a nation with John Kennedy at the helm, were on the verge of attaining the pinnacle of ultimate greatness. And now, he was gone. JFK. *Our* JFK. The young, dynamic, witty, leader of our nation, our charismatic president, was dead, murdered, assassinated. I felt as if I had lost a close personal friend.

That this man we so loved and trusted would be subject to a public murder was unthinkable. I felt the emotional whirligig of desperate denial alternating with the gut-wrenching panic accompanying the realization of the awful event. While I now know this as what comes with facing a personal and emotional loss, at that time it was new to me.

How...*how* could this happen? In America? We were the leading industrial democracy in the world, not some banana republic run by a nickel dictator.[3] Our governmental transitions are accomplished through elections, not gunfire. It was crushing. The world took on a surreal aspect.

---

[2] In 2015, I called Mr. Gates to invite him to our 50th year class reunion. We discussed the Kennedy assassination. When I mentioned he broke federal law by leading us in the Lord's Prayer, he responded "That's one of the finer laws I have broken in my life."

[3] I wrote this sentence decades ago. Presently (2019) it looks like it may be coming to pass.

John Kennedy's assassination was one of those rare events that forever marks a particular time and place to anyone alive at the time. History was no longer an annoying irrelevancy. We bore witness to it. As the members of our parents generation would always remember where they were and what they were doing when they heard about the Japanese attack on Pearl Harbor, each one of us would always remember where we were on the afternoon of Friday, November 22, 1963,[4] when we heard about John Kennedy's death. It is a bond, a common shared experience, a marker etched into each and every one of our lives.

The days that followed had an air of unreality to them as the events unfolded live before us on our television sets. That Sunday my family and I witnessed Lee Harvey Oswald shot to death by Jack Ruby in the basement of the Dallas jail. Good God, what the hell was going on in Dallas? It seemed like a wild west shoot out. This was reality TV decades before its time, complete with real bullets, real blood and real death.

The very first international satellite TV broadcast was on November twenty-fifth 1963. It was John Kennedy's funeral. There was no school that day. I watched the funeral on TV with my family, and the rest of the world.

We saw the images of little John Kennedy, Jr., saluting as the horse drawn caisson bearing his father's body went past. The skittish riderless stallion with the boots turned backwards in the stirrups seemed to sense the uneasiness of an entire nation as the funeral procession plodded along to the somber cadence of the muffled drums.

The relentless cadence and solemn timbre of the parade drums beating out their mournful rhythm seared itself so deeply into me that I can pick up a pair of drumsticks today and play it.

I will never forget that funereal military tattoo speaking of our young, dead president. The insistent relentless rhythmic dirge, marking time, propelling the funeral procession toward JFK's final resting place, Arlington National Cemetery, even as it marked the time that pushed us as a nation reluctantly forward to a now uncertain future.

The sound of the drums changed with the microphone position and camera shots. From far away, they echoed off the buildings, the hollow reverberance echoing the emptiness I felt inside, the void that opened up in my world with the loss of John Kennedy. Closer, they had an immediacy and presence that accented the gravity of the occasion, the funeral of a president elected by the people and removed from office, and from this earth, by a ruthless act of murder.

---

[4] September 11, 2001 would also be added to this list of defining events.

The drums bespoke a mournful chant of death ushering in the period of chaos and madness for which the American 1960's will forever be remembered. We didn't know it, but the brutal and senseless murder of John Kennedy, our young and vital president, our friend, was the harbinger of the tens of thousands of other equally tragic and senseless deaths which would follow.

The assassination of John Kennedy was the end of one age and the beginning of another. It was the moment where the decade transformed from sparkling brand-new, brighter, more modern and full of promise into a nightmare of assassination, alienation, war, and rioting in the streets. This day was a herald, a subtle hint, as it were, of what was coming. With John Kennedy's assassination we all became hostage to the 1960s.

Fully two generations have come of age since that day. Doubts about JFK's assassination still linger. In 1964 the Warren Commission determined that Lee Harvey Oswald acted alone. In 1978 The House Select Committee on Assassinations concluded that there may have been or probably were others involved in the assassination, a belief presently held by seventy percent of Americans.

John Kennedy, our president for just over a thousand days, was not with us long enough for us to really know what kind of a president he was. I remember him fondly.

While unflattering personal revelations about John Kennedy have surfaced over the decades, he charmed us and we loved him for it. He was so brutally torn from us. Life went on. School went on. The world went on.

CHAPTER 7

BEATLEMANIA ONWARD

The first time I heard the Beatles was on a Saturday night in the winter of 1964. Dick Orlandi was driving us in Pat Chamberlain's 1958 Ford. Five of us passed a bottle of Mad Dog around while heading out on Route 59. WKBW was on the radio. The DJ said "Here's one by England's newest hit makers, the Beatles!" followed by opening chords to *I Want to Hold Your Hand.* We were transfixed. The five note chromatic guitar run in each verse was the hook that just...*tripped...my...switch!* About the third time it came around Bill Wassam said "...wow...that music..."

Yes. That music...it was *GREAT!*

The Beatles dominated the Top Ten for months with hit after hit, sometimes occupying the top three slots at once. Coming just months after John Kennedy's assassination, the Beatles were more than welcome. Kids just lost their minds over them! It was the same thing Elvis had done a decade earlier. Their songs were different and fresh. The genius of John Lennon and Paul McCartney's songwriting was a beacon in the morass that was pop music!

Paradoxically, one thing the Beatles lacked was an identifying style. There was no "Beatles Style." The voices were the same and readily identifiable, but from song to song and album to album, you never knew what was coming! We were witnessing the emergence of musical genius. It was a genuine privilege. We did not know it at the time but the Beatles were on the cusp of an incredible musical renaissance and cultural upheaval. And they had LONG HAIR! Until then most people considered and only girls (and queers!) wore long hair! Boys sporting Beatles style hair started being seen in America. But the music...the music was transcendent. The winds of change were blowing. Seeds of rebellion were sown.

I kept my greased up DA[1] for another year, going Beatle style in fall of 1965 at Lock Haven State College. By 1972 my hair was halfway down my back. It was the times. The weirder things got, the longer everybody's hair got.

We had only one kid in our class who was hip enough to go full-on Beatle, Buddy Feit. He even had one of those Beatle suits with no lapels. As soon as he bought the Beatles first American album, *Meet the Beatles*, he commandeered a record player and we partied to the Beatles before the morning bell. The teacher shut it down, of course.

DRUM LINE

Our band director, Mr. Partchey left Hubber High[2] in 1963 to teach music at a college. He was an outstanding instructor, but his taste in marching drum lines was very conservative. We, being cocky hotshot drummers, wanted to use drum corps style marching cadences, muffling the drums with strips of felt and using antiphonal cadences[3] with snare and tenor drums. Mr. Partchey would not have it. The marching section was snares, bass and cymbals. Unmuffled. Tarumpity-dump! Period!

Our new director, Mr. Brzenski, let us do what we pleased. And we became *badasses!* Taking LP records of drum corps competitions, we would tape them on Brian Roebling's tape recorder. Practicing relentlessly, we stole drum cadences from championship drum lines. We were just goddamned *invincible!* We blew peoples' minds. Other schools couldn't come within a mile of the precision contrapuntal rhythms we used. Oh yes, we were just *too* hip and rhythmically precise. We wore white gloves and the tenor drummers twirled their mallets. We were completely in love with just how *fucking* cool we felt, looked, and *were!*

One of the several things we stole from the national champion Hawthorne, NJ, Cabelleros was a roll-off (the drum cadence that signals the band it is time to play) that had 4 beats of complete silence in the middle.

---

[1] The hip pre-Beatles hair style for guys was the style favored by juvenile delinquents: grease it ("Brylcream, a little dab'll do ya") and comb it back with no part and a nice pompadour curl at the front. A proper DA had the sides combed back, ever so streamlined, and long enough that the hair at the nape of the neck could be formed into an upward curl like feathers on a duck's tail. Termed "duck tail," it was commonly referred to as DA for "duck ass."
[2] Smethport was the county seat, the "hub," so our Athletic teams were the Hubbers!
[3] Contrapunctual rhythms

That seriously messed with people. Eight beats of cadence. Four beats of silence, the band still marching forward, no horns raised. Those four beats of silence were a major mind bender to those watching! Then, another eight beats of cadence to finish the roll-off. Horns up on the last two beats, *play!!*

If there is something cooler than a marching drum line, I don't know what it is! Well...maybe sex...or a rock n' roll band! In my senior year I was the drum captain. As a marching percussion section, we were *stoked!* The Hubbers were 6 &1 that season. The last football game of the season was at Port Allegany, our athletic rival. For the halftime show, Mr. B instructed us that both bands were to take to the field, play several numbers together and the Port A drum line was to march both bands off the field. The Port A. drum line was a typical "Tarumpity-dump" high school drum line. Here I was at my *last* high school halftime show *ever* and my hot shit drum line were going to silently march off the field to a shitty old cadence played by an inferior drum line? I don't think so! Before we took the field I gave the order, "Listen for my command!" The moment both bands finished the last number I shouted "Cadence!" and gave four rim shots. My highly disciplined drummers exploded with infectious rhythm and we marched the Port Allegany band off their own field! I figured I'd catch hell for it. Nobody said anything. *Haha!*

HONKY-TONKIN'

I got my first job playing music professionally in the fall of 1964. Every Saturday night I would go to the Columbus Club in Kane, PA and play country music with Gene Walker and Freddie Couch. Freddie had a daughter, Jackie, who always got up and sang a few songs with us, she was terrific! We made $12 apiece each night, and that was some *good* money!

Gene introduced me to his brothers, Bob and Dick, who had a rock n' roll band called The Blazers. They came to a couple practices and we jammed together. Ohhh, yes! Rock n' roll! I was hoping they would offer me a job.

My last job with Gene and Freddie was a memorable one. There were some big, burly woodcutters who used to hang out at the Columbus Club, and, of course, they would pick up the women there. We were playing the job as usual, and had another guitar player, Don McClelland, sitting in with us. Don was a legendary guitarist in the area, had a brand new custom made candy apple red Fender Jaguar and played like Chet Atkins. Don was also a legendary drinker and highly undependable, which is why he sat in with bands instead of playing a steady gig with one.

It was New Year's Eve and a fight broke out between two of the woodcutters over one of the women. Those two guys were giving each other a real working over, with one being knocked ass-backwards through a window like something out of a cowboy movie. Fights broke out nearly every weekend. They were usually over in a half dozen or so punches. Not this one! The old Italian guys who were in charge of the club (it was the K of C) ignored it and we kept playing. They never called the cops for a fight. As the exchange of blows raged on, Don packed up his guitar, put on his coat, and left with the woman they were fighting over!

Bob and Dick asked me to join the Blazers, which I did in a heartbeat. Playing with the Blazers was a grand experience. We would learn songs as soon as they were released. I remember the girls screaming when we launched into the Beatles' *Eight Days a Week* the same week it appeared in the record stores! I left the band after graduation because I was going to college in the fall.

OH MY GOD! I BROKE HER!

In the fall of my senior year I was dating an attractive blonde from Eldred, a town about thirteen miles down the road. Girls from other schools were considered exotic in the Pennsylvania small-town culture of the 1960s. I thought I might actually get laid!

We made out a lot. I loved feeling her soft breasts. They weren't really big, but they were "a nice handful," as we used to say. She never let me take her top off but she did let me finger her cooch. I remember the first time I ever put my hands in her pants and felt her pubic hair. I liked it. I fingered her. I was so inexperienced I did not know pussy smelled! When I took my hand out of her pants and got a whiff I thought maybe I put it in the wrong hole. So I did it again. Yep, I had the right one, the one on front!

We were parking one night in my dad's 1965 Chevy. She was lying on her back across my lap as I fingered her. All of a sudden she exploded, her hips pumping, her face contorted, she moaned and whimpered and writhed. I had never seen girl have an orgasm before, I thought I broke my girlfriend! What would I tell her mom? It turned out she wasn't broken, she was just fine! But she never reciprocated. I did not get laid and graduated from high school a virgin. Oh well. I gave it a good effort.

W. EUGENE JOHNSON

THE STAR SPANGLED LIE & THE CLASS OF 1965

Vietnam. I first encountered that name in sixth grade. There was an article in our Junior Scholastic magazine about Vietnam–which Mrs. Lindquist pronounced it "Vee-et Nee-am–portraying it as a tiny country beleaguered by the dreaded communists. Being as the USA was the good guys, we were going to save them!

At the time of Kennedy's assassination there were slightly less than 16,000 U.S. military personnel in the Republic of South Vietnam. Lyndon Johnson ran as a peace candidate in 1964 defeating Republican challenger and arch-conservative (for the time anyway), Arizona senator Barry Goldwater.[4]

In August 1964, the government informed America of an alleged incident in the Gulf of Tonkin involving North Vietnamese torpedo boats firing on the American destroyers, Maddox and C. Turner Joy. On August 7th, Congress passed the Gulf of Tonkin resolution. In April of 1965 President Johnson announced the commitment of U.S. ground forces to Vietnam, the Marines having landed at Da Nang on March 8th.

That week we had an assembly in the auditorium. A panel made up of teachers and seniors discussed this new and serious situation. The atmosphere was subdued, with less of the usual boisterousness and horseplay that always accompanied assemblies. Military involvement in Vietnam was now real. We believed this would be the war for our generation as World War II had been the war for our fathers' generation. Boys from all of the grades present that day, seventh through twelfth, would serve in Vietnam. More than a few would return maimed in body and wounded in spirit. Three of the boys in the auditorium that day would lose their lives there.[5]

Graduation was June 3, 1965. Twelve years of force-fed public education was coming to an end. There were a hundred thirty-two of us in our class, the largest class to ever graduate from Smethport.

Graduation is socially significant because you are cut loose to make major mistakes on your own. The thing is that no one should let you believe that you actually know anything yet. Nobody just out of high school really knows anything. These well-meaning but clueless citizens stand up there on the stage and lay all this crap on you. And, since they

---

[4] Some years back I was discussing 60s politics with someone who said "They told me if I voted for Goldwater we'd be at war within a year. I did and we were!"
[5] The Old Curmudgeon's Sage Advice No. 6

are the adults in power telling you, you believe it, right? An appropriate commencement speech would have been this: :

Well, kids, here you are, graduating from high school. You think you really know some stuff, don't you? Well, let me tell you right now, you really don't know shit! What you have is information. Information is not knowledge. Knowledge is experiential. You do not have experience yet. Now is when you are really going to start learning.

America doesn't work the way you were told in POD class. The old balding bastards in government who run this shit show work for the corporations, and they are going to make your generation trade your life's blood for corporate profits. They'll tell you the war in Vietnam is for God and Country, but that's just star-spangled horseshit with a side order of Jesus. Some of you will be shot to hell, some of you will be poisoned by your own government to the extent it will affect your offspring, some of you will die there, and some of you will be war widows before you are twenty. And many of you will just be fucked up for the rest of your lives, largely ignored by the Veterans' Administration.

Politicians who will sponsor this slaughter won't send their own kids over there, no way. But a lot of you poor small town chumps will go because you believe all that patriotic crap your dads and the rest of the WWII vets spew out on Memorial Day. You will get fucked up and fucked over, no matter what you do. And you won't even get the benefit of a kiss or Vaseline! So bend over, kids, here comes the weenie!

NEAR DEATH EXPERIENCE

We were doing that one fine Saturday afternoon on Route 46 between Smethport and Emporium. The Rolling Stones *"Satisfaction"* was blasting from the radio and we were all bopping and singing along with it. Barry's cousin, Keith, and I were in the back seat. Don Thomas was riding shotgun and Barry was hauling ass. We were taking Keith to his home in Emporium. The road had some gentle curves some dips, and rises but, in our estimation, was quite navigable at excessive speeds! We watched the speedometer...90... 95...100 ...110 ...120... *Holy Shit! He's got it pegged!*

It was hunting season and the area was full of flatlanders[6] who had hunting camps in the area. One such camp was ahead of us on the right. Until recently it was a gas station with a little store. The big oval 7-Up sign by the road, proclaimed "Lacheskey's Service" around the 7-Up

---

[6] A pejorative term used by locals for hunters from Ohio and Pittsburgh who come to the area during hunting season to pick up women in bars. They did some hunting too.

logo. The pumps had not yet been removed. We came up over a rise and in the distance we can see the station turned camp. There were 6 or 7 vehicles and about a dozen hunters. One guy coming toward us stopped and backed his pickup into our lane. *Oh shit!*

When we had wet snow in the winter, Barry, like all of us, would cut donuts[7] in the school parking lot and drift around every corner in town. In the next few seconds the skills he acquired doing this would be crucial. He let off the gas and gently applied the brake. His actions in the next few seconds would determine whether or not any of us had another birthday! We were flying like the proverbial bat out of hell and in *serious* trouble.

The Olds went onto the large gravel covered area surrounding the old station and drifted toward the pumps. *Oh shit shit shit shit not the fucking pumps!* Barry corrected the slide. We missed the pumps. People were jumping out of our way! *Holy screaming dogshit! Now we're headed toward two cars!* More corrections. *Oh fuck, not the goddamned TREE! NOOO!"* And since I had jerked off that morning I was in a state of mortal sin and was going to hell to boot! *Shit! OH MY GOD AM HARDLY SORRY...*Another correction and we spun 90 degrees clockwise and somehow ended up crossways to the road in a four-wheel sideways skid! I thought there was nothing left of us but headlines in the next day's paper!

"CARLOAD OF TEENAGE ASSHOLES KILLED TRAVELING AT INSANE SPEED AFTER RUNNING DOWN HUNTERS FROM PITTSBURGH!!!"

The day was not turning out so well. At least we weren't dead! That was positive!

We stopped some distance down the road. The left rear quarter panel sustained some damage from smacking a reflector by a culvert. Had we hit the culvert curb with the rear wheel, the car would have undoubtedly rolled over and over sideways for a half a mile! We got out, checked damage, and observed some pissed off hunters screaming epithets and walking in our direction. At least they weren't shooting! It was time to GTFO so we GTFO!

It is a wonder no nobody shit themselves. At least Barry didn't have to explain shit stains on the upholstery of his mother's car! The damage to the rear driver's side quarter panel? No problem. "Someone must have backed into it in a parking lot…" That's an easy lie. Shit stains? *Much more detail required.*

---

[7] Purposely spinning a car in circles on wet snow or ice, also called "cutting brodies."

CHAPTER 8

LIKE A BUG ON A WINDSHIELD

CAN'T HACK THE MATH

Lock Haven was an academic disaster. I should NOT have majored in chemistry, I couldn't hack the math. I did it because it was "expected of me." And we are under an obligation to do what "is expected" of us. Right? I collided with college math like a bug hitting a windshield. Freshman thermodynamics was a washout. Sophomore calculus? Fuggetit!

What I did not know at the time was that I had Lyme disease, and adolescents with Lyme disease have difficulties with mathematical abstractions, memory and other cognitive functions. I learned this in 2015 Oh well. At least I now know it wasn't ALL my fault. I had teachers, our (less than useless) guidance counselor, and my dad up my ass all through high school about my shitty math skills. Whenever I tested, math was my highest aptitude, so it just had to be my fault. At the time I just figured I was fucking something else up, you know, SOP. "You're just goddamned *lazy,* that's all!" was my father's take on the situation. I didn't know if I was lazy or not, but I knew I was a no-good shitbird. I must have been. They all told me so.

I told my father I couldn't hack the math and want to change my major to biology or earth science. Mistake. I should have just gone ahead and done it and told him later. He had a complete goddamned meltdown calling me a quitter and a bunch of other shit. What the fuck did he know about my situation? Nothing. He never fucking listened, he just bellowed. I was still at the stage in my life where I believed my decisions still needed parental approval. Always terrified by my father's fits of rage, I continued to major in chemistry, said "fuck it," and dropped out of Lock Haven entirely after my sophomore year.

The best thing I got out of Lock Haven was a couple friends and some experience with hypnosis after learning about it in a psych class. I took some books out of the library, read them, and started hypnotizing people. At the time it was party type stuff, later I got into the more esoteric aspects of hypnosis, specifically regressing people into a past life or six. Reading *"The search for Bridey Murphy"* was the first crack in the monolith of Catholic dogma and medieval bullshit I had inside my head. The two miserable years I spent at Lock Haven were worth it just for that.

One of the highlights was a dope bust in the fall term 1966. A girl gave her roomie a joint and her roomie turned her in. I wondered what she was doing with dope as I was not yet curious about marijuana. And a worker in the Piper Aircraft Factory located there shot and killed several co-workers in October, 1967.

BEER BUST 101

One Friday evening in the spring of 1967, my roomie, Mike Kolwinski, and the two guys from across the hall, Bill White and Bill Phillips, and I were BSing in our room in North Hall. Someone we did not know poked his head in and hollered,

"Hey, you guys wanna go drinkin'?"

We were off in a flash. There were six of us. And the funny thing was that we four didn't know the other two guys' names. All we had in common at the moment was the desire to get some suds in our bellies.

Jim Peters was – to us – an old man of twenty-one. He went downtown with us and we went to a bar where he bought us a six-pack apiece. We rewarded him by buying him one of his own. This was a standard practice. We left Jim off back at the dorm.

The driver pulled his Volkswagen beetle pulled into Hannah Park. We had just popped our beers open when car headlights came on behind us and a spotlight beamed through the rear window. *Shit!* It was the cops!

Two officers approached the car. The driver rolled down the window and produced his license and registration on demand.

"I smell beer," the officer said, handing the license and registration back to the kid behind the wheel.

"Open up the door and get out."

The driver complied. I was sitting in the seat directly in back of him. The officer pulled the seat in forward and shined his light in to see the quantity of 6-packs by our feet, and an opened can of Budweiser nestled neatly between my feet.

"Here it is," he said to his partner, then turning to me, "kinda goddamn stupid to pull into the park, wasn't it? All of you, get outta the car. NOW!"

The cops confiscated our beer. We were not handcuffed. They put four of us into the police cruiser and the other two[1] told to drive in front of the cop car to the police station. When we arrived at the combination police station/fire hall/city hall, marched us through the front door in single file: a cop, the four of us who rode down in the cop car, the second cop, and the other two fellows.

Once inside the building, we had to go to the left and into the police station portion of the building. We all did, except for the two fellows on the end. Instead of going to the left and into the police station, they walked straight through the building, out the back door, got in their car, and left.

The police, who were yucking it up about how damned dumb we college kids were for getting caught with the beer in Hannah Park. That was true. But they had not yet noticed they were missing two desperados. Yeah, we made a dumb move, but we could count to six! Besides this, and fortunately for me, they didn't search us for weapons. I was carrying a *huge* Italian picklock switchblade – purchased from classmate Dave Lamborn while he was home on leave from the Army, 11" opened up – sticking out of my pocket, but my coat covered it. I was very glad that they didn't ask us to make ourselves comfortable and take off our coats.

I experienced for the first time in my life, being "booked": fingerprints, and mug shots complete with the little sign on the beaded chain.

Dean of men was out of town. He hated my roommate and I. Not because we were assholes or anything...*hahaha!!* The feeling was mutual. The Assistant Dean of Men came down to get us out of our jam. Somewhat inebriated himself, he said, "Don't worry, boys," he said with a slight smile.

We all went to a Justice of the Peace where there was much ado about the fact that we wouldn't give them the names or talk about the other two guys who took off in the car! Hell, we *didn't* know their names!

---

[1] OK, so that's six people in a VW bug. That means there were seven of us in it when we took Jim Peters to get the beer. How did we do it? Who the hell knows.

We were each fined $25 plus $9 costs which none of us college students had on us. The Justice of the Peace gave us a period to time to pay, three weeks, I think.

The Dean of Men was on us like a ton of shit when he got back to the campus the following week. We were placed on disciplinary probation and had to write up a big report on how all of this happened and on and on and on... Our names and our disgraceful actions were written up in the local paper and reported on the WBPZ radio news *every half-hour for an entire goddamned week!*

I hitchhiked home the next day. I really didn't want to tell my parents about this new bunch of shit I was in. My friend, Mike Quirk, was attending St. Bonaventure University in Allegany, New York, about twenty-five miles from my home. I borrowed Dad's car and went to see if I could borrow the money from him. Mike wasn't in the dorm, so I went to the local college bars in Allegany. No luck there either. The only thing I found that night was the Allegany PD's speed trap. My dad's car was a new Mercury Comet with a hot V-8. I wasn't paying attention and got clocked at ten miles over the speed limit. They wanted ten fucking dollars, and I was broke. The two cops took me to the police station and jerked my chain around for a while. Finally, the officer agreed to let me go, but he would keep my driver's license until I sent the money for the fine. Well, it sucked but it was better than being in jail.

It was definitely not my weekend to get along with law enforcement, no matter which state I was in. Yes, both incidents were my own damned fault, but you do not consider things like that at nineteen. I ended getting the money for fines and expenses from my grandmother. The Allegany cops never did give me back my driver's license. They lost it. Sometimes you just keep stepping in shit every time you turn around!

I finished out the term and dropped out of Lock Haven State.

CHAPTER 9

THE ENDLESS BOOGIE – PART 1

After I dropped out of Lock Haven State College, I tried to get in the Navy and Air Force bands. The Navy was not auditioning drummers at that time. I went to Washington, D. C. and passed an audition for the Air force Band, but they didn't need any drummers at the time so I didn't enlist in the Air Force either.

For the rest of 1967, I worked in the toy factory in Smethport where my mother worked. Smethport Specialty Company made magnetic toys, the kind that has a face under a flat, square plastic dome and you put hair and beards on them by manipulating iron filings and a magnet. These "Woolly Willies" and "Dapper Dans" and a dozen or so other items were shipped from Smethport all around the world.

I ran the ovens that tempered the steel for the magnets. It was a damn hot, sticky job, but, it was a job. Every day I would fire the magnets in the ovens and quench them in tubs of Oakite to knock off the scale. I cut sheets of cardboard on a huge paper cutter and tumbled the powdered iron that went in the toys in a revolving tub with some chemicals. Sometimes Willard, one of the other three men employed there with about three dozen women, and I soaked long pieces of metal stock in solvent and would both have a cheap drunk from that for the rest of the afternoon. It wasn't a bad job, as far as jobs go, but nothing I wanted to make a career out of. Besides, all the women that worked there were either married or engaged. There were no available single women working there, none.

W. EUGENE JOHNSON

THE BRADFORD CREW

"*EU*gene," said my classmate Mia Fiorello one day, "you've just *got* to go to Bradford and meet some people I met there. They have the *neatest* parties! Oh God, these people are *so* cool!"

Well, with a glowing recommendation like that, I just had to see what was going on in Bradford. And so I met Ron Lattin and Jay Peterio.[2]

Ron was a good looking soft-spoken well-mannered individual with an excellent sense of humor. We share a penchant for partying and became good friends sharing many trips across the PA/NY line to take advantage of New York's drinking age of 18. Jay had just gotten out of the Army and lived with his parents in an apartment on Pine Street. Jay's parents would go away for the weekends, leaving the apartment in Jay's hands. There were always six or eighteen people hanging out at his place on the weekends and a party would be in progress. This was the place for the hippest people in Bradford. Part of this group were Lynn (blonde, stacked, vacant) and Lin (brunette, part Native American, generally wore more make-up than necessary). They were both attractive.

Jay's parties were just crazy as hell. Jay's mom used to refer to her apartment as "Mrs. Peterio's Home for Wayward Children." We partied 'til we dropped. Literally. Anyone who passed out was fair game for pranks. Bill Mandy passed out one evening and we stood him in the hall closet. Jay's mom came in and nearly had a heart attack when she opened the closet door and Bill tumbled out! Bill woke up, and, being a polite boy, simply said, "Oh, Hello Mrs. Peterio."

The house usually suffered no damage, but during one weekend party a kitchen walls was removed for reasons I can no longer remember. Jay's parents were understandably upset at this![3]

1967 was the heyday of the Summer of Love on the west coast. We didn't really know much about it, just the dribs and drabs that came through in the media. But we did try the great put-on[4] of 1967: mellow yellow, smoking dried banana skins. It was on the network news and everything, and we were determined to try it. I know if there had been some grass around, we would have all been smoking that too.

---

[2] The Old Curmudgeon's Sage Advice No. 2.
[3] A few years later Jay's father died of a heart attack while yelling at Jay.
[4] A "put-on" was something highly improbable being touted as true. The mellow yellow put-on was funny because all these establishment types would be trying to figure out how to keep kids from smoking banana skins and getting high on the fictitious compound 'bannadine." Not to mention what the United Fruit Company execs must have thought about a ban on bananas! More on this in Chapter 24.

The musical breakthrough of the summer was the Doors *Light My Fire*. AM radio was the only source of broadcast music for us at that time, and we had the greatest respect for any station that was hip enough to break the three minute limit imposed by their playlists and play the entire seven-minute album cut with the extended solos rather than the short radio version, less than half that length. This was the very beginning of what would become known as "album oriented rock" or AOR.

I had brought my good friend Barry Wilson into this circle of youthful miscreants. Ron played guitar. He and Barry and I picked up another guitar player, Mike Capinjola, and put together a band that summer, The Autumn Shadow, and played a couple of dances. I played drums. Barry played his mother's portable Hammond organ. The only reason it was portable was the it took four people to carry it rather than six or eight, I suppose. That fucker was genuinely heavy! We didn't have a bass player so Barry covered the bass parts on the organ. For a PA system, we used Barry's Marantz stereo, using his Ampex reel-to-reel tape recorder for an echo unit.

We were the first psychedelic band in the county. Barry mounted a switch on my kick drum pedal. We had blue lights on the band all the time, and whenever I smacked the kick drum, the blue lights went out and red lights flashed. Oh yes, we were definitely hip for McKean county!

Our repertoire included *Light My Fire, C'mon Down to My Boat, Baby, Little Bit O'Soul, Solitary Man, Live for Today Wipeout, Walk, Don't Run, Donna, Midnight Hour, Louie Louie,* (what are the words to that song, anyway?) and some others that slip my mind after more than fifty years. Rehearsals were in Barry's garage and were usually accompanied by massive partying with cases of Iron City beer, quarts from the Cow Palace in Limestone, NY.

Jay's parents bought a house about a block from the Bradford Police station and went on vacation for a week, leaving Jay in charge. And, of course, we partied for a solid goddamned week. There were teenage inebriates all over that house. Ron and I set up the drums and guitars. Gary Haynes brought his organ over (Barry Wilson was back at school that fall) and we had a week long blast. And when it was over, we cleaned up the house (all the walls being intact this time) and the place looked like nothing happened. All the while, the police drove by all day long. You didn't have to be necessarily cool to get away something, but you did have to be exceptionally stupid to get caught.

And speaking of stupid, I got very drunk one November night in Bradford with Ron and attempted to drive home. The result was that I rolled my '63 Falcon on a curve a few miles outside of town. Rolling a car over is quite an interesting experience which I do not care to repeat.

I was doing about eighty into a turn near the Pennhills Club that was good for about thirty-five. By the time I realized where I was, I knew I was in deep shit. Usually quite skillful at managing a car in a skid, I was too alcohol-impaired to pull it off. The rear end was fishtailing and I kept overcompensating. I knew it was going to go over. Sure enough, *ker-thumpity BAM,* it rolled over once and landed right side up in a sand trap in the golf course, gearshift in neutral, engine still running. It was a miracle I didn't hit one of several trees on that turn. The door handles were jammed into the doors, so they wouldn't open. The windshield and rear window were laying in the road and the roof was a bit lower. It was drivable so I went back to Ron's house and crashed for the night. Classmate Buddy Feit was home on leave from the Navy prior to shipping out to Vietnam. A hospital corpsman, and he came to Bradford the next morning and checked me out for concussion, etc.

WHILE SGT. PEPPER PLAYED

On a Tuesday night in December, the 12th to be exact, Ron Lattin called me up.

"Hey Gene, do you want to smoke some pot?"

Does a bear defecate in the forest? Does the Pope, by any slim chance, happen to be Catholic? At long fucking last! Yes. YES! *YES!*

"When and where, man?"

"C'mon over to my trailer."

I hitchhiked the twenty miles to Ron's trailer. His car was broken down at the time, so a friend gave us a ride to a local juke joint, Zirkle's, and we met Dave and Sue Hollander. Both from Bradford, Dave was in the army stationed near El Paso, Texas. Sue supplemented David's service pay by smuggling kilos of Mexican grass over the border and selling "lids," roughly an ounce of grass in a baggie, to GI's on the base where Dave was stationed.

We finished our drinks, got into Dave's car and started toward Ron's trailer. Sue took out a skinny cigarette twisted tightly on the ends and lit it. The car was immediately filled with an aroma not unlike burning autumn leaves. When I took a puff on it I filled my lungs with the pungent reefer smoke, coughing a bit, but trying to hold in the smoke. Yes, I was now into drugs, breaking the law. A felony? Only if caught.

We passed the joint around, smoking down to a small "roach" on the way back to Ron's trailer. I didn't get off.

"Hey Gene," asked Ron, "you high yet?"

"Don't feel a thing."

"Sometimes you don't get high the first time," said Sue, "it takes a couple of times."

Bullshit, I thought, *I want to do it tonight!*

We went into the trailer. David took out another joint and fired it up. We passed it among ourselves. After a couple of hits, I got a sudden rush, feeling like someone had tied my ass to a rocket and fired me into space! This was it! Ohhhhh...*yes!* I was *high*, but *not* fucked up! Better than beer? Fucking-*A!* I closed my eyes and it felt as if my eyeballs were revolving in their sockets and watched fireworks going off behind my eyelids. It was just plain goddamned fine! It was a groove, and I knew I could handle it.

We put the Beatles Sergeant Pepper on the record player and kicked back, grooving to the music and having occasional fits of giggling. It was a gas. But there was one prodding question in my mind: if grass was *this* groovy, *what* was LSD like?

BACK TO THE HALLOWED HALLS OF ACADEMIA

Epiphanies can occur in the strangest of places. I was in the Roxy in Portville, New York one evening in the fall of 1967 with Barry Wilson stuffing my face with pizza and swilling 10¢ drafts. Out of the blue, the thought came to me that I should go back to college. *Yes!* That was it! The next day I started writing letters. Lock Haven State College would have nothing more to do with me (surprised? Naahh...). However, I was accepted to carry 12 credits at a local college, the University of Pittsburgh campus in Bradford, Pennsylvania.

Looking at the present day campus of UPB, now a four year university, with numerous buildings and athletic fields, it is difficult to think how this sprawling modern institution started out as a two-year community college shoehorned into Bradford. Emery Hall, was the dormitory and housed the administrative offices as well. Classes were held in Main St. storefronts. I took a logic class in the old Emery Hardware building and an art class in the Hamsher House, a building near the hospital that formerly housed nursing students. A blue bus affectionately called "Old Blue" shuttled students between Emery Hall and Hamsher house.

Today only a paved lot remains at 5 Mechanic St. due to a fire some years back. Adjacent to what is now Emery Tower, once Emery Hall, it had been occupied by three story brick building housing storefronts on the ground level and two upper floors of apartments. A plaque on the heavy wooden door proclaimed the aging structure to be "The Mansion House." Once grand, it was past its prime when I rented the second floor front apartment above the Capitol Meat Market, while attending Pitt-Bradford during winter trimester, 1968. My front window overlooked Main St. and Veteran's Square.

Not yet having attained the age of majority, then 21, I should have been living next door in Emery Hall with the university *in loco parentis*. I was doing this on my own dime, my parents were not paying for it, so when I signed up I neglected to mention I was living on my own in my own apartment and not with my parents. I had *unsupervised freedom!* What could *possibly* go wrong with that?

MY PAD

My furnished apartment was two rooms, kitchen and bath for sum of forty-five dollars a month, utilities included. The living room had a couple of overstuffed chairs and some floor lamps and a nice, comfortable old sofa, couple of end tables and a coffee table. A bay window faced Main Street with a small wrought iron balcony that went to the bay window of the adjacent apartment. The bedroom, which you had to go through in order to get to the kitchen, had a double bed and a single bed. The kitchen had a stove and a counter, but no sink, the dishes had to be washed in the bathtub.

I had taken and passed my pre-induction physical the previous month. The Selective Service System's rules had changed (again!). The test I had taken a year and a half earlier was no longer considered a valid criteria of whether or not one should have a student deferment.[5] Now that I was enrolled as a full-time student was entitled to a 2-S student deferment. The reason I qualified for a 2-S was a one day delay in getting the information from my physical in Buffalo to the draft board in Bradford and I could not be given the requisite number of days notice to which I was entitled under law. I think it was thirty, I can't remember.

Shortly after moving into my pad, I gained a roommate, Terry Shirey, who worked at Howard Johnson's. We split the rent and shared the

---

[5] A senator's kid must have flunked it. Those rotten bastards would never risk their own in the folly of Vietnam.

place. For the month of January, I was fairly serious about my studies and was actually attending classes on regular basis.

Terry liked to party as much as I did. 5 Mechanic St., Apt 2, became the base of operations for general bacchanalia.

There was always an ample supply of beer, usually cheap quarts of Iron City, bought by the case at the Cow Palace in Limestone, New York, and illegally transported across the state line. Of course, there were occasional purchases of Yacht Club Ale ($2.98 for *a case* of 12oz. cans). We lived to party, and sometimes things got out of hand.

ROCK AND ROLL ALL NIGHT

One evening we embarked on what would become a spontaneous all night beer blast. The stereo was cranked up with tunes by the Beatles, the Rolling Stones, Cream, the Mothers of Invention, Fugs, and the Iron Butterfly. I was in the bedroom in an inebriated grope with Lin when the beer ran out.

There was a member of our Bradford crew, Greg Wixen, who was the epitome of a youthful hoodlum. Greg was medium built, about five-feet-six, brown greased back hair, a sort of long face and a dead front tooth that had turned black. His eyes were steel gray. Greg had a talent for burglary. He did not, however, have a talent for getting away with it. He had probably broken into every business on Main Street at one time or another and gotten caught every time.

I emerged from the bedroom about 3:30 in the morning to find everyone drinking from several cases of beer Greg had just liberated from the Bottle O'Beer warehouse a block from my apartment. There wasn't a whole lot I could do about it, so I figured what the hell. The party pooped out about 7:00 A.M. and I decided to get some sleep.

At 8:00 I was awakened by an insistent knocking at my door. I groggily opened it and was confronted by my landlord, Sam, and a police officer. *Oh shit!*

"Mr. Johnson?" the white haired policeman inquired.

"Yes?"

"I'm Officer Carbunkle. You are a student at the University of Pittsburgh here, is that correct?"

"Yes."

"I understand you had a party here last night."

I looked at Sam. He stood a head shorter than Carbunkle and didn't say word. I could tell by his face he was not at all happy.

"Uh...yeah."

"Well," he continued, "it seems that the Bottle O'Beer warehouse was burglarized last night. Around 3 a. m. individuals were observed entering this building carrying some cases of beer."

Oh shit! Think fast, and lie real good!

"Jesus!" I said trying to act genuinely surprised. "You mean there might have been some stolen beer at my party? Hey, I don't know anything about this. I was in the bedroom with a chick. When I came out there were some guys here that I didn't know, friends of friends, y'know, I think they might have been from Olean, but I'm not sure. I know someone said they brought beer."

"Then you don't know anything about the break-in?"

"No. I mean, I'm into partying, but not burglary. Hell, I wouldn't want anything to do with that. Believe me, if any stolen beer came in here last night, I don't know a thing about it."

"You sure about that?" He raised an eyebrow.

"Yeah, I'm sure."

"Do you mind if I come in and look around." He tried to peer around me.

I had opened the door only enough to talk to them and they couldn't see past me into the room.

I knew my rights. "You got a search warrant?"

"No. You want me to get one?"

I hesitated for a moment. "No. Come on in."

They were not ready for the sight that greeted them. There must have been twelve to fifteen people at my apartment partying all night long. There were empty beer cans everywhere: on the floor, on the mantel, on the tables, under the tables, on the couch, on the kitchen counter, on the tank of the toilet, on the stereo speakers, in the trash cans. Iron City, Schmidt's, Schlitz, Budweiser, Black Label, Labatt's, Genesee, Colt . 45, Piels, Yacht Club Ale...

The utter chaos of the situation saved my ass. What with the quantity of empty cans, there was absolutely no way to tell which were stolen and which were not! An empty can was an empty can. And none of them said "Hey, look at me, I'm stolen!" They couldn't see the trees for the forest.

Carbunkle turned to Sam. "Now here's a guy who has gotten caught in the middle of something without knowing about it." He looked back at me. "I think you're on the level. But if you find out anything, give me a call. OK?" He turned to leave.

Sam finally spoke. "You and me gotta talk." He glowered at me, turned and followed Carbunkle out the door.

I did not get in any real trouble with the police for the beer heist, but this was an incident that gave me a profile with the BPD as a n'er-do-well. Lacking much else to do, the Bradford cops started parking a cruiser across the street from my apartment at 8:00 P.M. observing the foot traffic into the building.

Later that week I was walking down Main St. and ran into David and Susan Hollander. I hadn't seen them since they had turned me on to reefer in December. David was home on leave prior to deployment to Germany. They had a generous supply of mind-altering substances and we went to my pad and partied all night. The brought some great records with them. This was my first exposure to Jimi Hendrix and the entire Doors first album. David had a stash of Preludin (European diet pills), and we got cranked right up on them.

Mr. Callahan, the Dean of Students, was a rather short, rotund man, bald and usually had a harried expression on his face. That might have been only when he was dealing with me.

The next day I was still speeding my brains out when Mr. Callahan, stopped me on the way back from class.

"Johnson?"

"Yes...?"

"We require all students who are under twenty-one and not living at home to live in the dormitory. Why are you in that apartment?"

"I don't live at home anymore. I'm independent. I'm here on my own dime."

"I want to see you in my office tomorrow."

I agreed to be there. I called my father to see if he could render some assistance. He came over and talked to the dean and explained that I was making my own way and he wasn't responsible for me. It worked! I was allowed to keep my party paradise! Oh, yes, victory was so sweet!

My circle of friends widened at UPB, and my apartment was soon visited by some students from around Newton, Massachusetts. Near Boston. David Sherman[6] was a thin, bespectacled young man with a keen sense of humor and an appetite for good times and good pot. Karen Wallerstein also frequented my apartment. Her cousin, Eric Hurwitz, while not a student, came to Bradford and fit in with our drinking and general debauchery. His ride was a dark blue '65 Ford that had a police interceptor engine in it. Damn! That car would haul ass! He let Ron Lattin borrow it one night and the cops goat after him. Ron would have outrun them if he hadn't run out of gas! Eric married one of the girls in our circle. Phyllis was from "Lon-Guyland." They had a friend called "Grub," who had the hair, beard and general appearance and demeanor to go with his name. Vern Grousley, a Beatle-ish looking bass player from Shinglehouse, PA, was there a lot too. They mixed well with the usual assortment of Bradford people who frequented my den of iniquity.

MARISSA

Ron Lattin introduced me to an attractive young woman by the name of Marissa. She had long, dark hair, dark brown eyes, a lovely mouth and lips and was nicely built. We took a liking to each other.

I had a couple of drunken gropes prior to meeting Marissa, but none with anything resembling passion. Marissa would prove to be my first experience with that. One evening we started to make out on the couch and she suggested that we go into the bedroom. Getting up from the couch, she took my hand and led the way. We melted into each other's arms and made love together for the first time enjoying warm intimacy of our lovemaking.

I watched her face, a young woman in the grip of pure sexual enjoyment, so lovely, framed by her dark tresses on the pillow. Marissa become more and more excited by the moment, her breathing becoming faster, deeper, then frantic. She literally exploded with orgasm. I had finger-fucked some of my girlfriends, and seen them cum but I had never seen anything like this lovely young woman at the pinnacle of sexual ecstasy. And because of ME! She grasped a corner of the mattress with each hand and pulled it damned near double up around her ears! I achieved my climax shortly after she did. Oh, yes! We lay there quivering, basking in the afterglow of our passion. She kissed my face and nibbled on my lips. "Nobody has ever made me cum like that before."

---

[6] The Old Curmudgeon's Sage Advice No. 2

I accepted the compliment. I could feel that self-esteem issue I mentioned previously start to heal itself!

The only problem is that she was sixteen and I could be found guilty of statutory rape for banging her. It bothered me–for about a tenth of a second! She was a gorgeous and sensual being, young woman. Beautiful and willing, I could not deny myself my desire for her. We just couldn't keep our hands off each other and were constantly screwing. I even got bold enough to go down on her. I hadn't really done oral sex, but I had read about how to do it in those paperback "marriage manuals" that were available on drugstore book racks.

More than one morning I awoke to pleasurable sensations to find Marissa in my bed naked and fellating me. It beat hell out of my alarm clock! She would skip school and come to my apartment for an all day fuckfest! Naturally, I blew off classes too.

In the ensuing fifty plus years, I don't believe I have ever met a woman hornier than Marissa. She was instantaneously turned on, and once turned on, had to achieve orgasm. She was positively voracious. That is to say, delightful!

She wanted me to meet her parents, so we went to her house one evening and did some chit-chat. We were alone together on the porch for a few moments. I walked over to her and looked into her eyes, kissed her, and reached down and gave her pussy a light stroke through her jeans.

She broke the kiss and looked deep into my eyes. "Don't *ever* do that unless you intend to *fuck* me." Yeah. Like she had to worry that I might not! We went back to my apartment and took care of that in short order. Life was positively grand!

Marissa was a picture of youthful feminine pulchritude. Her skin perfect, clear and without blemish, her eyes dark, seductive, and sensual. Her breasts were perfectly formed in proportion to her build, the appropriate produce reference being apples. Her nipples as pink as rosebuds. She had a slender waist and long, lithesome legs. Her pubic hair was somewhat sparse, like it was not finished growing in yet, formed a sexy little patch between her legs. She had the most perfectly formed little ass, sweet teenage cheeks which just begging to be kissed! I was completely intoxicated by the sheer beauty, sexiness and sensuality of this young and uninhibited creature.[7] We weren't in love, just fuckstruck over each other.

---

[7] In the midst of our fuck frenzy we did have enough sense to use birth control, EMCO spermicidal foam.

W. EUGENE JOHNSON

I'M LIVING IN A WHOREHOUSE?

Bill Allen was an older black man from Bradford who had played alto sax, on the road with Louis Armstrong back in the day. He sat in on some gigs I played. I had just started smoking weed a few weeks before I met him. I figured since he was a jazz man he was a pothead. After we finished a tune I lit up a Winston and hit on it like it was a joint. Bill, who was standing in front of my drum kit, instantly spun around, his eyes wide, and said, "Y'got any? My connection died ten years ago!" I didn't have any weed at the time, but over the years I did see Bill several times after that and managed to lay some smoke[8] on him whenever I did.

I came out of my Mechanic St. apartment one day as Bill was coming up the stairs. "Johnson!" he exclaimed, "what are *you* doing *here?*"

"Oh hi, Bill. I live here." I pointed to my apartment door.' "What are *you* doing here?"

Bill's eyes sparkled. "Oh, you don't know about this place, do you?" His voice had a playful taunting quality to it.

"What's to know?"

"Oh, well, you see, this place used to be a cat house. Some of the girls still live here and I'm going to see one of them! Catch you later," he grinned and proceeded down the hall.

My place of residence, the Mansion House, had once been a whorehouse. I have heard ugly buildings and old whores gain respectability as they age.

To quote Dirty Harry, "Marvelous..

---

[8] Weed, marijuana, grass.

Smethport Hometown Hero banner honoring Christian "Buddy" Feit for his service and sacrifice. Located along U.S. Route 6 in the Borough of Smethport PA.
Photo Credit: Barty Barton

CHAPTER 10

BUDDY

CLASSMATE, FRIEND, & MADMAN EXTRAORDINAIRE!

There occurred in January, 1968, an event that would stand out as being fundamentally influential on my lifelong political and social attitudes, forever coloring my world view.[9] I hadn't developed a political consciousness yet. Life was still an endless party and I wasn't taking anything too seriously.

Buddy, whose full name was Christian Franz Feit III, was one of my best friends ever. We had known each other since the sixth grade when I started attending the borough school.

Buddy was the class clown. His father was the Superintendent of Schools for McKean County. His mother had been my teacher for 3rd, 4th, and 5th grade at the East Smethport school. We both played drums in the school band and were in Boy Scouts together. We became quite good friends, sharing an interest in rock n' roll, cars, and, in our late teens, the consumption of vast quantities of beer. We developed this penchant for out-and-out hell raising that seemed to be all-consuming. The Sunday drag races was one of the high spots of our existence then, drinking our way up and back. We just didn't *give* a shit!

He was an outdoorsman, and loved hunting and fishing with his father. Buddy was the biggest Beatle fan I ever knew and was the first kid in town to get the first Beatles first US. album in the winter of 1964. He

---

[9] The Old Curmudgeon's Sage Advice No. 2.

even had one of those peculiar Beatles suits, the ones with no lapels. As Beatlemania was mounting, he commandeered a school phonograph one morning and we proceeded to party with the *Meet the Beatles* LP in our homeroom until the teacher came in and put a stop to it.

In 1964, it was generally assumed as biologically impossible – not to mention socially and culturally unacceptable – for men to grow hair long enough to cover their ears despite depictions of Jesus with long hair that we had seen all our lives.[10] Everyone who was the least bit "cool" still wore their hair greased into a '50's slicked back streamlined 1950s DA style, myself included. Buddy had the first Beatle haircut in town and used to get the hell harassed out of him at school, not by the students so much as by the teachers. I think this was a bit vindictive, as some of these teachers resented his parents and their positions within the school system. Buddy took a large ration of shit for his daring to be hip. True to his character, he didn't give a damn, or so he acted. I know the crap he was given for his general attitude and demeanor–being an individual–got to him much more than he let on.

Buddy's antics were legendary. For instance, we had a fellow in our class, Jack Case, who was tall and long limbed. While Buddy was driving his family's green Jeep Wagoneer down the street, Jack would reach across and take the steering wheel in his left hand while resting his head on his right hand, his elbow resting on the open passenger window and looking straight ahead. Buddy would then lean out the driver's window and wave at people with both arms while smiling with an idiotic grin!

One of the leisure time pursuits in which we all participated was doing things that could be characterized as impractical, impossible, dangerous and/or downright stupid with four-wheel drive vehicles. This would usually involve four to six persons, somebody's Jeep, several six-packs of beer and a reckless idea. About thirteen miles from Smethport is the Kinzua Viaduct – well, what's left of it, a tornado knocked a great deal of it down some years ago – the longest railroad bridge in the world. It rose three-hundred feet above the valley, as tall as the Statue of Liberty. It is now the Kinzua Bridge State Park. The sides of the valley are, to say the least, quite steep, and on the far side a footpath descends to the floor of the valley. Buddy decided one evening that he would take his parents' Jeep Wagoneer down this footpath. At least two people backed out of the deal, saying it was impossible. Bud, spurred onward by this challenge insisted that he would do it.

---

[10] "Who the hell do you think you are, Jesus Christ or something?" was an often heard epithet directed toward males with long hair.

The footpath had never, to anyone's knowledge, been traversed by a wheeled vehicle. It was narrow with brush on both sides and had many switchbacks owing to the steep hillside. The family Jeep did indeed descend that valley via the footpath using a technique developed on the spot especially for that purpose. It was rather simple, really. Buddy would come to a switchback and stop. Four guys would get out and get on the upper side of the Jeep. Buddy would gun the engine, pop the clutch and spin the rear wheels while the others pushed the rear end of the jeep around and Buddy could proceed to the next switchback. To my knowledge, no one has ever done this since then. But then…why would anybody want to?

Bud transferred to Lock Haven State College from Clarion State for the second semester of his freshman year after he enlisted in the Navy, which he would enter during the summer of 1966.

He and I continued our hell raising at Lock Haven. We would go all over the place in his blue Volkswagen beetle, drinking beer all the way.

On our of our weekend excursions, Bud and I were in Bradford going down Jackson Avenue drinking Colt. 45 malt liquor. While watching a young woman's shapely behind moving sweetly down the sidewalk, Bud rear-ended a car in front of us. I hit the windshield of his blue VW bug with my head and left a lock of my hair dangling from it. True to our semi-intoxicated form, we just…split! Like two damned fools, we took a right turn up a dead end street! Jesus, what a panic. We were not only drinking in a car, we were both underage to possess liquor in any form in Pennsylvania and this would be my second bust for this. We ditched the Colt . 45 in the weeds and went back down the street where we expected to be met by the people we had just rear-ended and be in a world of shit. They were nowhere to be found! What *amazing* luck! We went back up the hill and retrieved our Colt .45! Priorities, you know!

Having to explain the damaged windshield, we concocted a preposterous yarn about being "…run off the road by an oncoming car and…" It was really a bunch of silly shit. I don't think his mother for one moment believed any of it, but she never said anything. Perhaps she didn't want to know the truth if it took a lie that big to cover it up! We returned to LHSC the next day with another adventure to relate to our friends.

AWOL

College had not worked out for Buddy. He wanted to find his place in the world. His father had been and Army officer in WWII. Wanting to do something different that what his father had done, Bud joined the

Navy. He signed up to be a corpsman (medic). He attended training, passed, and was serving on active duty. He seemed to be doing quite well in the Navy. One day out of the blue, Buddy showed up in uniform with his sea bag at Lock Haven. I went over to him and shook his hand.

"Hey, it's good to see you," I shook his hand, "but what are you doing here?"

"I'm AWOL."

"You gotta be shittin' me, man. Why!?"

"I was home on leave and I was going back and I went to sleep in the bus terminal in Chicago. My wallet was in here," he indicated how it was folded over the waist of his pants under his tunic (there are no pockets in seaman's trousers), "and when I woke up it was gone. It had all my money and my bus ticket in it. I had no way to get back to the base. So I split. Started hitchhiking."

Jesus Christ! I both could and couldn't believe it at the same time. Bud never did anything half-assed, it was always full-tilt gonzo humungous. Nineteen-year olds are prone to doing things like that. But making a decision to commit a federal offense for which he could go to prison was a whole different thing.

I found a place for Buddy to stay for the evening at Lock Haven. He left the next day, hitchhiking up to New England to see an old girlfriend, Faith.

It bothered me to see him in trouble, and I knew he was in some truly deep shit this time. I was torn about what to do. While I knew little about real life, *i.e.*, outside of college or living with my parents, I did know that once you were in the armed forces, your ass belonged to Uncle Sam in the most literal sense. Bud had made a profound error in judgment by going AWOL. If he was gone long enough he would be declared a deserter and that would be federal prison for sure. I agonized over what to do. Bud was my friend, and I am loyal to my friends. He was also embarked on a disastrous course of action which he seemed keenly intent on making worse. I finally decided that the best course of action was to tell his folks. I called his mother and told her Bud was AWOL. She informed the Navy and Buddy was picked up by local authorities somewhere in New England and turned over to the Navy.

He was taken before Captain's Mast for discipline. He told me that in order to avoid more severe punishment he volunteered for duty in Vietnam. Marines don't train combat medics. Because they are part of the Department of the Navy, they use Navy corpsmen. It was such a typical Buddy Feit move. He wasn't sent over right away, however, he was stationed at St. Alban's Naval Hospital in New York City. He was home a few times over the summer and we did our usual thing: drink and raise hell.

He finally received his orders for Vietnam. He was to leave on December 9, 1967. I remember going over to his house the night before he left and wishing him well.

"Hey man, when you get back, we'll get drunk for a week!"

He looked at me and said "Yeah, you bet." There was no conviction in his voice. We shook hands and I left.

THE BAD NEWS

On the evening of the January 25, 1968, there was a knock on the door of my apartment in Bradford. I opened it. It was my parents. Mom had a very concerned look on her face.

"We have to talk to you," said Dad. His tone of voice was serious.

The three of us sat down. Mom didn't say anything. She glanced me and then my at my dad. He looked at me, then down at the floor, then back at me. "It's about your friend, Bud."

I knew what was coming next, but I still hoped it wasn't so.

"How bad?" I asked.

"All the way," said Dad.

I was stunned.

"Gener," said Mom, "we're awful sorry. We thought we should come over and tell you before you read it in the paper."

"When did it happen?"

"We don't know," Mom replied, "we just heard about it. Will you be all right?"

"I'll be OK, Mom. Thank you both for coming over and telling me."

We talked for a few minutes and they left.

I was devastated. This was the first time death had touched someone so close to me. Bud was dead. Damnit! And for what?

I went to the lobby of Emery Hall and called Mia at her college, charging the call to my parents' phone number. I got her dorm, identified myself and asked for her.

"Hello, *EU*gene?" She always put the emphasis on the first syllable of my name." How are you? What's happening?" She was so upbeat and cheerful, and I was going to give her news that would break her heart.

"Oh, God, Mia, I have some bad news. You'd better sit down."

"Good lord! What's wrong?"

"It's...it's Buddy...he's...dead."

"What?!...Oh my God! Oh, God, Eugene, they've *killed* him! They've *killed* him! Oh no! No! *Goddamnit! NO!*"

She was hysterical with grief. I do not remember how the conversation ended, except that it did. Some years later she told me that, in her rage, she tore the phone off the wall. That is an amazing feat, when you consider that she is just a wisp of a thing (at our twentieth year class reunion she wore the same clothes she wore in the eighth grade and did the twist).

I then called Faith, whom Buddy hadn't dated in some time, because I felt she should know. Bud's mother later related to me that she received a very nice letter from her.

The next morning I bought the January 26 edition of *The Bradford Era*. Buddy's picture was on the front page. The headline read "C. F. Feit III Killed in War." Still in shock, I read the article that followed.

SMETHPORT–Christian Franz Feit III, 20, son of McKean County School Superintendent C. F. Feit Jr., and Mrs. Feit of 508 King St., Smethport, was fatally wounded in combat in the early morning hours Thursday in Vietnam.

The youth according to word brought to the parents by Lt. Cmdr. George Rashley, Naval Reserve Training Center, Jamestown, N. Y., died at 8:46 a. m. aboard the U.S. S. Sanctuary, a Navy hospital ship.

Young Christian became the second McKean County youth to lose his life in Vietnam while serving as a Navy Hospital Corpsman. The first was a Bradford resident, James Keith Oxley, 21, son of Mr. and Mrs. Keith Oxley of 166 High St.

Corpsman Feit was serving with the Third Battalion of the 26th Marine Regiment, Third Division. He enlisted in the Navy on June 28, 1966, and was sent to Vietnam Dec. 10 1967. His last visit home was in November, just prior to shipping off to Vietnam.

(Associated Press reports Thursday that the 26th Regiment of Marines was under heavy Communist attack at Khe Sanh air strip, and it may have been in that fighting that the Smethport youth was killed.)

FLASHING BACK– COMING OF AGE IN THE AMERICAN 1960s

Christian was born in Kane on Dec. 28, 1947, to C. F. and Dorothy Bickel Feit. He graduated from the Smethport grade schools and in 1965 received his diploma at Smethport High School.

During his high school career, Feit was active in the band, Teen-Tones and the Smethport High School Chorus. In September of 1965 he entered Clarion State College. However, at the time of his enlistment, he was a student at Lock Haven State College.

He was a member of the First Methodist Church of Smethport.

Surviving besides his parents are a sister, Josephine, a student at Lock Haven State College, and his maternal grandmother, Mrs. Joseph Bickel of Mill Hall, PA, and several uncles and aunts.

Mr. Feit received the word of his son's death only a few hours after returning from Lock Haven where he had taken his daughter back to school after mid-semester vacation. He had been to Penn State University where he had attended a meeting. Arrangements will be under the direction of the Hugh G. Fry Funeral home here.

Three-hundred sixty-three words. My friend's entire life, the all too short span of twenty years and twenty-eight days, had been reduced to three-hundred sixty-three words. All the laughter, tears, love, friendship, camaraderie, joy and sorrow, everything he had ever known, everything he ever was, were reduced to ten paragraphs on the front page of *The Bradford Era*. Three hundred sixty-three words, his picture, and his memory were all that were left of my friend.

Hundreds of other similar stories ran in home town newspapers across America that week, each announcing the death of a native son, a kid everyone knew and liked, a young man with a future, a brave boy doing his duty. And how many fathers, mothers, sisters, brothers, sweethearts, wives, children grandparents, aunts, uncles, cousins and friends felt the irreplaceable loss of someone so precious to them? This was the effect of the Vietnam war on American society. Each death was like a pebble dropped in a pool of water. The ripples, the effects of each individual loss, emanated from it in ever expanding circles. This was repeated over fifty-eight thousand times as the flag-draped coffins returned American youths to their hometowns, to their families, and to the earth.

The event for which January 1968 is remembered was the Tet offensive. Hell was unleashed sweeping through Vietnam, consuming young American lives as a wildfire consumes prairie grass. America was beginning to awaken to the futility, tragedy and waste of this war, but it would take tens of thousands more deaths before it finally ground to a halt.

I went to Bud's parents' home a couple days later, after I regained some of my composure. His mother told me she knew the moment he had died half a world away. She awoke in the middle of the night with a disturbing feeling something was very wrong. When the government car pulled up to the house the next day, she knew. The Naval officer got out and started toward the house. She opened the door even before he got to the front the steps and asked, "Is he dead?"

"Yes," he replied.

In the days that followed, she received a letter from a fellow who was in boot camp with Buddy. He had been stationed on the hospital ship and was present when a chopper brought Buddy from Khe Sanh. He had been struck in the head by a fragment from a rocket. He never regained consciousness, nor did he suffer.

God. How awful. *Why*, I asked myself, *couldn't Bud have just been wounded? Why did he have to die?* But then I realized that if he hadn't died, he would have probably been a vegetable from massive brain damage. This would be no way for an active young man to live. He was always hunting and fishing and just, well, *being* so much in the world. It was an ironic blessing that my friend was dead. My wish that he might have survived his wound was selfish.

Another fellow Smethport Graduate, Class of 1966, Charles "Butch" Gregory, a Marine, was killed the following week. I knew him when he caddied at the golf course in Smethport one summer.

Gary Grassi, from Bradford, PA, was killed a couple of days after that. I knew him from Lock Haven State College. He had been the star quarterback on the Bradford Christian High School football team. There was a story that he had wired some flowers home to his fiancée prior to being killed. Ironically the flowers and a note written by him were delivered to her after she received the news of his death. He was posthumously awarded the Silver Star for actions he performed saving the lives of some men in his unit while mortally wounded himself.

Buddy's body came home on March 9, three months to the day after he had left for Vietnam. His parents had to look inside the coffin to positively identify the body as their son's. Mrs. Feit told me, "Gener, his head was twice its normal size from the trauma. The rocket fragment went through his left eye and into his brain."

The last two persons from Smethport to see Buddy alive were classmates, Ted Hyde, and Dave Murray, serving at Khe Sanh with the Marines. They saw Buddy around Christmas time, 1967. Ted told me the situation was grim and the Marines were preparing to face an overwhelming number of North Vietnamese forces. While medical personnel were not issued weapons as a rule, Bud was given an M-16, a weapon for which he had been given no training. Ted showed him how to use it. He said Bud looked scared when he saw him. Hell, who wouldn't be?

Dave Murray, Teddy Hyde, Christian "Buddy" Feit, all members of the Smethport, PA, Area High School Class of 1965, taken at Khe Sanh, RVN, around Christmas 1967. Dave lives in Florida, Teddy and Buddy are deceased.
Photo Source: Chris Murray

The NVA wanted to overrun Khe Sanh. General Giap, the commander of the North Vietnamese People's Forces, was running the show just like he did fourteen years earlier when, under his command, the Viet Minh overran the French forces at Dien Bien Phu, ending the French colonial occupation of Indochina. It was a very uncertain situation at the time, but massive American B-52 strikes prevailed and Khe Sanh was not overrun.

The names of KIA were listed in each issue of the U.S. military's GI newspaper, *"Stars and Stripes."* Years later while having a beer with

Ted Hyde in Smethport, he told me, "Y'know, Gener, if I read the name 'Eugene Johnson' in there, hell, that could be anybody, it wouldn't have to be you. There could have been a hundred 'Eugene Johnsons' in Vietnam. But when I read 'Christian F. Feit,' there was no doubt who it was. It could only be Bud."

In times of peace sons bury their fathers, in times of war fathers bury their sons. But, oh, what a devastating feeling it must be for a mother to look at a lump of dead flesh and know that a short time before it was her son, a living, breathing human being with feelings and emotions, a young man, her baby, born of her own body, someone who had such promise and who filled her with such pride. And now he is taken, she will never again hear his laugh or see his smile.

Sometime after the funeral, Mrs. Feit received Buddy's personal items and his medals from the Navy. She told me, "You raise a boy for eighteen years, and you try to love and do right by him. You nurse him through measles and chicken pox, cuts, scrapes, and broken bones. Then they send him off to war to die and they give you a handful of medals. And for what? I just…don't…think it's worth it."

"It's *necessary!*" my father thundered, "We *have* to do it." I was not so sure. I was starting to question the war. *Hey, hey, LBJ, how many kids did you kill today?* was now not just a chant I heard demonstrators shouting on the nightly news, it was something personal.

This was a most pivotal event in my life,[11] the beginning of my political consciousness, for I would dwell at length on this event, not just because of my personal bereavement, but because I wanted to understand for what my friend had died. Khe Sanh was abandoned. For what did Buddy lose his young life? What the hell was going on?

From the day I learned of Bud's death, I would never look again with trust upon the leaders of this country. I started having reservations about Vietnam since the previous summer. I would examine it much more closely now. This was the beginning of my political consciousness, of my cynicism and of an anger and inner rage that, while it has cooled somewhat for over a half century, has yet to abate.

It is always possible to fuck up to the point of getting yourself killed. In the 1960's, it was just a lot easier to do it. In his quest to find himself, to become a man, become his own person, establish his own place in the world, Buddy fucked up. He fucked up his way out of col-

---

[11] The Old Curmudgeon's Sage Advice No. 2.

lege. He fucked up his way into the Navy. He fucked up his way to Captain's Mast and fucked up his way to Vietnam. He fucked up and got killed for it.

SGT. CAMPBELL

With the advent of the internet in the 1990s, I set up some web pages and posted an early draft of this work. I also did some searching to see if I could find anyone who knew Buddy in Vietnam and who possibly knew how he died. All that any of us knew about Buddy is that he died at or near Khe Sanh on January 25, 1968. Mrs. Feit told me that he had been killed by a head wound from a rocket fragment.

I included this paragraph on my memorial page for Buddy:

There is some consolation–if there can be any at all–in the fact that it was Buddy's mission to save lives rather than take them. I will probably never know what happened just before he was hit. Did he expose himself to hostile fire while saving the life of another boy? Did his death spare some other family the agony of burying their son? Or was he just some poor bastard, a teenage soldier, standing in the wrong place at the wrong time, paying for it with his young life?

On June 12, 2001, I received this remarkable e-mail:

Dear Mr. Johnson,

My name is Carl Campbell and I've just finished doing something I don't normally allow myself to do—surfing the net, dredging up old and painful memories.

I came across, and read, chapter 5 of "Coming of Age in the 60's." I was struck with the profound impact your friends death had on you even after all these years. In one of the last paragraphs you said you would probably never know the circumstances of his death.

*In January 1968 I was the Platoon Sergeant of the 1st platoon, "K" company, 3rd Battalion of the 26th Marines. Christian Feit was my corpsman. I was 25 feet away when he received his fatal wounds. I can fill in those details **if you are sure you want to know**.*

I must tell you that the two or three times since Vietnam that I ventured into responding to a request (I know you didn't) from a loved one or interested party have been "bizarre" to say the least. So I don't do it anymore but, as I said, I was struck by the obviously profound impact your friend seems to still have on you.

Because of these past experiences, if you choose to respond, we'll need to establish some sort of rapport. When I came back from Vietnam, my own mother wouldn't talk to me about it. My dad just wanted to talk about his war. So I learned how to bury my experiences and I don't often dig them up.

In any case I admire your keeping your friends memory.

Carl Campbell[12]

He and I exchanged a couple of e-mails. He was class of 1960 but quit to join the Marines in 1959. He was 25 years old and a platoon sergeant at the time of Buddy's death, "an old man," as he described himself. He was in the marines for 10 years, a Drill Instructor for his last year. Serving on the San Diego police force, he retired to Missouri where he now spends his time "terrorizing the fish." He called me on Saturday evening, June 17, 2001. We talked for about an hour.

I told him that I never expected to hear from anyone who had served with Buddy in Vietnam.

"I'm not surprised," he replied, "he wasn't in my outfit very long."

"He left for Vietnam on December 9th so he couldn't have been in country for more than six weeks," I told him.

"Well, he was only with my outfit for three days. No one had a chance to get to know him. The only reason I knew his name is because I was his platoon sergeant."

He then described the situation. Kilo Company was stationed on hill 861 about two miles west of the main combat base at Khe Sanh. Hill 861 was shaped like a foot print. 1st platoon of Kilo company had been deployed between the arch and the little toe. A trench had been dug around the perimeter with the back higher than the front. Along the trench were fighting holes about the size of a queen bed dug waist deep and piled with sandbags.

Buddy was wounded on Wednesday. The Sunday prior to that, Kilo Company had received around 3000 rounds of mortar, artillery and rocket fire as well as a ground attack. Kilo company lost nine people the first night of the siege. One corpsman was killed and another wounded and medivaced out from the landing zone at the heel. That is when Buddy was sent up from the battalion aid station.

---

[12] This is not his actual name I could not locate him to get permission to use his name without violating his privacy.

"It happened on Wednesday and it was clear, so it must have been in the morning. At night it got so foggy you couldn't see your hand in front of your face. We were not under attack at the time. The NVA would just drop mortar rounds in at random to harass us. I was around a corner from two fighting holes that were about 12-15 feet apart and had taken off my boot and sock to air out my foot. I was leaning back and relaxing when I heard a mortar round explode nearby."

"Now, a rocket you can hear coming and you have a chance to take cover. With a mortar round, there is only a 'pop' from the launcher that you may or may not hear. Sometimes the round will get to you before the sound does. They have a high angled trajectory and just seem to drop in from nowhere with no warning."

"I put on my sock and boot and wrapped the laces around my ankle. Starting toward where I had heard the mortar round explode I met the platoon commander going the other way, he said 'You're going to have to deal with this one,' and kept going. He looked like he was going to throw up. I got to the first hole where Lance Corporal Frank Pennetti had been. The round must have landed either right on top of him or the wall of the trench. The only thing that was recognizable was his lower torso and legs. The rest of him was splattered."

"Then someone hollers 'There's two more over here!' Your friend had been evidently standing in the trench talking to PFC Kenny Goodman. They had been blown into the fighting hole twelve to fifteen feet away from the one Pennetti was in. Goodman was semiconscious and crying. He knew he was wounded but wasn't conscious enough to help himself. He had numerous shrapnel wounds and a broken arm."

"Feit was unconscious and had a diamond shaped hole near his left temple, as well as other wounds. He was spouting blood like a water fountain. We got them out of the hole and medivaced them from the LZ at the heel. Goodman died on the way to the hospital ship. Feit died the next day. He never knew what hit him"

Campbell told me that every time he is in Illinois he visits Frank Pennetti's grave. The way he contacted me was by entering the name "Christian F. Feit" into a web search and he came up with my memorial web page for Bud. He got my e-mail address from there.

He said his wife asked him why, after all the men he had seen die in combat, why, after all these years, the deaths of these three men affected him so deeply.

"I don't know why," he told me, "maybe because it was because I was wearing Pennetti's extra pair of fatigue pants. He was the only guy with an extra pair."

I am satisfied as to the veracity of what Mr. Campbell has told me. Aside from the fact that his demeanor on the telephone gave me the impression that he was genuine, I was also able to verify names and casualty dates of which he spoke from the K 3/26 web pages[13]. Besides, there was no reason for deception on his part. Generally when someone lies to you, they do it because they can gain something from it. Mr. Campbell had nothing to gain from lying to me.

So there it was. After all these years, I now know how and when Buddy died. He was just standing there and never knew what hit him. To this day I have never hit upon an acceptable "why."

BUDDY LOOKS BACK AT US

Buddy's story does not end here. In 2000, classmate Dave Lamborn, an Army Vietnam veteran and one of the first GIs on the scene when the VC overran the American embassy during Tet '68, told me he was certain he saw Buddy on a History Channel program.

"He was holding an IV bottle and turned and looked right into the camera," Dave told me. If anybody would find Buddy somewhere, Dave would be the one. He has been our Finder of Lost Classmates for our high school class reunions.

I related this to Carl Campbell during our telephone conversation. Campbell replied that this could very well be true as Bud would have been assigned to the battalion aide station at the combat base before he was shipped to Kilo company as a replacement." There were news cameras all over the place up there until the fighting started. Then I guess they found somewhere else to be."

Around Veterans Day 2004 I saw a program, "Unsung Heroes, the Battle of Khe Sanh," on the History Channel. About a minute into the program I saw the shot Dave Lamborn had described. A person looking a lot like Buddy and holding an IV bottle turns and looks directly at the camera. It is about a second and a half, and a particularly moving video clip not only because of the personal connection, but also because of the emotion in his face. I videotaped the program when it was shown again.

I played the tape, pausing it, studying the images of the young soldier who looked so much like Buddy. But was he *really* Buddy? Out of

---

[13] http://home. switchboard. com/KiloCo3rdBN26thMarinesVietnam. This is now a dead link.

2½ million Americans who served in Vietnam, what were the odds that this could *really* be *our* Buddy looking out at us from the TV screen, pictures not seen and not recognized by us for nearly four decades? Probably about even with the odds a particular young soldier could stand on a hill on a clear morning in Vietnam and be killed by a single piece of ordnance dropping from the sky.

I digitized the video and compared individual video frames to his senior yearbook picture. It certainly seemed to be him. Magnified details showed a similar facial structure, earlobe attachment and the shape of the chin with a small scar on the left side. Even the light refracted and distorted through the thick lenses of the glasses looked the same... But was it ...*really*...him? I *wanted* to believe it was him, but...I wasn't yet fully convinced. I had *rational* and *empirical* evidence, but *no emotional connection* to the person in those images.

A span of nearly four decades can jumble memories. You can look at a face you have seen thousands of times and not be at all certain who it is. But the odds were looking better. What were the chances of someone looking so much like Buddy also being stationed at Khe Sanh and being filmed holding an IV bottle?

Hospitalman Christian "Buddy" Feit at Khe Sanh prior to assignment to Kilo Company, 3/26 Marines on Hill 861 where he became a fatality on 25 January, 1968, 29 days after turning 20.
Source: "Unsung Heroes: The Siege of Khe Sanh © The History Channel

I e-mailed the pictures to Buddy's sister. At first she wasn't at all sure if it was Buddy. Then we each had an epiphany. I had printed Buddy's pictures and put them in an envelope. I happened to and peer into the envelope and saw the images upside down. Something clicked. That intuitive sense of recognition, the one that sorts out what you see and tells you what it is, said *"oh, there's Buddy"* in the same casual same way it would if I saw him driving down Main Street in his family's green Jeep we used to see him in all the time.

That same day I received an E-mail from his sister telling me she had a printout of the pictures lying on a desk upside down. She looked at it and recognized Buddy immediately. She told me "...now I don't know how I could ever believe it was *not* him."

I find it so remarkable that Buddy should be looking out at us in these images. Here he is, communicating with us after nearly four decades. I look at him and I see the face of an ordinary young man diligently performing his very difficult job amid extraordinary circumstances. He looks *so* very young, as were we all in 1968.

It is not surprising that Buddy, whose wonderful personality, outrageous sense of humor and insane antics had such an impact on us as our friend should also impact the producers of this program with the diligence in his expression as, soon to become a fatality himself, he attends to the needs of a wounded marine. This very short video snippet was just a cutaway shot, just a second or so, it likely meant nothing to the video editor except that it was a haunting image and entirely appropriate. To we who knew Buddy, it was like a miracle that we should see him again all these years later.

Decades after his death, Buddy looks directly at us, a spokesman for those who never survived the tragic carnage, terror, waste of valor and vain sacrifice that was Vietnam. Their faces appear in no film, the details of their final moments forever known only to themselves.

Buddy's short life and tragic death epitomized the *zeitgeist* of those dark and hopeless years which ended the 1960's. He became another unwitting human sacrifice to the gods of commerce, and his death and tens of thousands of others helped swell the coffers of the defense industry that was turning a profit on every bullet, bomb and body bag in Vietnam.

It was a catch-22. In order to survive the 1960's, you had to be able to make life and death decisions. But you didn't know what the hell they were. Some figured it out. Some got lucky. Some got dead.

In a small town, friendships and relationships are formed early and continue throughout life. We, the members of the Smethport Area High School Class of 1965, shared experience and developed a bond based on genuine care for each other. Many of us went to school together from first through twelfth grade.

I feel so very fortunate, so privileged to belong to a group in which the members have so much mutual affection for each other.

However, while we do have unusual cohesiveness as a class, we are still divided by Vietnam: those who went and those who didn't. It is a rift in our generation that will probably never heal. There are some class members who do not speak to others – and in particular me – and there is some bitterness. We are a microcosm of American society.

FONDLY REMEMBERED

At our thirty year class reunion in 1995, Buddy was remembered fondly and with sadness by all of us. Among class memorabilia posted on a bulletin board that evening was the poem I wrote in 1988, "For Buddy."[14] I was examining some of the items on the board when Denny Swartzfager, an Army Vietnam Veteran, was reading the poem. He looked at me and said, "You know, Gener, it was all for nothing. That's the damned shame of it. It was all for nothing."

Dan Nichols came up to me later and said "I read what you wrote about Buddy. Man, that's something that'll make your eyeballs sweat."

Dan had been a Marine gunship pilot in Vietnam. He and his wife Katy were both class members of our class. They had a stormy relationship all through high school. They had broken up at one point after graduation and Buddy had been instrumental in getting them back together. For many years they sent flowers to Buddy's grave every year. They have been together for over fifty years now.

Buddy's name came up while I was talking to Beth Albright, our Valedictorian, who was attending college in Pittsburgh at the time of his death. She lived three blocks from Buddy while growing up in Smethport. "I used to go to the airport whenever I knew someone from Smethport was going to Vietnam, and I would see them when they returned if I knew when they were coming in. When I saw Buddy off, I said 'I'll see you when you get back.' He replied, 'I don't think so.' He knew he was going to die."

At the time of our 25th year high school reunion in 1990 Mia, Lana Gunderson, and I visited Buddy's grave Kane, PA. I brought along a joint and a six-pack. Mia toked and poured a beer on Buddy's grave saying, "Well, Bud, if you won't come to the party then the party will have to come to you!" We celebrated him, drinking to our friendship and his memory.[15] We did it again at for the 50 year reunion.

For years after his death my relationship continued unconsciously. I would find myself thinking things, like, if I had just heard a particularly excellent new album, *Boy! Wait'll Buddy hears this.* Then I would re-

---

[14] See page v.
[15] The Old Curmudgeon's Sage Advice No. 5.

member he was dead. I don't suppose I knew how much I loved him until he was gone, twenty-eight days after his twentieth birthday, in Vietnam for less than two months. Part of it is guilt. I never answered the letters he sent me. I still have them. I was so busy with my life here that I could not take the time to answer them. I lived with a sense of shame from that self-centeredness for many years – Catholic guilt requires you always feel guilty, whether or not you are still a practicing Catholic. Some time ago I realized that it was perfectly OK, that's the way people are. I was a young man busy living my life.

For decades I fell into a depression around the anniversary of his death on the 25th. In 1988, I wrote the aforementioned poem, for Buddy, and suffered no depression. In the following years it returned.

This did not happen with the deaths of my own parents. Maybe that's because I expected my parents to die before I did. Death happens to parents. It's not supposed to happen to young men. Maybe that's another reason I have never fully come to terms with Buddy's death.

When I think of Vietnam, of the 58,130 dead, and of all the fathers, mothers, wives, lovers and sweethearts and children, I feel the rage, the frustration, the despair over a war forced on my generation by arrogant, cynical and greedy men. I can still feel the passion of that time running hot through my veins.

In 1983 when I visited the Vietnam Memorial in Washington, D. C. I felt no particular emotion as the memorial came into sight. However, the closer I got, the more I became aware of constricting, choking feeling. My God, how much room those names took up! By the time I got up to the wall, I realized I had arrived at America's own wailing wall. I felt as if I was being crushed by all the sorrow, the bereavement, the loss suffered by every single father, mother, brother, sister, son, daughter, spouse and lover of each one of the names etched on the wall. Of the four names I wanted to look up, I only made it to Buddy's. I couldn't see for the tears. I had to leave.

How I loved him, how we all loved him! I could have not loved Buddy more if he had been my own brother. And, to this day, I miss him. Sometimes I dream that he didn't die, is still alive, and comes to visit me. We talk, we laugh, listen to rock n' roll, drink beer and share good times. On occasion these dreams are so real I awake moved, feeling I have had a visitation from the dead.

Buddy's death affected me so very deeply, even to this day. It has taught me that you do not get over the loss of a loved one. Buddy's death created a void in my life in which my memories of him live on. Even more than 50 years on, there are times when it feels like it happened yesterday. As long as I draw breath, I will remember, miss, love, and honor my friend.

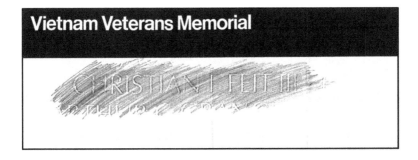

CHAPTER 11

THE ENDLESS BOOGIE - PART 2

One of the trending fads of the times was body painting. Well now, that just looked like it might be fun, so we had a body painting party, three couples. Someone brought a Polaroid camera. We painted and partied. I must admit, it was a rather sexist event, the men remained clothed painting the girls who were bare-ass naked.

Each of the girls had their picture taken on standing on a table in a corner of my apartment. Behind them was a backdrop formed by Richard Avedon's psychedelic Beatle posters and some Avalon Ballroom posters from San Francisco I purchased in a record shop. Added to this were psychedelic pictures clipped from "head" magazines of the day. It was the wildness and recklessness of the 1960's at its best, Bradford style.

Then, Marissa and Lynn decided to disrobe Ron, and Sue snapped pictures of the two girls as they attacked him, tearing his clothes off. General insanity ensued and everyone ended up…well…you know…

ATHSMADOR ABUSE

Of course there was some youthful recklessness and stupidity that accompanied our zealous hell-raising. We wanted to be hip and get high on drugs. Other than alcohol purchased in New York State, there were damn few recreational drugs in Bradford. However, some of the kids from Bradford found a ready source of hallucinogens.

Athsmador was a non-prescription medication for asthmatics. They were cigarettes that were to be lit and the fumes inhaled. They contained, among other things, belladonna and stramonium which were hallucinogenic and also deadly poisonous if taken in a large enough quantity. Lin and Lynn were into Athsmador, digging the crazy hallucinogenic high. Ron said it wasn't that bad!

As reckless as I was, I did, at times, display caution and I was not about to do anything so damned foolish – that would come later – because somewhere I learned about atropine type drugs and their inherent danger.

Lynn and Lin took some over the counter Contac cold medicine, emptied the capsules and stuffed them with the contents of the Athsmador cigarettes.

Bryan swallowed four of them. After not feeling anything for about an hour, he took four more. When he got off, oh man, he was really in space! He was MEGA fucked up for three days. We had to have someone babysitting him every minute. He would talk to the floor lamps, run into the doorways and even try to climb the walls. He was really out of it. There was practically no communicating with this guy, he was in another zone, another universe! You would say his name and he would recognize it, but you couldn't get him to answer you about anything intelligently. His reality was not the one the rest of us were experiencing, not at all.

I went to classes one day, a rare event. I told Lin and Lynn they gave him that shit and got him fucked up, so they were responsible, and to keep him safe and out of trouble. I returned after classes to find that the girls had split, having first bound Bryan hand and foot! Well, they did keep him safe and out of trouble! He had this pathetic look on his face. He still wasn't right when he left three days later and was seen talking to trees. He never came around my place after that, and I don't think he ever did drugs again.[1]

---

[1] The chemicals in Athsmador were similar to those found in Jimson Weed. I came across this from Robert Beverly's *History and Present State of Virginia,* published in 1705: "The James-Town [Jimson] Weed...being an early Plant, was gather'd very young for a boil'd salad, by some of the soldiers sent thither, to pacific the troubles of Bacon and some of them eat plentifully of it, the Effect of which was a very pleasant comedy; for they turn'd natural Fools upon it for several Days: One would blow up a Feather in the Air; another wou'd dart Straws at it with much Fury; and another stark naked was sitting up in a Corner, like a Monkey, grinning and making Mows at them...A Thousand such simple Tricks they play'd. And after Eleven Days, return'd themselves again, not remembering anything that had pass'd." Yep. That sounds like Bryan!!

THE ORACLE

I purchased a copy of an outrageous publication calling itself *The San Francisco Oracle*" from a record store The *Oracle* was a tabloid with a colorful front page featuring a supine nude female figure in yellow and blue. When I opened it up I was mind blown. I had never seen such a publication. Yes, this was *proof* that there was *something* going on! The pages were adorned with outrageous original art. Columns on some of the pages were not straight columns, but geometric shapes. Some pages were overlaid with colored designs. In some cases it was challenging to read. Ads were hand drawn, many in the psychedelic style, meaning they were difficult to read because the mind had difficulties making the necessary closure with the shapes, distinguishing the object form the field it is in. In other words, difficult to read if you were not stoned!

Subject material was widely varied: politics, drugs, sex, poetry, music, interviews with and articles by prominent counterculture figures such as Allan Ginsberg, Ken Kesey, Timothy Leary, Alan Watts, others. This was pure art disguised as an underground newspaper! It was the fulfillment of a dream by Alan Cohen, the publisher. I did not know at the time that I had gotten hold of an issue of one of the groundbreaking counterculture publications of the age. I immediately got a subscription. Just my luck there was only one more issue until publication ceased. Just the same, I had a little piece of San Francisco hipness right there in my very cool pad. I had no idea that in a year I would be there myself.

THE SPRING FROLIC

The annual spring social event at UPB was the Spring Frolic. David Sherman had arranged for a band from his hometown of Newton Centre, Massachusetts to play for the dance.

"*EU'*gene,"–he always called me by my full name and, like Mia, accented the first syllable–"you're going to like my friend Neal's band. These guys are good. And, dig this, he will bringing some dynamite weed with him. We are going to party!"

The following week David came into my pad, "Eugene, my friend Neal has a problem with his band. I thought maybe you could help him out."

"If I can. What's the problem?"

"Well, it seems his drummer is in jail and can't get out. Can you play drums for them at the Spring Frolic?"

"I don't see why not." I had been paying my rent and meeting incidental expenses playing drums on the weekends. I didn't happen to have a gig the night of the Spring Frolic.

"Now, seriously, Eugene, do you think you think you can really do this? This is important to me now." His voice took the tone that it did when he was very concerned about something.

"David, believe me, I can play rock n' roll." I didn't blame him for being concerned, after all he had never heard me.

"OK, but remember, I'm counting on you to not make me look bad."

Jesus, what a worry wart." Well, David, I'll do my best not to do that. All right?"

He was satisfied.

Neal's band arrived the day before the dance and I met them. Neal was a dark haired fellow with hair down over his collar. He wore wire rimmed glasses and had a Marine Corps dress blue tunic that he called his "Sergeant Pepper" jacket. Neal was the only head in the band. The keyboardist was Russell, a round-faced kid with John Lennon glasses. He played a Vox Jaguar organ and some guitar as well. Bruce, the bassist, was tall and had a brown Beatle moptop haircut. He was a very pleasant and outgoing fellow. Rhythm guitar was handled by Dave, who played a Vox teardrop electric twelve-string. As much as Bruce was outgoing, Dave was reticent, even sort of a sourpuss.

We unloaded their PA system and equipment, set up in the hall that was being decorated for the dance and started rehearsing that afternoon. We did some Young Rascals tunes, the Vanilla Fudge slow version of *You Keep Me Hangin' On,* some Hendrix, the Rolling Stones version of *Route 66*, the Kinks *You Really Got Me* (which had a neat segue into the Bo Diddley tune *Who Do You Love*), and a bunch of other stuff. The guys in the band didn't say a word. We just went from song to song. Finally we took a break.

I had to find out how I was doing. "Hey, Neal, uh…how am I doing…I mean, am I doing what you want?"

He and Russell the keyboard player started laughing. "Goddamn, man, you're fanfuckingtastic! I mean, don't worry. What you're doing is *great!*"

I was immensely relieved.

David had arranged for the band to stay in the dorm. Neal was the only one in the band who did drugs, so he came over to my pad with a bag of reefer and we proceeded to get wrecked. Neal was kneeling in the middle of the floor cleaning the reefer and rolling some joints when the door burst open and Bill Burlett lurched in. Bill was an aggressive juice-head who loved to fight. He was drunk as usual and looked at Neal hunched over in the middle of the floor.

"What…what the hell's he doin'?"

David Sherman, stoned and giddy, put his finger to his lips and replied in a loud whisper, "Shhh…be quiet Bill, he's …meditating. Careful, don't disturb him…if you do he's liable to…" David's eyes got big and he made an expansive sweeping gesture with his hands, "*freak out!* Be *very* quiet!"

Bill looked at Neal–who never looked up during this entire exchange–for a moment, shook his head and left. The party continued!

The next day Neal offered me a job with the band, "The Quiet," in Boston. This was it, a way out of Bradford and into a rock n' roll band. At that time, MGM was signing bands in the Boston area, trying to exploit the "Boston Sound". The most notable result of this promotion was a band called The Ultimate Spinach. He figured his band would have a recording contract in the next year and so on and on and on… Hell, it sounded good to me. Just getting out of Bradford had to be good for me. The police were breathing fire up my ass now and all I could see coming was trouble if I stayed in town. I agreed to come to Boston after finals in April.

NEAL GETS BUSTED

Neal had a pot dealing operation. He worked as a clerk in a bookstore in the Dedham (MA) Mall. His pot customers would call and order a paperback book to be placed aside. Neal would put book in a bag with the dope and put the customer's name on it. They would then come to the bookstore and he would hand them the bag. They paid him with a five dollar bill folded in half with the money for the dope folded inside it. He would unfold the fiver and put it in the register placing the other money aside, give them the change for the five and they would leave with their illegal goods.

It takes a certain amount of fearlessness as well as foolishness to run an illegal drug operation out of somebody else's legit business! But, damn, it was a well thought out operation. The only way for this to go awry would be for someone to get popped and roll on him.

Both Lin and Lynn liked Neal and, not coincidentally, his drugs. They both went to Boston with him. Lin was eighteen, Lynn was sixteen. As luck, or lack of it, would have it, Neal's pot dealing operation was compromised by a friend of his who rolled over on him after being arrested on pot charges himself. The two girls were arrested with Neal and another boy in the parking lot of the Dedham Mall. The news hit the local paper and radio. They were caught with a kilo of reefer and some speed.[2] When the police went through Lynn's purse, the found the picture of her wearing nothing but paint standing in front of the only collection of Avalon Ballroom posters in Bradford.

"And just what the hell is this?" inquired the arresting officer.

Lynn, never at a loss for words replied "It's me. Who the hell d'ya think it is?"

The picture was immediately sent to the Bradford Police Department so that they could deal with the den of depravity – which my pad obviously was!

Prior to Neal's bust, I, for no good reason, I took down the posters and rearranged various items of furniture in my apartment.

With the police cruiser parked across the street every evening, I advised my friends to use the back door to the building, which was out of view of the cruiser. At one point, someone had seen the police going through trash before it was picked up at the curb. I have no idea what they were looking for. Drugs? We had none to speak of. And if we did, we sure as hell wouldn't be throwing them in the trash!

Soon after the bust I received a visit from Sgt. Goodly, a Bradford police officer who had developed a genuine dislike for me. He was rousting me on a bullshit noise complaint. I knew it was bullshit because we hadn't been *making* any since the all night beer party incident. Disaster seemed close enough without bringing more heat for turning the goddamned record player up. Hell, we might have been wild, but not *completely* devoid of sense. As he questioned me, he was trying to look around me and inside the room.

I didn't know at that time about Lynn's picture having been sent to the BPD, but when I found out about it, it made perfect sense. She was only sixteen. The picture of her wearing nothing but the paint was taken in front of the *only* collection of Avalon posters in Bradford. If they could prove that the picture of her in front of the Avalon posters was had

---

[2] The Bradford Era, not being so good with drug facts, described speed as a "souped up form of the hallucinatory drug, LSD"

been taken in my apartment, they could bust me for corrupting the morals of a minor, not a small offense! Lucky again.

CHAPTER 12

THEY WANT US TO DO *WHAT?*

In 1968, civil disorder of a racial nature was on the rise. Recent years had seen tensions boil over in Watts, Detroit and Newark as they exploded with arson, looting, violence in the streets, and snipers targeting police and firemen. National Guard troops were called in.

In McKean County, although we saw it all on TV, it was like it wasn't real, it was more like it happened on another planet. After all, that wasn't something that could happen here…could it?

Bradford's National Guard unit was to be assigned to riot duty in Pittsburgh or Erie if necessary. In what would become the ultimate irony, April 1968 had been declared Riot Control Month by the National Guard.

National Guard, Company A, was composed of young men who had received no training whatsoever in crowd control. Being as rural McKean County was hardly populous enough to have a decent sized crowd to control let alone a riot to quell, Captain Shade, the commander of Company A, faced the problem of adequately training his troops.

Around the middle of March David Sherman came into my apartment in a very excited state.

"*EU*gene! Oh man, listen to this, you're gonna love it! Oh wow! Guess what's going to happen!"

I shrugged my shoulders. "I haven't the foggiest, David."

"The National Guard wants us to stage a riot, man, they actually *want* a riot! My God! Can you *believe* that? Oh, this is bee-*yoo*-tiful!"

Well...it did seem rather preposterous. "What are you talking about?"

"There is a notice up in Emery Hall that says the National Guard wants Pitt students to stage a riot so they can train the troops in crowd control. Oh shit! Isn't this great, man?" David could barely contain himself, gleeful at the prospect of being invited by authorities to stage some civil disorder.

I had to see this. We went over to Emery Hall. Sure enough, there was a notice on the bulletin board in the lobby that read

Company A, 112th Infantry Battalion of the Army National Guard requests the students of the University of Pittsburgh at Bradford to stage a mock civil disturbance for purposes of training National Guard troops in crowd and riot control techniques on Saturday, 8 April 1968, at 1:00 p. m. in the area in front of Emery Hall. Sirens will signal the beginning and end of the exercise. Signed, Captain Ellsworth Slade.

"See, I told you. Can you believe it?"

Dear God. David was right. They *wanted* a riot! The National Guard wants a riot? Nooooooo problem! It would be damned near patriotic, wouldn't it?

"Dig it, Eugene," David continued, "I talked to this kid here at Pitt, Chuck Foxly, he's coordinating this thing with the National Guard. He told me that they want us to use eggs and water balloons, bags of flour, stuff like that. The Bradford Police are going to be in on it too! Isn't this positively wild, man?"

Hmmm...an open invitation to pelt the National Guard and the Bradford Police with missiles...definitely an opportunity not to be missed...

Emery Hall stood at the intersection of Main Street, Mechanic Street, and South Avenue. Directly across from it was Veterans Square, a small park about 30 x 40 yards, overlooked by commercial buildings. It should be easy to confine a disturbance to this location. With the anticipated number of "rioters" at 50 to 100 students, Company A would have no problem handling them.

Naturally, I felt obligated to share this information with my Bradford friends. It would be a sin of omission to withhold poop about an event where it would be possible to serve one's country by staging a mock riot, and at the request of the authorities no less!

Ron Lattin came over to my apartment that evening. David and I told him about the guard's request.

"You gotta be shittin' me!" He stood there grinning and wide-eyed, an incredulous look on his face.

Terry Shirey came in about that time. He was in the guard unit, so we asked him.

"Oh yeah, it's true," he replied, smiling his goofy gap-toothed grin. "It's a training exercise. We're gonna kick your asses!"

The word spread like wildfire. Our friends told their friends and siblings who told kids at the schools in town who told all of their friends who told…

On April 4, Dr. Martin Luther King, Jr., was assassinated. Plumes of smoke billowed from cities across America as passions held in check by Dr. King while he was alive were unleashed with a savage fury by his murder.

Saturday, April 8th came. A few column inches buried at the very bottom of the front page of the Bradford Era informed the unsuspecting community of what was about to transpire.

A training session on riot control which will include a mock 'riot incident', will be staged beginning at 1 p. m. today in the Main St. - South Ave. - Mechanic St. area, by Company A, 112th Infantry Battalion, 56th Brigade, 42nd Infantry Division according to its commander, Captain Ellsworth Shade. "The session which was planned at least two weeks ago, will be in connection with 'Riot Control Month' of the National Guard, and will also be participated in by the local Police and Fire Departments." Capt. Shade says the plan calls for some 50 to 100 students to serve as 'volunteer demonstrators' and 'demonstrate on the street.' "The simulated incident is a fine training vehicle for the Guard and for local authorities," the commander stated. "Company A's two segments from Bradford and from Warren, will be represented by about 110 men." In many cities in this district, the 'riots' were staged within the last several weeks.

At a last minute meeting was held between Captain Shade and the Student Riot Committee,"[1] Captain Shade instructed the Riot Committee to begin rioting at 1:45p.m. – not 1:00p.m. as was published in the morning's Bradford Era – and the Guard would show up at 2:00 p.m. to quell the disturbance.

By 12:30 p.m. young people were gathering in Veteran's Square. Most were not Pitt students so they had no idea – nor would they have cared – the riot schedule had been pushed back forty-five minutes. At

---

[1] Really? A "*student riot committee?*" The mind doth boggle…

exactly 1:00 p. m. they hauled the benches from the square, barricaded the streets and started chanting and began behaving menacingly.

The police department, for whatever reason, neglected to close off the exercise area to pedestrian and vehicular traffic as originally planned. Unsuspecting pedestrians and cars were trapped inside the barricades completely unaware of what was about to transpire. Ah, yes, in the vernacular of the time, *the shit was going down!*

Minutes ticked. The "demonstrators" grew more threatening, milling about the barricaded square shouting and chanting. Getting into the spirit of things they started rocking some of the cars caught inside the barricades. Terrified occupants rolled up their windows not at all certain of what was going on around them.

At 1:30p.m. Lt. Hanley of the Bradford Police Department and Captain Shade came out in a jeep to reconnoiter the situation. Expecting a handful of students in the square, they faced a motley rabble of unanticipated size and disposition! Fully prepared to deal with 50 to 100 "demonstrators" in the square, there were 250-300 people behind the barricades. Some were civilians unintentionally trapped, but most were kids who were there to throw stuff. Kids from every neighborhood as well as some from nearby communities, were positioned on the rooftops of the surrounding buildings prepared to wreak havoc – as requested – with eggs, water balloons, paper bags of flour, and produce in various stages of ripeness. A couple corner groceries in the area reported being sold out of produce and eggs.

The sidewalks were full of bystanders, some of who came to watch, and others who were unaware of the riot exercise. The authorities were outflanked. The forces of chaos and anarchy held the high ground! It was an AMBUSH!!! BWAHAHA!!!

In a prelude to the main event, a single water balloon splattered on the hood of the jeep. Captain Shade ordered the driver to go back to the guard staging area where he conferred with Police Chief Zimmerman. They decided to cancel the exercise.

Captain Shade needed to communicate this to the Riot Committee students. However, the students on the Riot Committee with whom he had originally made arrangements were not only in the minority, they were behind the barricades amongst a couple hundred participants most of whom had no idea anyone was in charge of anything and didn't care anyway. It was a gorgeous spring day and they were there to throw stuff! Neither the Guard nor the Bradford Police had a public address system. Contingency plans involving aborting the exercise hadn't been considered and were, therefore, nonexistent.

ALL HELL BREAKS LOOSE

A lone sacrificial victim, a Bradford police officer, approached and, cupping his hands, shouted

"You are hereby ordered to disperse. This exercise has been called off. Go home."

Naturally, the "rioters" thought this was part of the exercise. I mean, what else could it possibly be, right? Veterans Square echoed with a resounding obscenity and a bombardment of water balloons, bags of flour, eggs and produce ensued. The melee was on! The police brought up a couple cruisers. An officer on a motorcycle tried running the barricades and was completely covered with eggs and flour! The "rioters," acting in character, met the police with "Get the pigs! Get the pigs!" Hapless civilian vehicles trapped inside the barricades were also egged and water bombed. The air was filled with a mirthful cacophony of shouts, whoops, shrieks, laughter and chants fueled by the exuberance of youth in springtime! Chaos raged on a grand scale!

My friend, Grub, whose nickname bespoke of his raggedy-ass appearance, was in his tattered army field jacket and standing in front of the entrance to Emery Hall. At the height of the fracas he was hurling eggs and water balloons when he heard someone address him. Turning around he saw a neatly dressed high school girl and her parents.

"Excuse me, sir. Could you please tell us where to find the admissions office?"

"Yeah. It's right in there," he replied in a matter-of-fact manner, pointing to the door behind him, "but it's closed today because we're having a riot." He then turned and resumed his bombardment.

City police, trying to keep things from getting worse, waded through Saturday shoppers and onlookers only to be met with showers of more fruit, eggs and flour. The kids on top of the buildings had the advantage of spotting any movement on the street by the police and directing fire at them. The mob on the ground were just *going* for it, targeting anyone and anything beyond the barricades!

Since pedestrian traffic had not been rerouted, civilians who were not part of the staged civil disturbance were unknowingly caught up in the riot zone. The original plan was that the Guard unit was to deploy and control the crowd with fixed bayonets held at throat level. Things were bad enough with the situation being out of control. Company A advancing on innocent civilians with fixed bayonets would open the door to panic and the possibility of serious injury. No sense in turning the debacle deadly. The sight of an advancing phalanx of bayonets could still give somebody's grandma a heart attack were she trapped in the combat zone because the police failed to seal it off beforehand!

In a vain attempt to end the exercise, the prearranged signal of two blasts on the city's siren was sounded. Those who knew what it meant didn't appear to hear and those who didn't know – most of the participants – could care less. Communication between the authorities and the "rioters" was nonexistent.

The fire department was sustaining hits on their truck which was standing by within projectile range, ready to turn hoses on the crowd if necessary.

A public address system was urgently needed. The police department in the nearby community of Foster Brook had one and their police chief had been convinced to bring it over. The Bradford Police addressed the rabble which was now running out of ammunition.

The mob finally dispersed around 2:00 p.m. Barricades were removed and the bewildered motorists caught inside the combat slowly drove through mess and left.

AFTER ACTION REPORT

The Monday edition of *The Bradford Era* reported the police convinced that the "rioters" that the exercise had indeed been called off and so they dispersed. Truth be known, munitions were depleted. There was nothing left to throw! When the fun's over, you might as well go home, right?

Nobody was hurt. No property was damaged, but there were some cleaning bills for police uniforms! The most serious casualties of the afternoon were the squad cars and motorcycle officer who rode through the barricaded area being covered with a mixture somewhat similar to pancake batter. The Bradford Era described the scene as looking like "a giant omelet."

Somebody had to clean it up. The National Guard troops, held back until the mob dispersed, were ordered to police the area. Cheated out of their role in the enormous amount of fun that just transpired – and to which they had looked forward as much as we did – they grumbled and bitched while cleaning up the mess. A student placed a stereo speaker in his window in Emery Hall and serenaded the troops with the patriotic strains of *"The Stars and Stripes Forever."*

The lead story in the Monday Bradford Era was "Local simulated 'riot' verges on real thing." University officials, ever conscious of the image of their new branch campus in the community, were quick to point out that they had told the students early on that the university "was not sanctioning their participation in the exercise, but wouldn't prohibit the students from taking part in it." They did mention that they thought perhaps an area away from the main part of the city would be more appropriate for such an exercise. The Era also reported that the city manager thought the police handled themselves well, bearing the brunt of the onslaught.[2]

THE TRIMESTER ENDS

Phil, who's band, the Potato Creek trio, I played in had a cousin who was the Bradford PD desk sergeant. His cousin asked him, "Hey, this guy Johnson, he plays in your band, right?"

"Yeah, Gener's played in my band for a couple years."

"Well...do you know anything about a body painting party? And pictures?"

"No," Phil lied. I had shown him all the pictures.

"Well, it seems there was a body painting party with some underage girls. We suspect there are drugs involved too. I'll tell you what, this guy Johnson is smart. We have tried our damndest to get something on him and can't!"

Well, now wasn't that a revelation. "Smart" had nothing to do with me not getting caught. I was *not* smart, I was *incredibly* reckless. The BPD just couldn't get their shit together enough to bust me. That qualified as my good luck!

I was sitting in calculus class when the door opened and Mr. Callahan peered in. He glared at me and turned to the professor whom he had just interrupted.

"Excuse me. I need to see one of your students immediately," turning to me, "Johnson! Out here in the hall. *Now!*"

Oh oh. In some shit... again. I complied, leaving the room and shutting the door behind me. "Yes, Mr. Callahan?"

---

[2] While attending UPB in the late 80s, I gave Dr. Vince Koehler a draft of the riot chapter, which he handed out to his '60s literature class. I asked him later how the students reacted to it.
"They didn't believe it was true. They said they didn't think the police could be that stupid," he replied.

His face was livid. He was obviously exasperated. He brought his finger up and shook it angrily in my face. "Johnson, I want you out of that...apartment of yours...or you'll *have to leave the university!*"

He was really steamed. "But, Mr. Callahan–"

"*No buts!* If you want to continue here, you'll have to move into the dorm. There is room for you if you wish to do so."

"But, why?" I said, with an air of complete and total innocence.

"Because *you're* giving the university a bad name! *That's why!*" His extended index finger wagged harder, emphasizing each word.

I was curious. It could have been the all night beer party which attracted the attention of the police. They now watched the front door to my place – to which they now referred as "the rat's nest" – after 8pm. I had my friends use the rear alley entrance. The dorm mother told the girls not to go near my apartment. That advice was ignored of course.

Or it could have been the Polaroid that made its way to the police department of a 16 year-old Bradford runaway apprehended in New England standing in front of the only collection of Avalon Posters in Bradford – mine – wearing nothing but body paint...or the door glass we accidentally broke at Zippo...or...no matter really. There were definitely enough valid reasons!

"I don't understand, what brought all this on –"

Jesus, I thought he was going to have a stroke! About one prime rib dinner away from a coronary, his face turned bright red and his eyes widened as he shook his finger in my face sputtering, "*Don't* even ask!"

Hell, I could take a hint. "OK. I'll take the room in the dorm."

"See that you are out of that place no later than the day after tomorrow."

Again I attempted a meeting with Mr. Callahan, my father, and myself. Mr. Callahan invited Officer Carbunkle who had a thick file folder allegedly containing information on me.

"Mr. Johnson," Officer Carbunkle said to my dad, "I'm certain you have seen the article in the paper about the girls from Bradford who were arrested in Boston for narcotics. They and other questionable persons," he tapped the file folder, "are known to frequent your son's apartment."

I was outgunned. Later my father said, "Once the cop came in with that file, there was nothing I could do." I have to give him credit, he wasn't upset in the least. But then, he was a hell raiser when he was young.

What a revolting development! My party paradise was going to have to shut down to save the good name of the University of Pittsburgh at Bradford.

There was about two weeks of classes left at this point. I paid for a room in the dorm, but never spent a night in it. Instead, Ron and I moved in with two young women attending the local beauty school.

Marissa and I, without a place to tryst, hung up our affair, but we did have one last fling. One evening I ran into her downtown. She was hot to trot and so was I.

"I wish I still had my apartment."

"I know a place we can go."

Indeed, she did. At the end of South Avenue, there was a condemned house that sat on the high side of the street above a retaining wall that was slowly collapsing. It was unlocked and all the furniture was still in it. It was just around dusk, and we went around to a side door an entered. The house was an older two-story house. With all the dusty furniture in it, it was kind of spooky. We went into an upstairs bedroom and made love on a bed. When we had finished and started to put our clothes back on, we thought we heard someone walking downstairs. We hurried to get our clothes on. Yes! There were definitely footsteps! We could hear them clearly.

"What'll we do?" Marissa whispered, her doe eyes wide with apprehension.

I was wondering the same thing. For me to be screwing a sixteen year-old was against the law. I could hear the footsteps on the stairs now.

"Ok," I said, "he's on the stairs. I'll go first and knock him over. Stay right behind me and don't stop, just run 'im over!" Marissa nodded her head in agreement.

We went over to the door. I looked at her and shouted "Now!" and we both went flying out the door, down the stairs and out the side door. There was nobody else in the house! Unless, of course, it was someone we couldn't see!

The trimester ended. Caren Wallerstein rented a station wagon with her father's credit card and to Boston we went.

All that fun took a toll on my grades. My grade point average for the trimester was .69 out of 4.0. I figured it didn't matter, I was leaving and never coming back. Never say Never. In 1981 my wife and I moved to Smethport from San Francisco. I returned to UPB in 1987 and made up for my poor academic performance by graduating *cum laude* by .026 of a grade point.

CHAPTER 13

BOSTON

THE SCENE

For a kid fresh out of the Pennsylvania boonies, Boston in 1968 was overwhelming. I had never lived in a major city or even been in one for any length of time. My friend, Caren, was a great help to me, taking me around Boston to find work. I got a job in a shop silk screening colonial patterned wallpaper and drapery. It was a cool job. I worked with a black guy, Curtis O'Neal. Curtis mixed the paints and he and I worked the screens on several tables, one of which was 50 feet long with five-foot square two-man screens.

Curtis was around forty, and a real nice, gentle man with a family. They lived in a housing project. Sometimes a couple of his friends, guys in their mid to late twenties, would stop by. I got to hanging around with them after work and smoking some dope with them. They said they were Black Panthers[1]. I don't know if they actually were or not. I doubt it, but they were very cool people.

There couldn't have been a much wider cultural gap between people than existed between these men and myself. I was pretty much a babe in

---

[1] The Black Panther Party (BPP), originally the Black Panther Party for Self-Defense, was a political organization founded by Bobby Seale and Huey Newton in October 1966. The party's core practice was its armed citizens' patrols to monitor the behavior of officers of the Oakland, California, Police Department and challenge police brutality. In 1969, community social programs became a core activity of party members. Black Panther Party members were involved in many fatal firefights with police. Government oppression initially contributed to the party's growth, as killings and arrests of Panthers increased its support among African Americans and on the broad political left. (source: Wikipedia)

the woods at that point in my life, a country boy just moved in to the city. Yet there was common ground enough between us that we could ride around the city in their old Buick, Curtis and I in the back seat, him rolling joints and passing them around.

I was in a state of cultural naiveté concerning race, and was willing to accept everyone I met with no prejudice. I say I was naive, because I expected others would do the same for me. It was certainly the case with Curtis and his friends, but I would find out this was not so true generally.

I was crashing in Neal's basement room in Newton Centre, taking the MBTA (Massachusetts Bay Transit Authority) to and from work. The first day I got on the wrong line and ended up way the hell out in god knows where. A very nice lady gave me directions on how to get back to Newton Centre. After about a week of staying at Neal's, I rented a room in the Back Bay area near the Prudential Tower. This was the most visible landmark in the city, and would serve as a point of reconnaissance when I wanted to figure out where I was. I took the MBTA out to Neal's for band practices during the weekend made the band gigs, frequently crashing afterwards on a spare bed in Neal's basement room.

THE MAYOR OF SHEPHERD AVENUE

One sunny Sunday afternoon in the beginning of May, I was at 14 Shepherd Avenue where I spent a great deal of my weekend time with Neal and his friends. Shepherd Avenue was a one block long, uphill, dead-end street off Huntington. On the edge of Roxbury, Shepherd Avenue was ethnically diverse, with working class whites, blacks, and hippies. 14 Shepherd Avenue, at the very top of the hill was a communal living situation. It was a large, first floor, three bedroom apartment and was the social center of the Shepherd Avenue head community.

The dominant personality at 14 Shepherd Avenue was J.C. Burkhouse from nearby Fitchburg. I had never met anyone like him in my life, I mean, I had seen the pictures of hippies in Life Magazine the year before, but this was for real! I would have to say he was the Mayor of Shepherd Avenue! J.C. was moving modest quantities of grass and acid. He was an outrageous (to me) appearing person, tall and thin, a mass of thick, dark hair framing his long face that appeared to sit on his shoulders and roll around like a ball when he moved his head. He had a bushy mustache, and always wore bell bottom jeans and western boots. The image of J.C. that I have in my mind is wearing a long sleeved knit shirt with red and white horizontal stripes, and a black leather vest. He was the epitome of the hip dude.

A guy called Big Jack also lived at 14 Shepherd Avenue. He was a massive human being, about six feet four, with light brown curly hair that seemed to explode from the top of his head and big mutton chop sideburns. Big Jack had an unusual intensity to his gaze, probably the result of his penchant for injecting methedrine.

Doug Mossey was another resident, a tall thin fellow, also from Fitchburg, with straight dark brown hair past his shoulders, rimless glasses, and a handlebar mustache that drooped below the corners of his mouth and served to accentuate his features. Some years later, I saw an underground comic character, Harold Hedd, who looked just like Doug!

The record collection at 14 Shepherd Avenue was astoundingly large, the result of four or five people pooling all their albums. J.C.'s stereo was awesome.

When I first arrived in Boston, I was such a hayseed I didn't even know such a thing as stereo radio existed. The first time I ever heard FM stereo was when I went to J.C.'s pad with Neal. We got stoned in the kitchen and I went to the living room where the music was coming from. I looked at the turntable and saw it wasn't on. Just then, an announcer came on.

"...that was *Statesboro Blues* from Taj Mahal's new album. How about that slide guitar? That was Jesse Ed Davis. Taj and his band are going to be at the Tea Party this weekend. I suggest everyone go hear them. This is WBCN, your FM stereo station here in Boston. Stick around for some more tunes." He segued into the intro to *Born to be Wild* by Steppenwolf.

Wow! What a revelation that was! Stereo radio, and it sounded so good, not the semi-shitty AM sound I was used to from radio stations where I grew up. How did they *do* that anyway?

SMOKE-IN ON THE BOSTON COMMON!

J.C. came into the living room. "C'mon. Let's go to the smoke-in[2] at the Common."

Smoke in? Hey...what's this? thinks I!

---

[2] An "in" was a protest event, a form of civil disobedience ."sit-ins" started on college campuses where a group of people with a grievance would all sit down in a public area to peacefully disrupt business as usual while making a point about just about anything: racism: college policies, the war in Vietnam, whatever. The "Human Be-in" in San Francisco's Golden Gate park in 1967, also called "The Gathering of the Tribes" was a peaceful gatherings of freaks celebrating life, peace, and freedom."Die-ins" were a form of war protest where people would protest war and nuclear arms by lying down as if dead. These peaceful gatherings were sometimes dispersed by cops cracking heads with their batons, first amendment be damned.

"Groovy idea." Neal was up and ready to leave.

I was new to this scene, just kind of tagging along at this point. In Bradford I had been a very hip dude. Here, I was just a hayseed from the sticks.

J.C. had a what looked to me to be a teenybopper runaway named Tina with him. Tina was a cute thing, blonde and built. She had been shacked up with J.C. for about a week. Neal, Big Jack, J.C., a sweet Swiss girl who spoke with a German accent and called herself Moonstar, and I all piled into Big Jack's VW van and headed for the Common.

I had to ask. "What's this deal with the 'smoke in'?"

J.C., who was riding shotgun turned around. "Oh man, it's a stoned groove. Dig it. Here in Massachusetts there's a law that states that it is a crime to 'be in the presence of narcotics.' So if there's a dope bust, the cops have to arrest everyone who is present on the premises. Y'dig? So, if people are smoking dope on the Boston Common, the cops would have to arrest everyone on the Common for 'being in the presence of narcotics.' And there's just no way they can do that." JC's face lit up with glee.

"So on Sundays, we all go down to the Common and blow weed right in front of the cops and they can't fucking touch us!"

The Boston Common on a weekend held the most amazing assortment of people. The scene of the massacre by British forces which helped precipitate the colonial revolution was still a place for free exchange of ideas. Political discussions and arguments were taking place among gray-haired men in their Sunday suits. Street preachers were trying to save souls, waving their Bibles and exhorting all within earshot to repent. Teenagers walked hand-in-hand. Lovers sat together under the trees, conscious only of each other. Enclaves of people of all descriptions were spread out over the historic Common.

Boston Police lounged in the sun on the hood of a paddy wagon on a rise overlooking the Charles & Beacon Street corner of the Common. We sat down about ten yards in front of them and proceeded to openly smoke grass. Sure enough, we were ignored by the officers. We were not alone. Many other small groups of heads were openly defying authorities by smoking reefer in the warm afternoon sun. What a trip! I had not been in Boston for a week yet and here I was smoking weed on the Boston Common in front of the police!

I eagerly took in the scene that was happening around me. I had never seen so many heads in my life. This was Boston's "Summer of Love," a wide open declaration of the advent of a new consciousness, a generation rejecting the values of their parents (or so it seemed). Hippie women circulated through the milling throng, the breeze gently blowing the long skirts they wore made from Indian chintz bedspreads, the musky scent of patchouli oil trailing behind them.

Costumes of various sorts abounded. A hippie couple were done up in full Native American buckskin regalia, complete with beadwork, fringe, feathers and smoking a "peace" pipe. Strings of beads adorned men and women alike. The soft sounds of guitars being strummed joined with the tinkling of tiny brass bells in ankle bracelets worn by some of the women. Resonant tones from a bamboo flute floated on the breeze along with the smells of incense, pot, and spring flowers.

The saffron robe clad Hare Krishna devotees were chanting, scalplocks dangling from their shaved heads, swaying in time to their shuffle-footed dancing, finger cymbals chinging away in time with the drums that accompanied their eons old Vedic refrain.

Tambourines could be heard coming from various locations, jangling away in time with cosmic rhythms known only to their players.

A black man wore an ocher dashiki that exploded in geometric splinters of intense red, yellow, green and turquoise. He wore sunglasses, his hair in an Afro, and sported a goatee. Blowing melodic refrains on an alto sax, he was accompanied by another black man, short fat, wearing black slacks, a light blue short sleeved shirt and a red beret, sitting on a bench playing a conga drum and chewing on a wooden match. Two others stood by, nodding in rhythm to the music and checking out the ladies who passed.

Kids, "weekend hippies" from the suburbs, circulated, wearing their new medallions and Nehru jackets bought with their allowances at the hip boutiques on Massachusetts Avenue and Charles Street. Their hair barely covered their ears.

Freaks were everywhere, discreetly selling joints, ounces of grass, hits of speed and acid. Spades,[3] looking so cool and detached, wandered through the crowds of longhairs, selling or trying to score reefer and maybe pick up a hippie chick.

Young men with obvious military haircuts were dressed in their civilian hip finery, enjoying a short leave and trying to fit in with the abounding head culture. Others wore their uniforms as they escorted girlfriends and fiancées through the Sunday throng. Poets distributed broadsides with verses printed on them.

---

[3] *spade* - an African-American, probably comes from the phrase "as black as the Ace of Spades." This was a non-pejorative term freely used in the longhair culture for black men who hung with white hippies. Black women were referred to as "spade chicks."

Moonstar, petite, befreckled, with long reddish hair and wearing an army field jacket joined our party. She gave Big Jack a kiss and put her arm around his waist. We lounged in the sun, pleasantly stoned.

A middle-aged man came up to us and started to focus his Nikon camera on our group. He was busy making adjustments when Big Jack spoke up.

"Excuse me sir. Would you like me to insert that camera in your rectum?"

The man lowered the camera slightly, looking incredulously at Big Jack, then brought the camera back up to his face.

"Hey, Mister! I asked if you wanted that fuckin' camera shoved up your ass! Go take your pictures somewhere else!"

The man again took the camera away from his face and looked at Big Jack.

"I'm fucking talking to you, man. Get your fucking camera out of here. *Got that?*"

The man lowered his camera and wandered off. Big Jack turned to Moonstar and me.

"Probably a fuckin' nark," Big Jack said as he took a hit of the joint we were passing around.

After making the point of inhaling illegal herb in front of the authorities, we got up and wandered around the Common.

People were gathered around a preacher, a thin middle aged man with wisps of gray hair combed over the top of his bald head and wearing glasses. Nicely dressed in a gray suit, he was giving an animated and forceful delivery of the gospel, waving his Bible as he did so. At the climax of his delivery, a tall wide-shouldered man, hair and beard long and unkempt, clothes dirty and with a glowering countenance emerged from the crowd to my left. He watched the preacher for a moment, then went up to him and roared,

"Oh *yeah?* What about the *war in Vietnam?*"

The preacher, stunned by the appearance of what must have seemed to him to be a demonic apparition straight out of hell, was speechless. The big man gave him a push and the Bible flew out of the preacher's hands and he landed squarely on his ass, glasses askew.

"*Ya fuckin' demon!*" the angry individual exclaimed. He walked toward the crowd, which separated in his path like the Red Sea parting for

Moses, and let him pass. The preacher got up, straightened his glasses and tie and continued to preach, albeit a bit more subdued this time.

I turned to J.C. "Who the hell was that?"

"Mad John. He's a burnout. That dude's been shooting up speed and acid together for a couple of years. I don't like him. I think he's an ear for the man. A fucking nark."

Mad John. He seemed like a character straight out of a Dickens novel. This was the nature of the times. Anything was possible. The more unlikely something seemed, the greater the chances you would run into it the next time you ventured outside. More often than not, it would come in through your front door, smoke your dope, raid your refrigerator, hit on your girlfriend, and pass out on your living room floor!

The Friday and Saturday evening scenes at the Common on the corner of Beacon and Charles streets were another matter altogether. This was not an eclectic scene like the Sunday afternoons. This was a very specialized gathering: a wide open drug market. On any given Friday or Saturday evening a crowd of perhaps two thousand people would be buying and selling every conceivable illegal substance available.

Many of the buyers were the kids from the surrounding suburbs in town to score their weekly ounce of grass and hit of acid, speed, whatever. A lot of runaways were attracted to this scene. Marijuana and LSD prevailed. Dealers would circulate among the crowd announcing their wares in low tones "…acid…speed…lids… acid…speed…lids…."

This was where the newest dope hit the street every week. Prices fluctuated according to supply and demand, a free market of psychotropia. It was, of course, rife with narks.

In the process of writing this book, I crossed paths again with J.C. Burkhouse after nearly forty years. He sent me a picture from 1967, looking ever so dapper. He told me,

"If you take a look at my eyes in that picture, wow, man…I don't know how much acid I did that day, but it was lot. The next day I flew out to LA and scored party supplies for the First Boston Common Smoke-In: five keys of grass! That was my idea. I set up and bankrolled that whole thing in the summer of 1967. And you know something, I brought that weed back in my checked luggage! The thought that I might get caught never occurred to me at all. I was going to do this very cool thing and that was it. I left no room in my mind for failure!"

"We put up posters and handed out flyers, but what really did it for us was that we were able to hook up with some college radio stations that put the word out in their news syndication. It was incredible, there were about 17,000 people there. People came from as far away as Chicago and Denver! We must have rolled ten-thousand joints! We had every color of papers, you know, the flavored ones, banana yellow, strawberry red, chocolate, and you know, Bambu and Zig-Zag, the yellow Zig Zag wheat straw...just boxes and boxes of them!"

"We passed out joints all day long. The cops couldn't do shit about it. You know, San Francisco was having their Summer of Love and we were getting high on the historic Boston Common!"

"My father, who was executive Secretary to Air Force General Curtis LeMay, wanted to kill me for that stunt especially because I was on the WBZ 11 o'clock news boasting about how everyone was smoking grass. The TV guys says to me 'How can you be sure they were smoking grass?' I said, 'Because I gave it to them!' Did I mention that my dad wanted to kill me?"

J.C. Burkhouse - "The Mayor of Shepherd Ave." 1967
Photo Source: J.C. Burkhouse

BOTH DOORS FLEW BACK!

The Quiet played one or two gigs a week. No bars, we weren't old enough. We gigged at park pavilions, high schools, whatever came along that wasn't a bar gig. We frequently played for fraternity parties on

Marlboro Street. Usually they were quite, you know, normal. But there's always that one time.

I don't know what the hell these guys were thinking. Can't remember the fraternity's name, Kappa Delta Phuckup will do. So Kappa Delta Phuckup had a keg party one Saturday night. A cover charge keeps the riff-raff out. There was no cover charge this time, you purchased tickets for draft beer once inside. Neal was doing acid that evening.

We were set up in a large room into which the double entrance doors opened. The stage area faced an adjoining room. All in all it made quite a nice party area.

We were into the second set and just pounding away on *Who Do You Love* when some asshole in off the street starts hitting on a frat brother's girl. She turns around to walk away, this guy grabs her by the elbow and spins her around.

"Fuck off, you *ass*hole!" she spits at him, throwing her drink in his face.

Oh shit oh dear! Here we go!

Her boyfriend steps up and spins the asshole around giving him what I am certain he thought was a good punch. It barely phased the asshole who then starts pounding the shit out of the brother. A couple other brothers tried to get this asshole off the brother whose face is now covered in blood. Friends of the asshole start mixing it with the brothers. Rock and roll and the sounds of human struggle as well as the crackling of furniture being broken and things being smashed were heard in the melee, at this point confined to the adjoining room.

Neal turns around, pupils fully dilated from the acid, and says "keep playing!" so we kept pounding out the Bo Diddly beat to *Who Do You Love*. Bruce's bass and my drums were fused into a throbbing syncopation that just *pounded* your skull! Neal's acid inspired riffing and feedback from his Rickenbacker guitar topped it all off! Yes! THIS was rock n' roll: a 110 decibel anarchical fuzztone apocalypse, the sonic meltdown of Western Civilization on Marlboro Street!!

Of course someone called the cops. Just like in the Chuck Berry tune, "when the police knocked, both doors flew back!"[4] The double doors burst open and here come Boston's finest, two abreast and batons at the ready. *Yee-haw!*

You did *not* fuck with these guys. They were all Irish, beefy, and ready to kick some ass! Once inside they engaged in some serious bone

---

[4] From "Round and Round" © Chuck Berry

crushing. A cluster of struggling cops and brawlers surged towards where we were set up. Somebody's beer got dumped into our PA amp, ruining it and blowing a fuse. All the other instruments stopped, so I launched into a Krupa type tom-tom solo, providing an appropriate soundtrack or the event!

One of the Kappa Delta Phuckups – I suspect the imbecile who planned this debacle – came up to me pleading "Will you PLEASE stop! You're not helping the situation!"

"I'm not being paid to help, I'm being paid to play drums!" was my smartass reply. But I did stop. Someone's ass was going to be in a sling over this, probably this poor bastard!

As far as spontaneous brawls go, this was top notch! It wasn't everyone bunching up together and throwing punches! I guess that is what we should expect, a well organized slugfest worthy of a fraternity from an institution of higher learning.

Other than the PA getting fried, it wasn't a bad evening. We made our money and got some good entertainment in the bargain! And Russell was compensated by the Boston PD for his fried Bogen PA amp.

DROPPING ACID

I first took LSD on Memorial Day, 1968. A group of us dropped[5] on Shepherd Ave. and went to the Common. As we approached the corner of the Common at the intersection of Beacon and Charles Streets, about a dozen Devil's Disciples[6] came roaring up on their choppers, popping wheelies before they parked. It was impressive.

The Disciples' leader rode a sweet looking knucklehead, nicely chopped in the 60's style: extended springer front end, ape hangers, sissy bar with a chromed Iron Cross at the top, upswept pipes, tear drop gas tank a deep shade of metallic maroon with the Harley Davidson name done in gold leaf. This beautiful machine was a piece of kinetic art.

In contrast to his classy looking scooter, he was a large bearded, hairy-armed dude with chrome sunglasses and a red bandanna headband. He had on a greasy T-shirt under his equally grungy colors, which featured a red devil's face with a leering grin framed by "Devil's Disciples M.C., Boston Massachusetts" on the rockers. It looked like he might have changed the oil in his chopper more often than he did the thirty-weight on his hair. An earring dangled from his left ear. The seat of his

---

[5] Means "took by mouth."
[6] This is not the "Devil's Diciples." which is a different organization entirely.

jeans was ripped and flapped in the breeze, giving everyone a view of his bare ass. He was going about his business as if nothing was wrong. Nobody laughed, and nobody pointed out his, ah, southern exposure.

Closing my eyes would bring a fantastic cascade of constantly changing geometric patterns. Listening to music was absolutely amazing. It seemed that I could connect directly with the music on an emotional level I did not know was possible. It was as if I could feel the emotions of the players as I listened to their music. This applies to recorded music as well as live performances. Live performances are more intense, because you are psychically interacting with the group consciousness of the band. They play. You dig it. They get a vibe that you dig it. They play more. You dig it more. And on and on.

We finished off by going to the old tower on Fort Hill before sunup and watching the city come alive, the elevated trains looking like lighted caterpillars traversing the darkness.

I took acid regularly. These psychedelic experiences started me on my spiritual journey. I augmented my acid tripping with reading. That summer I read "Damien," "The Steppenwolf," and "Siddartha" by Hermann Hesse. While these were interesting and worthwhile, I sought more esoteric reading and found the volumes on Tibetan Buddhism by the English scholar W.Y. Evans-Wentz and added "The Tibetan Book of the Dead," and "The Tibetan Book of the Great Liberation" to my reading. As years progressed I would also read "Tibetan Yoga and Secret Doctrines" and "Tibet's Great Yogi, Milarepa," all by Evans-Wentz. A series of popular paperbacks by a Tibetan Lama, Tuesday Lobsang Rampa, were also part of my reading as were works by Carlos Casteneda on native American spiritual beliefs and use of hallucinogens. "Magic and Mystery in Tibet" and "Tibetan Secret Oral Teachings" by Madame Alexandra David Neel became part of my collection of esoterica. Edgar Cayce books were in my library as well. I was a million miles away from Catholicism now.[7]

14 SHEPHERD AVE.

During one of my visits to 14 Shepherd Ave., Moonstar came over to me and said "I'm going up on the roof to get some sun. Want to come along?"

"Sure."

---

[7] The Old Curmudgeon's Sage Advice No. 4

We went to the roof of the house. Moonstar spread out a blanket and, looking me seductively, stripped down to a bikini bottom. She was petite and had a cute shape, red hair and freckles. Her breasts were ample, and she looked so sexy there in the Sunday afternoon sun.

She took a joint out of a leather stash bag and we smoked it. We started kissing. Coming on to the weed, our passion grew. "I want you to fuck me!" she said in her Swiss-German accented English (a real turn on)! Being too much of a gentleman to refuse a lady's sincere request, I made it with her right then and there on the rooftop. Got my ass bit sunburned!

The cops busted 14 Shepherd Ave. in June. The teenybopper runaway J.C. was banging had a wealthy father, who hired a private detective. She had since moved on, but some of her karma must have been still hanging around. It seems that the private detective took pictures of J.C. and her together. Her father was determined to cause problems for this hippie creep who was screwing his runaway daughter and pulled some strings with the Boston PD to get J.C. busted. One evening when I was (fortunately) not partying at 14 Shepherd Ave., J. Arthur Linsky, head of the Boston PD Narcotic & Vice Squad, raided J. C's apartment and took everybody downtown.

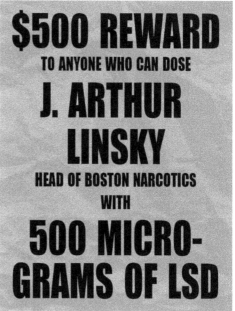

The police only found small quantities of marijuana, LSD and speed on the premises. J.C. and the others in the apartment were put on probation.

Shortly thereafter Shepherd Ave. got its own beat cop on Huntington Ave, hassling every longhair who went up Shepherd Ave. This pissed J.C. off. He had a handbill printed and distributed it on the Boston Common that said "$500 reward for anyone who can dose J. Arthur Linsky head of Boston narcotics with 500 micrograms of LSD." No one ever collected on it that I am aware of. I am certain Linsky was never dosed, but it was an interesting tactic. The beat cop left after a week or so, and life resumed as normal.

By this time, J.C. had a steady girlfriend, Laurie. She was a very sweet kid, about eighteen, and totally alienated from her mother with whom she was living. J.C., after the bust, decided to keep a lower profile and they moved to an apartment in Cambridge. I heard later he got stopped on his bike while holding some weed. He and Laurie split for San Francisco. Someone gave me his address and I tucked it away in my wallet.

By midsummer I was living in the bottom apartment at 1 Shepherd Avenue. I was sharing the apartment with Gene Hadlock, otherwise known as "The Raspberry," whom I met at J.C.'s. He was not into the hip scene because of any ideological reasons, he was there because he perceived it as "the thing to do." Raspberry played bass and did some song writing. We had some jam sessions back at 14 Shepherd Avenue, where I still spent much of my time. We fancied ourselves "The Shepherd Ave. Cartel."

Raspberry moved out of our digs after a month and moved in with a cute little chick named Debbie. They had an apartment on the other side of Shepherd Ave.

Another couple rented 14 Shepherd Avenue, Marius and Beth. Marius was a slender, young delicate featured black man. I don't know where he came from. He spoke with no trace of a ghetto or foreign accent. Beth was a white suburban runaway, pregnant with Marius' baby. As soon as they moved in they painted a huge magical sigil on the wall of the living room, professing to be into black magic. It was a protection seal, they said.

About five days after they moved in, the cops kicked the door in looking for J.C., now long gone. They searched the entire apartment, except for the room with the magic sigil on the wall, which they never entered. Go figure!

Jimmy was a tall black man who was a friend of Marius, a drummer and a Vietnam vet. No one talked about PTSD in those days. Jimmy was pretty much straight up PTSD'd to the max. I don't know what his MOS[8] was, but he could take a door of its hinges in a heartbeat. I got along with Jimmy, being a white kid playing drums and all. Jimmy was a cool dude and always had great weed. He laid a joint of Vietnamese weed on me one day. I smoked about half of it and couldn't get out of my chair for about six hours. He neglected to tell me the weed was laced with opium, Yah mon!

---

[8] Military Occupational Specialty

W. EUGENE JOHNSON

TAKE TWO, YOU'LL GET OFF FOR SURE!

In my youthful ignorance and recklessness, I bought some bright red caps touted as "psilocybin."[9]

"Take two, man. You'll get off for sure," said the dealer.

Get off I did! The experiences were more like horror film type trips, Bela Lugosi shit, such as a face-to-face encounter with a strange crustacean with a shiny caramel colored exoskeleton and eye stalks that inspected me, as if, perhaps deciding through which eye socket to suck out the contents of my skull. I walked into a dimly lit room and saw...something...out of the corner of my eye jump back into the shadows, hiding from me. I looked for it in the corner and it wasn't there, but when I looked away, there it was again, moving almost imperceptibly in my peripheral vision. Weird stuff. Physical movement became very difficult, as if walking in mud up to my knees. I wasn't scared, it was a "oh my, isn't this interesting" type of trip. It was interesting enough that I did it twice!

Years later, reading Carlos Castaneda's books on the Yaqui brujo,[10] Don Juan, I could relate to the types of experiences Castaneda described when he was writing about his experiences with some of the old brujo's powerful hallucinogenic alkaloid mixtures.

TRIPPING WITH TROTSKY

My world was full of unusual and interesting people. I met a fellow one day while riding the MBTA. He had wild looking hair, black, curly, grown out like a pointy black halo. His facial features were bi-racial, his skin almost a golden color. He had a scraggly mustache and goatee. His glasses had heavy black frames reminiscent of Buddy Holley. The thick lenses magnified his eyes, giving him an intense look. He wore an army surplus field jacket, a blue chambray work shirt and the ubiquitous bell-bottoms and boots. I always checked out the footwear of strangers I met to make certain they were not wearing black shoes. Narks wore black shoes. They might grow their hair and sprout a mustache and wear–what they considered to be–hip clothes, but they never got it that their black shoes were a dead giveaway.[11] We struck up a conversation about the

---

[9] The psychoactive component of many so-called "magic mushrooms" of the *psilocybe mexicana* type.
[10] sorcerer
[11] There is a cinematic allusion to narks with black shoes in the 1971 movie "Cisco Pike" where Cisco Pike (Kris Kristofferson) and Wavy Gravy (formerly Hugh Romney, from the Hog Farm traveling commune) are doing a twenty-kilo weed deal. When they meet with the buyers, a quick camera cut to the feet of the prospective buyers shows they are wearing black shoes. Kristofferson calls off the deal and he and Wavy Gravy haul ass leaving the weed behind in Wavy Gravy's truck. This movie is a microcosm

quality of grass and acid that were available on the streets. This was the usual ice-breaker conversation with longhairs. He said his name was "Leon."

Leon was a revolutionary, but not your run-of-the-mill wild-eyed Marxist, he was a protégé of Leon Trotsky, the Bolshevik revolutionary exiled from the Soviet Union and murdered by Stalin's assassin in Mexico. It also explained his appearance. He by God *looked* like Leon Trotsky!

He says "I have some great acid. Want to do some with me?" We dropped the acid and retired to my pad on Shepherd Ave.

Leon was quite garrulous.

"I'm half black and half Chinese. I'm a nigger-chink. Man, I'm all fucked up!" he said with a half-humorous delivery. "The blacks don't like me 'cause I'm half Chinese. The Chinese don't like me 'cause I'm half black. I don't fit into anybody's world so I became a revolutionary. The world needs revolution."

"Just look at the war in Vietnam. It is capitalist oppression for not only the Vietnamese, but for Americans too. No one is dying for American freedom over there. Vietnam is no threat to the United States. The reason the war is being fought is because it makes money for the capitalists who sell bullets, bombs and body bags to the government."

"Americans were warned. Eisenhower spelled it out clearly in his farewell speech when he talked about the military/industrial complex. Americans haven't listened. They are too busy watching sports and jerking off to Playboy foldouts while these rotten bastards plan wars that American kids will die in for no other purpose than to make money for war profiteers!"

"Poor young people are the cannon fodder for capitalist wars. If you are white and have money, you can get out of going to Vietnam. No members of Congress have their kids getting blown to shit in Vietnam. Everybody else is just fucked. The present setup with the voting age being twenty-one,[12] those who are expected to fight and die for corporate profits have no say, no power to affect any change through legislation. If you aren't old enough to vote, they don't give a flying shit about you. Meat for the grinder, that's all you are."

"I'm hip to that." I replied with an overused cliché. "I had a good friend killed in Vietnam in January. He was twenty. He was killed at Khe

---

of the times with a washed up rock star, a crooked cop and a hundred kilos of weed. It accurately depicts the zeitgeist. It also accurately portrays the connection between musicians and drug dealing.
[12] The voting age in the U.S. was changed from 21 to 18 in 1971 by the 26th amendment.

Sanh and five months later it's abandoned. What the fuck? He died for nothing. Two other guys I know were killed in the same week."

"Sorry to hear about your friends," Replied Leon. "It does go to show how the war oppresses everybody. But they didn't die for nothing. They died for war the profiteers, for profits for the merchants of death, American arms and munitions makers."

The weekly body counts of American soldiers KIA had topped four-hundred. I know the many people affected by Buddy's death. There were probably just as many for each soldier in the weekly body count. That is just so much loss, so much suffering, so many affected. And why discount the suffering of the Vietnamese? Did they love their families any less than we?

"LSD is an agent of revolution," he said, "it opens up your mind. People should take LSD. It is the enlightenment of the proletariat. And revolution is enlightenment. Enlightenment is revolution. LSD can take Trotsky's concept of permanent world revolution to cosmic dimensions. Weed can help, but I think it makes people too passive to have a proper revolution. LSD is the key for any modern day Trotskyite revolution."

We were smoking weed earlier so I asked "Leon, why do *you* smoke weed if it's so bad for revolution?"

"Well…it's not *that* bad!" he grinned. Even a revolutionary needs to… get mellow… once in a while! Even when I am mellow I'm still committed to the revolution!" He grinned his toothy grin and raised his clenched fist.

"Besides, drugs like weed and LSD are part of the revolution because they form an economy that operates outside of governmental control and regulation. It is like the glue that holds the counterculture together. And *that* is where the revolution will come from."

He continued. "I gotta say this about weed man. It does fit into the revolution in this way. Everybody that smokes weed has made themselves an outsider. If caught holding even tiny amounts they may face felony charges and prison. If you have to remain constantly vigilant because you are operating outside the law on a daily basis, you are experiencing alienation. You have become a member of a brotherhood of outlaws whose very existence challenges the establishment. Being an outlaw – someone whose lifestyle is outside socially accepted parameters social behavior and the outside the law – puts you about halfway to becoming a revolutionary Oppression is oppression, man. Oppressed people eventually revolt."

Being a peace and love hippie freak I said "Yeah, but revolution is violence. And violence is violence whether or not it is in a war or a revolution. People die. Lots of people. Innocent people."

"It is a question of what they are dying for," Leon replied. "You can bleed and die in Vietnam so the capitalists can make their profits. They make a profit on every bullet you shoot. They make a profit on every artillery round fired, every mortar round, every hand grenade. They make a profit on the bandages used to keep you from bleeding to death when you get shot to shit, on the fucking body bag they put you in and the flag for your coffin. They make a profit on supplying uniforms, tents, field rations, everything. The military is a huge giveaway program for the capitalists: the government gives them a mountain of money to make weapons and materiel that is used to support capitalism by killing revolutionaries in other countries. They buy all this deadly shit, blow things all to hell with it and then they need more deadly shit to blow more things all to hell with. That's what American kids are dying for in Vietnam. The Vietnamese don't want to take over the U.S. They just want foreigners to get the fuck out of Vietnam. *They* want *their* country back!"

Leon was on a roll. "That war is a human sacrifice of American kids. Americans believe all this red-white-and-blue bullshit and let the government send their kids to Vietnam for profits for the capitalists. The most fucked up thing about it is that Americans are blind to what is going on. They think it's still fucking World War Two and their kids are fighting for freedom!"

"You are concerned about violence in revolution? How about violence in *not*-revolution? What about the violence of the cops in the ghettoes? What about the violence of racism and what it does to people and society? What about the violence of drafting young men, lying to them about defending freedom and liberty and sending them off halfway around the world to kill people who pose no threat whatsoever to the United States? What about the violence of generational poverty and hopelessness? These all happen inside the United States. And where does it all come from? The capitalist class system!"

"At least if you die in a revolution, you are dying to end this type of class exploitation of the poorer classes by the moneyed class. You're not dying to make some rich fat fuck a richer fat fuck."

"Leon, my man, there is a lot of truth to what you say. Now, I'm no Marxist[13] but I can't argue against the existence of class warfare."

---

[13] Which was true at the time. The older I get the more I see validation of Marx's ideas, not so much the idea of a controlled economy but as a sociologist, an observer of human group behavior. I can't see a refutation for Marx's observation that everything comes about as the result of struggle.

"Just keep your eyes open, Gene. You'll get there. Evolution leads to revolution. Let your consciousness evolve."

Leon was an ideologist. Never once did he talk about revolutionary violence itself, he talked in generalities about "the revolution," but not about making bombs.

"Trotsky correctly said the revolution has to be worldwide and continuous. There is revolution in Vietnam. We need revolution here as well. We need it everywhere, but here in the U.S. especially. As the forces of capitalism and the military-industrial complex become stronger the closer this country comes to being the biggest threat to world peace."

"Really?" I inquired." What about Russia. Isn't Russia a threat?"

"Oh, *fuck* Russia!"

"Fuck Russia? Isn't Russia a revolutionary communist state?"

"As it stands, the Soviet Union is neither revolutionary nor communist. It is a totalitarian state that barely resembles anything socialist. Thanks to 'Comrade' Stalin."

"Oh?"

"Yes. And this is where Trotsky broke with him. Stalin believed that socialism could be achieved one state at a time. Trotsky insisted the revolution had to be continuous and universal. International revolution. Simultaneous. Stalin won the struggle and you see what the Soviet Union has become."

"Russ–the Soviet Union is still a threat to peace, is it not?"

"Yes."

We tripped all night discussing revolutionary politics and drugs. I never got the feeling that Leon was trying to convert me, I think he had a need to explain himself. He felt rejected, penalized for being bi-racial, truly something over which he had no control. He probably didn't have any friends. I can see how prolonged exposure to Leon could wear you out pretty damned fast!!

This became his reason for wanting to change the world. We all wanted to change the world. Some of us still do.

Leon split around daybreak, when the acid wore off. I never saw Leon after that.

FLASHING BACK– COMING OF AGE IN THE AMERICAN 1960s

PARTYING WITH THE HUNS

The Huns were a biker club with chapters in and around Boston (although in 1968 Boston, "bikers" were called "bikees"). I got to know them through Doug Mossey who became a member in July. At his initiation party, which happened at 14 Shepherd Ave., they pierced Mossey's ear with a rusty nail. From what I could see, the Boston Huns were really a bunch of nice guys trying their best to be badasses. They were not serious individuals.[14] They liked smoking weed and dropping acid and frequently scored dope from us. Any intersection of the longhair and biker cultures concerned drugs. Many times we partied all night at 14 Shepherd Ave. with the Huns. Usually it was lots of reefer and a few bottles of Mateus, the combination of which resulted in purple hallucinations! There was never any trouble, at least with the Boston chapter.

The Fitchburg Chapter was a bit rougher. Ritchie and Thing from the Fitchburg sometimes came to Boston and partied with us. Thing gleeped[15] Ritchie's scooter. Now, *real* bikers *never* fuck with another member's scooter. This caused contention within the chapter, but it never spilled over to where it affected citizens. I do not remember how or if it was resolved.[16]

THE BOSTON TEA PARTY

One of the local psychedelic dungeons was The Boston Tea Party located at 53 Berkeley St. Formerly a synagogue, the name itself was a pothead double entendre, a play on words referring to marijuana, referred to by beats and jazz hipsters as "tea," the pungent smell of which wafted over the crowd at the Tea Party. Attending the Tea Party was a weekly event.

The lineup consisted of local bands, a supporting act, and the headline act. The first acts were inevitably semi-crappy garage bands imitating Cream and performing endless guitar solos.[17] I'm sure that these local bands worked cheap–to the benefit of the promoter–and got some good exposure–to the benefit of the band. Besides, every musician has been in a band that sucked. I know I have!

The rock venues were the electric churches of the head community, cathedrals of rhythm, the meeting ground for everyone who was into

---

[14] A "serious individual" is a sociopath who will kill you in a heartbeat without giving it a thought. The Devil's Disciples had a lot of serious individuals. The Huns had none.
[15] To gleep is to steal
[16] Bikers refer to non-bikers as "citizens."
[17] As much as I liked Clapton - and *loved* Cream - I would have to say that was Clapton's one musical sin, encouraging every guitar player in the known universe to solo endlessly regardless of skill level!

peace, love, dope and rock n' roll. You didn't even need money in your pocket get in. You could start at the door and work your way to the end of the line panhandling for change as you went. By the time you got to the end of the line you would not only have the price of admission–a modest two or three dollars–you would likely get a joint and tab of acid laid on you as well. It was possible have a superb evening of social interaction and rock n' roll involving no cash of your own!

The headliners were the top name acts, short of the superstars (*i. e.*, Hendrix, Joplin, Dylan). British acts often made Boston their first stop on their tour of the colonies.

The first act I saw at the Tea Party was the Jeff Beck Group. Beck had left the Yardbirds and formed his own band consisting of Mick Waller on drums, Nicky Hopkins (who recorded and toured with the Rolling Stones) on piano, Ron Wood – now playing guitar with the Rolling Stones – on bass, a then unknown singer, Rod Stewart, and Jeff Beck blazing on guitar.

At that time, Taj Mahal's band showed up a great deal of the time as the second act, and they were great. There has never been a band since that has had the style of Taj's band in the late '60s. The arrangement for *Statesboro Blues* on the album was the inspiration for Duane Allman's version a few years later.

Throughout the summer the Tea Party was visited by the likes of the Byrds, The Flying Burrito Brothers, John Mayall's Bluesbreakers, Fleetwood Mac, The Electric Flag, Savoy Brown, Chuck Berry, The Grateful Dead, blues acts like B. B. King, Buddy Guy, Albert King, Muddy Waters, Magic Sam, Big Mama Thornton, the Memphis sounds of Sam & Dave, the Mar-Keys, Booker T and the MGs, lesser known groups such as Cat Mother and the All Night Newsboys, Aum, Rhinoceros, Fire and Ice, Quill, the Ultimate Spinach, the Beacon Street Union, and many more I can't remember. I wanted to hear something different, I didn't really know what it was, but I kept searching, listening for it in every band I heard.

LED ZEPPELIN

In January, 1969, our friend, Mescaline John, who worked at the Tea Party, told us." There's this new British band going to be at the Tea Party next week, Led Zeppelin, supposed to be pretty good."

They didn't even have an album out yet, so all the local head station, WBCN, could say about them was "…the guitar player is Jimmy Page, formerly of the Yardbirds…"

The Tea Party ran bands on Thursday, Friday, and Saturday nights. We tried to get in on Friday and Saturday and the place was sold out. They held the band over until Sunday, January 26th, and we managed to get in. The opening band was called Raven. Never heard of them before or since and I don't remember them at all. All I remember is that when Led Zeppelin took the stage, from the first thundering chords of *Good Times, Bad Times*, I heard it, the *sound!!*

That show was an astounding experience. While Led Zeppelin would go on to become one of the most successful acts of the '70's, they were unknown, on their first U.S. tour, and we were seeing them in a small venue.

The Tea Party was on the second floor of a former Jewish Synagogue, a high arch over the stage emblazoned with "Praise Ye The Lord." The accompanying light show covered the walls with the colorful and fluid shapes of immiscible colored oils between sheets of transparent materials on overhead projectors pulsating to the beat, along with black and white film clips of trains rushing at you and – for Zep – the Hindenburg disaster. We were only about forty feet from the stage.

Prior to hearing Led Zeppelin, I sort of knew what I wanted to hear, the sound. In The Quiet, we were arranging the Yardbirds tune, *For Your Love*. I suggested to Neal, the lead guitarist, that during the chorus, the bass double the guitar line, a 1-3-5-6 eighth note boogie line, over a 5-4-1 chord change. "Oh no. We can't do that. The guitar and the bass never play the same thing." Hey, I was the drummer. How would someone who only hits things with sticks understand music, right? Well, this is precisely what Led Zeppelin was doing, and to great effect. This is the "heavy sound" every hard rock band since Led Zeppelin has emulated.

I saw a lot of good bands back in the day. Did I say "good" bands? *Fucking outstanding* is more like it. Jimmy Page is the best guitar player I have ever breathed air in the same room with. His playing was rock n' roll pyrotechnics. To be there and hear and see him play was…wow…just wow!

There are very few times in my life I have had my mind blown by some new music. Zeppelin did that. They were utterly unique. Zeppelin thundered like no other, with the guitar riff doubled in the bass line forming a sound so thick could feel it sticking to you as it washed over you. Then came Page's the acoustic picking, very nice contrasts and blends. Their heavy-handed blues goes without saying anything. Zeppelin played over four hours that evening with only a single album's worth of material!

I was captivated by the music of Led Zeppelin from the very first. Their blend of rock, blues and Celtic music was unique. Coupled with their instrumental prowess, Led Zeppelin was an irresistible force. The "heaviness" of Zeppelin's sound was unmatched at that time. Still is.

The British are great at slam-you-up-against-the-wall rock. Zeppelin combined this with eminently listenable blues riffing creating a wall of sound that just *consumed* you! Led Zeppelin was the embodiment of overstatement. And then again, Page could sit on the edge of the stage and entrance the audience, gently tickling Celtic inspired melodies from his 6-string acoustic guitar.

I saw Led Zeppelin again at the Tea Party the week of May 29, 1969 while completely blasted on some orange sunshine acid a couple of days before my departure on a journey that eventually landed me in San Francisco. Shit! Zeppelin on acid was damned near a *religious experience!!*

They got called back for so many encores they ran out of tunes and just jammed on anything they could think of: Chuck Berry's "School Days" and a ton of other rock and roll oldies! Page's seamless riffing just carries you away on the rhythm, and Plant's soul–shattering shrieks and the relentless inevitability of excess heaped on the excess that preceded it and you have Zeppelin's approach to subtlety: there was none. At their hardest they were the equivalent of a kick in the teeth, and yet still bring it down to something soulful, soft, and ...almost...quiet, like Page's acoustic *Black Mountainside.* Then they would hit you with the jackhammer staccato of *Communication Breakdown!* Just goddamned amazing.

I read in some guitar magazine where an alleged rock pundit pontificated on Jimmy Page's sloppy playing is. Right. If Page is sloppy, he is magnificently so. That criticism was likely written by some rock n' roll wannabee who can't dickfinger a C chord!

RUNAWAYS

The head scene in any city – and most cities had one by the summer of 1968 – was a refuge for runaway kids. There just *so* many! Wherever there was a public gathering of longhairs there were bound to be runaway kids. I don't know what they were running away from or where they expected to go. These things were generally not discussed. Looking back from a vantage point of over fifty years, and knowing what I have learned about the world since then, there is little doubt many of these kids were fleeing abuse of one sort or another. Some were gay and had been tossed out of their homes by parents.

At a party at Marius and Beth's one weekend there appeared a face I hadn't seen before, a tall girl with long, frizzy red hair. She seemed to be quite shy and retiring. By the time Sunday evening rolled around, she was looking rather dejected. I went over to her.

"Hi. I'm Gene. I've seen you here all weekend, and right now you're not looking so good. Is something wrong?"

She looked at me. Her eyes were green. "Yeah. I came here from New York this weekend with my boyfriend. He split and ditched me. I don't really know anybody here and have no place to go." Her voice had a sexy huskiness to it. "My name is Lori."

She was a runaway. Since the Raspberry got married, I was alone in my pad. Lori moved in.

Lori returned from an afternoon of panhandling at the Common day with a small, dark-haired dark-eyed beauty who went by "Sunshine."

A third young woman joined our situation within the week. She was another sixteen year old, a delicate little blonde named Bonnie and came from a moneyed family somewhere in New England. She had one of those very elegant upper-class accents. A very intelligent young woman, she was immersing herself in the head culture to get away from her mother, whom she hated. She also moved in.

Now, contrary to popular conceptions about free love, there was coerced sex in the head culture. Much of this occurred with runaways having to trade sexual favors for food and shelter.[18] This was not my scene. Nothing was coerced, of course, but, ah, donations were cheerfully accepted!

It was a sort of "cozy" situation. The girls stayed with me in the apartment under no obligation, save that everyone had to contribute something to our communal living situation. They would panhandle or work from time to time as waitresses or maybe bum some grass from a dealer and sell it on the street or on the Common.

Although she had no accent, Sunshine had a German passport and was not a U.S. citizen. She had me keep her passport stashed between the floor joists in the basement where I also kept a dope stash.

She was a sweet kid who wanted adventure and soon took off with a group of people to go out to the Midwest and get some wild marijuana. It grew wild there because it was cultivated during WW II for rope because the Japanese had the hemp growing centers in the Pacific.

---

[18] A bumper sticker of the day said "Gas, grass or ass, nobody rides for free."

They took off. In about a month I received a postcard from Sunshine with an Ohio correctional facility address on it. It seems that, indeed, they had found their dope and gathered an entire U-Haul trailer full of it.

On the way back they pulled into a motel near Akron, Ohio. The trailer was not pulled all the way off the roadway, and a state trooper stopped to tell them to move it. One of them was standing in front of the opened door to the trailer when the trooper approached. Busted![19]

We corresponded for the next few months. She got probation and was placed with a family that owned a restaurant in which she worked. We lost contact when I moved from Shepherd Ave.

While the girls were still living with me, there appeared on Shepherd Avenue one day a short, stocky fellow with wild black hair and beard and a huge gold earring looking for all the world like a pirate. He was driving a red Mercedes convertible and his name was Danny. The Mercedes was stolen.

"Some guy gave it to me," he said, "he stole it and was paranoid he was going to get busted with it, so he told me to take it." Such were the times.

One evening my friend Neal went someplace with Danny in the Mercedes. A few hours later, Neal returned, alone.

"Wow, man, that was close."

"What happened?"

"We got pulled over by the state troopers. The ran the plates on the Mercedes and found out it was stolen. I told them I was just hitchhiking and they let me go."

"Where's Danny?"

"In the cooler."

Neal was on probation. Had they checked him out, he would likely have had to do his suspended sentence for the grass bust back in Dedham. He got lucky.

EDGAR'S HEARSE

Much of the summer of 1968 was spent tooling around New England in Edgar's 1957 Cadillac hearse. Edgar was a hip black dude from Fitchburg who looked – sort of – like Jimi Hendrix. His hearse was the

---

[19] And the shame of it is that the "wild marijuana" they harvested was wild hemp, and was pretty much useless for recreational use.

perfect party vehicle, complete with an 8 track tape deck and huge stereo speakers. Hitting the road in the hearse was to be in a party on wheels.

Barry was an acid dealer in our group who rode a green metal flake Harley chopper. We would hit the four lane and Barry and his lady would ride beside the hearse. We would pass joints and bottles of Bali Hai wine back and forth between the hearse and the chopper on our way to Hampton Beach or some other party town.

KENNY BAIRD

Kenny Baird was another individual I met at 14 Shepherd Ave. He rode a blue 500cc one lung Beezer.[20] A sweet machine indeed! He ran in biker and doper circles. He was a slightly built fellow with dirty blonde hair that was not too long, and a trimmed mustache and goatee. Kenny was an extremely pleasant individual. His wife, Andrea was nice too. She was somewhat zaftig[21] and had a gorgeous ass! J.C. Burkhouse took a liking to Kenny's bike. Kenny sold it to him, and then pulled an outrageous stunt.

He stole a police bike from a policeman's home. He walked it out of the driveway, pushed it down the street a bit, then lit it up and roared back past the cop's house! Over the winter he chopped it. Now, I have no clue about how you go about getting paperwork to get a stolen bike on the street, but Kenny evidently did. He was cool enough to hang with the Devils Disciples. I am certain they had expertise in this area!

A bunch of us, including Kenny and Mossey on their choppers, headed to Provincetown one weekend to party.

We pulled into a restaurant on the way down and had a bite to eat. It was full of citizens, and they were checking us out like we were from the moon. On the way out, Doug and Kenny gave them a real treat by turning around before going out the door and doing the "lip lock," frenching each other in full view of the restaurant full of citizens! Two hairy bikers in an open mouth tongue kiss, well, that's a good way to fuck with citizens' heads! And this was 1968, mind you. Attitudes were a LOT different then. It was the first time I had ever seen something like this myself. It was…different.

Once in Ptown Kenny got into an altercation and the cops cuffed him, stuffed him and hauled him off. . That was the last we saw of him

---

[20] A 500cc single cylinder BSA Gold Star, a British made bike.
[21] Yiddish, plump, somewhat full figured

that weekend. I figured he'd end up doing time when they ran numbers on his chopper.

We got back to Boston on Sunday afternoon. I went over to Kenny's apartment that evening to see if Andrea had heard anything from him. She had not. We smoked a joint and one thing led to another and we ended up in a nice sweaty, reefer fueled fuckfest. [22] Hey, just helping out a friend's wife in her time of need! She made the first move. She and Kenny had an open relationship. What was I going to do, say no? And, yes, her naked ass was indeed gorgeous!

Kenny showed up on Shepherd Ave. Monday afternoon.

"Holy shit! I thought for sure you would go away for your bike!"

"Oh hell, I wasn't busted on my scooter. Some guy got in my face and I decked him. Cops grabbed me immediately. My scoot was right where I parked it before they grabbed me!"

PARTYING WITH THE DISCIPLES

One day Kenny says to me, "Hey Gene, I'm going to the a DD party. Wanna come along?" Well, hell yes, I did!

I don't remember where their clubhouse was but I do remember the "party favors," glass ampoules of liquid pharmaceutical methamphetamine that were given out at the door. I was not into injecting speed so I gave mine to Kenny. There was lots of booze, speed, cocaine, smack, a controlled substance free-for-all. They had a rock band cranking out noise and it was a generally rowdy good time. The women were... outrageous!

The Devil's Disciples were definitely not a group to be fucked with. Their drug of choice was crank.[23] The disciples partied heavily and always had great quantities of meth, dynamite reefer, and oceans of beer. Rough-talking biker women, tattooed and attired in black leather, would show off their ample titties, flashing the men and smiling, occasionally dropping their pants and shooting moons.

Biker and head subcultures were two separate things, and the rules of conduct, such as they were, were not to be confused. A free love attitude prevailed among heads. A guy could hit on any chick–and *vice versa*–and that was OK. Bikers, on the other hand, regarded their women a

---

[22] Also called "dope balling."
[23] Methedrine

property. Hitting on a biker's old lady could result in a crippling injury. And some of these biker women loved to flirt with other guys just so they could enjoy watching the ass kicking that would surely follow.

There was a constant parade of people going in and out of the clubhouse bathroom to shoot up speed. In my entire life, the only place I have seen case lot boxes of ampoules of pharmaceutical grade meth was at the Disciples clubhouse. They were serious about this shit!

Kenny and I were just standing there, already ripped to the tits and pulling on a joint. The band was cranked and people were dancing. There is this couple dancing near us. He weighed probably 260, stood about 6'2", hair past his shoulders, scraggly beard and wearing DD colors. It was obvious he was nobody to fuck with. His old lady[24] was grooving to the music. She was an attractive brunette with an…ample… bosom. He looked over at us and then pulled his old lady's shirt up exposing her *perfect* grapefruit sized titties bouncing in time with the music.

"Hey" he hollered to Kenny and me, "whaddya think of them tits?"

Well, they certainly met with *my* approval. But this guy is a genuinely serious individual. *Is this a trick question? Am I going to get my ass kicked no matter what answer?* I remained silent.

Kenny grinned and responded, "Those are some mighty fine tits!"

The DD's attention turned to me." How about you? Whadda you think of 'em?"

Mock-up of Boston Chapter Devil's Disciples colors

Taking the cue from Kenny, "Those are mighty fine tits in*deed!*"

"Yeah, I think they're mighty fine tits too!" he said with an ear-to-ear grin, then he pulled her top back down and they continued to boogie!

---

[24]Bikerese for girlfriend, significant other, main squeeze.

"That's Crusher and Spider," said Kenny." She has a spider tattooed on her ass. I've seen him pull that any number of times! And she *does* have mighty fine tits!"

Inarguably correct! The rest of the evening was a blur. That's all I remember of it.

CHAPTER 14

CRISIS OF CONSCIENCE

THE WAR

By the summer of 1967, the war in Vietnam was going in such a strange enough direction that any goodtime party idiot – like myself – couldn't help but notice it. The message was slowly getting out that nothing was being accomplished there. Protests were mounting all over the country. Well-known people were publicly coming out against the war. I couldn't put my finger on it yet, but *something* was not right.

That summer, classmate Dick Orlandi, a Marine, came back to Smethport from his thirteen month tour of Vietnam. I had known Dick since first grade. I went to his house one afternoon to talk with him. I wanted to know from a firsthand source what was going on in Vietnam from something other than the standard newscasts and wire service articles. I was becoming suspicious and I wanted to hear about Vietnam from someone who had been there.

Dick's father, Mark was in the room. He had been in the Marines in World War II, drove a truck on D-Day, was an American Legion member and a real super-patriot. Dick showed me his pictures from 'Nam and we started talking about the war.

"Tell me, Dick," I asked him, "Is there really something to be accomplished by our being in Vietnam? I mean, is this thing going to be militarily successful or will it result in a chickenshit deal like Korea?"

Mark, who had been listening to our conversation intently, exploded, "What the hell do you mean, 'chickenshit deal?' We did *exactly* what we set out to do in Korea. We stopped the *goddamned* communists!"

"Look," I said, turning to Mark, "it doesn't look that way to me. It was more of a military stalemate that resulted in an armistice. And what I am asking Dick is if the war in Vietnam is headed in the same direction."

Vietnam GI [Underground GI newspaper] May 1968

Source: Archives and Special Collections at the Thomas J. Dodd Research Center, University of Connecticut

Mark was hot. "What the hell is wrong with my 'country right or wrong?' It doesn't make a *god*damned bit of difference what you or anyone else thinks about the war! If the government says it's necessary, *then it is!*"

It was obvious to me at that point I was going to find out nothing more than I already knew. I said good-by to Dick and left. More than 50 years on, Dick and I are still friends.

WESTMORELAND'S INCOMPETENCE

General William Westmoreland, commander of U.S. Military Assistance Command, Vietnam (MACV) told President Johnson, "I am absolutely certain that whereas in 1965 the enemy was winning, today he is certainly losing."[1] On November 21, 1967, LBJ had Westmoreland repeat this to a televised joint session of Congress.

The Tet Offensive at the end of January, 1968 brought the war to a new level of intensity and controversy. Tet was a huge military defeat for the Viet Cong and NVA forces. However, the fact of the newly built U.S. embassy in Saigon being overrun by VC sappers who killed the Marine guards there, and the well-coordinated attacks on military installations throughout the Republic of South Vietnam, did not strike most people as the actions of an enemy was on the verge of defeat. This was not lost on the media, or the people of America who viewed these events on the nightly news in their living rooms. The life-long effect of Tet on myself was the fact that three young men I knew had died in it.

This cartoon from the May, 1968, issue of "Vietnam GI," an underground publication by active duty GIs accurately sums up Westmoreland as a commander. Westmoreland willfully ignored accurate intelligence about the enemy troop buildup prior to Tet given to him by the CIA. In a conversation with Dan Nichols, high school classmate and Marine gunship pilot in Vietnam, he characterized Westmoreland as "the stupidest, most useless son-of-a-bitch on earth. He got a lot of guys killed for no good reason."

BLOOD AND POLITICS

In April, plumes of smoke billowed from burning cities across America in the wake Martin Luther King's assassination. The National Guard sought to restore order throughout the nation. I asked myself, *is this is America?*

Robert Kennedy held out to us the hope of bringing peace and unity to America. He wanted to end the unpopular war in Vietnam. He did not

---

[1] Losing, W. (2018). Westmoreland tells media the communists are losing - Nov 21, 1967 - HISTORY.com. Retrieved 10 March 2018, from https://www. history. com/this-day-in-history/westmoreland-tells-media-the-communists-are-losing

have quite the charisma of his older brother, but I, and many others felt he would be the man for the job. Someone had to get America back on track. His seemed like the only sane voice amidst the cacophony of star-spangled verbal diarrhea that so freely flowed from the pie holes of self-serving politicians.

On the morning of June 5th, I saw the Boston Globe in the vending boxes on my walk to work. Robert Kennedy had been assassinated after winning the California primary the night before. Good God! Where was this all going to end?

I had a hard time believing that this was the same country that in 1960 had so enthusiastically welcomed the election of John Kennedy and had looked forward to a new decade, a new era. What had happened to America? All of the people to whom my generation looked to as heroes were dead at the hands of assassins.

Baby Boomer's found themselves in the unenviable position of being called on to fight and die in an undeclared war in Vietnam while having no political voice. The age of majority was 21. If you were under 21, the politicians didn't give a flying fuck what you thought about anything because you couldn't vote. We were expected to just shut the fuck up and go to war because we were told to do so.

It is futile to attempt to work effectively within a system that is set up to buttfuck you. To effect political change in the United States, you must either (1) vote, (2) lobby Congress, (3) or purchase it by being a corporation and "lobbying" congress, *i.e.* bribing the greedy, dishonest sons-of-bitches.

As a generation we could do none of these things. The powers that be would not listen to us. Our feelings and our opinions did not count. All the while, the death toll mounted in Vietnam and the re-useable aluminum flag draped caskets carrying young dead Americans came home to the neighborhoods of America. There was absolutely no legal path for those expected to fight in Vietnam to have their voices heard.

Over fifty years ago Robert Kennedy, our last hope for peace in Vietnam, was torn from us by an assassin. The presidential choices were Hubert Humphrey, Richard Nixon and George Wallace, all pro-war candidates. Nixon won. Deaths in Vietnam would double before his "secret plan to end the war" ended the US combat role in Vietnam. What lay before us on June 5, 1968, was a black hole of rage and despair.

The war-mongering fucks running the country refused to listen to members of the generation being maimed and slaughtered half a world away. The spokesmen who held out hope for America in that decade –

John Kennedy, Martin Luther King, Bobby Kennedy – were all gunned down, publicly murdered. The attitude of the antiwar movement bent toward *OK, so if you won't listen to us when we are being reasonable, you will at least notice us because we are rioting in the streets!* The Rev. Martin Luther King said before he was murdered, "Riots are the language of the unheard." Fucking A.

It was not difficult, in that surrealistic time, to think that America was becoming a police state.[2] The term "fascist" was freely used in the underground newspapers hawked by longhairs on the street corners. Three years before, when I was still in high school, "fascist" meant a Nazi from Hitler's Germany, or one of Mussolini's blackshirts, something from another era, a bygone time. Now it meant a lot of people, from the cop on the beat and the riot squad, to members of Congress, the President, and their masters, the corporate industrialists, bloated on profits from trading blood for money.[3] From the point of view of the Vietnam generation, action in the streets was not at all inappropriate. This growing antiwar sentiment was giving the war-makers of the establishment fits of raging paranoia.

The antiwar movement was taking on a new consciousness. It wasn't just a bunch of college radicals and unwashed longhaired drug-drenched malcontents (as the media seemed content to portray it at the time) parading around with signs and chanting obscenities at police. Prominent personalities involved themselves. Dr. Benjamin Spock, the distinguished baby doctor, spoke out against the war at induction centers and was arrested. Heavyweight boxing champion Muhammad Ali, even though he had been promised a safe term in the service doing morale boosting fights and the like, refused induction into the U.S. Army. He was stripped of his title, had his boxing license rescinded for five years and was sentenced to five years in jail, and received an avalanche of hate mail. It was at this time Ali made the statement, "No Viet Cong ever called me 'nigger.'" After three years of legal wrangling, the courts reversed his conviction on appeal and reinstated his title.

As the flag-draped coffins came home, one American family at a time were starting to see that their sons were dying in a war that seemed to have no strategy, no purpose, and no end. The GI's had a term, "wasted." If someone was killed, they were "wasted." The use of that term was never more appropriate.

---

[2] Unfortunately, this is truer now in 2019 than it was then.
[3] And it hasn't changed a goddamned bit in fifty years.

The zeitgeist was one, I suppose, of moral assessment. An entire generation was questioning authority, calling into question the legitimacy and the morality of the U.S. military involvement in Vietnam.

When I started taking LSD, reading Herman Hesse and Evans-Wentz, I was having transcendental experiences, a feeling of the unity of and with all creation. I saw a similarity between this chemically assisted transcendental experience and the Buddhist belief in the oneness of all, in which all beings are connected by their own essential divinity.

This was what Christianity was supposed to be about but definitely was not. The churches, with very few exceptions, like the Quakers, supported the war. Young men were supposed to go and kill other young men "for God and country." Certain aphorisms of the counterculture made a lot of sense, like the hippie aphorism "fighting for peace is like fucking for chastity." The whole world seemed like it had been turned inside out. Nothing was the way it should be, whatever the hell that was, anyway.

THE WAR CHURCH

The Catholic Church supported the war in Vietnam. Anything that was anti-communist was good in the eyes of the church.[4] A good example was the missionary medico, Dr. Tom Dooley, before we knew he was a CIA stoolie (the rhyme is unintentional but appropriate). The Nunz held him up to Catholic youth as a hero, the "spirit of Christ working in the modern world." They used to show us movies about him in Catechism classes.[5]

Later I would wonder how many people he helped murder through his involvement with the CIA. Was it as many as he had helped with his medical mission? What was the sense of ethics here? The CIA were bloody handed murderous sons-of-bitches. Would Christ have been a CIA snitch and pinpointed people for assassination?

The Catholic Church, for all its mouthing about being "the One True Church of Jesus Christ, the Son of God" has always been a bloody organization. During the Vietnam war it was referred to as "the war church."[6]

---

[4] Even Nazi war criminals, who were aided by the church in escaping justice in WWII.
[5] But they neglected to tell us he was also a homosexual. I don't think that was a trait of his the church wanted us to emulate despite the longstanding wholesale buggery of altar boys by priests. I am not judging, just citing facts.
[6] Myra MacPherson, *Long Time Passing, Vietnam and the Haunted Generation*, 1984, New American Library, p. 119.

The Catholic Church did not support conscientious objection to Vietnam. Why should it be? The Catholic Church has a long, sanguine history of killing in the name of Christ, starting with Emperor Constantine, who saw the cross and the words "In Hoc Signo Vinces"[7] in the heavens, causing him to stop butchering in the name of paganism and started butchering in the name of Christ. Then there were the bloody Crusades – which were really wars to open up trade with the East – the Borgias and their murderous, whoremaster popes, papal wars, The Inquisition, papal sanctioned witch burnings, and so on.

The Nunz had taught us that, as far as the church was concerned, the Mosaic commandment, "Thou shalt not kill,"[8] did not apply to cases of self defense, capital punishment and "just" wars.

Fuckface...oops...I mean *Francis* Cardinal Spellman helped get America involved in Vietnam. He sucked up to Nixon when Nixon was Ike's VP and got the first American aid and advisors sent to the Republic of Vietnam after the French got their asses waxed at Dien Bien Phu in 1954. The French, who had colonized and ruled Vietnam for about a hundred years, left behind a Catholic Vietnamese minority who ruled over a Buddhist majority and were the heirs to the colonial system instituted by the French. It was to the benefit of this privileged class of Catholic Vietnamese that things should remain *status quo* with foreign economic interests sucking the country dry of its resources. And this was fine and dandy with the Roman Catholic Church.

Spellman, the Archbishop of new York, was the Military Vicar of the U.S. Armed Forces for Roman Catholics. He wanted the United States involved actively in Vietnam as a measure to stop the spread of communism which, if left unchecked, would diminish the church's sphere of influence. Another concern was to keep the Catholic minority in power over a Buddhist majority. In 1966 he said the Vietnamese conflict was for the "defense, protection, and salvation not only of our country, but… of civilization itself."[9]

The North Vietnamese, definite Marxists; didn't see things that way. National elections were supposed to be held after the French left, but they were canceled because it was feared that Ho Chi Minh, the dirty commie, would be the victor.

Seeing the nation and the world in the shape they were in, I figured that the people who said they knew what was going on and what ought to

---

[7] "In This Sign You Shall Conquer," and a made-up fairy tale for the credulous if ever there was one.
[8] Accurately translated from Hebrew, this commandment is "You shall not do murder."
[9] Francis Cardinal Spellman visits South Vietnam
"Francis Cardinal Spellman Visits South Vietnam". 2019. *HISTORY*. Accessed May 9 2019. https://www. history. com/this-day-in-history/francis-cardinal-spellman-visits-south-vietnam.

be done didn't know a damn thing more than I did. And, if they didn't know what the hell was up, all the people who had been telling me all my life what was right and what was wrong were probably full of shit too.

At the age of twenty, I decided to regard everything I had been taught up to that point as being false. I discarded, or at least tried to discard, all my former beliefs and attitudes. I did not realize it at the time, I still kept my idealism, sense of justice, personal integrity, and sense of commitment. I thought this was because of my religious training and inspiration from John Kennedy. I now believe these were inborn as part of my character.

I saw society failing. I could not recognize America as the same nation which had seemed so positive and so full of optimism eight years earlier. I, like many other socially and politically alienated youth of that time, was dropping out, starting over, searching for answers. I just wanted...the truth... Hell, truth is truth, isn't it? How difficult could *that* be?

ME AND MY UNCLE

In June of 1968, I received a notice from the Selective Service System Local Board 101 in Bradford informing me I was reclassified 1-A, which means the U.S. Government saw no reason why I, too, should not be sent to kill or be killed. I hadn't thought about the war much since Buddy was killed in January. It was less abstract to me because of his death, but not yet a part of my day-to-day reality. Now it was looming because I was going to be called upon to participate in it. Being drafted was a sure ticket to Vietnam. They needed fodder for the green machine, warm bodies to be turned into corpses for the financial gain of the military-industrial complex.

In July I received my notice to report for induction. Having taken, and passed, my physical the previous December, this was it. I had to make a decision that would affect the rest of my life. This was my invitation to the party from my Uncle Sam.

I was in a state of complete social and political alienation and had pretty much decided that I was under no circumstances going to be a part of the war. Even in my state of alienation, this was a decision not easily reached, as duty to one's country was a value that was instilled in me at home, in my public education, and the general culture. If a crisis of conscience was required for official admission to the turbulence of the 1960s, this was mine.[10]

The war was wrong, this I knew. I did not want to participate in it, not so much for reasons of personal safety so much as for philosophical, moral, and spiritual reasons.

Having become thoroughly psychedelicized, I had experienced my consciousness outside the physical confines of my body. Was this what death like? Did it show me the spirit survives beyond the physical body? What really concerned me, though, was whether or not I would be required to take the lives of other human beings, people, with whom I had no quarrel, and who could not possibly pose a threat to the United States.

I was no conscientious objector, nor was I a pacifist. While not a violent person myself, I would not hesitate to use deadly force in defense of myself or others. I knew there were things for which sacrificing one's self is necessary for a greater good. Vietnam was not one of them.

I could have probably enlisted and gotten into an MOS[11] that would have kept me from of participating in the killing part of the war, but that was not enough. Through my developing spiritual consciousness, I had become aware that we human beings are spiritual entities dwelling in fleshly bodies, completely unaware of their own spiritual nature. We are spirits having a physical experience.

War is the ultimate evil undertaking of man: spiritual beings, unaware of their innate spirituality, blowing each others' fleshly forms to bits on battlefields, or, as G. I. Gurdjieff wrote regarding World War I, "...men who are asleep killing other men who are asleep." I felt that if I served in the military in any capacity whatsoever, I would be adding my own energy to the forces that kept the killing, destruction and suffering going.

I knew that in many other nations, people who rebelled the way we, the freak culture, were, would be killed. Such a thing had just recently happened in Mexico City, where the army massacred scores of students at a demonstration. They weren't shooting students in America – yet.[12] I appreciated the Constitution and the Bill of Rights, but America was not being threatened in any real way by what I and many others increasingly viewed as a civil conflict among the Vietnamese.

Who the hell was the government – or anyone else – to tell me I had to go half the world away and kill people who had done nothing to me

---

[10] The Old Curmudgeon's Sage Advice No. 8
[11] military occupational specialty
[12] That would come in 1970 at Kent State University in Ohio, Jackson State in Mississippi and South Carolina State.

and were not likely to? We were supposed to be making Southeast Asia safe for democracy, yet we were backing a repressive regime in Vietnam, one that clearly did not represent the majority of the people. A Catholic minority was oppressing the Buddhist majority. Was this a "fledgling democracy" that America needed to defend? *Fuck* no!

Stories of atrocities by U.S. and ARVN troops were also starting to circulate in the underground media. I grew increasingly suspect of the news doled out by the conventional media.[13] But even then, weighing only what was reported in the straight[14] media, I saw many reasons to question the war.

No one then or since has ever answered the question "What was the objective of U.S. involvement in Vietnam?" It was not to capture and hold territory. Buddy was killed in January 1968. The position he and 729 others died defending was abandoned in July, 1968. What the hell was this? It made no sense at all.[15]

America had gone mad. The most absurd was commonplace. There was violence in the streets at home and violence in Vietnam.

American forces had staged a vicious counterattack following the Tet offensive. After the village of Ben Tre was virtually destroyed, an American Major said to journalist Peter Arnett, "It became necessary to destroy the village in order to save it."[16] This was Orwellian doublespeak straight out of *1984*.

Colleges and universities became the spawning ground of political unrest, centers of sedition with many campuses lit by the glow of burning ROTC buildings.

"Ask not what your country can do for you...," John Kennedy's words echoed in my mind, "...rather, ask what you can do for your country." What could I do for my country? *Not* go to war. The war was *wrong*. There was no justification for sending America's finest young men off to die in a foreign war with no end in sight. We were told there was a "light at the end of the tunnel." If there was, it was headlight of a locomotive hurtling headlong toward us in the dark.

Yet, I would fight in a war if it were *necessary*, for I also loved my country. I saw a distinction between "patriots" and those who loved their

---

[13] The term "corporate media" had not yet entered the national lexicon.
[14] If something wasn't "hip," it was "straight"
[15] This question was answered in Col. Harry G. Summers book, "On Strategy." Summers explained that while there was tactical superiority on the part of the U.S. in almost every situation, there was no strategic objective, except for a vague idea of a return to a status quo. Tactics win battles, strategy wins the war. So there was in fact no strategy and therefore no objective. It was a monumental clusterfuck from beginning to end.
[16] "Major Describes Move". New York Times. 8 February 1968.

country. "Patriots" were blind to all reason, acting solely on the emotional level red-white-and-blue flag-waving jumping-up-and-down whistling-Yankee-Doodle my-country-right-or-wrong bullet-head mentality. I loved my country and was disturbed to see it rent by the war abroad and civil strife ay home. It seemed that the forces of darkness and oppression were attempting to bludgeon our generation into submission to the state. The blood of young men with no say in the political process was being traded for corporate profits by the greedheads of the corporate oligarchy.

Where to look to for guidance? Well, I was a Boy Scout. The Boy Scout Oath starts with "On my honor I will do my duty to God and my Country." So, exactly what was one's duty to God and country? Were preachers and politicians the sole arbiters of duty to God and country? Were we supposed to be automatons who blindly did their bidding?

Then there was Davy Crockett. Every American kid knew about Davy Crockett. We all had coonskin hats and idolized him as an American Hero. In his book *The Strawberry Statement*, James Simon Kunen suggested that Walt Disney, as rabid a right-winger as ever breathed, inadvertently contributed to the radicalization of the baby boomer generation by making us aware of Davy Crockett's motto

"I leave this rule for others when I'm dead;

Be always sure you're right – THEN GO AHEAD!"[17]

Now, I am not going to claim that this was consciously on my (or anybody else's) mind at the time. These were, however, something we had all absorbed through movies and TV. Yes. They were absorbed into the collective consciousness of America, no doubt having an effect on our generation, no matter how subtle it may have been.

THE BOSTON DRAFT RESISTANCE GROUP

"A 'No' uttered from the deepest conviction is better than a 'Yes' merely uttered to please, or worse, to avoid trouble."

–

— Mahatma Ghandi

I needed to find resources. Perusing a copy of the Cambridge underground newspaper, *The Old Mole,*[18] I found a listing for The Boston Draft Resistance Group in Cambridge, just across the Charles River. It

---

[17] As quoted in *David Crockett: His Life and Adventures* (1874) by John Stevens Cabot Abbott
[18] The name comes from this: "We recognize our friend, our old mole, who knows so well how to work underground suddenly to appear: the revolution," – Karl Marx

turned out that Edgar had also received his notice for the same induction date, August 21st. We traveled in his hearse across the Charles River.

Going to the address given in the paper we found a small office suite on the second floor of a brick building. There was a huge black omega[19] painted on the glass in the door. Edgar and I tered. An attractive young woman was operating a mimeograph machine. Her hair was blonde and straight, hanging past her shoulders. She was wearing an ankle length cotton print dress, typical of the hip fashion of the times. She turned around when I entered and I saw she was wearing a white button with a large black omega on it.[20]

> **CONTINUING EVENTS**
>
> Boston Draft Resistance Group.
> Draft counselling noon to six,
> Mon.-Sat. Till 9 on Thurs. 102
> Columbia st., Camb. 547-8260
> Draft Counselling, Friends, 5 Longfellow Park,
> Cambridge, M-F, 2-9 876-7939
> Cambridge Rent Control Campaign,
> Meetings, Thurs. 7:30, Sat. at 1
> 595 Mass Ave. 868-1580
>
> Draft Trials: In Federal Buidling, Post Office Sq. Trials are postponed and changed so often, intentionally sometimes, to prevent people from attending, it is impossible to list dates. Call Carol Neville for specific information. 227-8337.
>
> 1968 Cambridge MA "The Old Mole" SDS ppubllication
> Boston Draft Resistance Group
> Source: University of Michigan

"Hi. Can I help you?"

We explained our situation to her and she called a young man out of another room.

"This is Phillip Ramsey," she said as he came over to me and shook my hand with a firm grip, "he's going to Harvard Law School, he'll be your counselor," and she smiled.

Phillip had shoulder length brown hair, a mustache, and wore a T-shirt emblazoned with the omega resistance symbol, denim bellbottoms and western boots. We went into the other room and remained standing. He looked over our induction notices.

"OK," he said to me, "you are no longer a resident of Bradford, Pennsylvania, right?"

"No, I live in Boston."

---

[19] Omega is the electrical symbol for resistance, It was adopted by draft resistance groups as a symbol for draft resistance.
[20] The omega is the electrical symbol for resistance and was adopted as the symbol of the draft resistance movement.

"For how long?"

"Since classes at the Pitt Bradford campus ended in April. I came to Boston then."

"Good! You are now legally a resident of Boston. The first thing you have to do is transfer your local board to Boston. Your old local board actually has no jurisdiction over you in Boston. That way we can deal with your situation from here." He went over to a filing cabinet, opened it and pulled out a form. "Fill this out and send it back to your local board immediately. It will buy us another month. That's how long it will take for them to process the paperwork."

"We are also going to need copies of your draft board files from..." he looked at my notice again "...Bradford."

"How do I get those?"

"Just ask them. Selective Service Law entitles you to make copies of your records. Just go in to the draft board office and ask for them. They have to let you do it. It is Selective Service law. Understand?"

He addressed Edgar, "Edgar, you are already a legal resident of Boston and have already passed your physical. You don't have the extra month that Gene does."

I asked, "So, Phillip, what *do* we do?"

"The way to stop this war," he said with great conviction, "is for enough people to refuse induction into the U.S. Armed Forces so that the Federal Court system will become clogged with draft cases."[21]

This was not exactly what we wanted to hear.

"Here is how you do it. They have you in a line. At some point they will tell you to take a step forward. At that point, you will be considered inducted into the U.S. military, and you will no longer be subject to civilian law. When they tell you to take the step forward, refuse to do so. And don't let them trick you by saying 'why don't you come over here and we'll talk about it?' You take a step forward to talk to the sergeant and you are in the Army," Phillip explained. "And if you take the step for-

> Richard M. Nixon, former boy wonder and Vice President, was elected President of the United States of America on November 5th, 1968. The USA is a large country lying between Canada and Mexico. It is ungovernable.

Nov. 16 1968 Cambridge MA "The Old Mole" SDS publication
Source: University of Michigan

---

[21] This strategy in fact worked according to Myra MacPherson in her book, *Long Time Passing: Vietnam and the Haunted Generation.* Doubleday 1984

ward, you will be subject to the Uniform Code of Military Justice, and that is a whole different ball game. I cannot give you advice that will help you at that point, you will be in the U.S. Armed Forces and it will

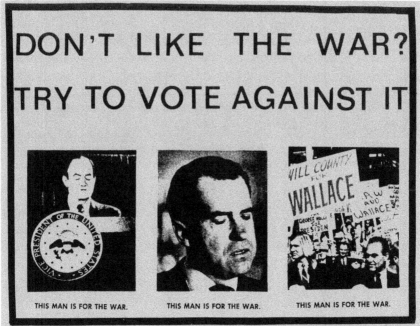

Source: "Vietnam GI," an underground GI publication, 1968. All three candidates, Hubert Humphery, Richard Nixon, and George Wallace, supported the war.

be too late. Even better, when they tell you to take the step forward, take a step backward."

I was listening intently. Edgar seem somewhat nonplussed.

"When they realize you're serious about refusing induction, you will be escorted off federal property by military police. In about 90 days, an indictment will be handed down charging you with refusal to be inducted into the U.S. armed forces. This is, of course, a federal offense. If you are convicted, and it is quite certain you will be, you will have to serve time in a federal prison."

"How much time?"

"Two years is what federal judges are currently handing down. This may get shorter as they run out of space in prisons for draft resisters."

I didn't feel like risking going to jail any more than I felt like going to war. And I really didn't want to go to Canada either. Actually, that thought pissed me off. Who the hell were these assholes to drive me out of *my* country because I wouldn't go halfway around the world and kill people who pose no threat to this nation whatsoever? *Fuck* 'em!

"OK, that's one idea," I replied. "Got any others?"

"Well, we could try getting you a letter from a psychiatrist that would say you are unsuitable for military service. That might work." His tone of voice was doubtful.

Edgar and I left the Draft Resistance office and headed back to Boston, smoking a joint as we crossed the Charles River. That is the last time I ever remember seeing Edgar, we were to be drafted the same day. I have wondered about whatever happened to him.

Pondering my situation, I knew this: if I were to try to convince the military I was mentally unsuitable for service, it would be far easier to convince strangers in Boston than people who had known me all my life, like my father's boss, Milt Hodges, the postmaster in Smethport. He had signed my induction notice.

My apartment had no telephone. The nearest one was in a booth in the back of the Triple-A Superette on Huntington Avenue. It was unavailable during the noon hour because the owner was making book.[22] I called my parents during the first week of August.

"I hear you got something in the mail." My father's tone of voice was upbeat. He thought military service would straighten out my rebellious attitude, make a "man" out of me. And, most importantly to him, cut my hair!

Well, here goes. "Yeah. That's a bunch of crap."

"What do you mean by that?"

"I mean I'm not going."

"Not going...?"

"There's no way I am going to fight that goddamned war, Dad. I refuse to be a part of it. It's wrong."

"If the *government* wants you to go, then, by God, you *go!*" This was the angry tone I usually heard from him just before getting my ass kicked.

"That's not going to happen."

"You really feel that way, do you?"

"Yes, Dad, I do. The war is wrong. I will not be part of it."

---

[22] Take bets

There was a hesitation, then he spoke firmly and deliberately. "In that case, at the end of this phone call, I no longer have a son."[23]

"OK. That's on you, then, Dad."

He hung up. My father had disowned me. The "generation gap" was now an undeniable fact in our family. We certainly weren't the first family to be split apart by the war in Vietnam, and we certainly wouldn't be the last.

In 1968, my father was a 43 year-old World War II Navy veteran and past commander of American Legion Bucktail Post 138 in Smethport. He had no idea of where I was coming from, and it was useless to try to tell him. I knew from past experience he would not listen. While this turn of events bothered me, I had more timely things to attend to.

ROAD TRIP!

I packed my suitcase and proceeded to hitchhike back to Smethport. I needed to get my draft records. I had no trouble getting a ride out of Boston with a salesman. We conversed for a couple of hours before he dropped me off.

"Hey, you know, you gotta be careful of them 'hippies'," he said.

I thought this was amusing. I was wearing John Lennon glasses, a tattered army field jacket, bell-bottomed denims, cowboy boots, a yellow silk paisley scarf and hair to my shoulders. "Is that right?" I replied.

"Yeah. They take that, uh, LDS stuff, y'know."

LDS? Oh God, This was rich indeed! "Yeah, I've...I've heard of that...L...DS...stuff."

"Yeah, well, you gotta be careful. That shit makes you crazy. Don't let 'em give you any of that crap. End up in a goddamned mental hospital. Turns you loony."

LDS makes you crazy...I'll make damned sure I never become a Mormon. "It sure sounds bad. I'll remember that." I tried to sound grateful. After all, he was giving me a ride and, he thought, some good advice as well.

At some point the conversation got around to politics.

"Yeah, George Wallace. He's my man." said the driver.

The thought chilled me.

---

[23] Years later my sister told me that she remembered our father crying only two times. One was when Grandma died, the other was after a phone call with me. I am certain it was this call.

"Wallace doesn't put up with a lot of bullshit. And he won't fuck around in Vietnam like the candy asses we have in Washington now. Goddamnit, he'll get this country straightened out. He'll take care of the goddamned niggers, too."

Good Christ! I couldn't believe what I was hearing. I knew Wallace was running as an independent candidate, but I didn't think there would be a lot of support for him outside of the South. Shit, I run into a random guy in New England and he's a fucking Wallace freak! Were there a lot of people who felt like this? I had been hanging out only with other longhairs, so I was somewhat culturally isolated. Sweet fucking Jesus! America might be in deeper shit than I thought!

That evening, I was thrown off the New York State Thruway by a state cop (after being searched and after he ascertained I had enough money on me to not qualify as a vagrant) and had to thumb through a series of small towns. Some of my rides were only for a mile or so. I looked so strange that people would give me a ride just to find out what the hell I was! They were all good-natured. There were no threats on my life or anything like that.

That night it rained like crazy. I spent the night curled up in the doorway of a store in Attica, New York. Shortly before dawn I was rousted by a town cop who gave me a ride to the city limits and told me not to pass through there again.

I was then visited by the County Sheriff, who had been alerted about my presence by the cop who had just run me out of town. It turned out he was originally from McKean County, too, so we shot the shit for a while and he let me go on my way.

I was in Belfast, N. Y. by the middle of the morning. Another New York State trooper – no doubt alerted by some local resident upset that some alien life form was hitchhiking through town – saw me and brought his car to a gravel-skidding halt across the road from me and got out.

"Just what the *hell* do you think you're doing?"

"Trying to get home, officer," I said as innocently as I could.

"Get your ass over here."

Must be his wife refused to give him a blow job this morning. "Yes-sir." I complied, picking up my suitcase and trudging across the road.

"Lemme see your ID."

I produced my PA driver's license.

He looked at it, then handed it back." Now tell me just what the hell you're doing."

"It's like I said, Officer, I'm trying to get back to Smethport, Pennsylvania. That's my home town."

"Where you comin' from?"

"Boston, Massachusetts."

"Boston, huh?" He looked me up and down. "Whaddya do there?"

"Play drums in a rock band."

"Oh...a rock band!" He hesitated for a moment. "Say, you ever smoke any of that... marra-wanna?"

I decided to fuck with his head. "Sure, I smoke it all the time," I grinned.

His face, which had been impassive up to this point, became animated. "Oh yeah? What's it do for you?"

"Gets me high, feels real good!" I replied enthusiastically. He's probably getting a hard-on, I thought, thinks he's finally going to make a drug bust!

"But, I mean, how does it feel? Is it like...whisky?"

Typical fucking juicehead! "Oh no, it's better than whisky. No hangover. Doesn't make you run into walls or fall down. *Great* stuff."

"Yeah? You really like it huh?"

"Hey, I *love* it!"

"Got any on you?"

This asshole thinks I'm as dumb as he looks! "Not a chance!" I smiled broadly.

His expression suddenly got serious. "Yeah, well maybe I oughta see that pack of cigarettes you got in your pocket there!" He pointed to my Winstons.

"Sure, Here." I handed them to him. He looked through them and, finding only Winstons, handed them back.

"Lemme see what's in that suitcase."

"I'm telling you, I'm clean. You're gonna get no dope bust with me," I told him as I opened my suitcase.

After going through the clothes I had packed, he had me empty my pockets Finding no narcotics, he admonished me to not pass that way again and let me go. It started raining again, so I called Barry Wilson in Smethport to come and get me, which he did.

I had planned to crash at Barry's house because I didn't think I was welcome at home. I was no sooner in the door of Barry's house when my mother called on the telephone. She was crying. "Gener, come home. Please. Please come home."

I was amazed, "How'd you know I was here?" My apartment didn't have a phone, I knew she couldn't have called anyone in Boston. Barry's mother probably told her.

"I...I just thought you'd be there... I guess. Please come home, will you?" She was crying.

"Mom, I don't think Dad wants to see me. He's really pissed. If I come home, there's just going to be more trouble. I don't need the shit kicked out of me this week."

She cried harder and pleaded more. This whole thing was tearing her up. My mother loved both of us and was distraught at the rift between my father and I. Not wanting to hurt her any more than she had been already by this thing, I agreed to go home.

My father glowered at me when I came in the door, said "You look like a goddamned bum!" and stormed out. I heard the car start and tear out of the driveway. Mom hugged me and sobbed.

My father was genuinely perplexed by my behavior. I would not cut my hair and I did not want to go into the army. He figured I must be crazy.

The next day he announced, "I've made an appointment with the psychiatric center in Ridgway. I'm taking you there the day after tomorrow."

"Hey, thanks a lot. That's going to help my stay out of the Army. I appreciate that, Dad." This puzzled him even more.

The following day I hitchhiked to Bradford to secure copies of my draft files. The Selective Service office was on the third floor of the Hooker-Fulton Building on Main Street. A long counter divided the room in two. Official posters with Selective Service rules and patriotic propaganda posters were on the walls. The walls on the other side of the counter were lined with filing cabinets. Two women sat facing each other at two oak desks pushed together in the area behind the counter. They looked to be in their sixties and regarded me with shock and disbelief. I went to the counter.

"Just...what...can we do for you...sir?" said one, in a tone of voice that conveyed purest contempt. She had her gray hair pulled back into a bun and pursed her lips in disapproval.

"I'm here to copy my draft files," I said.

"What!?" she said loudly and with mock surprise.

"My draft files, Ma'am, I'm here to...copy...them."

"What for?" she demanded icily.

"Because I do not intend to become a participant in the Vietnam war. In order to prevent this, I need to copy my draft files."

The second lady, still sitting, chimed in, "Oh, so you don't believe in the draft, is that it?" She had her head tilted up, looking down her nose at me.

"Ma'am," I was being as respectful as I could, "it doesn't really make any difference what I believe. I am not here to debate the war or politics with you. Now, may I please copy my draft files?"

"You certainly may *not!*" the first one shot back. "Those are *government* property." She came up to the counter and faced me. "You absolutely may *not* copy them!"

Being polite not getting me anywhere. I leaned forward over the counter and put my face close to hers.

"Now see here, lady, it's time to cut through the *bull*shit! Those are government files which happen to contain information on *me*. I *am* entitled, under Selective Service Law, to make copies of those documents if I so desire. You can either hand them over to me immediately or I will come back here with a lawyer and you by God *will* hand them over. *Got it?"* I was bluffing, I didn't know any lawyers in Bradford.

Taken aback by my sudden change in demeanor, her eyes widened. She looked back at the other woman, still seated, than back at me and spoke, "Well...I don't know –"

"Then get on the *God*damned phone and find somebody who *does* know! You are in *violation of Selective Service law* by denying me access to those records! *Do you understand me?"*

Looking at me open mouthed, she gingerly stepped backwards to her desk, sat down and called a colonel with the Selective Service System in Harrisburg. He told her that, yes, under the law I was indeed entitled to copy those documents.

"But you have to do it here. Those papers cannot leave the office," she told me.

"Fine with me. You can copy them on your copy machine."

"I don't—"

"Don't start the bullshit again, lady. You just got told by your superior that I am entitled by law to copy those records. Since I can't take them out of this office, then *you* have to copy them for me. It's not a difficult concept to grasp."

"It will cost you –" she hesitated "– a *dollar* a page!"

"Fine. *Do* it!"

Having secured the necessary documents, I went back out on Main Street to hang out in front of Nick's Red Hots when I saw classmate Bill Wassam. We had graduated from high school together and were good friends. Bill was a positively brilliant individual. He had just completed his bachelor's degree in chemistry from Clarion State College in three years and had been accepted for graduate work at Princeton University. There was, however, a slight snag. Student deferments ran out after the bachelor's degree, and the green machine needed more cannon fodder. He was scheduled for induction on the same day I was, August 21st.

"The war is total bullshit, man," I told him, "there's no reason you gotta go. Look at what happened to Buddy. He got fucking blown away, man. Butch too. For what? I'm supposed to go the same day you are. No way, man. I'm not fighting their fuckin' war for them. You don't have to either. Come on back to Boston with me. We can get you out of this."

Bill gave me a look like I was crazy. "Uh, no, I don't think so I'm going to try to get into chemical warfare or something."

"Yeah, well, good luck, man" I said and we went on our separate ways.

SEEING THE SHRINK

The following morning my father and I made the half-hour drive to Ridgway in total silence. Once in the office, he proceeded to tell the psychiatric social worker, Mr. Olson, about my general weirdness. I added nothing to what he said, except to agree with what he was telling Olson. He was not at all exaggerating. He just plain didn't goddamn understand what was going on with me. How could he?

I almost felt sorry for him. I mean, what the hell, World War II was a completely different deal. Any GI who went to war in the 40s knew that the war would end when Allied troops marched through the streets of Tokyo and Berlin, and not until. Total victory over the enemy forces was the goal, nothing less.

In Vietnam, nothing was that clear, nothing at all. Victory wasn't even a goal in Vietnam. There was no talk of our troops marching victoriously through the streets of Hanoi. All that was desired was a return to some nebulous *status quo* of an independent non-communist South Vietnam. These thoughts went through my mind as I watched my father explain the situation.

Olson indicated to my father that he wanted to talk to me alone. My father left the room. I took the initiative. "Look here," I said, drawing my chair close to his desk, "I'm not crazy. I know my father thinks I am, but that's because I don't want to cut my hair or go on the army. He just can't handle it."

Olson, who looked to be about thirty-five, was a clean cut fellow with light brown hair and thick, dark rimmed glasses. He sat back in his chair, placed the fingertips of both hands together, said nothing and raised his eyebrows. I continued.

"The plain fact is that there is no fucking way I am going in the service. Vietnam is a mess. I lost a very good friend there in January. At Khe Sahn, which has since been abandoned. And for what? Not one goddamned thing as far as I can tell. We are destroying entire villages of civilians and creating free fire zones in which anything that moves is killed. I am not going to be a part of that."

"I see," he said, "What kind of drugs are you taking?"

"Grass and acid. Hashish. Some speed once in a while. I'm into mind drugs, not body drugs. Downers, heroin, shit like that doesn't interest me. Neither do needles. Needles are not recreational, they are death."

"I see."

He dropped the professional crap at that point and we spent the next fifteen minutes just talking. He was a rather hip dude, surprising, as he was stuck in the hills with all the red-necked flag-waving patriots.

I was preparing to leave.

"Do you want some…mood elevators?" he asked

I couldn't believe it. Olson was offering to legally give me some dope! "No thanks, I told you, I'm not into speed, but I appreciate the thought. But if you got any grass I might be interested." He smiled and shook his head "no." I was sure he was lying.

My father went in for a private conference. We made the return trip in silence. I have no idea to this day what he told Dad.

While I was home, my mother and I had a conversation about politics.

"Well, actually, we like George Wallace. I hope he wins. I think he'll do a good job."

Fuck me Jesus! There it was again, and from my own mother! There was, indeed, a chance that America was in deeper shit than I thought.

TIME IS RUNNING OUT

I arrived back in Boston with two weeks to go before my impending induction. Returning to the Cambridge Draft Resistance Group, there was nothing in my file that would help me avoid induction. I was cynical enough by this time to figure that the Selective Service System was just another government bureaucracy. I had already used their cumbersome jurisdictional procedures to good advantage to buy some time. I figured I could utilize their inherent phobias of the freakier aspects of the counterculture, and, perhaps, some (un)controlled substances, to render myself unfit for military service.

Phillip got on the phone and started calling of psychiatrists he had who were sympathetic to the draft resistance movement. It seemed that every sympathetic shrink in Boston and the surrounding area was on vacation for the month of August. On two other days I went back to see Phillip with the same result. I was up shit's creek without a canoe, let alone a paddle.

In an act of desperation I went to the mental health clinic at the Massachusetts Mental Hospital, not too far from where I lived, and tried to con a doctor into thinking I was crazy. No good. He saw right through it.

The psychiatric social worker in Ridgway. Olson, had given me his card and told me to call him if I needed anything. I called. He, though sympathetic, was also unable to help me.

On Monday, the 19th, two days before induction, I went back to Cambridge. I got lucky! Phillip found a psychiatrist on Beacon Hill, Dr. Benninger, who would do the deed. Hot damn!

I was flat-assed broke at that point. Phillip gave me a dollar and I took the MBTA to the Park Street Station and found my way to the doctor's office. He wrote the letter, making me out to be a Class-A fuck up with beaucoup authority problems, a drug abuser and libertine. He covered all the bases! He wanted twenty-five dollars, but being as I was broke, he said I could pay him when I could. It turned out I never did.[24]

I formulated my strategy for dealing with my impending induction. With the letter from the doctor, I would convince the army I was unsuitable for military service. Failing that, I would refuse induction. When the indictment came down, I would go underground. If they wanted me, the FBI was going to have to look long and hard for me. *Fuck* 'em! It was a desperate set of alternatives, but then those were desperate times and I was a desperate young man.

There were thousands of refugees of various sorts in the hip underground. How many longhairs had wants or warrants out on them one could only guess. The underground nature of the freak culture made it the perfect outlaw refuge. All you had to do was throw away your razor, let nature take its course and change your name to "Sunshine." Last names were not necessary and, in fact, very rarely used. Part of this was basic pothead survival. Social cohesiveness, relative anonymity, and a liberal tolerance of others were a good thing for many. It didn't take too long until a person had no resemblance at all to their last school picture (or mug shot!). It was like a bottomless pit which would swallow up fugitives from justice, injustice, parents, the FBI, private detectives, or anything else.

The FBI had absolute fits trying to deal with this. Trying to locate a specific individual who had immersed himself (or herself) in the murky underground head culture was like trying to nail Jell-O to a wall. Since individuals were largely untraceable in the underground, the feds usually settled for harassing their families on a regular basis. Many people were regularly visited by FBI agents asking questions about a son or brother or other relative who had evaded the draft, had deserted from the military or was on the run from a federal warrant of one kind or another. Yes, the freak culture was the perfect outlaw hideout.

I received much moral support from my friends during this time. I had sympathetic left leaning friends in Smethport, college students on summer break especially my lifelong friend Mia. In Boston, David

---

[24] Some months later I would read in the Boston Globe about Dr. Benniger being busted for helping men evade the draft. No good deed goes unpunished. God bless that man.

O'Brien and Jeanie Loudon, who lived at 40 Kempton Street, were a fortress of strength for me.

I stayed up all night with Dave and Jeanie before I left for the induction station at the Boston Navy Yard. We smoked grass and took some "Christmas trees" (100mg. dextroamphetamine sulfate capsules). As I left, David gave me four more. I thanked him, took two and put the other two in my pocket.

THEIR GAME. THEIR RULES. I WIN. FUCK 'EM!

Armed with the letter from Dr. Benninger, a head full of amphetamines, an "attitude" and carrying a bag with a change of underwear and my toothbrush as per Selective Service System instructions, I reported at 6 a.m. to the Boston Navy Yard as ordered.

Following signs, I entered a building and walked into a room with rows of chairs. Several young men were already waiting there. A stocky sergeant sat at a desk at the front of the room. Speeding my brains out, I walked up to him.

"I got a letter from my shrink—"

"WHAT'S YOUR NAME?"

"Johnson. I've got a letter from a shrink. I think —"

He shuffled through a stack of manila folders and then looked up. "WALTER E.?"

"Yeah, that's me. Now I've—"

He thrust the folder into my hands. "STICK IT IN THE FOLDER, SIT DOWN IN THE THIRD ROW!"

Thinking to myself, *Well, Gene, this is where your attitude act starts*, I took a seat in the fourth row.

"GODDAMNIT! I SAID THE *THIRD* ROW!"

I got up and casually plopped myself in to a seat in the third row, giving him my best "fuck you" look. The look on his face told me he understood. His glare was even badder than Rod Steiger's, and I had always thought Steiger had the baddest glare on the planet! I was scared shitless, but I didn't dare let on.

Soon there were about forty of us nervous young men waiting in that room. Edgar was not among them. The sergeant got up and barked,

"ALL RIGHT! LINE UP. RIGHT HERE!" He indicated the left aisle of the room. "MOVE IT. *NOW!*"

The rest of the fellows fell over themselves getting into line. I didn't. I waited until they were all lined up and casually sauntered over to the left end of the line and stood. The sergeant swaggered down the line as he continued barking at us. His voice, tinged with a southern twang and a military cadence. .

"AFTER YOU ARE THROUGH WITH YOUR INDUCTION PROCESSING YOU WILL TRAVEL BY BUS TO FORT JACKSON SOUTH CAROLINA. YOU WILL ARRIVE THERE AT ELEVEN-HUNDRED HOURS AND YOU WILL ENTER BASIC TRAINING FOR THE ARMY OF UNITED STATES OF AMERICA."

Oh yeah? Not me, mo'fuck!

"IS THERE *ANYONE* HERE WITH A POLICE RECORD?"

As he looked up and down the line, I was the only one with a hand up. He walked over, took my folder and put a large red "X" on it with a grease pencil. Again, I gave him my best "fuck you" grin when he thrust the folder back into my hands. *So far so good.*

We were filed into another room and told to strip down to our undershorts. There was a walking hairball with women's lace panties on. The induction center personnel completely ignored his attire. I am sure they had seen this many times before.

The next stop was a window where we gave our folder to another soldier. When it came my turn, he asked,

"Is there anything that has changed since you had your pre-induction physical?"

"Yeah. I got a letter here from a shrink."

"Is that right?" His tone was most unconcerned. "Well, son, this is all kind of *sudden*...isn't it?"

"Hey, a lot of shit happens in eight months. Check it out. My physical was last December."

He knit his eyebrows and opened the folder. After shuffling through the contents and reading the letter, he returned the folder to me and, with a look that suggested loathing, motioned toward a door. "Go in there and wait. The doctor'll see you."

I opened the wooden door, the kind where the top half has the dimpled glass you can't see through, and walked through. It was filled with genuine fuck-ups, phony fuck-ups and hopeful fuck-ups. Right on schedule!

I sat beside a sallow, unhappy looking youth. He looked at me as I sat down. There was no conversation at all. Everybody just sat staring straight ahead. I was speeding like crazy and broke the silence.

"This must be where they send the misfits, huh?" I said to the anemic looking youth. Mistake. He proceeded to tell me at length the entire history of his chronic asthma. The door opened, the doctor stepped in and told the kid to shut up. I was glad. He took the guy on the end of the bench into his office and we all slid down.

I surveyed the assortment of faces: chubby, thin, acne-ridden, peach fuzz, scraggly mustaches. Each face concealed a terror, the uncertainty of what was going to happen to them, fear of the unknown.

The minutes ticked off. In the door the young men went, one after another. A few others came in and sat at the end of the line.

"Next."

It was my turn. *Fucking-A. Here goes everything!* I got up and entered the inner office with the shrink. He was a Navy officer. I was trying to look casual, you know, very nonchalant. It's tough to do when you're nearly naked and mightily twisted on amphetamines.

"Have a seat." I sat in the chair in front of the doctor's desk. My heart was pounding, I could feel the blood pulsing at my temples. *Be cool, Gene, be cool.*

He took my folder and looked it over, extracted the letter from the shrink and set the other papers aside. As he read, I pretended to be unconcerned, all the while watching his face out of the corner of my eye. His eyebrows knit several times and he managed a headshake at one point. He sighed and laid the letter on the desk. Leaning back in his chair, he spoke.

"Well, Mr. Johnson, what do you think of going into the armed forces?"

Attitude. Cop the attitude, man. Still looking away from him, I hesitated a moment, then turned my head and looked him in dead straight the eye. "It's bullshit."

"You don't like the idea of military service, then?"

I was still giving him the deadeye stare. "*Fuck* no."

"And just why is that?"

Thinking of the contents of the letter, I responded. "I don't particularly fucking care about being told what to do *any* of the time, let alone *all* the time."

"I see." The man's face was impassive, just like a cop. He was good, I couldn't read him. "What about drugs, Mr. Johnson. What kinds of drugs do you take?"

"Well, mostly grass and acid. Smoke some hashish when I can get it. Did some opium a couple of times. Some speed too." *Like right now, asshole.* "I dig mind drugs, y'know. Expanding my consciousness. That's where it's at."

"What about heroin?"

"Bad scene, man. I'm not into that shit. And I'm not into needles, man. . uh…not my idea of recreation, y'know?" *Pace your rap, man, you're really cranked. Too easy to run on and on. To easy for the shrink to see through. Slow down, man, keep cool. Don't blow it! Have to keep cool.* "I mean, y'know, people who're into that shit are fucked up, y'dig?" *And I am obviously not, ha ha!* "That shit brings you down. Down is not where it's at. I like to expand my consciousness, not diminish it. Y'dig…?"

"Well…how often do you take. . LSD…Mr. Johnson?"

"Whenever I feel like it. That's usually three, maybe four times a week." Slight exaggeration. Once or twice a week was more like it. I didn't want to um…*abuse* it!

"How long have you been taking LSD?"

"Let's see…" I struck a thoughtful pose, not too obviously exaggerated, though. *Keep in character! Got to stay in character!* "About a year…year and a half…I guess." More like three months, really.

"What…does it do for you?"

"Depends on what's going on, what kind of acid it is, who I'm tripping with. Acid is cosmic, though. That's why I like it. I mean, tripping my brains out on some good acid is just about the grooviest feeling I can think of. The colors…the hallucinations…I just…*dig* the shit out of it."

"I see. Have you ever had any…uh…flashbacks…from your LSD experiences, Mr. Johnson?"

"No, not really. I think it'd be a stoned groove though."

He looked puzzled. The impassive face was showing a reaction. *Yes!* This was the first indication that my act might be working. "I don't understand…"

"Hey man, more bang for the buck! Y'dig? I'd be getting more mileage out of the drugs I paid for, get it? Kind of like a free ride, a free trip! A bonus from my travel agent!"

Looking at me, he raised his eyebrows slightly, sighed, leaned forward, and picked up the letter and looked at it. "Tell me...Mr. Johnson, what about...sex?"

"What about it?"

"What do you, ah, like...?"

I grinned. *He must have gotten to the "polymorphous sexual behavior" part.* "Most anything depending on the circumstances. Or anyone. Whatever..."

"But ...what is your preference...you must have a preference?"

I looked him square in the eye. "I have a liberal attitude and a sense of adventure. *You* figure it out!"

He looked at me, his expression tightening a bit. Glanced at the letter again, then back at me, "if you were inducted into the military, do you think you would continue your pattern of disruptive and irresponsible behavior to the point of being court-martialed?"

"Hey, I wouldn't, y'know, plan on being court-martialed, but if it happened, hell...it...uh...wouldn't surprise me. Not a fuckin' bit. Y'dig?"

"You think you'd have trouble following orders in a military situation?"

"Depends."

"Depends...on what...?"

"Lotta stuff, I suppose..."

"Can you be...more specific?"

"OK." I leaned forward and spoke deliberately. "I don't like the idea of serving in the military. I don't like the fucking war and I don't have anything against the Vietnamese. One of my best friends was killed at Khe Sanh. That was in January. Khe Sanh was abandoned in June. So, *you* tell *me*, just what the *fuck* did he die for?"

I didn't have to act to deliver that, I spoke from my heart. He looked straight at me. No response.

"That's right. For fucking *nothing*. That's what the fuck he died for. Nothing. Not a *god*damned thing. The fucking army wants to turn me into a killer? Not a problem. Give me a weapon. Then have some asshole tell me it's *my* turn to die...for nothing." I leaned forward slightly for emphasis. "I'll *know* which mother*fucker* to shoot!"

I leaned back, holding his gaze. I was speeding my tits off, scared shitless, and hoping I wasn't showing it.

He gave me one last long look, then scribbled something on one of the forms in the folder, closed it and handed it back to me. "Report to Station 14."

I took the folder and left his office not knowing whether or not my act had worked. I found a sign designating Station 14. My mind was going a million miles a minute as I ambled up to it and handed the GI my folder. Was I going to have to refuse induction? Would I have to go underground? Would I have to live the rest of my life looking over my shoulder for the FBI?

He opened it, looked at a form and reached for a rubber stamp. "Well, Johnson," he stamped the folder and looked up at me, "you're unsuitable for military service." He placed my folder on a pile of folders to his right. "You can get dressed and go home now."

I was stunned! I didn't dare let on, of course, but I HAD DONE IT! HOT GOD *DAMN!* I was a FREE MAN! I had met the green machine on its own terms and it *rejected* me! The army *didn't fucking want me!* It was *their* fucking game played by *their* fucking rules and *I* fucking won!

I took the MBTA to Park Station and went to the Common where I hung out for a few hours, rapping and smoking dope with friends, then I swallowed the other two Christmas trees that were in my pocket and walked back to Shepherd Avenue.

Down past the "Peter Bent" (the Peter Bent Brigham Hospital on Huntington Avenue) Jeanie Loudon spotted me.

"Gene!" she shouted from across the street, "What happened?"

"I'm a *fucking* reject!! Can you believe it? I pulled it off! They *don't fucking want me!"* An older woman down the street from Jeanie heard my exclamation and gave me a dirty look over her shoulder.

Jeanie ran over and gave me a big hug. We went back to her and David's place to tell David.

I called home that evening. My mother answered.

"Hello Mom!"

"Gener! Where are you?"

"It's not where I am, Mom, it's where I'm not. I am definitely not in the army. And I am not in trouble. Not with the government or anyone else."

She was quite confused by this turn of events, but relieved that I wasn't in trouble and that I wasn't causing any scandal for the family by getting my name in the paper.

I didn't blame her for not understanding what was going on. She had lived in McKean County all her life. Her father died when she was under two years old. When she was fourteen, World War II broke out. She quit school at fifteen to go to work. With all that had gone on in her life, she had little time for politics. Her generation understood that the government was trustworthy, an institution looking out for the best interests of the American people. It was no wonder at all she was naive to the politics behind the events of the 1960s. Hell, it was confusing for anyone.

This was a landmark achievement in my life and the real beginning of my independence. I had struggled with my own conscience and made a moral decision. I acted on that decision and influenced events relevant to that decision that drastically affected the course of my life.

But, what about that Navy psychiatrist? Was he really taken in by my act, Yard? Or was I the one guy a week he let go? I don't know. I never will.

A couple of weeks later, I bought some issues of *"Vietnam G. I.,"* an underground paper being hawked by a street corner vendor in Copley Square. It was written and published by GIs and veterans and was distributed in Vietnam as well as stateside. The Army considered publications like this to be contraband.

It contained a picture of four American GI's displaying two severed Viet Cong heads, the decapitated corpses in the foreground, one with the gore facing the camera. The soldiers had the faces of the All American Kids Next Door, posed as if displaying the results of an afternoon of game hunting. I cut the picture out and an article on Khe Sanh and sent them to my parents. The article carried no byline. I enclosed a letter:

Dear Mom and Dad,

I know you are concerned and distressed over my decision to resist the draft and not go into the military. Here are some things from an underground paper written and published by GI's who either are in or have been in Vietnam. They should know what is going on over there. We are not getting this kind of news in the states. This is what the GIs who are serving in Vietnam are saying about the war. Remember, Khe Sanh is where Buddy died. And take a good look at the picture, too. Is this really what you want me to do? I don't think so.

Your son,

Eugene

The above picture shows exactly what the brass want you to do in the Nam. The reason for printing this picture is not to put down G.I.'s but rather to illustrate the fact that the Army can really fuck over your mind if you let it.

It's up to you, you can put in your time just trying to make it back in one piece or you can become a psycho like the Lifer (E-6) in the picture who really digs this kind of shit. It's your choice.

From "Vietnam GI" underground publication May 1968

I didn't expect this to change my father's mind about the war, but I wanted him to get a look at something other than *The Bradford Era's* war reporting edited from the AP and UPI wire services and accompanied jingoistic editorial garbage and the bullshit on TV. I thought since the piece was written by GIs, he might pay closer attention. He never mentioned it to me but it must have made some impression as I found the letter and clippings in my father's things after he passed away in 1994.

FLASHING BACK– COMING OF AGE IN THE AMERICAN 1960s

While the ever escalating war raged in Vietnam, the 1968 Democratic National Convention in Chicago became the scene of a police riot.[25] Thousands of young Americans disenfranchised from the American political process tried to voice their feelings on the war and were beaten bloody in the streets for their efforts. Marius, Beth, and I watched the television with disbelief as Mayor Daley's forces of repression brutalized young people with enthusiasm. It was ghastly. We all took this personally. Right there in the streets of Chicago we all felt we were seeing what our nation would like to do to us. Just fucking beat us to death! It was a time to be nervous. And we were.

Khe Sanh

One thing that really pisses you off in Nam is the way the brass plays around with the lives of GIs. Take Khe Sanh, for example.

Last winter General Westmoreland and the other generals were talking about the *offensive* importance of Khe Sanh for mounting attacks against NVA infiltration. But after they discovered that the 5600 marines at Khe Sanh were surrounded by 20,000 NVAs, they suddenly switched their propaganda from an offensive to a *defensive* line.

The generals tried to use their strategic screw-up to rally the American people so they could get more GIs sent to Nam. As one marine general put it, "If we leave Khe Sanh, where do we stop? The South China Sea?"

The result of all this was 2300 GI casualties. And for what?

On June 27, MAC-V officially admitted that they had already begun to abandon Khe Sanh. The reason given was that recent increases in NVA strength have made it necessary to keep U.S. troops more mobile. They also mumbled about a new strategic approach which would allow infiltration to be checked without a large forward base at Khe Sanh. In other words, they said Khe Sanh wasn't militarily significant. *300 GIs died just for the hell of it!*

We probably wouldn't even know this much if it weren't for John Carroll, a reporter for the *Baltimore Sun* who broke the news in a June 24 dispatch from Khe San. When the "secret" broke in the States, the brass reacted by lifting Carroll's accreditation for "breaking security."

As Carroll put it, "The move is no secret among the men at Khe Sanh, nor is it hidden from the NVAs in the hills overlooking the once-besieged base." To *the brass, "breaking security" means telling the American people what everybody else —including the NVAs— already knows!*

Khe Sanh is a good example of what the Nam is all about and why we should get the hell out.

From "VietnamGI" Underground publication 1968

---

[25] As determined by the Walker Commission."The special commission appointed to investigate the protests at the 1968 Democratic Party Convention (see August 28, 1968), known as the Walker Report, issued its official report on this day. The report characterized the violent events as a 'police riot' directed at protesters." Tourek, Mary. 2013."Walker Report Finds "Police Riot" At Democratic Party Convention". Today In Civil Liberties History. Accessed June 5 2019. http://todayinclh. com/?event=walker-report-finds-police-riot-at-democratic-party-convention.

CHAPTER 15

GEORGE WALLACE MUST DIE!

DRUG-ADDLED PSYCHO-MUTANTS

"I think we oughta shoot the fucker," said Arjuna.

"Oh, c'mon man! That's *bull*shit," said Paul, "you can't just *kill* people!"

"Well, what the *fuck?*" Arjuna shot back. "That's what he'll do to *us!* That's what they've been doing to anyone who opposes their trip. Look at what happened just this year with Martin Luther King and Bobby Kennedy. Shit man! You got a *better* idea?"

Every week we had psychedelic adventures as we shed our normal perceptions and entered the surreal realm of the psychedelic, fantastic, and sometimes stupid bordering on insane.

Somebody who is dosed on acid can have their heads copped by people who are inclined toward being manipulative. It's sort of like the "imprinting" that happens with baby ducks: they think the first living being they see after they hatch is their mother. When you are tripped out on a heavy psychedelic like LSD, someone can walk in to the situation and manipulate you into believing that a line of purest absolute bullshit is the ultimate insight into the nature of the universe. If it happens repeatedly, the result is brainwashing. Charlie Manson and his band of psychedelic cutthroats are a prime example of this type of imprinting.[1]

Our weekend acid parties were more often than not just plain good times: partying, rock n' roll, general weirdness and sex. There were a few times when someone came through the door who would just rip off the whole scene by laying some kind of a weird trip on everybody and then split. I did not, at the time, understand enough about the psychological dynamics of psychedelic voyaging to know what was happening. None of us did. We were just *doing* it.

One evening, five of us settled into my apartment for a night of psychedelic adventure. Marius and Beth from 14 Shepherd Ave. were there. Debbie, a neighborhood resident with long, dark wavy hair, very full, parted in the center and falling over her shoulders. Her eyes were a deep, liquid brown, and she was wearing a colorfully embroidered Mexican peasant blouse that showed off her ample bosom. Her bell-bottomed jeans were fashionably patched. Paul was there, too. He was a real, good-hearted, impressionable, rather thin, curly-haired young man who had just gotten into the freak scene and was growing a beard.

We put on some tunes and smoked some grass. We all had a respectable buzz on when Marius took a baggie out of his vest pocket and started doling out capsules of LSD. This particular batch was called "white lightning," clear gelatin capsules filled with white powder, allegedly made by the legendary West Coast acid chemist, Augustus Owsley Stanley III.

We were getting off when in the door comes a dude who went by various names including "Arjuna," "Jesus Christ," and "Jimmy." He gave a new meaning to the concept of identity crisis. This week's featured personality was Arjuna, the warrior hero of the Bhagavad Gita and friend of Krishna.

Arjuna's brown hair was parted in the center, wavy and down past his shoulders. He had a handlebar mustache, a short beard, wore denim bell-bottoms and cowboy boots, a red bandanna around his neck and a denim jacket. This particular evening he was tripping on acid and speeding. We started talking politics and soon the conversation got around to George Wallace. He was going to be in Boston for a rally on the Common the next day, October 9.

Debbie handed Arjuna a roach we were finishing up. "So who do you think will be the next president?"

---

[1] This type of mind control was also part of the CIA's MK-ULTRA program.

"I don't know. The Republicans will probably nominate Nixon." He adjusted the roach in the clip and handed it to Marius.

"Think he'll win?"

"I don't know. Maybe."

"What about the Democrats?"

"Gene McCarthy was our peace candidate," said Beth, taking the last hit on the roach and putting the clip on the table.

"Even if he had been nominated, I don't think he could win." Arjuna took out a baggie and some Zig-Zag papers out of his a small leather pouch that hung from his belt and twisted up a joint.

"I don't either" said Beth, "and the war is such a bummer."

"Yeah," I said, "three guys I knew were killed there in January."

Beth looked at me. "That's fucked."

"Yeah, I'm hip to that!"

Arjuna lit the joint, took a hit and passed it to Marius." I'll tell you what scares me. George Wallace."

"Yeah, that dude is scary, all right." Marius hit on the j. "He sure don't like us 'colored' folks."

"He's going to be in town tomorrow. Big rally at the Common," said Arjuna.

"Yeah?" Marius handed off the joint to me. I took a hit and handed it off to Beth.

"Do you think he's got a chance of winning?" Beth sounded concerned.

"More than a chance," said Arjuna.

Beth seemed concerned. "You think so?"

"Fucking-A. He'll get the hate vote. There's a lot of hate in this country."

"Oh, I don't know about that," said peace-and-love Beth, passing the joint to Debbie.

"C'mon, Beth!" said Marius, "Get real. Do you think Vietnam is the result of peace and love? He damn sure wouldn't end the war."

I spoke up. "Hey, my parents would vote for him. My mother told me that. And they're not from the south, they live in Pennsylvania. And if they feel that way, there's an awful lot of others who feel the same."

"Yeah?" Deb passed the joint to Beth.

"For sure."

"Yeah, and you can kiss the civil rights stuff good-bye." said Marius as he hit on the joint Beth passed to him.

Beth lit a stick of incense and waved it slowly back and forth. We were coming on to the acid and watched the glowing ember leaving orange neon trails in the air. "What do you think'll happen?" she asked.

CHEMICALLY ENHANCED LUNACY

Paranoia was starting to rev, like a turbine slowly turning, at first an almost imperceptible rumble, but it was there, building.

"He's a fucking Alabama redneck. Anything could happen."

"Well, he's got no use for blacks, and less for freaks. That's for damn sure."

"What'll you think he'll do?"

"Concentration camps."

"What?!"

The turbine was turning faster, the rumble was becoming a roar.

"Yeah, concentration camps. The government has 'em already built. They'll just round up all the freaks and put 'em in concentration camps."

"Holy fuck!"

"Oh, c'mon, man. That's bullshit!" said Paul.

"You think so? Look what they did to the Japanese in World War II. Besides, Wallace is from the South. Fucking Alabama. They don't give a shit down there." Arjuna's eyes moved around the circle of people as he spoke. "Hell, it's no big deal for them to lynch people. Look at what happened to those civil rights workers in Mississippi, the fucking KKK just shot 'em and buried 'em in a fucking mud bank."

That was fact. It had happened only four years earlier.

"A lot of people see longhairs as pure trash, something to be gotten rid of. They'll just kill us off like Hitler did the Jews."

"You mean gas chambers–?"

"I doubt that," said Arjuna, "they'll probably let the Army use freaks for target practice. Or the National Guard."

"Holy shit!"

The roar of the turbine was becoming a whine, rising in pitch and intensity.

"Yeah. Dig it." said Marius, "If Wallace wins, we're fucked."

"But, do you think he'll really win?" said Debbie.

Arjuna lit another joint. "Most people want the war to go on –"

"And most people don't like freaks. They sure wouldn't miss any of us," agreed Marius.

"Shit, that's scary."

"Fucking-A."

"How many people do you think will really vote for him?" asked Beth.

Marius looked at her. "How many straight people do you know who hate 'niggers and hippies'?"

Silence. Far too many people fell into that category.

"What'll we do?"

"If he gets elected, it's our asses."

"If he's dead he can't be elected," said Arjuna.

"But what can we do? We can't just sit here and let all this shit happen!" said Beth.

Arjuna responded, "We gotta waste his ignorant redneck ass."

"But…it's wrong to kill," said Beth.

"Not if someone's gonna kill you."

"I don't know –"

"Look, would it have been wrong for someone to kill Hitler? I mean, what if some Jews would have gotten together before all that shit happened and offed[2] him. Would that have been wrong?"

"Well no –"

"Then what's the problem? Let's kill the motherfucker. It's the only way we can save ourselves."

We all looked at each other. There was silent agreement. We were convinced, while ripped to the tits on LSD, we were following a correct and reasonable course of action. We were going to alter American political history and save ourselves from certain extermination. Yes, we were

---

[2] To "off" is to kill in the left wing vernacular of the day.

going on a mission to kill George Wallace, Governor of Alabama and candidate for the Presidency of the United States. What could possibly go wrong with this plan?

The turbine was shrieking now. We were beyond logic. The paranoia was now tangible, cold clammy fingers of fear reaching into us and chilling our souls.

The absurdity of our decision never occurred to us. Here we were, a bunch of tripped out freaks, stoned on our asses in the middle of the night, in the clutches of drug-induced paranoia bordering on psychosis, and we had just made the momentous decision to alter the course of American political history by wasting George Wallace at the suggestion of someone who was most likely a true schizophrenic even when he *wasn't* stoned.

It seems so improbable now.[3] However, it was not *all* madness. It was 1968. In America, political assassination and murder was becoming a common method to be used by the desperate for preventing political and/or social change. In the last four months alone we had seen the assassinations of Martin Luther King and Robert Kennedy. If the forces seeming to oppose us were so desperate, should we not be equally desperate?

We certainly didn't hate George Wallace. We just wanted the motherfucker dead because his presidency would be an existential threat. George Wallace was going to be the next president of the United States and turn the country into a police state. It was our duty to kill this man. Yes, by God! We were going to ***save America!***

A ROLLING CLUSTERFUCK

There was a logistical problem, however.

"Who's got a gun?" asked Arjuna.

We looked at each other. Nobody had a gun. We were peace freaks. What the hell did we need a gun for?

After a moment of silence, Debbie piped up, "Hey, I know a dude in Cambridge that deals smack. He's got one."

"Oh yeah? Think he'll let us borrow it?"

"Let's go ask 'im!"

---

[3] I wrote that several decades ago. Now, in 2019, America has a president who is an openly racist and intolerant, a misogynistic sexual predator, a completely amoral piece of shit. Nothing is improbable.

What a fine bunch of conspirators we were. Not a one of us had even fired a handgun. Someone, I don't know who, had a car. I don't know how the hell any one of us could drive, but someone did. We piled into the car and headed out in the middle of the night to secure a weapon with which to murder the visiting Governor of Alabama.

We drove down Huntington Avenue, took a left onto Massachusetts Avenue and crossed the Charles River into Cambridge, the lights making liquid patterns as they passed through my field of vision. Looking out the rear window of the car I observed Massachusetts Avenue moving, swelling up behind us in a slow molasses-like undulation that formed a rooster tail behind us.

Debbie went up to the dealer's apartment in Cambridge to ask him for his piece. The rest of us stayed in the car. Looking back over more than fifty years that have passed since that time, I can imagine the conversation she might have had with, the dealer.

"Hi, Debbie, uh, howya doin'? It's 3 a m., y'know."

"Yeah, I know. Say, can we borrow your gun?"

"Well, I don't know. What do you need it for?"

"We're going to shoot George Wallace tomorrow on the Boston Common."

"Hey, shit, no problem. Just remember to bring it back when you're finished. And don't use up all my bullets. OK?"

"Oh wow, man, thanks a lot."

"Hey no sweat. Glad to help. Any time you wanna assassinate someone, just lemme know."

"Yeah. See ya later. Peace."

The dealer, wisely, did not let her have his gun. I remember the single-minded purpose we had in our murderous conspiracy: we had to find a gun to kill George Wallace.

Determined to carry out our task, we pestered everyone we know who might have a gun or might know someone who had a gun. Come sunup, we were still looking for a gun. The rally was to start at eleven o'clock in the morning. At five after eleven, we decided to abandon our search for a weapon and go to the Common. If America was going to be saved that day, someone else was going to have to do it. We couldn't find a gun.

The only parking space we could find was on Charles Street, a couple blocks away. We walked to the Common. It was incredible. I had never in my life seen more cops in one place at one time. There was an entire wall of battle-clad tac squad cops with helmets, goggles and riot shields, truncheons at the ready, their faces grim humorless visages, just waiting for someone to fuck up so they could break some skulls. They formed an impregnable barrier between Wallace's podium and the sea of people who came to hear him speak. Secret service men in gray suits, wearing sunglasses, Uzis concealed, surveyed the crowd from strategic positions. Only the most foolhardy – or, in our case, drug impaired – would attempt to breach such a barrier.

For a few moments, my psychedelic state transformed the line of police into centuries of Roman legionnaires, formed up in an impenetrable phalanx behind their shields. The sun glinted off helmets, swords and spears at the ready to repel barbarian hordes. Then they metamorphosed back into Boston cops, the swords and spears became night sticks and riot batons.

Any attempt on George Wallace's life that day would have been nothing less than sheerest suicidal folly, a task suited only to lunatics – a description that did not exclude us.

George Wallace was not assassinated that day, or even that year. In the light of the situation at hand – and the fact that the acid was wearing off – our determination to bring about the discorporation of George Wallace in order to prevent him from becoming an American Hitler evaporated.

In fact, the rally was ending as we arrived, we didn't even get to hear Wallace speak. The local antiwar community was well represented. Newspapers reported that Wallace received the most hostile reception of his campaign that day. One raggedy-ass hippie, features obscured by the huge ball of hair that sat on top of his shoulders, carried a sign that read, "Give Georgie some acid!" It was certainly good that never occurred to us, for unlike the firearm we lacked, LSD was something we had in abundance! There's no telling what kind of trouble we would have gotten into trying to expand Wallace's consciousness instead of extinguishing it! But then, the thought of George Wallace in 1968 ripped to the tits on LSD, assuming the podium and proclaiming the oneness of all creation and the brotherhood of all mankind while disrobing behind the line of cops is amusing!

Wallace's appearance in Boston was met with more protests against him than any other stop he made during his campaign. Good for Boston!

Nixon won the election. Vietnam remained a charnel house. Before the American involvement ended, fatalities would more than double.

Arjuna showed up at Shepherd Avenue about three months later, using yet another name, quite drunk, saying "beers is good for you." He said he was going to California to join the Hell's Angels. That was the last time I ever saw him.

WHAT KIND OF DOPE WAS ARTIE DOING?

George Wallace made his second and last bid for the presidency in 1972. I was glazing a window in the back room Boegershausen Hardware in San Francisco and listening to KGO when a news flash came on that a man named Arthur Bremer had shot George Wallace at a rally. I thought back to 1968 and wondered what kind of dope Artie was into.

Of the millions of people who heard about Artie, there were likely precious few who had a first-hand understanding of the thought process that brought him to his murderous course of action. I did because I had been in that exact place. Good thing we never found a gun!

Hubert Humphrey won the Democratic nomination. This brought no relief to disaffected American youth who saw Humphrey as the champion of the party with whose approval the police thugs beat people until blood ran in the streets of Chicago during the convention. "Dump the Hump" was the popular catch phrase. Dump him for what? Nixon was the Republican candidate. With Johnson not running again because of the war, the Democrats looked pretty weak. And Hubert Humphrey, well, he just wasn't impressive. It looked to me like Nixon was going to win. God, how depressing a thought that was.

CHAPTER 16

FALL & WINTER 1968-69

SANTA'S HIPPIE HELPERS

A guy walked up to me on Shepherd Avenue one day. "Hey, Gene, hey man, what's happenin'?"

I did not recognize him. I looked incredulously at this short-haired, clean shaven individual.

"Hey man, don't you recognize me? It's Danny!"

Hell, no, I didn't recognize him, he was a walking hairball that looked like a pirate the last time I saw him. "Danny, Jesus, I thought we'd never see you again! How'd you get outa jail?"

"Shit, the guy who owned the Mercedes was so glad to get it back he didn't press charges. They let me go scot fucking free!" He was grinning ear to ear.

Danny moved in to my pad. I was living there alone and could use someone to share the rent. Danny settled into the Shepherd Avenue head scene. I got a day job at the Mutual Home Club Plan in Brookline where I spent the day packing toys into boxes to be shipped to customers in various parts of the eastern United States. The Mutual Home Club Plan was an interesting environment.

I had found the job through an ad in the paper. It was a family business operated by three Jewish brothers who recruited housewives to have toy parties over the east. Hostesses would take orders from their guests. We would pack and ship them.

The people who worked there boxing up the orders were three middle-aged women, Kitty, Rosie, and Elaine, and an old[1] guy, Eddie. Another older guy, Joe did maintenance and handled receiving. I was the only freak working there until I brought Danny in. Then one day, Sol, oldest of the three brothers, came up to me and, because they were shorthanded, asked if I knew of any other people who needed jobs. Hell, that was easy! I went back to Shepherd Avenue at lunch time and recruited Danny, my redheaded friend, Lori, and a freak couple, Jeff and Joni. Jeff was quite tall and thin, no beard, and had brown hair parted in the middle that formed a ball on his shoulders. Joni was short with long dark brown hair that had a slight wave to it. I don't think I ever saw Joni without a smile.

The Mutual Home Club Plan in Brookline became the meeting place of two entirely different cultures. To the usual banter of the regular workers was added an FM radio tuned to WBCN and the patchouli aroma that followed Joni wherever she went. There were occasional clashes, such as when Eddie threw a fit after listening to Wilson Pickett scream the ending to *Hey Jude* for the third time in one day.

"Turn that goddamn screaming off! Jesus Christ! That's not music, it's nothing but noise!" I could see his point!

But things usually went pretty smoothly. Of course, we all went back to Shepherd Avenue for lunch and sometimes smoked some good reefer and were too stoned to return to work for the afternoon. But all in all, it was a very laid-back time. Ben gave me a bonus at Christmas being very appreciative of the employees I had brought in to the business when he needed them.

I became acquainted with a young woman by the name of Nancy Alfred who lived at 14 Shepherd Avenue with the newest tenants, George Harmon and his girlfriend, Heidi. Nancy and I became lovers and she moved into 1 Shepherd Avenue. Nancy was a very sweet girl slender, lovely skin, with long brown hair which she frequently wore in braids. She had beautiful brown eyes, eyes I could look into for hours. We did acid together and would make love while high. Although we were not wildly passionate together, we had a tender relationship.

Nancy was originally from southern California. Her parents were divorced. She was really close to her mom, and told me at length how

---

[1] Ha! He was probably thirty years younger than I am now!

groovy and hip her mother was. Her mother had a boyfriend and they had a cabin near Lake Tahoe.

"My Mom is so neat," she would say, and proceed to tell me about her mom's pot stash, clearly labeled "marijuana."

"Reverse psychology. My mom thinks that no one would ever believe it's really grass!"

She recounted to me how she had gotten pregnant when she lost her virginity. "My mom arranged an abortion for me. She said it was the same guy who performed abortions for [Walt Disney star] Annette Funicello."

I was falling for Nancy, but she wasn't really looking for a long term relationship. I suspected this, but I knew it for sure when we were sitting on the bed one evening, I reading a book, and Nancy writing a letter to a friend. I glanced out of the corner of my eye and saw her write "I'm living with a dear, sweet Virgo, but the situation is getting sticky." I knew at that moment that she wouldn't be with me for long. It hurt me for sure, but I didn't say anything. I wanted her to stay, I liked her a lot. I also knew enough about her to know that she would do what she wanted and there was no use trying to get her to do otherwise. Why should she? Why should anybody? I decided to take the situation as it was and just enjoy what we had.

She got a letter from her brother the first of December and he was going to be in Massachusetts for Christmas. She was excited about seeing him and pleased that they would spend Christmas together. I said good-bye to Nancy and made plans to go back to Smethport shortly before Christmas of '68, ready to turn on the world.

ACID IN THE ALLEGHENIES

About a week before Christmas I took a bus out of Boston. I had a pound of Mexican reefer and a hundred hits of acid. Committed to the cause and philosophy of the psychedelic age, I was an acid evangelist, an LSD soaked hippie tripster, out to turn on the world! Oh yes, peace and love, 60's style, were about to descend upon my sleepy home town nestled in the snow covered Allegheny Mountains.

A party happened at my friend Mike Quirk's grandfather's house. Mike was attending St. Bonaventure University in nearby Allegany, New York, and stayed at his grandfather's during breaks. The party was a rather spontaneous affair. We just called a few friends and classmates and the word spread in a flash!

By nine o'clock in the evening, there must have been eighteen or twenty people there. Wine, beer and whiskey flowed freely from a makeshift bar tended by my friend Mia's high school age brother and a friend of his. I was astounded to see pot was being smoked openly by the sons and daughters of the leading members of the community. Smethport was turning the corner!

The stereo was playing jazz (Mike was a jazz pianist and despised rock n' roll!). People dropped in to score reefer and acid from me. Caution was pretty much thrown to the wind.

The Griffiths lived next door to Mike's grandfather. They had several young daughters who were having a slumber that evening. Not wanting our wonderful revelry broken up by something as highly inconvenient as a drug bust, we were careful to keep the party confined to the house.

Mia had two friends with her who attended Gannon University, a Catholic men's school in Erie. One of them, Brad, would be her future husband. The other, Joe, was a friend of Brad's. Joe got shitfaced. About eleven o'clock we couldn't find him. A search of Elmer's house proved fruitless, so we started looking outside, very quietly. Joe, who was too drunk to stand, was found roving found about on his hands and knees in the snow. We brought him back inside where he passed out peacefully.

The party continued. Most of the people left by about one in the morning, only Mike, Jack Case, Barry Wilson and I were left. I turned them on to their first hit of acid.

There was much myth, misinformation and lore about LSD. Reports said you could "...hear the grass grow...see the color of sounds..." and so on. There were also (incorrect) rumors that it would cause chromosome damage. Quirk was a smart-ass and, as everyone was getting off, said "Hey Case, can you feel your chromosomes change?"

We were peacefully buzzed from the acid when some late arrivals came in the door, Ted Hyde, Paul Maynard and Eddie Henderson. Ted and Paul were on leave from the Marines. Eddie was a student at Edinboro University. They were smashed to the gills. We were gathered in the living room gathered around the stereo. Amazingly enough, we were still able to converse at that point.

The conversation, such as it was, got around to politics and the war. This was a sensitive area. I had the feeling there might be a bit of friction here, as Jack and Mike were campus organizers for the SDS (Students for a Democratic Society). Mike was a born instigator. He was also one of the most intellectually gifted people on the planet, carrying simultaneous majors in mathematics, chemistry and philosophy. Mike did not have a lot of common sense, however. He goaded the two Marines with direct criticism of the Vietnam situation. Jack Case, who had just dropped out of the seminary, was grooving to some jazz, wearing headphones. Taking them off, he said "Don't you think the war in Vietnam is a waste? They're making you guys die for nothing."

Paul was sitting near Jack with a can of beer in his hand. He was a highly decorated two-tour Marine with three purple hearts, two of them earned on consecutive days and was having difficulty staying upright. "Oh yeah? Y'wanna go outside and throw a few?"

Eddie was equally drunk. "If my country called me…I'd be proud to go."

Ted was sitting on a couch with the young woman in his lap. "I've seen too many good men die."

"The military doesn't care about you guys." Said Mike.

I interjected, "Look at Khe Sanh. Buddy was killed there and so were a lot of other guys. And now it's been abandoned. What is that?"

Ted, a veteran who lost most of his hearing at Khe Sanh, answered, "Gener, you don't understand the kind of war that's being fought over there." That was true, but not in the sense Ted intended.

"If my country called me…I'd be proud to go, "said Eddie.

Paul commented, "…y'wanna go outside and throw a few?"

About that time, Jack Case looked straight at Paul and said, "Typical fucking Marine."

I was sure we were going to be wearing our guts for a necktie. Ted, Paul and Eddie eventually left without any mayhem occurring.

About 3 a.m. Mike's grandfather, Elmer, in his 70s, appeared. "What are you boys doing here?"

I didn't have any good answers, so I didn't give him one. He tried Mike. Mike also gave him a blank stare. Barry was too tripped out to give a shit and giggled when the same question was put to him. He didn't bother asking Jack. Elmer wandered about not knowing what to make of our wasted condition, then returned to bed. We referred to Mike's grandfather after this as "the walking Elmer."

The next morning I got a call from Dave Lamborn. He had gone to the post office in the morning. Mr. Griffith, father of the girls who were having the slumber party next door to Mike's grandfather's house was a postal clerk.

"Did you hear about the pot party at Quirk's last night?" he asked Dave directly. Dave had been at the party, leaving just before we dropped the acid.

"Pot party? No. Don't know a thing about it."

"Well, my girls saw a guy crawling around on his hands and knees outside. He must have been high on pot to be acting like that."

Fucking great. The one guy that was falling down shitfaced drunk was spotted and mislabeled as being high on pot. After the phone call I hid my stash in a grove of trees near the house.

After the New Year Barry drove me back to Boston, Jack came with us. We went to the Tea Party and saw B.B. King. A great way to start the new year!

WE ALL LIVE IN A YELLOW SUBMARINE

After the holidays I had a job waiting for me at New England News as a shipping clerk. I got this job through Ben, one of the brothers from the Mutual Home Club Plan because he was impressed with the way I brought in my friends to work there when they were short on packers.

Nancy moved on in January and Lori Mallon moved back into 1 Shepherd Avenue. She introduced me to Jerry Bruner. He was a freak for sure, but didn't have long hair because he was a medic in the Army Reserves. My mental picture of Jerry is of a guy about six feet tall, and medium build. His face was round, his hair dark and would have formed ringlets had he let it grow much longer. He had a bushy mustache that drooped and bushy sideburns framed his face. Jerry always had sunglasses on, and was usually smiling (think of Elliot Gould in M.A.S.H.). We both enjoyed smoking good dope and tripping on acid.

Jerry and I set out on one of our psychedelic adventures one Friday night by scoring some acid on Beacon Hill. We each dropping a couple of tabs (blue flats) and walked to Fenway Park. By the time we got there, we were getting acid rushes up the spine.[2] We got on the MBTA and started back to Beacon Hill. The ride was most amazing that evening as we came on to the acid quickly once on the train and started peaking almost immediately. The train seemed to be traveling on amorphous undulating tracks that floated in space, assuming absurd patterns, even corkscrewing like, a theme park roller coaster. It was an interesting ride!

---

[2] There are more details about the physical and psychological/psychic effects of LSD in Chapter 33

We were stoned to the point of being telepathic and sat there goofing on the whole thing together. We managed to get off the train at Park Station. Emerging from the underground, we walked around until we saw Beacon Hill Theater was showing "Yellow Submarine." Hey, the Beatles cartoon flick! *Yes! Let's do it!* We got in line. A remarkable thing happened, I found myself following three different conversations going on around us as well as talking to Jerry.

By the time I got to the ticket booth, I was stoned to the point of hardly knowing where I was. What's more, the girl in the booth was wearing a lot of makeup and I started hallucinating on it. She was a very attractive young woman with an exquisitely sculptured face and high cheekbones. Her eye makeup and rouge became multi-hued blotches that first grew, then broke up into tiny geometric shapes that sparkled like tiny jewels, then turned vile, rendering her face into a hideous countenance of psychedelic/schizophrenic nastiness. I was transfixed. She was talking, but I couldn't respond, my concentration was totally absorbed by the fantastic transfiguration occurring in front of my eyes.

"Gene. Gene. Hey man..."

I became vaguely aware of my name being called.

"C'mon man, get your wallet out and pay the lady."

It was Jerry, standing to my left trying to break through my psychedelically one-pointed concentration on the vision I was experiencing.

"Hey, c'mon man. You're holdin' up the line..."

I was able, with Jerry's coaching, to get my wallet out and purchase the tickets. We ventured into the darkness of the theater and experienced "Yellow Submarine" while thoroughly psychedelicized. Ah, yes, it was a groove indeed!

Jerry and I shared several psychedelic adventures. With our common interest in mind altering substances... we started doing some small time casual dealing in acid, grass, and hashish.

A few days after Nancy moved out, I was awakened by someone banging on my door in the middle of the night. It was a Western Union guy with a telegram for Nancy. I gave him her new address and went back to bed. About midmorning there was a door knock. It was Nancy. She looked terrible.

"Gene," she asked, "can you please get me high? I really need it."

"Sure, c'mon in." We sat in the kitchen and smoked a joint.

Tears started rolling down her cheeks. "Gene, the most terrible thing happened. My mom killed herself!" She broke down in tears. I held her tightly and felt the sobs wracking her body. After a bit she sat up and looked at me with those beautiful, even when tear-filled, brown eyes. "She took pills. And here my brother and I left her alone at Christmas!" She collapsed again in tears. I just held her a let her cry. I had no idea what else to do. My heart ached for this poor woman.

I remember Nancy saying, "The thing that really get me is that she's going to have to go through this all over again in another life," referring to karma incurred by suicide. She stayed for about an hour. She thanked me for getting her high and left. I never saw her again after that. She was a sweet gentle soul. I can still see her beautiful, liquid brown eyes.

CHAPTER 17

THE HEROIN PLAGUE

FOLLEN STREET

I moved out of Shepherd Avenue because the building had been sold. Lori had moved on. Jerry and I rented an apartment on Follen Street in the Back Bay section.

Follen Street dead ended off St. Botolph Street. It was a run-down neighborhood and the rents were cheap. The ethnic makeup of the area was mixed with just about equal populations of black, Hispanic, and freaks, and some small enclaves of Gypsies here and there. Oh, and *lots* of smack heads.[1]

Follen Street was lined with three and four story flat roofed brick apartment buildings with bay windows facing the street. Ours was 22 Follen St., No. 4, rented from the Waltham Realty Company on St. Botolph Street, on the top floor of a four unit building on the right hand side of the street right next to the railroad track and chain link fence. The high-speed express between Boston and New York City thundered past at 6:30 every morning. A chain-link enclosed walkway ran over the tracks connecting Follen Street with Carleton Street in the Columbus Avenue section.

---

[1] Junkies

I remember the realty company because the office manager was evidently a dominatrix and wore thigh-high black leather boots with stiletto heels, a black leather mini-skirt and fishnets to work.

An alley ran between the apartment buildings on the left hand side of the street about halfway down where trash accumulated. The hard drug orientation of the neighborhood was evidenced from the "speedball" graffiti spray painted graffiti in three foot high letters over a row of trash cans.

While Follen Street was a slummy neighborhood, the Columbus Avenue section across the tracks was the ghetto. It reeked of poverty, human degradation and depravity. Black men in foppish attire commanded their stables of prostitutes from their ostentatiously appointed Lincolns and Cadillacs. The young black women wore miniskirts revealing shapely legs, and spike heeled shoes, purses slung on their shoulders and used as a prop serving to further the sexual swagger of their shapely derrieres as they paced on their corners. Bewigged and strung with gaudy costume jewelry, they wore dark red lipstick which contrasted pleasantly with their dark complexions, rouge on the cheeks and vile hues of metallic blue, green and lavender eye make-up. All male passersby were propositioned.

"Hey, Honey, y'all wanna party? Wanna have some fun?"

For all my alleged "hipness," I was still at this point a young man of rather limited sexual experience, and was quite embarrassed by the whore's blatant sexual come-on. I was actually embarrassed! I would walk past staring straight ahead, saying nothing.

"Whatsamatter white boy, you all 'fraid of me? You don't wanna talk to me?" Her voice carried mild irritation.

I had no comeback. Hell, I just wasn't used to having a woman proposition me, I had only lost my virginity a year earlier. I ignored her and kept on walking, pretending not to hear.

"Oh, I see, you got that long hair. Must be you don't like womens."

Cars would park along the street, visited by a constant stream of people who would go to the driver's window and money would be exchanged for a small glassine envelope.

The Columbus Avenue area was rife with violence borne of poverty and crime. Prostitutes trying to work independently or on the wrong corner would have their faces slashed by rival pimps or other prostitutes. Drug-related shootings and stabbings were routine.

It was entirely a heroin culture. On Columbus Avenue there was a small pharmacy where I used to purchase items from time to time. On one of the counters was a large bowl full of "binkies," baby pacifiers with a big rubber bulb. These were not purchased by mothers who need them for their children, but by heroin addicts who used them for their outfits, the home made syringe preferred by hardcore dope shooters.

The preferred tool of injection was an outfit made from a binky and either the barrel of a disposable syringe or a plastic eyedropper. The syringe or eyedropper would be cut off so it was about an inch and a half long. The cut end would then be heated in a flame until it softened, then mashed down on a cool surface so a flange formed on the end. The binky was then slipped over the flange and a disposable hypodermic point fitted on the end. In the case of an eyedropper, a piece of matchbook cover was often used as a shim for a tight fit.

The reason for the use of this type of outfit was because of the injection technique – the ritual – preferred and performed by junkies.

SMACK CITY

The winter of 1968-69 saw the Boston head scene awash in heroin. A death trip, it spread like a plague. From my vantage point as a non-junkie in the middle of all this, it seemed that every groovy acid head who was tripping out on peace, love, and LSD during the summer of 1968 was nodding out on smack in the winter to keep warm. And, yes, it was cold that winter.

Scoring junk (heroin) was as easy as breathing air. There was deadly, 100% pure China White, compliments of the CIA and U.S. military involvement in Vietnam,[2] morphine syrettes meant for combat medic use were diverted from military supplies, morphine tablets pilfered from hospital and pharmaceutical supplies, Mexican brown skag,[3] and the usual Mafia powder.

---

[2] From *The Politics of Heroin in Southeast Asia: CIA Complicity in the global drug trade*, Alfred W. McCoy, p,21. ."American diplomats and secret agents have been involved in the narcotics traffic at three levels: (1) coincidental complicity by allying with groups actively engaged in the drug traffic; (2) abetting the traffic by covering up for known heroin traffickers and condoning their involvement; (3) and active engagement in the transport of opium and heroin. It is ironic, to say the least, that America's heroin plague is of its own making." See also from *The Agency Of Fear: Opiates and Political Power in America*, Edward Jay Epstein, p. 149."While attempting to suppress narcotics, the federal government had inadvertently become a major supplier of narcotics. When the Nixon administration first assumed office, In 1969, It will be recalled, it was discovered that agents in the New York office of what was then the federal Bureau of Narcotics had become the leading dealers in heroin in the United States and were protecting the operations of illicit dealers (who in turn were providing them with their sacrificial "arrests"). Most of these agent-dealers were subsequently indicted, fired, or relocated."
[3] heroin

It was a bad time for longhairs in Boston. The powers that be in Boston had decided there was to be an all out assault on the burgeoning head culture. Since the middle of the summer, longhairs had been the particular target of police patrolling the Boston Common.

Toward the end of the summer the freewheeling drug market at the corner of Charles and Beacon streets was shut down. There were no arrests. As I stated before, there was a law in Massachusetts at the time that made it a crime to "be in the presence of narcotics." If they arrested anyone for dope they would have had to arrest everyone on the Common. Police on foot, on motorcycles, in squad cars and on horses simply descended on that corner of the common and forced them out. From then on the cops worked over any longhair caught lurking on the Common, tossing them into a waiting paddy wagon and taken to the Charles Street jail. The judge would then give the battered beatnik a choice: spend more time in jail or leave town. It was quite an effective hippie-control measure and accounted for the departure of quite a few freaks from the Boston area.

Any longhair who might pause to talk to someone on Beacon or Charles Streets adjacent to the Common would be admonished by a blue and white TAC Squad[4] cruiser to "move it," or even receive some lumps at the discretion of the officers in the cruiser. This happened to me several times.

The overwhelming majority of cops in Boston were big and beefy, tough motherfuckers who just loved beating the shit out of people. If people weren't available, freaks would do nicely! After all, who would complain about a few lumps and bruises on some un-American-commie hippie- freelove- clap- carrying- peacenik- longhair- faggot- ass- atheist-dopers?

In those days, before the formation of the Drug Enforcement Agency by President Nixon, the Federal Bureau of Narcotics handled federal drug law enforcement. There were two feds who made their contribution to the anti-hippie pogrom by grabbing freaks at random off the streets and taking them to the John F. Kennedy Federal Building for "interrogation." A couple hours later, the unfortunate victims were tossed back out on the street with assorted lacerations and lumps, and bruises. These were agents Mahoney and O'Brien. They were well known throughout the hip underground which was a source of surprisingly accurate poop as to what was up with the cops.

---

[4] Tactical Squad

The BPD was grabbing longhairs off the streets for no reason. One fellow I know, Ollie, was a harmless peace freak whose daily costume was clerical, closely resembling the Pope's getup with the short cape. The cops grabbed im up and took him to the Charles Street jail. The official story was that Ollie hanged himself there. Ollie was not a suicidal person. We were all convinced the fucking cops murdered him in retaliation for his wearing of (Catholic) clerical vestments.

THE SHIT ROLLS DOWNHILL

A young narcotics agent, Agent O'Brien, had been working undercover the previous summer. He had successfully infiltrated the Boston drug underground and had been making buys all through the summer and fall of '68, setting up dealers for a massive sweep in the spring.

He had also infiltrated the Devil's Disciples' drug dealing infrastructure. His cover was blown and they beat the snot out of him, nearly killing him. After he got out of the hospital, he and Mahoney started busting everyone he had ever met in the Boston drug scene.

My gig at New England news was easy and low pressure. I could do it stoned, and I did. It was close enough to walk to work. I would smoke a joint on the way to work, smoke a joint on my morning break, then another at noon, another on my afternoon break, then one on the way home. Unfortunately, it went belly-up, so Jerry and I got into some small-time dealing. Initially, we were moving pounds of grass, ounces of hashish and 100 hit quantities of acid, lightweight stuff, goodtime dope.

MARIJUANA BY MAIL

My friend Mike Quirk was attending St. Bonaventure University in Allegany, New York. He drove to Boston one weekend in January, 1970 and scored a key of grass and fifty hits of acid from me. We developed a system where Mike would mail envelopes full of cash to me, I would score the dope and ship it to him. This was waaaaay before the USPS monitored for weed. All you had to do was wrap it securely, package it well, and send it parcel post. I shipped an order a month that went to Room 212, Falconio Hall, at St. Bonaventure!

NEEDLE FREAKZ

Jerry hooked up with Dawn, a pleasant and attractive smack shooter. I knew that Jerry had done some heroin himself from time to time.

Lori told me that she and Jerry sometimes chipped[5] together. With Dawn around, he started using on a regular basis. It wasn't very long before Jerry got heavily involved in using and dealing heroin. This brought more junkies and junkie karma into our orbit.

I was still dealing grass and acid, but Jerry was moving a lot of smack, two bundles[6] – fifty ten dollar bags – a day. He and Dawn were putting most of the profits into their arms. The heroin trade now dominated what was going on at our Follen Street pad.

I had the opportunity to try heroin many times. Rebecca, one of Dawn's smack head friends was always trying to turn me on to it. "C'mon, Gene! Do a bag. You'll love this shit. C'mon."

No fucking way. While marijuana was a substance whose bad effects were chiefly limited to the amount of legal trouble it could cause for you and LSD did have certain psychological risks, heroin was death. And it wasn't just the heroin, it was the preferred method of administration: injection directly into a vein.

Whereas pot and acid were social drugs, shared among users, injectable drugs such as heroin and methedrine–there was very little cocaine in circulation then–were solitary in nature. Junkies had to prepare their drug for injection. The first step in this ritual was locating a suitable vein for injections I saw people shooting up many times, and not once did I ever see a skin pop (muscle injection). To all of the users I knew, this was a waste of good junk. The way to go was to "hit a vein," inject it directly into a vein, to mainline, getting the maximum effect. To someone who was getting sick,[7] it was also the quickest way to calm their monkey[8] down.

Depending on how long a person had been using, locating a vein could be difficult. Arms were usually the preferred area, starting near the elbow and working down the forearm. The more a person used, the more they developed calluses or "tracks" on the areas where they injected. I saw some hard-core users with callused tracks looking like snakes on their forearms. Wrists and the back of the hand were also injection sites. Legs could be used too. The vein was made to stand out by "tying off" with an old necktie or something similar.

---

[5] To "chip" or to "have a chippie" was to use heroin in a regularly but infrequently enough to preclude getting a habit.
[6] A "bundle" was twenty-five small glassine envelopes, "bags" in junkie vernacular, about an inch square bound with a rubber band. They sold for a dime ($10) each.
[7] "Getting sick" means starting withdrawal
[8] Referring to the "monkey on the back," a habit.

Street dope was usually stepped on[9] with quinine and rarely more than 10% junk.[10] Emptying the contents of the glassine envelope emptied into a "cooker," usually a tablespoon, but frequently a top to a quart sized Coca-Cola bottle, a small piece of cotton was placed in the cooker and heated until the powder dissolved. It was then drawn into the outfit through the cotton, which filtered out impurities.

Cottons were saved for the inevitable eventuality that the user be out of junk and out of money to buy more junk. The cottons would then be boiled in a spoon in an effort to extract enough residual junk from them to stage off getting sick.

Once the outfit was filled with the heroin solution, the spike was inserted into the vein and pressure put on the rubber bulb and the mixture squeezed into the person's bloodstream.

I began to see that there was more to this process of injection than merely getting the drug in to the bloodstream. After the outfit was empty, pressure was let off the bulb, allowing it to fill with blood. It was then forced back onto the vein with pressure on the bulb. Junkies called this "booting." I observed people repeating this process over and over again. The needle was an addiction as strong as the drug for some people, whom we called "needle freaks." It seemed that they were having sex with themselves via the needle, fucking themselves with a spike, sort of an esoteric form of masturbation. Jeff (of Jeff and Joni) was a needle freak.

Instead of internet memes we had underground newspapers. One of them printed this "Richard Nixon Memorial Toilet" page encouraging people to decorate toilets with it! Mock-up photo.

"I dig the shit out of shooting!" he told me, "hell, I'll even shoot up plain water!" I found it to be plain goddamned creepy. More than fifty years after the fact, I still feel the same. I wonder how many of the

---

[9] "stepped on" = cut, diluted
[10] "Junk" = heroin

needle freaks I met are still around to look back over fifty years. None I'd wager.

There was a certain macho attitude among smack shooters about how they performed the injection ritual. Rebecca was nineteen, blonde, petite, and good looking when she was cleaned up.

"Yeah, I'm hahd," she would say in her Boston accent.

Propping her right foot on a window sill, she would rest her right elbow on her knee and tighten a scarf around her arm with her teeth. If the vein didn't show itself immediately, she would tap the area with two fingers of her left hand which was holding the outfit – she was a lefty – until they popped out. She would then inject herself, boot several times, then sit in a chair leaning against the wall, nodding for hours. This was not what I considered a recreational type of drug. I wanted nothing to do with shooting dope. I think that is partly due to Doc Hockenberry and the big needle that scared the crap out of me when I was four. Thank you, Doc!

There was another unsavory aspect attached to the use of heroin. I am not sure if this was an effect of the heroin, the quinine that it was usually cut with, or both. Shortly after shooting up, the user would be compelled to empty the contents of their stomach.

"Hurry up in there, I gotta blow lunch!" was frequently heard shouted from the hallway outside the bathroom as someone else was getting sick in the "Richard Nixon Memorial Toilet," (declared to be such by a page from a local underground paper taped to the bottom of the lid!) Then the hall window would open and the hapless heroin user would ralph out the window. From the pedestrian walkway over the railroad tracks leading to Carleton Street, a huge puke stain could be seen originating from the hallway window of our fourth floor apartment.

Jerry had a high school buddy of his, Frank, whom we referred to as "Frank the Crook." Frank was scary. He had this demented gleam in his eye, the kind that told you he would undoubtedly murder someone before he met his own misguided end. This was borne out by the fact that he always carried a revolver with him and liked to wave it around while ranting about how people shouldn't fuck with him. Frank wasn't a hippie, didn't have long hair and didn't use drugs. He was simply a small tie crook and genuine goddamned psycho.

FLASHING BACK– COMING OF AGE IN THE AMERICAN 1960s

COZMIC DAVE

Cosmic Dave was the epitome of the hippie dude: about 5'10', slender, long wavy dark hair parted in the center falling past his shoulders, a thin handlebar mustache and sunglasses. He maintained a houseboat in Sausalito, California. Making transcontinental runs – I don't know how he smuggled the dope – he always had kilos of excellent weed. He also had a taste for fixing heroin. He stayed with us for a while, then rented a pad on Beacon Hill that was his base of operations when he was in Boston.

I came in one afternoon from doing some acid dealing and Jerry handed me a joint.

"Check out this weed, man."

I lit the number and took a good hit and held it in. It had that unmistakable flavor of fine Mexican weed, specifically Acapulco Gold, and a good head rush to go with it. Yes, this was some fine reefer.

"Good shit. Where'd you get it?"

"Frank and me went over to Cozmic Dave's. Dave wasn't there and I turned to leave. Frank says 'Wait a minute,' and took a credit card out of his wallet and opened the door to David's apartment. He went in and ripped this shit off. Two kilos of it. Nice, huh?" Jerry's smile turned up the ends of his bushy, drooping mustache.

Shit! I knew that heroin was a drug that was not conducive to boosting one's intelligence, but I didn't realize Jerry was this fucking low. Ripping off another dealer's stash was the pits.

Two days later Cozmic Dave stopped by. There was always a bowl with cleaned weed in it in on the kitchen table. Anyone could roll a joint anytime they wanted to. Cozmic Dave twisted himself up a doobie, and, lighting it, took a hit. When he tasted the weed, his eyebrows knit and he held the joint in front of him, staring at it. I am certain he knew that was his weed. This was *not* good.

The Boston scene had become a nightmare of depravity and violence. The bad drug karma was spreading. Rebecca's sister, Jennifer, was living with Peter, a meth dealer, on Beacon Hill. He usually had a pound or so in his apartment. One day Jennifer showed up at our place speeding her brains out.

"Oh shit, we got ripped off big time! They kicked the fucking door down and came in with badges and guns!

Jacked up on meth, Jennifer babbled a steady stream. I couldn't figure why she didn't pass out because she never seemed to stop to take a breath!

"They were fucking cops, man! They threw us up against the wall. One put his fucking gun in my ear. I heard him cock it. I thought that was the last thing I was ever going to hear! I figured he was going to blow my fucking brains out. I pissed my fucking pants! I've never been so fucking scared in my life! Oh, Christ, Peter had a half a pound of speed, they took it and all our money, eight-thousand dollars!

Cops? Maybe. Narks on the take were nothing new. Likely as not they were junkies ripping off dealers to support their habits.

The kids from the suburbs coming into Boston to score dope were victims of junkie hustlers.

"Yeah, I saw these two kids from Newton on Charles Street," said the ratty looking hippie who bought some junk and was fixing in the kitchen. "They told me they wanted to score a key. I told them I knew a dealer, but he was paranoid so they would have to give me the money and wait for me in the lobby of his apartment building. So I took the cash and went up to the roof, crossed over to the next roof and took the stairs back to the street. They're probably still waiting!"

COCAINE BLUES

Jerry had certain connections at Suffolk Downs, having worked there on and off for a number of years. He and several of the people at the Follen Street pad took jobs as trainers at Suffolk Downs. After the horses had run, they needed to be walked for a while to keep their muscles from stiffening up. People who did this were called "trainers." It was not a highly skilled position, according to Jerry.

Jerry claimed to know a lot about the New England horse racing scene from his experience there.

"It's all fixed," he explained to me one afternoon as we smoked a joint. "The whole thing is mob run. It's all figured out down to the odds and the last dollar paid at the betting window. You see, the jockeys can't bet. That's the law. But they give me their money to me to place bets for them. I would place my money on the same horses because they knew who was going to win. It's a mob run system."

I was completely alien to this type of thing, not knowing anything horse racing or mutuel betting.

"It's a good place to make dope connections, too," he continued. "The jockeys are all these little Puerto Rican and Cuban guys. They gotta keep their weight down y'know or they can't ride. Now, a lot of 'em do speed. Some have connections for cocaine."

Cocaine was, in the late 1960s, not yet a plentiful narcotic and considered exotic. It was impossibly expensive. Jerry came in one day from Suffolk Downs.

"Gene, I got great news. I set up a coke buy with this Cuban jockey, Luis. Oh man, this is fuckin' great!" He was excited.

We took the MBTA to Suffolk Downs the following Monday to do the deal. Now, going to the track on a Monday is a real experience. Only the hard core racing fans went to the track Mondays. They are totally involved in the dynamics of gambling. It was something to watch them go at it.

If Jerry ever made money on the horses, it certainly was from tips and not his own betting instincts. I had watched him drop hundreds of dollars at the betting window.

"C'mon. It's time to meet Luis." I followed Jerry to an area near the stables where we were to meet our connection. "He'll be here in a minute. Wait'll you meet him, he's a groovy guy and he's a *good* coke connection."

About that time I saw two big uniformed police officers dwarfing a little Cuban guy in racing silks. The Cuban guy looked at Jerry as they approached.

"Oh shit!" said Jerry under his breath, "C'mon, let's get the fuck outa here."

Luis was busted. The cops had raided his apartment that morning and found the coke. They grabbed him after his race. There went our coke connection. We split.

DIRTY DEALS DONE CHEAP

Rip-offs were becoming the rule in the dealing scene. Grass was scarce, the previous year's harvest was nearly gone. The annual grass drought had set in. Exorbitant prices were being commanded for kilos of mediocre weed.

There were a couple of shifty characters, Ritchie and Chuck, who come to our pad. They were a pair of gat junkie lovers who had just done a short stretch and had been out of the joint long enough to get strung out again. They claimed to have a connection for some good reefer, but said it had to be serious weight,[11] at least a ten kilo deal, their connection wouldn't move anything any smaller. We rounded up the money to make the buy. We wouldn't be making much on the deal, just a kilo for ourselves. They were late for the deal and didn't have a phone of their own. A chick named Diane was taking their calls. I called her from a pay phone.

"Diane, this is Gene. Jerry and I are supposed to do a thing this afternoon with Ritchie and Chuck. They're late. You seen 'em?"

"Gene! I overheard them talking. Those dudes are setting you up for a burn. Watch it!"

I had a feeling about this from the start. I told Jerry.

"I'll take care of it."

Ritchie and Chuck were late and I had a deal for several hundred hits of acid to do so I left. When I returned several hours later only Jerry and Dawn were there.

"What happened?" I asked.

"I gave 'em to the 'sidewalk bikers,'" Jerry smiled.

"What'd they do with 'em?"

"Fucked if I know."

The "sidewalk bikers" were a street punks we knew who hustled gays and liked to do drugs. They dressed in black leather jackets and engineer boots and carried Filipino butterfly knives that they were always playing with. They looked the part of bikers but had no scooters. Jerry knew them and occasionally hired them for errands. Their commission was usually an ounce of grass or a couple grams of hash. It was cheap labor. They had been marginally involved in the deal we were setting up with Ritchie and Chuck.

The leader was a blonde guy named Terry. I asked him when I saw him a couple of days later what they did with Ritchie and Chuck.

"Took 'em out into the woods and left 'em."

Lori Mallon had moved into 10 Follen Street with a black fellow named Ron. Ron was from a Philadelphia middle class family and was in Boston shooting dope in the ghetto. He and Lori were an on and off thing. Sometimes she would come and stay with me for a week or two. Relationships were quite fluid within the head culture.

---

[11] "weight" = a significant quantity of drugs; "intent to distribute" quantity. Felony weight.

FLASHING BACK– COMING OF AGE IN THE AMERICAN 1960s

Lori was "chipping," meaning shooting heroin but not enough to get strung out. Ron managed to get strung out. Lori came to me one day when Jerry and the junkies were not around. Her chipping had (finally) given her a habit. She asked me to sell her heroin. I refused for two reasons. First, that was Jerry's business and none of mine, it was his stash and his cash. Second, I wouldn't sell her – or anyone else – smack even if I could. I wasn't in love with her, but we had been friends and sometime lovers. She was a person I genuinely liked. She became angry and cussed me out, "self-righteous asshole" being the nicest thing she called me. This was disheartening and just made it clear that the heroin karma was piling up, looming, ready to engulf us like an avalanche of shit.

WHO'S THAT NARKING AT MY DOOR?

Jerry's bust was inevitable. While the scene on Follen Street was entirely centered around heroin, it was an irony that the event that led to Jerry's federal problems was a grass deal that didn't even involve cash. Jerry scored two keys of grass – felony weight – took them over to George and Heidi's and hacksawed a slice a slice off each brick, his commission on the sale. George then picked the bricks up off the table, turned around and handed them to this other guy. They did not know the buyer was agent O'Brien, the undercover fed who would soon be nearly beaten to death by the Devil's Disciples after his cover was blown. Was this Jerry's karma for ripping off the two kilos from Kozmik Dave? Hmmmm…

On the Friday of Easter weekend, I was relaxing at the Follen street pad, smoking some reefer and listening to Led Zeppelin with another acid dealer, a guy named Rick. Jerry and Dawn had gone to Jerry's parents for Seder.

There was a knock at the door. I opened it and was taken aback to see a man in a blue suit.

"Hey, Jerry said I could get some…stuff…here."

"Some…stuff…?"

"Yeah man, Jerry said it was OK."

"Forget it."

I closed the door.

"Who was that?" asked Rick.

"Some dude in a blue suit. Had to be a narc. Wanted to buy some …*stuff*…from me."

A few minutes later there was another knock. I opened the door and was met by the sight of two men in suits. The one on my left was in his fifties, slightly pudgy with a ruddy complexion and wore a gray suit. He was holding a warrant in his right hand and, in his left hand, a wallet displaying a badge and ID identifying him as Agent Mahoney of the Federal Bureau of Narcotics (Nixon had been president for three months and had not yet established the DEA).

On my right and slightly behind him was a younger, preppie looking fellow with some freshly healed wounds on his face. I knew this had to be O'Brien. Shit. This was it. Busted.

"We've got a warrant for a guy who lives here by the name of Jerry. Where is he?"

I was stunned, I couldn't talk. I thought of what was on the premises. At least the main junk stash was located in back of Mahoney under the steps going up to the roof. There were two boxes of disposable hypodermic points too, which Jerry, a medic, had procured from the Army reserves.

"Hey, c'mon kid, where is this Jerry guy?"

I was still speechless. Mahoney looked at O'Brien then turned back to me. He must have read my mind.

"Hey kid, I don't have a goddamned search warrant. This is an arrest warrant for 'Jerry.' We don't care what you're holding, we don't want you. All right?"

That was just what I needed to hear. My power of speech suddenly returned. "Jerry? There's no Jerry here."

"C'mon, we know he lives here."

Bullshit. If they don't know his last name, they don't know where he lives. "You got the wrong place. I don't know any Jerry."

"Well, we're coming in to have a look."

I was in no position to argue. They pushed past me and went quickly through the other rooms. Mahoney went onto the dining room where Rick was.

"Hey, Mahoney! Howyadoin' man? Shit, I ain't seen you since New York. What's happenin'?" hollered Rick.

"Wha...holy shit! What the fuck are *you* doin' here?" came Mahoney's response.

From the conversation that followed, it was apparent Rick was present when a bust went down in New York some months earlier. Just what we needed, a reunion. Shit.

About that time Robert Plant started belting out *Dazed and Confused* (how appropriate) from the stereo.

"Turn that noisy shit off and get your ass in here! Chrissakes, how can you stand to listen to that crap?" hollered Mahoney.

I turned the stereo off and went into the dining room.

The two G-men were standing on either side of a low table which had a bowl on it containing a quarter pound of cleaned weed. They were two stereotypical Boston Irish cops, right down to the Catholic Boston College rings they both wore. Rick and I sat on a mattress on the floor which served as a couch.

I felt like I had slipped into a psychedelic space-time warp and fallen into a cop movie. Mahoney must have stayed up late every night watching all the reruns of the old Highway Patrol TV show. He had Broderick Crawford's hard-boiled cop persona down pat. It was ...almost... funny.

Mahoney was giving Rick and I a hard time, telling us what assholes we were and how easy it was for him to get informants in the head culture.

"Sure it is. Just like Bull," said Rick, referring to a black guy we knew from the street dealing scene. "He worked for you guys last summer didn't he?"

Mahoney looked a bit surprised that one of his stoolies was that well known. "Yeah. He did." He looked at me. "You need a job kid? You can work for us." He looked back at Rick. "So could you."

"Thanks, but I'll pass. It's not my bag," I replied.

O'Brien Just stood there wordless, trying to look badass. He was a good looking man, freshly healed scars on his face notwithstanding, in his mid to late twenties, clean shaven and dark hair with a Brylcreem sheen to it. He wore a dark blue blazer, white shirt, a red tie with the miniature handcuffs tie-tac, of course, (ever see a nark without one?) and the standard issue black shoes. Cops always wore black shoes. He hooked his thumbs into his belt and opened his jacket far enough so we could see his handcuffs and gun. Wow. How impressive.

He finally spied a rent receipt with Jerry's name on it.

"No Jerry here, huh?" He handed the paper to Mahoney.

Mahoney glanced at the receipt and then gave me "the look".

"Where is he?"

When you can't think of a good lie, tell the truth, they won't expect it. "At his parents for Passover Seder."

"Don't give me that bullshit. Just how goddamn dumb you think I am?"

I was tempted to answer honestly. Instead, I said, "Hey, you asked, I told you. You don't want to believe it, fine."

"Where do they live?"

"I don't know." In Brookline, asshole, but I'm not telling you.

He gave O'Brien a glance and then looked back at me. "If I find out you called him before we get to him, I'm coming back for you. Understand?"

Fuck you. I said nothing.

He bore in on me and scowled." Hey, kid, you understand me? I mean it."

"Yeah. I hear you." *Fuck you again.*

"I didn't ask if you heard me, I asked if you *understood* me!"

"Oh hey. Yeah, right, I understand." *Fuck you three times, Jack.*

He and O'Brien headed for the door. I followed. When Mahoney reached the door, he turned around and pulled the string on the light in the narrow hallway. He put his puffy face next to mine and squinted. The blood vessels on his bulbous nose looked like a road map. In the glare of the bare bulb, he summoned up his best Broderick Crawford badass cop attitude and said,

"I want to get a good look at your face because I'm not going to forget it. And I don't want you to forget mine either." He paused a moment for dramatic effect, then turned and went out the door without turning out the light.

Junior G-man O'Brien scowled and gave me his best "that goes for me, too!" look as he sidled past me and closed the door behind him. *Good riddance. I hope you slam your dick in a car door!*

I watched from the window as they got in their car and left. I immediately went to the apartment on the first floor to use their phone. A mellow hippie couple lived there. Mahoney and O'Brien had been at their door and harassed them too. This confirmed my original suspicion that they really didn't know where Jerry lived, they just went from apartment to apartment hoping to get lucky.

I called Jerry at his parents place and told him the feds were on their way to arrest him. He decided to stay put, at this point it made no sense to run. Mahoney and O'Brien handcuffed him during Seder in front of his parents and took him downtown to the JFK Federal Building. He was out in two hours.

When I got back up to the apartment, Rick had some numbers twisted up and we turned Led Zep back on, kicked back and got blasted, goofing on our encounter with the feds.

I wondered if Rick was an ear for the man. I don't recall ever seeing him after that evening. Which may only mean he thought it prudent to avoid locations where the feds were likely to show up. If I were him, I wouldn't come back to Follen Street. No way.

I regarded this experience as an indication that I should get the hell out of Boston. Soon.

CONNIE

Robert Leightman was an intellectual acid head, intelligent, articulate and well read whom I had met at the Common over the summer of '68. summer. You could have very interesting discussions with him about literature, art, politics, social issues and the like. Robert was not a hippie superfreak. He was a perfectly normal looking dude, clean shaven with short hair. He was, however a connoisseur of high quality LSD. Robert always had the best acid in town.

Robert was the epitome of the hip acid dealer, just the right combination of brains and paranoia to keep himself out of trouble. He was an ethical and groovy person, too, not just a jive-ass super-hippie dope dealer.

At one time Robert lived on Windsor Street in Cambridge. One evening he took a cab home. When he went to pay the driver, the cabby said to him,

"You know, Buddy, we're supposed to report anyone going to or from this address to the cops".

Robert got back into the cab and went to his girlfriend's apartment. She went over to his place, packed a bag for him and they both went to Spain. He usually ended going to Europe about once a year whenever he thought he was getting hot with the police. As far as I know, Robert never got busted.

Then I met Connie. She was a friend of Jerry's. Connie went with Jerry and I one Sunday afternoon in April to score some acid from Robert Lehman. We spent the rest of the day together at the Cambridge Common, sampling our purchases, smoking hash and listening to rock bands at the free Sunday concert. We ended up spending the night together followed by a whirlwind hippie romance. Smoking hashish all day long, we dropped acid together two or three times a week. We felt like we were the last acid heads in a city that was on a massive heroin nod.

We managed to groove in the middle of the generally depressing scene that was going on. Connie was dealing hits of acid and grams of hashish in the Boston Public Garden. It was a fairly together scene. While longhairs were forbidden to enter the Boston Common, the Public Garden, right across Charles Street, was not off limits. We even had our own narc, an overweight middle-aged black man who sat on a bench reading his paper. Occasionally he would peer over the paper at the head scene through a pair of tiny binoculars. It is possible he wasn't a nark, maybe he was a private detective trying to track down a runaway. We referred to him "our nark" nevertheless.

The assortment of street people was typical of the times. "Mad George" was yet another wandering batshit crazy psychedelic messiah convinced he was Jesus Christ. George was another casualty of combining meth and acid. He was harmless, just kind of a pain in the ass at times, especially when people refused to take him seriously as Jesus. He was a tall thin beardless youth with hair that hung straight to his waist. I don't know what color it originally was, but at the time I met him it was a pronounced orange, the result of some experiment in hair coloring gone awry. He was an absolutely incredible blues harp player. He would sit there and just wail away for hours, the dude could really blow, unfortunately he was a schizoid mess.

George would occasionally fly off on a tirade for not having his divinity acknowledged. "You'll see! And you all be sorry! I'll show you all, when I come back with my wings on! You'll see!" I never did figure out the part about the wings, I think maybe he had Jesus and the Archangel Michael confused. And he said he was going to fry everybody's ass at his Second Coming!

"C'mon George, sit down and be quiet. You're upsetting people." Connie would tell him in a calming voice. George obeyed.

Mescaline John was there every day, peddling his capsules of white powder. Walrus was a straight looking dude who loved psychedelics. There were a few scrufty teenage runaways. The cops didn't roust anyone unless they did something exceptionally stupid in front of them, like sell a baggie full of pills or grass. With winter over, the Public Garden was a nice change from the smack infested hippie ghettoes.

Shortly after I got involved with Connie, several incidents occurred at the Follen Street pad which reinforced my decision to find a way out of Boston. The first was when this scrungy looking dude scored two bags of smack from Jerry, sat down at the kitchen table and did them up.[12] He no sooner took the spike out of his vein than he quit breathing, turned blue and fell in a heap on the floor. Rebecca, Jerry and I got him into a cold shower, got him breathing and slapped him into consciousness. He left a while later under his own power.

There were two good reasons for getting him out of there. First, if you can save someone who is in danger of dying – even if the dumb bastard did voluntarily pump poison into his own veins – you are morally obligated to do so. Second, the laws in Massachusetts at that time stated that if a person overdosed on an illegal drug, everyone who lived on the premises where it occurred could be charged with accessory to murder. In no way did we need that shit.

The next incident was a couple days later. Dariah was another young woman who came to stay in our den of iniquity. She was a friend of Dawn's, not particularly attractive and hadn't been getting any. One Sunday she brought some guy and had one night stand. The following day I was out doing a deal with a couple keys of reefer when he came back in the next afternoon with a revolver and cleaned out cash and dope from the apartment. He didn't get it all, our main stash located outside the apartment in one of the steps going up to the roof.

The thing that put the icing on the cake was the afternoon I came back to our apartment to find that Jerry had acquired a large stash of orange sunshine acid. Jerry the junkie? With LSD?

"Where did you get this stuff man?"

"Oh, Frank got it for me. He ripped it off from Robert."

Fuck me! Jerry had Frank steal Robert's acid stash! Karma was coming toward us like a tsunami of shit!

---

[12] Injected them.

CHAPTER 18

GETTING OUR KICKS ON ROUTE 66

TIME TO GO

It didn't long for Connie and I to become close. She had been a nurse in Florida who lost her nursing certification after getting herself strung out, first on speed and then on downers. She had a place in Cambridge – squatting in one of the dorms at Harvard University, not sure how she managed that – but spent most nights with me at the dope dive on Follen Street. Our relationship was balanced: sex in the morning, sex in the evening. Sometimes sex in the afternoon too!

The trafficking in heroin at 23 Follen had increased since Jerry's bust. Enforcement of narcotics laws in many cases resulted in increased narcotics traffic because a dealer, once busted and out on bail, had to hustle to get money to pay a lawyer and therefore would redouble the effort to sell more dope. Jerry had to pay a lawyer now so the heroin action on Follen Street increased. It was an all too common death spiral.

One day Connie said, "Gene, me and some friends are going to Colorado. Would you like to come with us?"

And of course I accepted!

My friend from Smethport, Barry Wilson, showed up unexpectedly. Connie, Barry, and I went to see Led Zeppelin at the Tea Party on May 26th. We dropped orange sunshine acid.

The opening band was Zephyr, some heavy acid-rockers from Denver whose lead guitarist was Tommy Bolan.

It was a truly psychedelic, absolutely mind boggling show! When Zep finished their last set, the place went wild with people calling for encore after encore. Once again, Zep ran out of their own tunes and did tremendous jams on some blues, Elvis, and Chuck Berry tunes. Yeah! Led Zeppelin on acid rates as the best concert I have ever seen, almost a religious experience.

Joe Moretti was another member of our band of fugitives and adventurers. Joe was from Springfield, Massachusetts, a slight fellow with brown bushy hair, glasses, and a scraggly beard. He played a nice Guild six-string flattop guitar and was into Dylan and Donovan.

Dickie was a massive looking hippie dude with shoulder-length blonde hair and a blonde beard, looking for all the world like a Viking. He was one of the gentlest persons I have ever met, under most circumstances anyway.

I suppose that the person with the heaviest reason for splitting Boston was a friend of Joe's who went by the name of Fitzie. He was a real quiet guy, serious, and had brown hair parted in the middle, about half way to his shoulders and a short beard. His eyes were bright blue and penetrating. Fitzie was the only name any of us knew him by, and there was a reason for that.

This was 1969, and the meat grinder in Vietnam was consuming American progeny at the rate of hundreds a week. Fitzie had been drafted. He told us, "I figured what the hell, I can handle two years in the Army, so I reported to the induction center and took the step forward. Then this Marine sergeant came into the room and picks every third man for the Marines. He picked me. I figured 'fuck this shit!' got off the bus at the first piss stop on the way to Parris Island and never got back on."

Fitzie wasn't just on the run from the local draft board, as so many were at that time, having taken the step forward he was a member of the armed forces and subject to the Uniform Code of Military Justice, not civilian justice. He was a deserter. The stakes were court martial, dishonorable discharge, and time in Leavenworth. Fitzie was genuinely on the lam from the government. If we didn't know his last name, we could be of no use to the FBI if they came looking for him. And we wouldn't even have to lie.

This is how the five of us were on that warm, sunny spring day in May, 1969, when we pulled out of Boston in Connie's 1968 robin's egg blue Chevy van and headed west.

We took turns driving smoking Connie's fine, dark brown Afghani hashish, and sleeping. Our mascot, a half-grown female black and white cat, "Kitty," spent most of her time stretched out on the dashboard snoozing in the warm sun.

The background music for this trek blared from the radio as we careened westward: *Pinball Wizard* by The Who, B. B. King's *The Thrill Is Gone*, and the Beatles' *Get Back* . Boy, could we relate to that! We were getting back to where we belonged alright, by getting the hell away from Boston! We were footloose and fancy free, stoned and rolling down the highway like Ken Kesey and the Merry Pranksters. If Kerouac and Cassidy were the Dharma Bums, then we were the Karma Bums, and good karma at that!

I had never been further west than Youngstown, Ohio, and I was loving the vast and varied beauty of the countryside as we rolled on. The people we met along the way were terrific. We experienced no hostility. Folks were pleasant and friendly wherever we went. It was reassuring to see that the whole country wasn't like the heroin horror show we had left behind us.

Picking up Route 66 in Chicago, we followed it down south. So anxious were we to put distance between us and the bummer in Boston that we didn't stop to stay overnight anywhere until we got to Oklahoma. We pulled into a campground and found that, out of hundreds of campers, we were the only longhairs in the place. We took advantage of the shower facilities to get cleaned up and then just wandered around checking out the place. At one point, Joe and I were standing in front of the little campground store drinking Cokes and being stared at by everyone. We overheard someone remarking about the "hippies." Joe turned to me and said in a stage voice,

"Y'hear that, Gene? They got hippies here. Imagine that. Wonder where they are?"

Several of the onlookers just shook their heads and walked off. No one really spoke much to us, but no one hassled us either.

TEXAS PANHANDLE ENCOUNTER

Our end-to-end traverse of Route 66 offered no end to meeting interesting people. We met one on the Texas/Oklahoma border one evening. Cruising through the warm evening just after dark with the windows down, we were laughing, listening to the radio and just grooving along when we saw this fellow alongside the road trying to flag a ride.

Now, to understand how he happened to be there, you have to know something about the liquor laws in Texas. Many of the counties in the northern part of Texas were dry. You couldn't get a drink of liquor unless you belonged to a private club. Well now, this fellow apparently did not belong to any clubs in Texas, so he hitched himself a ride into Oklahoma to get a proper snootful. He was, as far as we could tell, quite successful. I mean, this fellow was staggering-shitfaced-falling-on-his-ass drunk!

Slightly built, he wore jeans, a western style shirt, the ubiquitous cowboy boots and hat carrying a denim jacket. He was having rather a difficult time staying on his feet as he put this thumb out. We passed him. Connie said, "Shall we give him a ride?"

"Well, he sure as hell isn't going to get where he's going by walking," said Dickie. I stopped and backed the van to where he was because he didn't look like he was capable of walking far enough to catch up with us!

Connie was sitting in the passenger seat. She slid over onto the engine cover between the front seats and the cowboy climbed into the passenger seat. He was a skinny, hawk-faced fellow, probably, in his thirties, and was appropriately thankful that we were giving him a ride. He would have probably been there until morning had we not stopped. After he got settled into his seat, he looked around and began to take stock of the situation.

"Well, I'll be god*damned!*" he muttered, "a bunch of hippies! I'm gittin' a ride from a bunch of god*damned* hippies!"

He wasn't being nasty or anything, it was just a matter-of-fact comment. I'm sure in the Texas panhandle vernacular of 1969, "god*damned"* went with "hippie" like "Ford" went with "pickup truck."

"Yessir," he muttered to himself, "a bunch of god*damned* hippies."

Connie made some small talk with him, mostly where we were from, where we were going, stuff like that. I was watching him out of the corner of my eye as I drove. He was looking Connie over pretty carefully. I figured what was going through his mind was the same thing that most any other redneck or straight dude thought at the time: *Aha! A hippie chick! They believe in free love, I'll bet I can get an easy piece here!*

The conversation between he and Connie died down, and he sat there fidgeting in his seat. After a few minutes, he said

"Uh, ma'am, uh, kin I ask yew a question?"

"Sure" she replied, "what do you want to know?"

"Uh, ma'am, do yew, uh, have a boyfriend?"

Oh shit, I thought, here it comes!

"Yes I do," she replied, gesturing toward me, "This is Gene. He's my boyfriend."

I leaned forward and turning toward him gave him as big a sillyassed stoned grin as I could manage. At the time, my hair was down to my shoulders, I had no facial hair and was wearing John Lennon style glasses. I must have looked as freaky as hell to him. He gave me a look that said, *what's she see in that weird looking thing?* He scooched down in his seat and adjusted the brim of his hat and looked straight ahead. After a few more minutes, he started glancing sideways at Connie again, then he said,

"Uh, ma'am, kin I ask yew another question?"

"Why sure, go ahead."

"Uh, Ma'am, uh, are yew, uh, are yew a virgin?"

"Why no," said Connie in a matter-of-fact manner, "I'm not a virgin."

At this reply, the cowboy again scooched down in his seat, adjusted the brim of his hat and stared straight ahead. I was grinning to myself because I knew something was definitely going to happen before this was all over with. He was quiet for a few more minutes, then,

"Uh, ma'am, kin I kiss yew?"

"No, you can't kiss me. I told you Gene is my boyfriend."

With that, the cowboy sprang into action. He reached both arms out and grabbed Connie by the shoulders, pulled her into him and planted a big one right on her lips! In a flash, Dickie tore out of the rear of the van, reached over the seat and grabbed that poor, skinny, drunken cowboy by the collar of his western shirt, and ripped him away from Connie. He lifted that poor surprised bastard halfway over the back of the seat, spinning him around until they were eyeball-to-eyeball, noses almost touching, and snarled "If you *ever* do that again, I'll *kill you!*"

Words do not exist to describe the look of surprise and abject terror on that poor man's face! He underwent one of the fastest personality changes I have ever seen. After Dickie relaxed his grip on him, he settled down in the passenger's seat and wouldn't even look in Connie's direction. After riding this way for a couple of miles, he slithered over the seat, not looking at Connie, got into the back of the van and proceeded to make friends with Dickie. I guess he figured that if there was a hippie that big and that mean in the world, he would much rather be his friend than his enemy!

We pulled into Amarillo and stopped at a Taco Bell. When we left, our passenger was passed out face down in a plateful of tostadas.

Route 66 stretched out before us in the warm Texas night. We lit another bowl of hash, turned up the radio, laughed about the cowboy and drove off into the night with the breeze on our faces. America lay before us, and we were experiencing it all!

SANTA FE

This was the old Route 66, the first transcontinental highway in the U.S. There were opportunities to meet all kinds of interesting people. We stopped at a gas station/market/restaurant and there as an old guy there who had to show us the biggest groundhog he had ever shot, he was positively ecstatic. We also stopped to do some horseback riding.

We proceeded westward. Seeing a landscape so flat was something novel to me. I thought the prairie was flat, but parts of New Mexico are as flat as a tabletop. You could stand up and think that you were the tallest thing for as far as you could see. And that was a considerable distance.

We left Route 66 and headed north to Santa Fe. Santa Fe was a picturesque town with a lot of adobe construction, the "old west." We headed to the Santa Fe Plaza where the local heads hung out. Native Americans sold jewelry and crafts in the shadow of a monument that commemorated the heroes of the wholesale slaughter of the "savages" in the nineteenth century.

The Santa Fe scene was appropriately laid back. We got a campsite in the Santa Fe National Forest cooking over an open grill and sleeping in a three-sided log shelter.

Jemez Springs, about an hour away, had been recommended to us. It was a volcanic hot spring on hillside. Longhairs were frequently busted at Jemez Springs for nudity. Proper citizens of the Southwest were not used to the sight of naked longhairs with bouncing titties and dangling genitalia and, since if you squinted real hard and looked across the ravine through the brush, you could barely make out the sight of naked bodies, the New Mexico State Police issued numerous citations for public nudity.

"Yeah, I got busted out there last week," said Ralph, a head with long blonde hair, mutton chops, and a booming voice who spent most of his time at the square. "I was lounging in the water when some lady and her daughter came in and there I was with no clothes on. They called the cops. Makes me wish I had a big ol' hard-on when they walked in on me!"

We made a couple of trips to Jemez Springs but did our bathing in cutoffs as we didn't need the hassle of being busted for public nudity. Connie wore a T-shirt too. Contrary to a lot of perceptions about the longhair culture, not everyone was into nudity and group sex, and Connie certainly was not. If she was going to be nude, it would be with only one other person – me!

There was a very short rain shower almost every afternoon while the sun was shining. It was most interesting to be lounging in the hot spring while it was raining, the drops forming a mist that rose from the surface of the water.

Ralph went to Jemez Springs in the van with Joe, Dickie and Fitzie one afternoon while Connie and I stayed in Santa Fe. When they returned, Ralph wasn't with them.

"Oh, he got busted for indecent exposure…again," said Joe. "The cops took him away."

One afternoon we dropped acid and went to a Native American pueblo, I do not recall which one. A signs at the entrance said taking photographs was forbidden by the U.S. Government. We toured the village in the van. I was struck by the abject poverty I saw. No wonder the government did not want photos taken. I also thought it must be demeaning to these people to have people gawking at them as they drove through their village. It was uncomfortable.

One of our excursions took us to White Sands, the U.S. Government weapons testing area. High, chain linked fences topped with barbed lined the sides of the road. Government signs warned that deadly force could be used on trespassers.

BAD WEED & PARANOIA

We were running low on cash, so we decided to head for Boulder, Colorado. The logical thing to do, from the point of view of who we were and what we were into, was to sell drugs, the economic mainstay of the counterculture. We knew there was a head scene[1] in Boulder and we figured we could score some grass there and sell it in Albuquerque.

The trip to boulder was my first view of the Rocky Mountains. Indeed, they are most impressive, the "purple mountain majesties," magni-

---

[1] The counterculture had its own grapevine that was fairly reliable as far as info on local scenes, drug availability, and so on went.

ficent sharp, jagged naked rock, jutting thousands of feet into the sky. In my early years I had heard people refer to the Alleghenies in which I had grown up as "mountains." They were mere hills, the Rockies were *real* mountains. I thought of my grade school geography books, where the Appalachian Mountains were labeled "old worn down mountains" and the Rockies were "young rugged mountains!"

Supplies of Mexican grass grown the year before having been depleted and the annual grass drought was on. Inside of an hour in Boulder, Dickie and Joe found someone willing to sell us some homegrown. We paid a hundred dollars for two pounds it. We placed it high on a rock outcropping overlooking the highway to dry in the sun. We proceeded to hang out for a couple days, retrieving our contraband on the way out of town. We bagged it and concealed it in the laundry basket underneath the clothes.

We were headed toward Albuquerque, quite pleasantly stoned and grooving along. Connie was driving, Joe was napping using the grass stash for a pillow. We passed a New Mexico State trooper's car parked beside the road. We were holding weight. A slight ripple paranoia went through our collective consciousness as we passed the trooper's car. Peering out the rear window, we saw him pull out and start following us. *Shit!*

"Hey, the cop's on our ass!"

"That's OK," said Dickie, who was in the passenger's seat, "just be cool."

"He probably doesn't want anything," said Connie, a hopeful tone in her voice.

I knew we would be fucked if the trooper looked in the laundry basket. We had no money for bail if we were busted. Being as we were practically vagrants anyway, any bail would be too high. We were definitely looking at jail time if he found our weed!

I tried to casually look out the rear window, without appearing to be overly concerned. If he wasn't interested in us, we didn't want to give him any indication that we were concerned that he was following us.

The light came on.

Fitzie was looking out the rear window. "Oh shit! His light's on. God*damn*it! Better pull over!"

Connie put the turn signal on, pulled the van off the road and stopped. She took out her wallet and got the registration out as the trooper stopped behind us. Joe was still snoozing.

"All right, everybody be cool," she said, "I'll do the talking." We agreed.

The trooper came up to the open driver's window. "Good afternoon, officer," said Connie pleasantly, "What can I do for you?"

"I'd like to see your license, registration and financial responsibility card, Miss." He peered inside the van at the rest of us. We were silent.

"Why, certainly." She complied.

He looked at the cards, looked back at Connie. "Just a minute." He looked at the rest of us. "You folks stay put, OK?"

So, put we stayed! The collective feeling was a telepathic *oh shit!* He walked around the van and peered at the plate, then walked to the cruiser and got on the radio. We sat silently in the van. Words weren't necessary for us to communicate at that point. Any outlaw who has stayed out of jail knows you have to keep your shit tightly wrapped in the presence of the man.

I learned this skill while tripping one cold, snowy night in January, 1969. Four of us visited some folks in Roxbury, not too far from Shepherd Ave. We were leaving. I got into the seat behind the driver. The driver started the engine. At that moment a police cruiser passed us and stopped at stop sign about 30 yards away. Immediately I feel this BIG paranoid vibe from the driver. I don't know what he was holding but I was holding about a hundred hits of acid I had just scored that afternoon. Our driver immediately shut off the engine and turned off the lights. *So* fucking uncool! The back-up lights on the cruiser come on and it starts backing up. *Oh shit!* Then the cruiser stops, the backup lights go out, and it drives off.

With a "see you later" I exited the car. Only a few blocks from my pad, I got out of the car, shut the door, turned around and my fully-dilated pupils come nearly face-to-face with a beat cop walking down the street! I remember the thought *just be cool and go about your business* flashing through my psychedelicized consciousness and walked past him not making eye contact. Jeezuz! What an adrenaline rush! YES! You can get away with damned near anything if you look like you belong where you are and don't call any unnecessary attention to yourself.

So there we were, our telepathic mantra: everybody be cool... don't anybody fuck up... everybody be cool...don't anybody fuck up...

He returned to the van with the license and registration. "Miss Allen, could you please explain to me why you have a Florida driver's license, your van is registered in Massachusetts and you are in New Mexico?"

Oh, shit.

Connie had a wonderfully nonchalant delivery. "Oh, I was working as a nurse in Florida last year. I went to Boston last winter and bought the van there. I didn't live there long enough to qualify as a resident so I was ineligible for a Massachusetts Driver's license. We are on a vacation out here in the southwest. We've never been here before, you have a *very* pretty state, you know."

Good work, Connie! She sounded so sincere. Hell, she was. It was all true. The little bit of flattery toward New Mexico was a nice touch. Just so he doesn't get interested in the contents of the van!

"Well, everything is in order. You folks have a nice time while visiting our state," *...and be sure not to stay too damned long...* went unspoken but the feeling was there.

Handing the license, registration and insurance cards to Connie, the trooper touched the brim of his hat and went back to the cruiser. As he got back inside the cruiser, we broke silence.

"Fucking A!"

"Goddamn, that was close! Shee-it!"

"Nice work Connie!"

The noise woke Joe up. "What's up?"

"We just got stopped by a cop while you were napping on the stash, man!"

Joe raised up and looked out the window as the cop drove past. "Oh shit, that's the cop that busted Ralph last week at Jemez Springs. He probably remembered the van with the Massachusetts plate and wanted to check it out."

That explained his interest in us. *Damn!* We were lucky.

We set up camp in the Santa Fe National Forest, this time we were not at a regular campsite. We just found a nice place and camped there, setting up a tarp for shelter and building a fire pit of rocks. We even had our own little horned toad too!

W. EUGENE JOHNSON

WHERE'D JOE GO?

The next day we set out for Albuquerque to sell our dope. We had just enough money to get there. We took a young woman we met in Santa Fe with us, Morningstar, a Native American who had friends we could stay with in Albuquerque. An acid head herself, she told us her mother preferred peyote,[2] the traditional southwestern Native American psychedelic sacrament, over acid.

The University of New Mexico is situated along Lomas Boulevard in Albuquerque. The large grassy quad was a typical 60's head scene, lots of young people with long hair and colorful clothing, guitars, flutes, and incense wafting on the breeze. We set up shop under a tree on the grassy quad in front of the university. Joe had his Guild flattop with him and wandered off to do his minstrel thing. Dick and Fitzie circulated and let people know we had grass for sale.

The high mountain reefer we had purchased in Boulder was *bad*. And I do not mean, "good" bad, it was simply awful. Shitweed. I don't know if you got a buzz from the reefer itself or perhaps from oxygen deprivation at having to smoke so much of it to feel anything! We did, however, have the only reefer concession in town. In a spirit of fairness, we let everyone who was interested try a joint before they bought. Surprisingly enough, nobody who sampled it refused to buy. Ten dollars for a generous baggie full was a bargain. There were a couple of greasy-haired motorhead type dudes who were so struck by the quantity for the price that they, over our objections, bought three bags without tasting it.

We sold all the grass before dark and left the quad. Joe was still playing his guitar and told us he would catch up with us later. We went with Morningstar and partied until we passed out, crashing on the floor of an adobe house.

The next day we couldn't find Joe. No one had seen him. We went to a dented can discount store, stocked up on food and then to a laundromat. Still no Joe. While we were in the laundromat, in came one of the guys who was with the dude who had bought grass the night before without trying it.

"You people are in some shit!"

Connie responded. "What's the problem?"

"You ripped my buddy off."

---

[2] lomphora williamsii, a cactus that contains mescaline.

"We didn't rip anybody off," Dickie responded.

"That shit you sold him wasn't good weed at all."

"We never said it was," I told him, "we offered to let everyone taste it, but your buddy was in too much of a big goddamned hurry to buy it that he refused a taste."

"Yeah, well, my buddy's pissed. He's got a gun and he's looking for you."

Shit. We were sitting ducks in the laundry. I checked the door in back. It was locked. Not good. And this dude could lead him right to us. This was a situation that could get out of hand very quickly.

Connie always kept a cool head. "We didn't mislead you or your friend," she said in the same reassuring manner she used with the trooper, "you tell him to meet us in the quad in an hour and we'll give him his money back on any of the grass he has left."

He seemed surprised. "OK, you just better be there." He left.

As he left in his car, Fitzie spoke up. "You really gonna give him his money back?"

She looked over her glasses as she folded clothes. "*Fuck* no. We're splitting." She smiled.

"What about Joe?" asked Fitzie.

"I don't know about Joe," said Connie, "I'm not going to hang around here if there are people with guns looking for us. If you want to stay and look for Joe, go ahead."

When we arrived back at our campsite Joe was there, crashed out under the tarp. Dickie started razzing him, "Lookit Joe! The travelling troubadour! He must run into some good pussy last night! Plum tired him all out. Poor fucker."

Fitzie chimed in. "Hey man, was it good? She keep you up all night?"

"Charmed the panties of some sweet young thing with his velvet voice and his guitar. A regular rock n' roll star. God*damn!*" said Dickie.

Joe stirred form his sleep and raised himself up on one elbow. He looked like hell, his eyes were bloodshot and he was shaking. "Where the fuck you been?"

"We might ask you the same thing," replied Connie.

"Well, I wasn't gettin' no pussy, I can tell you that. I was hiking in the Sangre De Christi Mountains."

"What the hell were you doing there?"

"Some people you sold that ragweed grabbed me up and dumped me there. They weren't too fuckin' happy about the dope you sold 'em."

We all looked at each other.

"Joe, what happened?" asked Connie.

"Well, after you guys split, these three dudes came up to me and laid this trip on me about that ragweed you were selling. Hell, I told 'em I didn't have anything to do with selling it. They were mad as hell, said you stole from 'em and all, ripped 'em off."

"We know who they were. We ran into one of 'em this morning. Said one guy was after us with a gun. We told 'em we would meet them on the quad and give them their money back," said Fitzie.

"Did you give 'em their money back?"

"Shit no." said Connie. "We split. They were too greedy to try the weed anyway Fuck 'em."

"Well, I'm damned glad you didn't give 'em their money back. Anyway, they took me way out into the mountains and dumped me there. I had no fucking idea what was going down. I thought they might off me. They just stopped and told me to get the fuck out and drove off. I had no idea where I was. Walked for a while, and finally a pickup truck comes along. I flagged it down, it was two Indians. I told 'em what happened, and they laughed like hell. Said I was walking the wrong way. Told me to get in and gave me a ride back to the highway."

"Jesus. I don't know what was worse, walking around lost in the mountains or riding with them. They were passing this bottle of whiskey back and forth, sloshed to the gills, and offered me some. Hell, I don't drink and I said I didn't want any. So they start getting an attitude because I won't drink with' em. Shit! It was scary as hell riding with them dudes cause they were so fucked up, careening around those narrow mountain roads, so I drank. I figured what the fuck, falling off the mountain and dying in a fiery crash wasn't any harder to do drunk than sober!"

"We made it to the highway about daylight and I hitched a couple rides back here. And now I got a fuckin' hangover. Oops, gotta go! Got the heaves." Joe jumped up and ran into the bushes and retched.

We spent a couple weeks in and around Santa Fe, making occasional cautious forays into Albuquerque. On the summer solstice, 1969, we headed the van down Route 66 toward Los Angeles. Connie had relatives in Long Beach. At a gas station somewhere in Arizona we encountered The Hog Farm, a mobile Hippie commune traveling in a psychedelic painted school bus. We shared some dope with them and they shared peanut butter and jelly sandwiches with us.

The desolation of the Southern California desert had a magnificence to it. We were headed for Connie's aunt and uncle's place in Long Beach. When we got there, we didn't stay long. Her aunt took one look at the situation – Connie, a lone woman accompanied by four longhaired males – and told her, "You'd better get out of here before your uncle gets home." We split, heading north to San Francisco.

CHAPTER 19

THE LEFT COAST

ARRIVAL

The first time I ever saw the fabled Haight-Ashbury was June 21st, 1969. We came into the city from Los Angeles at about 6:00 a.m. and headed for Golden Gate Park. There were people crashed out in sleeping bags under every bush and tree in the park, or so it seemed.

We took a cruise down Haight Street, the hippie Mecca. It looked like a war zone. The collective consciousness of Haight Street was always affected by whatever the drug of choice was at the time. Acid had been gone as the major drug of choice since 1967. When we arrived, it was pretty much given over to meth and smack. The groovy head shops were gone. Many store fronts were boarded up. Meth had taken its toll, replacing the peace and love of the acid days with paranoia and violence. The only people we saw were speedfreaks: skinny, unhealthy looking people with bad teeth, walking around in the cool of the dawn.

We cruised around for a while and saw the Drogstore[1] Cafe on the corner of Haight and Clayton was open. We were low on cash and had to earn some money. A head in the Drogstore Cafe told us that the Haight Switchboard on Fell Street was a good source of day jobs. We went there immediately. Even at eight in the morning the Switchboard was a full

---

[1] A bit of Haight Ashbury history. During the Summer of Love in 1967, some hippies opened up a café where there previously was a pharmacy. A sign proclaiming it "The Drugstore" was still hanging outside, so they called it "The Drugstore Cafe," The city made them change the name since it was not a pharmacy, hence, "The Drogstore Cafe"

blown freak scene, with heads and space cases. Joe had some print shop experience and found a day gig with a shop on Fillmore Street near the Marina called The Paisley Penguin. The Switchboard turned us on to the idea of selling underground newspapers, particularly the *Berkeley Barb*.

THE HAIGHT-ASHBURY SWITCHBOARD

Switchboards were resources for the freak community. Serving as communication hubs, a switchboard was a place where freaks and street people could find survival resources. You could find day labor jobs, get a Chamber of Commerce map of the city, find out where you can crash for the night, get a free meal, free clinics, birth control, basic street survival stuff. The Haight Switchboard also had a message system where people would leave messages for individuals and the weekly *S.F. Good Times* would print a list of names with waiting message with the disclaimer that this messaging service could not be used to locate people who did not want to be found. Many people did not want to be found: runaways, deserters, those on the run from the FBI over the draft, criminal charges, whatever.

SWITCHBOARDS

Haight-Ashbury: 1820 Fell St., 387-3575.
Mission: 848 14th St., 863-3040.
Berkeley Free Church: 2200 Parker, 549-0649.
Marin Switch: PO Box 1386, San Rafael, 456-5300.
Help Unit: 421-9850.
Chinatown: 421-0943.
Diggers: 863-9718.
East Oakland: 532-2135
Huckleberry's for Runaways: 3830 Judah at 43rd, 731-3921.

San Francisco Good Times, Aug. 28, 1969
Source: Archives and Special Collections at the Thomas J. Dodd Research Center, University of Connecticut

SURVIVAL

The rest of us booked on over to Telegraph Avenue in Berkeley. We were pretty broke and needed money with which to purchase newspapers. Connie said "Let's panhandle." Now, I had donated money to various panhandlers, I had never considered doing it myself. It was, to my way of thinking, begging. But, we needed some money so I joined in with the rest of the crew and "spare changed" passersby.

Having never done this before, I had the chance to observe peoples' reactions to being hit on for pocket change. Some would just ignore you. The smiling stoned heads would usually give you a few coins, or – maybe even lay a joint on you! Straight people would either ignore you, look at you with contempt, or dig in their pockets and give you their coins. I found it curious that the people who did that seemed to give off this embarrassed vibe, like they felt guilty at having more than us raggedy-ass panhandlers. I didn't like doing it, I have never done it since.

We soon had enough cash between the four of us to go to the *Berkeley Barb* office and purchase newspapers which we sold on the street corners of Telegraph Avenue. We paid seven cents a copy and sold them on the street for fifteen cents.

We picked Joe up from the Paisley Penguin in the late afternoon. One of the longhairs who worked there, Charlie, said we could park the van where he and his lady, Polly, lived on Teddy Avenue in South San Francisco. We crashed there in Connie's van and got cleaned up in Charlie and Polly's bathroom.

We continued to sell *Berkeley Barbs* on the street for several days. I was not getting along with Joe, we constantly bickered with each other. They wanted to go back to Colorado, I, for no reason I could think of, decided to stay in San Francisco. I didn't know it at the time, but I would be there for the next twelve years. I said my good-byes to Connie.

I stayed one last night on Teddy Avenue crashing on the couch. Charlie and Polly, were real mellow San Francisco heads, older than us, in their thirties. They had quite an assortment of animals that all had the run of their house: a dog, couple of cats, birds and a super friendly gray and white rat. I awoke with the rat on my chest the next morning. He just wanted me to pet him.

I had my duffel bag and about $13 in my pocket. It was summer. I

FUCK MOTHER BELL

Spit on a penny and run it through the nickel slot until it sticks. Keep adding spit. After about five or six times it will stick. Then bang or shake the phone until it drops . . . with a ding! Make your local call.
—courtesy World Rip-Off Conspiracy

S.F. Good Times 11/68. Street survival. It was hip to scam the phone company. A friend of mine had a phone credit card. He gave me his number and I would change a digit and use it call all over the country. Can't do that anyore!
Source: Archives and Special Collections at the Thomas J. Dodd Research Center, University of Connecticut

was in San Francisco. I never expected to be in San Francisco, nor did I plan it. Here I was, on the precipice of something new. It was positively grand!

Polly dropped me off on Haight Street. I was truly lost, I didn't know what to do or where to go. I went to the Haight Switchboard and got a free Chamber of Commerce map of the city and hung out on Haight Street and Golden Gate Park for the day. I got a free ticket from a church to crash at a flophouse south of Market Street. It was a wino scene, a real bummer.

J.C. BURKHOUSE

The next day I dug into my wallet and found J.C. Burkhouse's address, 945A Valencia Street. I got my Chamber of Commerce map out of my duffel bag and checked out the bus routes. After a breakfast in a south of Market greasy spoon, I caught a 26 Valencia bus, got off at twentieth street and searched for 945A.

This was the Mission District of San Francisco. Ethnically it was turning from Irish to Latino (although the term in use at the time was "Chicano.") It was a pleasant sunny morning. I didn't see the house number, so I asked an older gentleman standing in front of 945.

"Oh, you lookin' for J.C. ?" he asked.

"Yes, I'm a friend of his from Boston."

"Well, I'm Mr. Kelly. J.C. rents from me. Right over there," he said, pointing to a pastel green wooden door set back between two buildings with 945-A on it. I opened it and saw a narrow walkway between two buildings. I followed the walkway back to a door and knocked on it. The door opened and there was J.C.

He grinned from ear to ear. "Well, I'll be damned! *Gene!*" he exclaimed and stepped forward to give me a huge hug. "Laurie!" he called, "Come here! Look who's here! It's Gene! From Shepherd Ave!"

Laurie came out and gave me a similar hug. God! It was so good to see some familiar faces! I had found some people I knew!

Their apartment was impossibly small, just one room, a tiny kitchen and tinier bathroom and a fenced-in porch in back. Even with only that little bit of space, they were willing to share it with me and wouldn't hear of me going anywhere else.

Laurie had a job clerking in a store. J.C. and I went to the top of Twin Peaks, the hills that held the fog back from this Mission district, keeping it sunny most of the time. J.C. laid a white capsule on me and took one himself. We tripped pleasantly all afternoon.

J.C.'s apartment was only two blocks from Dolores Park which was adjacent to Mission High, the very tough Latino high school. J.C. wasted no time introducing me to his circle of friends. Denny Vargas and his wife, Joyce, and some other people lived in a rambling flat on Linda Street, a dead-end street nearby. Denny drove a gray early model Morgan that had a wooden chassis.[2]

Rodney was a member of this group. He was a dealer, specializing in quantities of grass and hashish, and white capsules of MDA, an amphetamine derivative chemically related to mescaline and most definitely psychedelic. It was passed off as synthetic mescaline. This is what J.C. and I had tripped on.

We had "capping parties" at Denny's apartment. Rodney would come over with several pounds of his "mescaline" in large plastic bags. We would all pile in a car and go to the Hub Pharmacy on Market Street. The four of us would go in one at a time and each get two boxes of a thousand 00 gelatin capsules and two two-pound jars of USP dicalcium phosphate. The black dude at the counter was definitely hip to what was happening.

"Hey man, you wanna buy some...ah...vitamins...to put in those capsules?"

"Naw. It's cool, man. We already got our...vitamins. But thanks anyway!"

He smiled back as I paid for the purchase and left. Hell, it was perfectly legal, there weren't any laws against buying empty capsules and a harmless chemical.

We would then go back to Denny's apartment and cap up some "super caps" for our own use, a half-dozen each, of straight uncut MDA Then, Rodney would put the "mescaline" in a large bag and empty the dicalcium phosphate into it and shake it up to cut the product. We would then spend the afternoon stuffing capsules with powder from a large bowl in the middle of the table, licking our fingers occasionally and getting quite ripped. This happened every couple of weeks. Rodney would give me a generous baggie of caps to sell on the street for pocket money.

---

[2] The Morgan Car Company is a family owned British manufacturer of automobiles founded in 1910, still in business today.

FLASHING BACK– COMING OF AGE IN THE AMERICAN 1960s

STEPHEN GASKIN AND THE MONDAY NIGHT CLASS

"There's only one church and your membership button is your belly button," — Stephen Gaskin

Steven Gaskin and the Monday Night Class at the Family Dog on the Great Highway, 1970; the faces of a generation with a hunger for spirit.

Source: NY Times

"Stephen is such a groovy dude, man. Wait'll you meet this guy, you'll love him, Gene." J.C. was quite enthusiastic.

"So, what are these classes about?" I asked.

Laurie chimed in. "Oh, Stephen talks about all kinds of things! Energy, spiritual stuff, tripping. It's really neat. He has classes every Monday night. You have to go with us!" I was *definitely* interested.

The next Monday we took the bus out to Ocean Beach and the Family Dog, a rock n' roll dance hall. There were about fifteen hundred longhairs milling about, the *ultimate* head scene! San Francisco! This was where it all started! These folks were the *real* dropouts, people who hadn't had anything to do with straight society in years. I felt like I had arrived at the apex of the counterculture and felt at home among these kindred spirits!

Many of the women were dressed in flowing ankle length dresses made from imported Indian chintz bedspreads. Their hair was long and straight, except for natural curls or waves. There were a lot of bearded men in overalls or jeans. The ubiquitous hippie dogs were running about, many were Labrador retrievers wearing red bandannas with their collars. Entire families were in attendance, hippie moms and dads with babies and little kids.

The vibes in the room were good, it felt comfortable. The people were smiling, and very friendly. There wasn't a paranoid vibe in the place.

A tone pierced the layers of pot smoke and conversation. I looked around and saw two men sitting on a small platform near the center of the back wall. One had a full blonde beard and the other had a light brown hair and a scraggly goatee. He was blowing a note on a conch shell. Everyone sat down and started a long "aaauuuummm." I sat down alongside J.C. and Laurie and joined in. The psychic energy present in the room was amazing with everyone tuned in to the aum. It was like riding a big warm wave. The aum lasted for a couple of minutes after which everybody was quiet.

The man with the scraggly beard was Stephen Gaskin. I listened intently to Stephen that evening, fascinated by his intelligence, his sense of humor and his amazing ability to cross reference a seemingly infinite number of subjects from myriad sources. I don't remember what he talked about that night, but I do know that I was convinced that I was in the presence of someone who really *knew* some things.

Stephen was a genuine holy man, a living saint. The Monday Night Class was about spirit and religion. And how to just *be*. Stephen was the road chief, the head of this weekly spiritual conclave. He was the teacher. Everybody was welcome. Anybody could participate.

Stephen was not just an average dope-soaked hippie off the street. He was a speed reader and, for a period of time, checked six books out of the library every day. He read one on the way home, read four at home, and the remaining one on the way back to the library the next day.

He had been an assistant professor to the semanticist, S. L. Hayakawa, at San Francisco State College. Here is an excerpt from a San Francisco Good Times newspaper interview with reporter, Black Shadow.

Monday night about 1500 beautiful freaks descend on the Family Dog to sit crowded on the floor ...The rap is mostly about energy flow, but it manifests itself as everything from vegetarianism to Tibetan yoga,

General Semantics, rock, vibrational vector analysis, and what to do when you're on acid and your lady turns into a green spider and wants to kiss you. Steve offers instruction in getting high. And staying there.

Shadow: "How did you get on the trip in the first place?"

Steve: "I was teaching General Semantics and creative writing at State College...and discovered that I didn't want to be a writer...I needed to make a living somehow...So I...started teaching...I started seeing all these people the ones I wanted to talk to not showing up any more. They were leaving school, dropping out, going away. They were the ones who were interesting, and I wanted to know why they were leaving. And I fell into dope and strange companions."

"...I found that acid had taken a lot of things that I had thought were me, and left a set of skills....although I didn't have anything to teach any more...I began to find that there were things I wanted to tell people, and I decided to use the skills I already had. I had been pretty deep into General Semantics, and studied communication a lot."

"I started The Class at the experimental college at State...as an instrument of communication and research. As it grew, and as I processed more information and more energy, I had to learn how to handle the energy in order to be able to hold a bunch of people together. So I came into the energy sort of sideways I hadn't started off on that. And now I can't think of anything else worth doing." [3]

When the S.F. State Revolution[4] happened, the politics got too heavy and the class moved into some churches, the Straight Theater on Haight Street for a while, and then, finally, at the Family Dog dance hall on the Great Highway.

Politics was not something Steven espoused at the time, viewing it as too materialistic, putting effort into material stuff instead of spirit. In the late 60's, a lot of the counterculture was into left wing politics, which were heavy and leaned toward revolutionary violence.

Later in life Stephen came out in favor of everybody voting. In 2000 he ran for the presidential nomination by the Green Party, losing his presidential bid to Ralph Nader. His campaign statement declared: "I want it to be understood that we are a bunch of tree-huggers and mystics and peaceniks. My main occupations are Hippy Priest, Spiritual Revolu-

---

[3] San Francisco Good Times, September 4, 1969
[4] The Black Student Union and a coalition of other student groups known as the Third World Liberation Front (TWLF) led the strike, which began Nov. 6, 1968 and ended March 20, 1969. Clashes between the strikers and San Francisco Police tactical squads made national news. www.sfsu.edu/news/2008/fall/8.html

tionary, Cannabis Advocate, shade tree mechanic, cultural engineer, tractor driver and community starter. I also love science fiction."[5]

The Monday Night Classes were church in the truest sense of the word. We were taking communion together, communion being the common union of all the energy and vibes of all the people gathered. So, it was *real*. There *is* a purpose to gathering together in the name of God,[6] for that's what these people were doing. Stephen's raps were sermons, but unlike any sermons I had ever heard before.

The Monday Night Class It was a peer group. Stephen was the focus, not because he had some paper credential, but because he was plugged into what was going on and smart enough to talk about it intelligently without being any kind of high priest. He was one of the peers in the group, the most articulate one.

The Monday Night Class sometimes got heavy. Stephen, formerly a combat Marine who had taken and returned fire in Korea, was completely nonviolent, maintaining that violence was not where it's at on any level. That wasn't easy sometimes.

Along about 1970, Timothy Leary, the LSD guru who had been busted and sentenced to ten years for possession of a joint of marijuana, broke out of prison with the aid of the Weather Underground. Fleeing to Algeria where he took up with fellow political exile, black militant Eldridge Cleaver. He issued a manifesto which was printed as a handbill and turned up at the Monday Night Classes. It's main theme was revolution and stated something to the effect of "…killing a policeman is an act of love." One guy wanted go get up on Stephen's stage and read it. Stephen had read the handbill. Not wanting to promote violence, he didn't want this guy to read it. The guy with the handbill insisted and climbed onto the stage. Stephen took hold of him and tried to get him off the stage. As they were grappling in front of everyone, someone hollered,

"Stephen, what do we do about violence?"

Stephen, red faced from his exertions with the man, replied, "We're finding out right now, man!"

People should be skeptical of gurus and so-called spiritual teachers. There are people who are out to do a bad number on the world. Two examples are the Charlie Manson and the Rev. Jim Jones. This is where

---

5 Stephen Gaskin, Hippie Who Founded an Enduring Commune, Dies at 79
Nytimes.com. (2019). Stephen Gaskin, Hippie Who Founded an Enduring Commune, Dies at 79. [online] Available at: https://www.nytimes.com/2014/07/03/us/stephen-gaskin-hippie-who-founded-an-enduring-commune-dies-at-79.html [Accessed 1 Dec. 2019].

[6]Or whoever and whatever God might be.

you have to know how to distinguish truth, and that is not easy. There is a definite guideline for it, though.

Someone asked Stephen, "How do we know when someone is speaking the truth about spiritual matters?"

"It says right in the Bible, 'you shall know them by the fruits of their labors' Dig it. If a preacher has fancy houses, Cadillacs and Rolex watches, chances are that's what he's in it for."[7]

Stephen on revolution: "You don't need to bring down the government, man! Take over the government's function. Do for yourself."[8]

A lot of the talk at Stephen's classes was about drugs. Stephen was into mind drugs: grass, LSD, peyote, mushrooms. People wanted to know about things that happened while tripping. Psychedelic drugs are a device that can be used to remove the barriers that exist between the conscious mind and unconscious mind. Telepathy and transfiguration as described in the bible were subjects that frequently came up. Tips were shared on how to trip safely.

Much of what was discussed was about energy. Energy is attention, or more correctly, what you use to pay attention with. Where you put your attention is where you are putting your energy. What you put your energy into becomes more of a manifestation. Like playing a guitar or, loving your baby. The more you do it the, better you get at it.

Stephen's Monday Night Classes had a profound effect on me. Psychedelics became a sacrament. When I first started taking LSD, I thought perhaps this might be the original purpose of communion in the Christian Churches, something ingested that produced a change in consciousness, like some local mushrooms, or rye fungus![9]

The subjective experience of the oneness of all things, the sutratman,[10] of the Hindus that which binds all the universe together seemed to reinforce Christ's command to love one's neighbor as one's self because one's neighbor was, in fact, one's self. My personal experience with it was that we are all one, the only part of us that is separate is our physical bodies.

Having experienced this, I saw where the moral imperative about the sanctity of life as propounded by Jesus, Buddha and other spiritual masters originated. For people to cause injury to one another is for an

---

[7] Personal recollection
[8] Personal recollection
[9] Bread made with rye infected with a fungus, ergot, produced an LSD type of experience. In the middle ages entire communities were seized by manias that were caused by ergot poisoning.
[10] the "thread self" of the Hindus that which binds all the universe together. It is the spiritual element that permeates all creation binding all into one. It is the root of the English word "suture,"

organism to injure itself, like a crazed animal gnawing off one of its own limbs. For any man to do wrong or do injury to another has an effect on the quality of life in the universe for all. And for one person to kill another is the ultimate violation of the sanctity of life and spirit and a contradiction to the oneness of all. This was a reinforcement of conclusions I reached myself during my soul searching concerning the draft.

There was a feeling that I experienced being in Stephen's presence that I have only felt in the presence of two other individuals: Swami Satchidananda and Baba Ram Dass (formerly Dr. Richard Alpert, Timothy Leary's colleague at Harvard). Those three are the only people who claim to be spiritual who I ever felt actually were. I never got that feeling from any priest or bishop. Not a one. And not from Leary either. He was an LSD clown, interesting and entertaining, but lacking a commitment to the truth. Full of shit.

I continued to attend Stephen's Monday Night Classes until his family and others formed The Caravan in October, 1970. Twenty-five converted school buses toured with Stephen as he did speaking engagements at churches, colleges and universities all over the country.

The Caravan returned to San Francisco four months later and the class convened at the Family Dog and what was to be the final Monday night Class. We did the "aum." Stephen then looked around silently, then said something to the effect of, "We've done all we can do here. Let's just go."

The class adjourned, the hall emptied, and the Caravan left San Francisco for a second time, ending up in Summertown, Tennessee. They founded The Farm, the largest and most long lasting hippie collective in America. It is still in existence today as a co-operative.

Pundits in the media wonder from time to time whatever happened to the spirit that started in the youth in the Haight. The answer has been in front of them for decades. The Farm is exactly that. It wasn't perfect by any means, but it proved durable.

Stephen passed away on July 1, 2014 From natural causes at the age of 79. What I learned from Stephen has proven to be true. I loved him and celebrate him as the only living saint I ever had the privilege of meeting.

HEROIN KARMA

One fine sunny Sunday afternoon while I was grooving around on Haight Street, I heard a familiar voice holler "Hey, *Gene!*"

Could it be…no…yeah…oh shit! I turned around and there was Rebecca, the "hahd"[11] little blonde smack shooter from Follen Street in Boston.

"Gene, hey man, whattyadoin' here?"

"Uh…Rebecca, wow, uh…this is quite a surprise. I'm doin' all right. How are you?"

"Fallin' apaht, man, fallin' apaht." This was her standard answer. To me, it meant she was still shooting dope.

"How long you been here?"

"'Bout a week. We had to leave. You had the right idea, man gittin' the fuck out. The cops busted the place five days after you left. They found ten bags of smack and planted five bags of coke just for good measure. Jerry's in the hospital with hep.[12] Whole scene's fucked up, man. Hey, c'mon up!"

She led me to a second floor flat. There was Cozmic Dave, Rebecca's crazy goddamned speed freak sister, Jennifer, and Peter, her meth dealer boyfriend. This was just fucking great! The same scene that I had left in Boston had followed me to three thousand miles to the Haight! They all seemed glad to see me, I was about shell-shocked. Shit, double shit, and *triple* shit!

"Jerry's a fuckin' mess, man," Cozmic Dave told me, "after the second bust on Follen Street, his dad bailed him out and then put him in the hospital for hepatitis. Jerry started gettin' sick and left the hospital to score some smack. Dude is fucked up, man."

"Dawn's in jail," said Rebecca, "she couldn't make bail. Hadda go cold turkey."

I stayed for a while and then left. Rebecca hit me up for a buck on the way out. It was my last one but I gave it to her. That was the last time I ever saw any of those people. I don't miss them a bit.

Having given up my last dollar, I lacked bus fare, I started down Haight Street toward Market to go back to J.C. and Laurie's apartment. It was a very pleasant sunny day, a good day to walk. I was walking down a hill on the 1000 block of Haight Street just past Buena Vista Park, approaching Divisadsero Street. Three slender black teenagers were approaching me on the same side of the street.

Oh Shit! They're gonna fuck with me! flashed through my mind.

---

[11] Bostonese for "hard,"
[12] Hepatitis, from needle sharing

I remained walking straight ahead. They were close enough so that the only way I could avoid them was to cross the street, which would be a bad move and too obvious. I was at least in a relatively open and sunny space where I was, easier to be visible to others if some shit went down. I figured it was better than being in the shadows on the other side of the street. Glancing at the approaching trio sidelong, I casually edged closer to the curb. The three youths moved from being in a bunch to presenting a phalanx across the sidewalk. I pretended to ignore them and continued walking, hoping I could get by them. The one nearest to me sidled over and stood squarely in front of me.

"Hey my man, man, y'all know where I kin cop a lid?"[13]

"No man, I don't even know anybody who's holding. There's a grass drought right now. Sorry man. I can't help you." I started to go around him. He took hold of my right arm.

"Hey, hippie dude, I think we better have us a talk. My man here has a gun on you."

Oh shit!

He motioned with his head to the youth to my right who opened the light jacket he was wearing and revealed a revolver he had pointed at me. It could have been a toy or a water pistol, but I was damned sure not about ask if it was real.

"Sure man. What do you want to talk about?"

"Over here, mo'fuck" The third one was now at my left and took my arm. They escorted me over to the front steps of an apartment building.

"Siddown." They sat me down between them, the one with the gun stood directly in front of me, the piece under his jacket.

"Le's talk 'bout money. Yo' money."

"It'll be a short conversation. The reason I didn't take the bus is because I don't have bus fare."

"Yeah, lessee yo' pockets, hippie dude. You jes' might be holdin' some dealing' cash on you. Y'all look like a mo'fuckin' rich hippie dope peddler to me."

Christ! I hope they don't shoot me because I'm broke! flashed through my mind. "Be my guest."

They quickly rifled my pockets and wallet. I had a grand total of 7¢.

---

[13] "Lid" = baggie with about an ounce of weed in it.

They looked at each other. "Fuck this dude man. He ain't got shit. Mo'fuck's jes a broke-ass mo'fuckin hippie," said the ringleader. Letting me keep my 7¢, they got up and started up the street.

"See you 'round dude."

Their conversation continued as I sat there regaining my composure.

"...mo'fuckin' hippie was flat-ass broke, man...."

"...fuckin' hippies ain't got no money man..."

"...Jive-ass mo'fuck'..."

"...*Shee*-it..."

I continued back to J.C. and Laurie's apartment. It wasn't until later told J.C. what happened that I realized the gravity of the situation. J.C. had managed to score a couple of joints of good weed. We smoked one and it calmed my nerves. This was my first experience with being mugged. I was happy to be alive and uninjured.

The events of the afternoon gave me something to reflect on. I felt that this was the final severing of my ties with the scene in Boston and the people associated with it. I was convinced, and still am, that there are no coincidences in life. Every event that occurs in the universe is the result of all events that have occurred before it and influences all events that occur after it. The whole thing with the Boston people, the heroin karma, and the three black kids with the gun were related.

I split Boston to get away from the smack scene. So here I am across the entire goddamned continent in a room with some of the same assholes I traveled three thousand miles to get away from. Rebecca panhandled my last dollar. As a result I was on foot to be set upon by youthful brigands.

Sometimes it isn't what you did that causes unpleasant karmaic shit,[14] sometimes It's who you are hanging out with. The universe is a stern teacher. I got the lesson. Stay away from those people. They are fucked up and will fuck up everyone they meet and everything they touch. Even if you do something nice for them it will bite you in the ass.[15] I never saw any of those people again.

---

[14] The Old Curmudgeon's Sage Advice No. 3
[15] The Old Curmudgeon's Sage Advice No. 8.

FAYE

Rodney, the dope dealer, took an apartment, 3666 20th Street, between Valencia and Guererro Streets just around the corner from J.C.'s pad. He was gone most of time putting together drug deals. His apartment was full of expensive stereo equipment and, of course, grass, acid and other head goodies – including a suitcase with 50 pounds of hashish in it at one point. He needed someone to look after the place, so I stayed there, crashed on the couch, listened to his stereo, ate his food, and smoked his dope. And I fucked his girlfriend too. Faye Rosenstein was from Milwaukee, a dark-haired, dark-eyed slightly zaftig,[16] and delightfully passionate.

One morning after Rodney left for a two day drug buying trip, Faye and I were alone in the apartment. We smoked a joint and imbibed some of Rodney's "magic water" from the jug in the refrigerator. Rodney always said it was synthetic THC[17] but it was most likely some form of MDA.[18]

Faye came up to me and looked at me with her beautiful dark eyes. Without a word we fell into each other's arms. She was wearing a dress that was an Indian print bedspread with elastic at the top to hold it up above her ample breasts. She kissed me voraciously. I needed no further encouragement.

I felt her lovely ass through her dress as she pressed herself into me. I nuzzled her ear and kissed her neck. Her breathing became harder and she was almost immediately uncontrollably hot. She pulled the elastic down over her (lovely!) breasts. The dress dropped to the floor. Faye was gorgeous, nicely tanned all over. We went into the bedroom and lay down, I turned her over on her tummy. I kissed her neck and down her back while caressing her, running my fingers lightly up the back of her legs and over her ample ass. She moaned and shivered as I did so, such a delightful sight!

I lay on her, kissing her neck and back, working my way down her back. I kissed her lovely cheeks, embracing her above her knees and covering her ass with kisses. I reached under her and, brushing my fingers over her pussy lips, rubbed her clitoris. I turned her over and started performing cunnilingus on her. She moaned a lot, especially when I licked her clitoris. She undulated her hips and called my name, becoming

---

[16] Slightly plump. Same as "pneumatic" in Huxley's "Brave new World."
[17] Tetrahydrocannabinol, the active ingredient in marijuana
[18] There we were, taking a mind altering drug without knowing what it was. Was this stupid? Most certainly. Do I recommend it? Hell no! Why did we do it? We were young and reckless. It was the zeitgeist to explore the limits of human consciousness.

more aroused as I fluttered my tongue on her clit. She had a huge orgasm in my face.

Faye's sexual appetite was considerable, and she was quite uninhibited. We smoked dope and made love the entire day in every room in the apartment and in the shower. We spent the night together at her apartment a couple of times as well.

Faye gave me a little memento of our trysting. Several days later the last time we were together I found some discomfort while urinating one morning and figured I had a dose of the clap, so I went to the San Francisco VD clinic.

VD is a great equalizer. There were about ten people there when I went in, white, black, Hispanic, male, female. I don't remember any Asians. Now, there are a lot of doctor's waiting rooms you can be in and people will carry on conversations. Not so in a VD clinic. What is there to talk about? Everyone knows why you are there. The waiting room was dead silent.

The doctor examined me and determined that I did not have the clap. I had NSU (non-specific urethritis). I was referred to a free clinic where I was given some pills. Problem solved!

CLAP CLAP

The city's clap clinic is growing along with the free-love generation. Since the Summer of Love in '67 the clinic's facilities at 33 Hunt St. have been too cramped, and they've finally got the Board of Supervisors to approve their move to 250 Fourth St., between Howard and Folsom.

Love needs care, and it is provided fast, free, and confidentially any weekday.

1969 San Francisco Good Times clipping
Source: Archives and Special Collections at the Thomas J. Dodd Research Center, University of Connecticut

THE CAPTAIN

It was, I suppose, indicative of the times that you never knew what was going to happen next. For instance, one evening I was sitting around Rodney's pad mellow on some weed. I listened to Voco's (Abe Kesh) outrageous rhythm and blues show on KMPX, one of the Bay Area head stations. I looked out the window and saw the huge washing machine agitator, aka Grace Cathedral, which was under construction. I was quite mellow listening to Elmore James playing *The Sky is Crying* when the door opened and I saw a uniform come in. Well, shit, this gets me a bit excited, an adrenaline rush. Then I see it's not a cop. It's an Army captain in a class A uniform and Rodney's right behind him.

"Hey, Gene, this is Malcolm Riederman. We went to high school together." I shook hands with Malcolm.

It turns out Malcolm is shipping out for 'Nam the next day. He's not at all bummed out, though, he says, "Hey, when I come back from 'Nam, I will *be* Mister *Reefer* Man "I'm bringing back a footlocker full of Vietnamese weed. I'm gonna get rich off that shit."

"Don't they search your stuff when you come back to the states?" I asked.

"Naw, only the enlisted guys," he says, hitting on the joint and passing it to me, "I'm an officer. They won't fuck with me." He grinned.

I never saw him again. I have wondered if he made it back, and how Vietnam may have changed his life. And if his dope plan worked for him. Hell, I hope Malcolm made a million dollars! Even a jillion!

3,4,5-TRIMETHOXYPHENETHYLAMINE

Mescaline is the psychoactive ingredient found in the buttons of the lomphora williamsii, peyote, a cactus used as a religious sacrament by Native Americans in the southwest, a highly regarded psychedelic. There were a lot of capsules on the underground drug market purported to be mescaline, but were really either MDA, which is a psychedelic amphetamine structurally related to mescaline, or plain old LSD. Occasionally some large capsules would appear there were filled with a brown vegetable substance, allegedly peyote buttons which had been dried out and ground up.

"Tell you what" said Rodney as he toked on a joint, "I'd really like to get some synthetic mescaline."

"Can't your chemist make it?"

"He's too busy cooking MDA."[19] Says he can make a lot more MDA for the effort and materials required for mescaline."

"Wouldn't that price synthetic mescaline out of the market?"

"Synthetic mescaline is not a street drug, it is a psychedelic connoisseur's drug. Them that want it will pay the asking price. Like the rich heads in Marin County! Fuck, they have lots of money! If I have something exclusive – and especially if it is exclusive – there's a lot of 'Haha I've got something you don't' one-upmanship that goes on with these

---

[19] 3,4-Methylenedioxyamphetamine (MDA), is an empathogen-entactogen, psychostimulant, and psychedelic drug of the amphetamine family that is encountered mainly as a recreational drug. In terms of pharmacology, MDA acts most importantly as a serotonin-norepinephrine-dopamine releasing agent (SNDRA). Due to its euphoriant and hallucinogenic effects, the drug is a controlled substance and its possession and sale are illegal in most countries. including the U.S. (source: Wikipedia)

people. They'll pay the asking price whatever it is just to impress their friends. If you can afford a Porsche you can afford synthetic mescaline!"

True enough! There were a lot of Porsches in Marin County!

"I have a chemistry background, Rod."

He perked up. "Really? You have a degree?"

"Naw. I have 20 credits though, four semesters of 5 credit chem courses. Class and labs five days a week. Heavy duty."

"Do you think you could cook mescaline?"

"Given the right ingredients and equipment, hell yes!"

"What would you need?"

"I'd need the synthesis method. That would list the required chemicals as well as tell me what equipment is need for the process."

"Where do you find that?"

"The Journal of the American Chemical Society. Libraries have them. Just check the annual master article index and look up what issue we need."

Rodney and I consulted back issues of the Journal of the American Chemical Society to find a practical synthesis method. [20] It was fairly difficult and low yield, but that made the market value of the resulting psychedelic higher, a drug for connoisseurs. The raw materials necessary were unregulated and easily obtained through chemical supply houses as was the necessary lab equipment.

It would have been easier to set up an LSD laboratory, but the starting ingredient, ergotamine tartarate, was tightly controlled and difficult to obtain. You had to have an overseas connection for it, and we didn't have that. Besides, that base was covered. There were a lot of acid chemists around.

The lab was taking shape. We had a location in an old warehouse in Dogpatch, the industrial section near Third and Army streets. I went with Rodney and we purchased the glassware, pressure vessel and other necessary equipment. I was in the process of getting it set up when Rodney got busted on a shitty little two pound grass deal. He had been set up by a cheap B&E[21] artist with a smack habit that I had known peripherally while in Boston (amazing how these people kept showing up). I told Rodney to be careful when doing anything with this guy because he had

---

[20] A New Synthesis of Mescaline, Makepeace U. Tsao, J. Am. Chem. Soc.' 1951, 73 (11), pp 5495 – 5496, DOI: 10. 1021/ja01155a562, Publication Date: November 1951
[21] Breaking and entering

a way of getting busted by the cops and then cutting a deal, rolling over on anyone he knew who was dealing. Sure enough, he had been busted by the SFPD and set Rodney up. That was the end of the lab because Rodney's resources went into legal fees. I have no idea whatever happened to Rodney, I never saw him after that. He had resources that would have allowed him to leave the country.

STANYAN STREET

Rodney moved out of the apartment on 20th Street but I stayed behind, squatting and paying no rent, coming and going as I pleased. I found myself wanting the steady company of a woman. Stephen Gaskin periodically had picnics on top of Mount Tamulpias across the Golden Gate Bridge in Marin County. The picnics were a massive gathering of Monday Night Class people for a day of peace, love, music, excellent dope, good vibes, nudity for those who wish, and a good time for all. I had decided that I would meet a woman at one of these head picnics.

In August of 1969, being of a particularly cosmic state of mind at one of these picnics – due to the ingestion of one of Rodney's "super-caps"– I was standing in a certain spot and told myself that when I turned around, I would see the woman I was intended to meet. When I turned around, I saw a slender woman with long, straight black hair sitting near a rock. I went over and started a conversation. Her name was Anita. We smoked a joint and walked to a nearby rise, lay in the warm afternoon sun and smoked another joint. I kissed her hesitantly. She responded. We necked. I caressed her breasts, meeting no resistance from her. Her breathing quickened as I gently kissed her neck and darted my tongue in and out of her ear. Yes, I was going to get lucky!

We rode back to her apartment with two of her friends, Philip and Susan, who lived a couple blocks away from her on Frederick Street, kitty-corner from the Hari Krishna temple. We spent the night making love.

She didn't let me see her nude, she was in bed and under the covers by the time I washed up. I got in next to her and felt her warmth. A single candle beside the bed, which was two single mattresses on the floor, pushed together, gave us enough light to see each other's faces. I explored her body with my hands and lips. We both became extremely aroused and engaged in an intense lovemaking session.

When I left the next morning, she gave me her phone number. I called her the following week and went over to visit her. This visit ended with us smoking some grass and making love. I visited her regularly. We went to bed each time.

I found Anita to be quite attractive. She was five years older than me, 26, and worked as a secretary for a radiologist, Dr. Gold, at the University of California Medical Center on Parnassus Heights up the hill from the Haight. She had a pleasant smile and a slender build. I found

Anita in Golden Gate Park, 1970. The park was right across the street from her apartment building. We would go for walks there every Sunday. I wish I knew what she was saying to me when I snapped this shot!

her freckles totally charming. We got along quite well, especially in bed. In a few weeks, we were getting along well enough that she asked me if I would like to move in with her. I did.

Anita kept me. I was essentially a "hippie gigolo." I certainly didn't mind. We would make love, no, I take that back, we *fucked,* sometimes four and five times a day. One of us would say to the other, "Hey, wanna fuck?" and away we would go! I can only think now how one does not fully appreciate the stamina one has in youth! She told me that she had not found many men who could bring her off. I could and she appreciated it. She showed me letters she wrote to friends extolling my ability to bring her to orgasm time after time. It's good to have references!

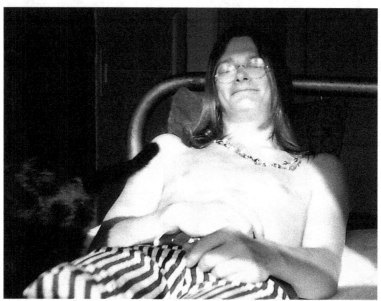

The Author pleasantly stoned in a warm sunbeam, 776 Stanyan Street 1970.
Cristabel Kitty exiting on the left! The beads are now a part of a macrame wall hanging my wife made. Anita snapped the pic.

We spent many hours exploring our mutual sensuality and doing a lot of "dope balling," smoking a joint of some good reefer and coming on to it during foreplay. Not enough is said about the aphrodisiac properties of weed. The combination of reefer and sexual stimulation made for explosive simultaneous orgasms. We generally used the missionary position, and finished our orgasms together with her legs in the air.

Anita was the most vocal woman I had ever bedded up to that point. One afternoon as we were making love, and for no reason that I can think of, I reached under her ass and inserted a finger into her rosebud as she was crossing over the threshold of orgasm. She screamed out loud as if in pain! I was not prepared for this explosion of noise and passion and stopped in mid stroke.

"Am I hurting you?"

"Oh, God! Uhhh! No!! AHHH! It doesn't hurt! OHHH!" she replied, between gasps. I resumed the stimulation. She writhed with ecstasy and continued screaming. I was truly amazed and tremendously turned on by her intense orgasm and, let's just say it ended well for both of us![22] Jesus, what a ride!

Anita was the first woman to request that I take her through the back door. I had never even considered this before, but, being as I was *such* an open minded gentleman, I complied with her request. She told me of a poet, Tim, whom she lived with for a while in Texas after her marriage to Sandy Lockett went to hell.

"He was hung up on me not being a virgin," she said. "He wanted to fuck me in the ass because nobody had fucked me there before. He just wanted to fuck part of me that was still virgin, I guess."

Anita was hung up on getting older. At 27, her breasts sagged a bit (although not unattractively so) because, she said, she was born missing a tendon that most women have which holds their breasts up. She also had a bit of spinal curvature. Previously she had posed nude for life drawing classes at San Francisco State. The teachers liked having her for a model because of this slight spinal deformity, it made her more difficult to accurately draw.

I enjoyed her body, she had long, slender legs and a very pleasing behind. Her breasts were not unusually large They were proportioned just fine for her build.

She also enjoyed having me perform cunnilingus on her. I loved going down on her. We favored the "queen's position" for this, with Anita lying on her back and me lying with my head between her legs. It was a pleasure to service her with my tongue, licking her vulva, tongue-fucking her and finishing her orgasm by licking and sucking her clitoris until she came, writhing violently and clenching her thighs around my head with such force I thought she would crush my skull! More than once I got a bloody nose! The little flesh part under my tongue would hurt for a day after one of these workouts! The knowledge of female anatomy I had gained in my adolescent years of jerking off to paperback "marriage manuals" as came in handy! Her orgasmic response to our lovemaking was passionate and ecstatic.

Anita was the product of a middle-class Jewish upbringing in Brooklyn. She despised her mother, who had been a rather domineering influence in her life and she had hoped that Anita would get a Ph. D. and marry a doctor or lawyer. She had sent Anita to Bryn Mawr in that effort. Anita wanted nothing more than to be able to work to survive.

---

[22] What I didn't know at the time was that the pressure of my finger in her back door pressed my penis up against her G-spot – something of which I was completely ignorant - triggering her intense orgasm. *Yee haw!*

"At Bryn Mawr, we had to be in every evening by nine o'clock." She told me, "It was a strict rule. When we asked our house mother why, she told us, 'Because if you stay out after nine o'clock, you girls will get pregnant.' Knowing that, we always made sure we got our screwing done before nine o'clock!"

She had been married to a fellow from Texas, Sandy Lockett, road manager for the popular psychedelic band, the Thirteenth Floor Elevators. She described her relationship with her in-laws. "'Yankee Jew-Bitch.' That's what they used to call me behind my back. I took about as much of that shit as I could then split."

Anita stayed in Texas for a while, then returned home to her mother. "I just wanted nothing more that to be able to get a job," she told me, "so my mother agreed to send me to secretarial school. I just wanted some goddamned practical skills. My degree in literature doesn't mean a whole shitty lot as far as getting a job goes. Anyway, she began immediately scheming to get me into graduate school. One day she laid it all out to me how I was going back to school to get my doctorate. I was so pissed that I packed up and left." She continued, "Before I got on the bus out of New York, I called her up and told her 'Mother, if I could kill you and get away with it, I would.' "

Whew.

She had gone from relationship to relationship, with occasional returns to her sweetheart from her high-school days, Louis, with whom she had been sleeping since she was sixteen. He was living just south of San Francisco.

We settled into a comfortable existence living on the edge of the Haight with her two cats and went to Steven's Monday Night Classes and Sunday Sunrise Services, smoking a lot of dope and dropping acid together.

I was into doing psychedelic artwork at that point, doodling for endless hours with colored pens. The drawings I made are still in a folder with the Stanyan Street address on them. My psychedelic flights of fancy resulted in multi-layered geometric mandalas, something Anita referred to as "psychedelic pointillism."[23]

I think it was in the 90s there was an anti-marijuana TV spot[24] that showed a group of doctors in surgical gowns in the operating room smoking weed and joking, the message being "what if that joint were in somebody else's hand, like your surgeon, your lawyer or your local policeman?" It cracked me up because in 1969 Anita and I would buy pounds of weed from Michael Ferguson across the hall and sell it to doctors and residents at the University of California Medical Center where

---

[23] Portions of some of these drawings have been incorporated into the cover of this book.
[24] https://www.youtube.com/watch?v=EumbZzk2rXU

she worked. We started doing this in October and had no problems with availability. The price had risen to $200 a pound. Keys (1 kilogram bricks) were pretty much a thing of the past.

As to "your lawyer or local policeman" smoking weed, lawyers definitely smoked weed and could afford the best. And cops ALWAYS had the best dope because they took confiscated it from those they arrested.

I was told by a former Lewis Run, PA officer that, in the 1980s, there occurred a situation where cops were pinching weed from a stash in an evidence locker until there was none left for which to prosecute the offender!

MICHAEL FERGUSON

Michael Ferguson and his five year old son moved into the apartment across the hall at 776 Stanyan St. I guess if you were going to use a word to describe Michael, it would be "dapper." Michael was an original, a real piece of San Francisco head culture. I never really knew exactly who Michael Ferguson was until later, when books were being written about San Francisco in the '60's. At the time, he was just the guy across the hall.

Michael was the founder of The Charlatans, one of the original San Francisco head bands, veterans of the legendary Red Dog Saloon in Virginia City. With Robert Hunter – who went on to being the Grateful Dead's lyricist – Mike Wilhelm, Richie Olson, and Dan Hicks, Michael was the piano player. They were acid-head Edwardian dandies who sported stiff collars and straw hats. Michael was slender with somewhat receding over the collar length sandy hair, and mutton chops. There was no big deal about Michael, not to him, he was a totally laid back dude.

He had been the proprietor of the first ever headshop, the "Magic Theater for Madmen Only"[25] on Divisadsero St., just north of Haight St. He had stopped running the shop years before. He wasn't playing any music either. His scene was him and his son.

Michael's living quarters were elegant in the sense of the Edwardian hip funk 60's. The whole place was a collage of groovy, collectible, rare, wonderful stuff. The wide doorway between his living room and dining room was bordered with satin brocade curtains, something like you might expect to see in a turn-of-the-century house of ill repute. His mantel was covered with carefully arranged antique/hip clutter. A fan shaped display of Nazi swastika stick pins adorned a small crystal vase on the mantel This little display understandably freaked Anita out when she saw

---

25 Taken from Herman Hesse's novel, The Steppenwolf.

it. An old Homburg covered with all manner kinds of cloisonné fraternal pins hung on a hat rack.

A picture frame seemingly full of mounted butterflies hung on the wall, except that when you got up close to it, it was butterfly shapes made by unrolling roaches[26] and gluing them onto paper in butterfly shapes. There were a some pictures of Michael and the Charlatans.

Michael's ex-old lady lived in the other apartment across the hall next to Michael's. She was a junkie, and a skinny black who always wore shades lived with her. There seemed to be a lot of sadness in Michael, and I think a lot of it came from Gracie. I think he really loved her, but she was into her junk.

"Yeah," Michael remarked to me one day, "Gracie just floated off on a heroin cloud."

Michael drove a nice looking maroon Mercedes sedan. It was classy, as was everything about him. I never asked Michael what he did because it was evident he was dealing. His connections were cool. I was at his apartment once when some guys came in and gifted him with a several bricks of choice weed straight from the planeload of reefer they had flown in from Mexico!

I met a most unusual character there one evening, a really stoned-out hippie dude who was short, probably about five-foot-two, and had long, brown frizzy hair that seem to rest on his shoulders like a big fuzzy ball and hung nearly to his elbows. His beard was equally outrageous, split and coming to two large points. He peeked out of the middle of this mass of hair through rimless granny glasses.

Now, of all the intoxicants man has found on planet earth, I would have to say that hashish is the finest. And this dude had lots of it. We smoked some, shot the shit and he finally got around to telling Michael what he had been up to. It turns out, he made this particular hash himself. He had gone to Afghanistan and apprenticed himself to a hashish maker for several years!

Michael's son's room shared a wall with our bedroom. One time when Anita and I were scoring grass from Michael, she mentioned the noise from his son's bedroom.

"Well," said Michael, with a grin and a twinkle in his eye, "I hear some pretty strange noises coming from your room, too."

---

26 The end of a joint too small to continue smoking

I tried not to laugh. Anita turned red and fell silent. When we went back to her apartment she remarked, "Jesus Christ! *That* was embarrassing!"

Michael had been in the antique business some years earlier. He told us, "It was a cool scam, There were all these old houses in Texas, you know, the people had moved during the depression or died and these houses were just sitting there full of antiques. I had women working with me and they would go in the houses and load up the furniture. I'd truck it out to California and sell it. I always had women working for me, because they would do what they were told and not screw it. I did that for a few years."

After I moved out of Anita's apartment I went back to visit Michael from time to time. I spent many enjoyable hours in the company of this utterly unique individual.

Eventually I lost touch with him. It was sad, years later, to read of his death in Hank Harrison's book, "The Dead" (about the Grateful Dead). Michael was a diabetic. He went blind, then had to have his hand amputated, then his leg, then his kidneys failed. I will always remember him, ever the hip dude, always ready with a joke, eyes twinkling, meticulously rolling perfect joints containing the finest reefer ever smuggled across the Mexican border. It was a real privilege to have known this intelligent, genteel man.

TOMMY AND GEORGE

The apartment building in which we lived had eight units and some interesting characters. Our upstairs neighbors were Tommy and George. They were black, gay, and tailors by profession. These guys were *really* into clothes! I have never seen more outrageous getups that the ones these guys would sew for their friends! They were the original black acid queens, with wild drug fueled parties that screamed and bitched all weekend.

I didn't really know Tommy well, but I talked quite a bit to George who bought ounces of weed from Anita and I. George was a sort of stay-at-home but Tommy, who used to be Little Richard's personal tailor and who used to tour with him. He wore lipstick, eye makeup and outrageous outfits that could embarrass a pimp. Tommy had a sister, Coxcee, who also bought weed from Anita and I, for her and some of her friends.

Their apartment was burglarized at one point, a lot of their clothes were stolen. George was talking to me one day shortly after that." I'm so depressed," he said, "I only have twenty-four pair of shoes left." Only *twenty-four* pairs of shoes? The mind boggles. They were great and very interesting guys!

OPERATION INTERCEPT

When I arrived in San Francisco in the summer of 1969 there was no weed available. None. There was a "grass drought." While I was crashing with J.C. and Laurie, J.C. came in one day and said with a big grin, "Hey man, I just copped a nickel[27] of weed on Haight Street!"

We sat on either side of a tiny table that was underneath a window in the kitchen. J.C. rolled a joint and we smoked it. Nothing. He rolled another one and we smoked that one. Same. Just then J.C.'s tabby cat, Kitty, jumped through the open window onto the table and started rolling around on the remains of the nickel bag J.C. had just bought. Well, it wouldn't get *us* high, but Kitty was just elated because it was evidently Class A catnip! Like I said, there was *no* weed in San Francisco that summer!

Weed is scarcer in the summer than in the winter because summer is when it is growing! The harvest is in September. The market responds accordingly to this cycle and the market responds accordingly. This cycle is no longer a big factor on the weed market because there is so much weed grown indoors and hydroponically.

September of 1969 I was living with Anita on Stanyan Street. KSAN was keeping us up to date on the Nixon administration's new anti-drug project, "Operation Intercept," an all-out drive on the smuggling of drugs into the U.S. from Mexico. Counterculture news services picked up on it and news of it was broadcast on head stations nationwide.

Operation Intercept was launched at 2:30pm. Pacific Daylight Time on Sunday, September 21, 1969. By late afternoon, the Tijuana crossing traffic was backed up for six miles.[28] Exasperated motorists stuck in the dust and heat blew their horns. "Hear that?" One customs agent remarked to a radio reporter, "They're playing our song!"

This happened at thirty other border crossings as well. Economic impact was felt on both sides of the border as tourism and commerce was hampered Everybody bitched. There were demonstrations against Operation Intercept in Mexico.

---

[27] $5 bag
[28] "The 1969 Marijuana Shortage And "Operation Intercept"." Druglibrary. org. N. p.' 2017. Web. 9 Aug. 2017.

FLASHING BACK– COMING OF AGE IN THE AMERICAN 1960s

From The San Francisco Good Times, September 11, 1969, byline Jim McGuirk:

God was the first person reached for comment on the government's campaign against Mexican marijuana. The Justice Department announced the death last Friday of George Emrich, 44, the chief US narcotics officer for Latin America. [29]

George met the inventor of marijuana under the ocean off Acapulco when he was hit by a wave and pulled out to sea by the undertow. He was walking fully clothed along the beach with two other oinkers, plotting against the weed, when the wave struck.

Despite this omen, Operation Intercept was launched this Monday along the Mexican War cease-fire line. But a car-by-car search at the border failed to uncover any significant quantity of dope.

However, Mexicans on their way to work and tourists are delayed more than four hours in traffic stretching for miles behind customs offices. The economy of the border depends on American tourists dropping dollars on the Mexican side and 'green-carders' and braceros supplying cheap labor on the American side.

Pressure is now being applied to the Mexican government to protest this potentially disastrous interruption of commerce.

The Justice Department's plans to attack the grass farms themselves (electronic surveillance and nausea sprays) is unlikely to deter the small farmer, for whom marijuana is the only cash crop he can depend on.

In Los Angeles, Tim Leary announced his own four-point 'Operation Turn-On,' its main theme being grow your own. The California gubernatorial candidate predicted the government's 'persecution of 30 million pot smokers' would have no effect on the growth of the psychedelic revolution in this country.

At the Customs mail facility in San Francisco, all leaves have been cancelled and employees have been forced to work overtime to open all packages of foreign origin. But all this is not likely to end the supply of good old Mexican grass and force us to rely on our own agrarian skills. As one police border scout lamented, 'There are areas out there where a small army could cross without detection.

Operation Intercept was a spectacular and counterproductive failure, abandoned October 11, twenty days after it began,

---

[29] This is true. It actually happened!

From July 1, 1968 to June 30, 1969, United States customs officials had seized 57,164 pounds of marijuana, about 150 pounds per day.[30] During the three weeks of Operation Intercept, they had seized 3,202 pounds of marijuana, about the same amount per day. Operation Intercept had enormously inflated marijuana publicity, but had not significantly increased marijuana seizures. How much smuggling increased elsewhere as a result of the transfer of customs officials and narcotics agents to the Mexican border is not known.

Not everybody thought it was a failure, quite the opposite. Drugs were piling up south of the border. This was before the advent of drug cartels with their unlimited financial resources. In the days before the rise of murderous drug cartels, marijuana was trafficked by people who were more entrepreneurial than criminal. Despite new FAA radar equipment, smuggling by air really – pardon the pun – *took off!* Previously, there was a planeload here and there, a single engine Piper Cubs, Cessnas and the like, but now larger planes were coming into their own for dope smugglers.[31] By 1971 they were using DC-3's and Lockheed Lodestars. There were rumors of a British WWII Lancaster bomber flown by a former RAF pilot! Flying low to avoid radar they disgorged their cargos of contraband at abandoned airstrips or in the desert.

Long after Operation Intercept aerial smugglers continued to use the techniques pioneered in September 1969. The Law of Unintended consequences came into play forcing smugglers to be more resourceful, resulting, ironically, in increased drug traffic overall.

UCLA did a study to determine whether there had actually been a marijuana shortage sufficient to curtail marijuana use before and during Operation Intercept. Government officials announced on October 23 that marijuana was scarce enough as to be almost unavailable at UCLA. The study did not bear this out. Half the respondents said their frequency of marijuana use was below normal at some time between May and October 1969, as a consequence of the extremely limited availability of marijuana.[32] The other half were smoking marijuana at their customary frequency despite the annual shortage that preceded Operation Intercept and despite Operation Intercept itself.

"Operation Intercept" was a marked failure, and the KSAN news director, "Scoop" Nisker, made great sport of how all it did was piss off the workers who had to cross the border daily to and from their jobs. If there was any effect on the supply of weed on the street as a result of Opera-

---

[30]Robert Berrellez, Associated Press, in the *Reporter Dispatch,* White Plains, N. Y.' October 1, 1969.
[31]New York Times, October 2, 1969
[32]W. McGlothlin, K. Jamison, and S. Rosenblatt, *Marijuana and the Use of Other Drugs,* Nature (London), 228 (December 19, 1970): 1227-1229

tion Intercept, I didn't notice it. The media reported that grass prices were rising because of limited availability due to Operation Intercept. It is far more likely that more people were smoking weed![33]

THE HOLY MAN JAM

The Family Dog was a rock n' roll dance hall on the Great Highway. Managed by Chet Helms, it was a popular rock venue taking the place of the Avalon Ballroom after the City Supervisors harassed it out of existence. I saw many bands there many times. Unlike Bill Graham's venue, The Fillmore West and Winterland, The Family Dog was not afraid to accommodate the esoteric wanderlust of its audience demographic. This is where Stephen held his Monday Night Classes.

Notable was an seven day event on October 3-9, 1969, the last three days of which became known as "The Holy Man Jam." This was a unique mixture of rock n' roll and appearances by spiritual leaders of various sorts. This is indicative of the thirst the freak culture had for real spirituality, not just the mumbled incantations, empty prayers and pious platitudes offered by society's approved forms of worship.

Featured acts were performances by the Hare Krsnas ("Hare Krishna" chanting), Middle Eastern music, Osceola, It's A Beautiful Day, Phoenix, The Golden Toad, Malachi, Afterglow, San Francisco's Radical Lab, Floating Bridge, and more.

Lecturers included Timothy Leary, Alan Watts, Stephen Gaskin, Michael Lorimer, Master Choy, Sufi Sam, Chiran Jeev, Allan Noonan, Asoke Fakir, Jim Kimmel and Jud, John Adams and Magana Baptiste, Sebastian Moon, Tup Fisher, Dr. Warwick, Swami Satchidananda, Pir Vilayat, and Schlomo Carlebach, and many others.[34]

I attended two nights and saw, among others, Stephen and Timothy Leary. Stephen was, well, Stephen. Leary was a clown. Entertaining to be certain, he had declared his candidacy for Governor and spoke about his campaign, part of which was a bumper sticker reading "I'm a head. Are you behind?" In early 1970 he was convicted of marijuana possession and sentenced to ten years.

---

[33] In Capital, Marx states that a commodity has value because of the labor invested obtaining it. Risk adds another dimension of value to a transaction. I guess Marx didn't have any dealers in illicit substances in his personal orbit. I wonder, did he and Freud ever do cocaine together?

34 The Sampradaya Sun - Independent Vaisnava News - Editorials - September 2006 Harekrsna.com. (2019). The Sampradaya Sun - Independent Vaisnava News - Editorials - September 2006. [online] Available at: http://www.harekrsna.com/sun/editorials/09-06/editorials652.htm [Accessed 28 Nov. 2019].

CHAPTER 20

THE MUSIC

ROCK N' ROLL COMES OF AGE

Rock n' roll of the 50s and early 60s consisted of innocent teenage love songs and up tempo tunes with nonsensical lyrics. It was unpretentious dance music. Many rock n' roll hits were covered (a euphemism for "stolen") by white artists borrowing from black rhythm and blues artists.

The desegregation of America started with music. Little Richard's *"Tutti Frutti"* was downright scary to white parents when they heard their kids playing his records. Good God, he was a NEGRO. Their kids were enjoying NEGRO music! What if their daughters wanted to date a NEGRO? OH NO!

So along comes the Caucasian Crusader, Pat Boone, who has a hit with *"Tutti Frutti"* getting more airplay with his shitty, completely uninspired cover than the song's creator because he was white and Little Richard was not. Rinse and repeat. This was done many times with many songs by many artists.

The nature of the music changed as the 1960s unfolded. There was a lull in rock n' roll between the death of Buddy Holly in 1959 and the advent of the Beatles in 1964. Once the Beatles established themselves in U.S. there followed a flood of bands from Britain that became known as "The British Invasion," The Dave Clark Five, The Rolling Stones, The Animals, Gerry and the Pacemakers, The Who, Pink Floyd and many more. This was the beginning of an incredible musical renaissance. Rock n' roll was now transatlantic with groups cross-pollinating musical styles and influences. The music blossomed into a renaissance.

Folk music was also on the scene. It was acoustic, no electric guitars or drums. Following the lead of elders Woodie Guthrie and Pete Seeger, folk music lyrically themed toward peace, freedom, justice, equality, and civil rights. These values were considered "communist" by broomstick up-the-ass-flag-waving right-wingers).

Bob Dylan carried this tradition on with his protest music, music with a social message pointedly critical of the status quo. Music with ideas and ideals. *Dangerous* music! Dylan emerged as the premier folkie and is now considered the most important 20th century American poet.

Rock n' roll and folk music were like oil and water, they did not mix. People by and large liked one or the other. When Dylan showed up at the Newport Folk festival in 1965 playing an electric guitar and backed up by an electric band, he was booed. Many said he had sold out. Dylan may have lost his hard core folkie fans, but he gained the wider rock n' roll audience. It was a shrewd move.

The Byrds started what became the Los Angeles folk-rock movement with sweet vocal harmonies and Roger McGuinn's distinctive chiming 12-string guitar and a hit Bob Dylan's "Mr. Tambourine Man."

Music was becoming more attuned to events of the day. "Abraham, Martin and John" by Dion lamented the assassinations of Abraham Lincoln, Martin Luther King, Jr., and John Kennedy. The Byrds had a song about JFK titled "He Was a Friend of Mine," echoing a popular generational sentiment. David Crosby was fired from the Byrds for being too political at their live performances.

The 60s generation also discovered the blues. Suddenly there was an interest in black blues performers who had been screwed by record companies and gone under appreciated and unpaid. They found their audiences turning white and being very appreciative.

Curiously enough this happened because of the British bands like the Rolling stones and Fleetwood Mac. America was racially and musically segregated. the Brits got their hands on as many records by blues artists as they could and drew upon them to form their own interpretation of the blues.

The Rolling Stones were aghast when, on their first U.S. tour, they found out that Americans by and large did know about or care about blues giants such as Muddy Waters and Howlin' Wolf. They helped spark a blues revival allowing many underappreciated blues artists to get some recognition and make some money before their time was up.

In the late 1960s instrumental proficiency increased exponentially. This was most apparent with blues bands like the Paul Butterfield blues Band and The Electric Flag in the U.S. and British Cream and Fleetwood Mac. The culmination of this was Jimi Hendrix who changed the role of the electric guitar forever.

In 1967 the Doors came on the scene with the long organ improvisation in "Light My Fire." By the end of the decade absolutely mind blowing performances were common, with groups like Led Zeppelin raising the bar dramatically.

The use of marijuana and psychedelics expanded the music lyrically and musically.

There is a great story told by Bob Dylan about visiting the Beatles in their hotel room on their first U.S. tour. Upon hearing *"I Want to Hold Your Hand"* Dylan mistook "I can't hide" for "I get high." He thought the Beatles were smoking weed and he brought some with him. As it turned out, the Beatles were not yet potheads. Bob Dylan changed all that! What a moment that must have been, Bob Dylan getting the Beatles high for the first time! I'd loved to have been a fly on the wall...

Young people loved rock music, as rock n' roll came to be called. Their parents hated it. It had universal appeal to youth everywhere and added to what was called the "generation gap."

What started in Haight Ashbury was occurring worldwide, with rock providing the soundtrack while reinforcing and promoting the values of their generation. Some artists were held in such universal esteem that the release of a new album became a major cultural event. The Beatles, the Rolling Stones, Bob Dylan, and Crosby, Stills, Nash and Young fell into this category.

Between 1963 and 1968, music went from doo-wop love songs with sweet harmonies to edgier, more rebellious and profane with Detroit's MC5 exhorting their audience to "Kick out the jams, motherfuckers!"[1] The Beatles went from "I want to hold your hand"[1] to "why don't we do it in the road."[2] Bands like The Jefferson Airplane and Country Joe and the Fish released material that was blatantly drug oriented as well as carrying social and political criticism. The Airplane inserted the street phrase "Up against the wall, motherfucker" into the song *"We Can Be Together."* GIs in Vietnam were singing Country Joe's *"Feel like I'm a' Fixin' to Die Rag,"* which reflected their feelings about being sent to fight in the endless, useless war in the lyric

"One, two, three, what are we fightin' for?

Don't ask me I don't give a damn, next stop is Vi-et-nam.

And it's five, six, seven, open up the pearly gates.

Ain't no time to wonder why, whoopee, we're all gonna die!"[3]

---

[1] © Lennon & McCartney
[2] © Lennon & McCartney
[3] From "Feel Like I'm a Fixin' to Die Rag," © Joe McDonald

Rock music became a unifying, glue holding the disparate and chaotic elements of the counterculture together. The electric guitar blasting sonic chaos through a stage full of amplifiers bigger than refrigerators became a weapon to be wielded against the powers that be.

And the best thing was, The Man could not fucking understand it! For a while MGM Records, in an attempt to boost sales – they only had one decent act, the Animals – used the positioning statement "The Man can't bust our music." That was true. The Man didn't clue one as to what effect the music was having as a social and political force.

With its appeal to youth and the tsunami of cash it generated, rock became an irresistible force. It didn't matter that it promoted sex, drugs and revolution. There was too much money in it to care.

This brings to mind Soviet Premier Josef Stalin's statement, "When we hang the capitalists they will sell us the rope we use." Rock music was promoting revolutionary values – yes, values guaranteed under The Constitution and Bill of Rights were revolutionary because they were missing in American society – that could be the undoing of capitalism. It mattered not. Capitalism benefitted hugely from selling music promoting of values that could threaten their very existence. While none of this has come to pass, capitalism enabled rock music in becoming an irresistible ideological force.

Here is a point about the counterculture that has been missed by many. Despite antipathy toward unchecked capitalism and a government that refused to hear them, the youth rebellion of the 1960s was not a communist conspiracy. Hippie fr4eaks did not hate their country. They wanted America to be what it was intended to be under The Constitution and Bill of Rights, a nation of free and equal citizens not subject to governmental tyranny. The counterculture did not oppose American values, rather, it opposed values and practices running counter to The Constitution and Bill of Rights: racism, discrimination, and the Vietnam war, which they viewed as a war of choice fought to make money for the defense industries and not a war of necessity.

The counterculture spawned many movements: feminism, gay liberation, the American Indian Movement, ecological movements, solidarity with the Black Panthers and other organizations opposing racial and ethnic discrimination, and an overwhelming desire for desire for world peace in this unstable nuclear age.

Freaks were labeled as "communists" and told "America, Love It or Leave It!" by Nixon's "silent majority" who goose-stepped along equating "my country right or wrong" and other authoritarian jingoistic bullshit with The Constitution, Bill of Rights, and the flag.

Sometimes it got up close and personal. I remember reading in the early 70s, I think in Rolling Stone, about Pacific Gas and Electric, a blues rock band from Los Angeles, with an interracial lineup, cutting their tour short after being assaulted in the south by the Klan.

The undeniable proof of the innate patriotic nature of the counterculture was when Jimi Hendrix took the stage at Woodstock and played the Star Spangled Banner. No one booed. Five-hundred thousand people, all opposed to the war, smoking grass, tripping on acid and whatever else was available, and there were *no* catcalls for the National Anthem! That is because each and every one of those kids loved America.

The shared experience of LSD defined the values of the counterculture. Music was the expression of those values, keeping and disseminating them. Half a million young people holding those values came together at Woodstock for three days in peace.

"Straight" society with its war in Vietnam and general repression of dissent and it's loathing of the counterculture stood in diametric opposition to all of this. In terms of Marx's dialectic, the conflict of two opposing ideas out of which emerges a new idea, the music helped set the stage. It was just so goddamned magnificent that Marx himself would have said "Bring it on *motherfuckers!!"*

Phun with Photoshop - partying with Karl at Woodstock

THE FILLMORE WEST

Bill Graham's Fillmore West was located on Market Street at the Carousel Ballroom. J.C. introduced me to a fellow from Fitchburg, MA named Bob, who was in the Army. He said he had been a disc jockey and radio announcer, fucked up and transferred to the infantry. He was to ship out for 'Nam the next day. He was scared. As a last blast, he said he would take J.C. and me to the Fillmore. Bill Graham's shows usually had three bands each playing a two sets.

The opening ACT for this show was The Loading Zone, an R&B band from Berkeley. Chuck Berry was the second act, and Jethro Tull the headliner. I had seen The Loading Zone several times before, they always put on an excellent show. Chuck Berry, of course, was Chuck Berry. He was backed up by the Loading Zone[4] and played his red Gibson ES-335 through a pair of Fender Twin Reverb amps. Tull was the headliner, and deservedly so. They were playing through Hi-Watt amps bigger than most doorways!

Their drummer was Clive Bunker, a most amazing dude. The standard drum kit for rock bands was a huge twin kick drum set, many tom toms, cymbals and so on. Bunker was using a four piece jazz kit with only two cymbals, hi-hat, wood block and cowbell. The dude was outasight! Oh yes!!

We went home stone cold straight as there was not a stick of reefer to be had in the city that week. I said good-bye to Bob, and thanked him for the concert and wished him luck. He was definitely sweating about shipping out for 'Nam.

The following afternoon, I went over to J.C.'s. Bob was there. "Shit! What's up man? You AWOL?"

"No way. Dig it, I was waiting at the airport, and wasn't going to board until the last minute. An announcement came over the PA system that all those who had not yet boarded my flight should not get on board. The guys who got on are on their way to 'Nam. I don't have to go!" I thought it was a weird story, but that's what he told us.

He was elated, and I don't blame him. We celebrated by going to the Fillmore again that night for the Tull lineup. Afterward, we ran into Ian Anderson and the guitarist, Martin Barre, on Market Street and talked with for a while.

---

[4] Chuck never traveled with a band, he always used locals for backup. His songs were such a canon of rock and roll that everyone knew them. Rolling Stone critic, Lester Bangs put it this way: "If you are going to play rock and roll, Chuck Berry is a door you have to go through."

Bob's story sounded fishy. I lost contact with J.C. Burkhouse over the years. J.C. and I reconnected a while back. I ran this past him.

"Oh yeah," he said, "That story is totally true. Bob was a complete fuck up. He was a huge asshole. And he's my brother-in-law. He lost his radio announcer gig through some dumbass thing – I don't remember what, there were too many – so they were transferring him to the infantry. He asked my father if there was anything he could do. My father worked for Curtis LeMay.[5] Strings were pulled. They couldn't have just one guy taken off the plane, so they pulled this stunt. How, I have no idea. But Bob got his ignorant ass saved. Now, do me a favor and don't *ever* bring his name up again."

This anecdote serves as another example of how those with connections could obtain preferential treatment regarding Vietnam.

Bill Graham also put on shows at the Winterland auditorium, formerly the headquarters of the Ice Capades. This was a much larger venue than the Carousel. Glass containers were not allowed inside, kids were mixing reds[6] and wine, getting trashed and puking on concert goers. As you got your ticket and walked into the venue an imposing black security guard patted you down so fast you didn't know it happened until it was over. One evening my girl friend Anne and I were going in – I think it was the New Riders and the Grateful Dead on the bill – and in a micro second this guy patted me and had my Sucrets tin full of rolled joints out of my jacket pocket. Before I could think "*oh shit!*" he opened it, inspected the contents, closed it and handed it back to me saying "Enjoy your evening, Sir," with a big grin. He was very skillful!

There was hippie-dippy bullshit over the music promoters, chiefly Chet Helms who ran The Family Dog, and Bill Graham who ran the Carousel Ballroom (Fillmore West) and Winterland. "Oh, Bill Graham, he's on a money trip," people would say, "all he cares about is money." Then the light shows went on strike wanting as much money as the bands got. There were picket lines and lots of bad vibes. Chet didn't draw as much fire as did Graham. What the hell, these guys were businessmen, musicians are not free, and music is not free. Peace and love are free. Concert admissions require cash.

---

[5] The retired Air Force general, "bombs away with Curtis LeMay," who supervised the WWII firebombing of Japan and was George Wallace's VP running mate in 1968
[6] Seconal, red capsules, downers

FLASHING BACK– COMING OF AGE IN THE AMERICAN 1960s

THE ALTAMONT FREE CONCERT

Dec. 4, 1969, San Francisco Good Times clipping advertising the concert to be at Sears Point. The Altamont Speedway was chosen with less than 24 hours before the start of the concert.
Source: Archives and Special Collections at the Thomas J. Dodd Research Center, University of Connecticut

The Rolling Stones decided they wanted to do a free concert during their 1969 U.S. tour. Originally they wanted to hold it in Golden Gate Park. The city would not issue a permit for it, so the search was on for a suitable concert site. The concert was scheduled for December 6, 1969. Anita and I kept KSAN tuned in all the time to get details. The Sears Point Raceway was announced as the concert site. That deal fell through and the search for a suitable location continued. It was less than 24 hours before the concert was supposed to start and a site had not yet been found.

The announcement came that the concert would take place at the Altamont speedway in Livermore, across the bay from San Francisco. Chartered school buses provided rides to and from the concert. KSAN said the buses would be along the panhandle on Oak Street. Anita and I had a cooler with a picnic lunch, and I rolled a pocket full of joints. We took some blankets too.

The scene on the buses was anarchy, like something out of an S. Clay Wilson drawing. It's like 8:00 in the morning and the party is *on!* Our bus was a crowd of hippie freaks of every size and description in full-tilt-boogie mode.

Joints were passed, pipes were shared, jugs of wine made the rounds. The air was heavy with a mixture of marijuana smoke punctuated by pungent of patchouli oil and the delicate scent of stick incense and the occasional whiff of body odor. The overall mood was buoyant. Everyone engaged in pleasant conversation. Someone played an acoustic guitar, a tambourine jangled semi-rhythmically. A bamboo flute and the ching-

chinging of finger cymbals added to the joyous cacophony. Good God! It was positively *glorious!*

Attire was typical of the freak culture at the time. Bell bottom jeans were ubiquitous on the men. Many of the women wore them as well while others wore long flowing dresses made from chintz bedspreads imported from India printed with intricate designs in shades of red, yellow and green. These garments were simple, a bedspread sewn into an appropriate sized tube and secured in place with elastic around the top and held in place by the wearer's ample breasts! It was December, and the weather could get cool, so many had warm jackets and blankets to sit on.

Hair styles were outrageous, with some looking like hippie hairballs. Anita referred to as "Jewish afros." Others had pony tails, a single braid and all manner of facial hair. Some had long frizzy hair to the middle of their backs, a few hippie chicks wore long straight blonde hair accented with a single skinny braid on one side, just everything imaginable. Members of both sexes wore beads and hippie jewelry of every description with many of the women favoring jingling brass wrist and ankle bracelets from India. In the seat directly on front of us were two hippie women entwined in each other, casually making out. Everybody was up for a good time!

And the bus drivers…OMG…it was SO funny! They all looked to be young to middle-aged petite Chinese women wearing their very prim

> The Rolling Stones will be giving a free concert in the park on December 6," said Glynn Johns, recording engineer for the Stones. "We're just wrapping up negotiations now." We were talking to Johns last Wednesday night at the Family Dog benefit held at Fillmore West.
>
> "The concert will be filmed and recorded," Johns said, "with all proceeds going to some charity." He added that he wouldn't be recording the concert himself though, since he had to be back in England for his brother's wedding.
>
> Over the past week rumor of the Stones' concert has spread all over the country. In Los Angeles they are planning caravans already. But so far no one had contacted the S.F. Park Department for permission to use the facilities.
>
> Peter Ashe told us there are several problems in the way of a permit although he didn't categorically say that it will be denied:
>
> First of all the time is short. The Wild West and the Moratorium gave two or three months notice. There are tremendous problems of public safety and sanitation, he said.
>
> Secondly, in early September there was a temporary cessation of rock concerts by decree of the Park Commission. They allege it was necessary due to the incidents of violence and firearms in the past.
>
> And lastly, there has never been a rock concert in the park with over 30,000 in attendance. Ashe feels that the Stones could draw as many as 200,000.
>
> Nov. 27, 1969 San Francisco Good Times
> Rolling Stones Free Concert
>
> Source: Archives and Special Collections at the Thomas J. Dodd Research Center, University of Connecticut

and proper and pristine blue-gray chauffeur uniforms, with dark piping and chauffeurs' caps. Staring straight ahead, it was as if they dared not look back at the scene behind them. Those poor ladies must have been scared to death. Or maybe they all knew kung-fu! Anita thought it was a delightful cultural incongruity. I wonder, did they get a contact high? Overall, the journey was weirdly pleasant. Or pleasantly weird. Something like that!

Everybody was pretty well-buzzed by the time we disembarked at the concert site. The weather was going to be warm, but not uncomfortably so. We were in the middle of the crowd. A freak show ensued. There was the enormous Latino dude – he had to go at least 300 pounds – tripping his brains out who, running all over the place was bare-assed naked. All during the run up to the start of the music you'd see him blissfully walking, skipping, dancing...he was having a pretty good time! The people he was trampling were not so pleased, but he was among fellow acid heads and was tolerated. As on the bus ride, flutes, tambourines, drums and guitars added to the pleasant din of the crowd. The sound crew was tweaking the sound system. "God's Eyes" of various sizes made of colorful yarn could be seen here and there in the crowd looking like military standards for cohorts of hippie freaks. Marijuana smoke and incense wafted on the breeze. The overall mood was upbeat and festive.

At the 1967 Human Be-In in Golden Gate Park, Hell's Angels volunteered to do security and provide lost child services[7] and were generally helpful, contributing to the success of the event. So, who should you call to run stage security at Altamont? Why, the Hell's Angels, of course. And pay them in beer. What could *possibly* go wrong with a plan like that?

The Altamont concert was doomed to be a disaster from the start. The lack of planning resulted in the stage being too low to keep it from being overrun by a surging crowd. There were no barriers and no way to manage the crowd. The stage was at the apex of this enormous mass of stoned humanity. The Maysle brothers film, *Gimme Shelter*, clearly shows people being pushed by the crowd toward the stage. All day long there were calls for people to move back so as to make room down front. The crowd complied, at least the part of the crowd distant from the stage. We picked up our stuff and moved back several times that day.

Anita and I were in the middle of this of drug drenched multitude later estimated at 300,000. Santana was the first band up. It didn't take long for trouble to start. The naked tripping fat dude somehow offended

---
[7]*Human Be-In, Haight Ashbury 1967 | John McCarty.* (2016). *John McCarty.* Retrieved 2 April 2018, from http://www. johnmccarty. org/human-be-in/

the Hell's Angels down by the stage and they beat him bloody, knocking his teeth out with pool cues.[8] Hell's Angels mixed it up with people in front of the stage. During the Airplane's set, a Hell's Angel knocked singer Marty Balin unconscious when he tried to intervene. The festive feeling was quickly turning ugly. All day long there were pleas from the stage for the fighting to stop.

We couldn't see the trouble from where we were, but we could feel the nasty vibe building. The film makers, the Maysle brothers, and their film crew had been shadowing the Stones on their tour shooting footage for a movie. In their film, "Gimme Shelter," Hell's Angels, pool cues flailing, are seen beating the bejesus out of hapless folks in front of the stage.

Some Angels parked bikes in front of the stage. Predictably, the crowd was pushed forward knocking some of the bikes over. The Angels responded by beating the living shit out of them. People who got on the stage were thrown off it and stomped by Angels. The music was interrupted by these incidents all day long.

The escalating violence reached its climax during the Stones' set. They stopped and restarted *Sympathy for the Devil* because of violence in front of the stage. As they started into *Under My Thumb* a black man, Meredith Hunter, had an altercation with an Angel in front of the stage. Hunter pulled a revolver and was stabbed by one Angel and mercilessly stomped by others. It was caught on film: a gun in Hunter's hand, the flash of the Angel's blade.[9] The Stones stopped the song while Hunter was evacuated. No one knew he was dead until the next day.

The Stones set proceeded. The Stones finished with *Street Fighting Man* and everyone gathered up their stuff and split. I don't know how we found our way back to the buses in the dark, but we did. I give Anita credit for that.

No one knew of Hunter's death until the next day. KSAN had extensive coverage including interviews with Hell's Angels President, Sonny Barger, and other principals involved. The aftermath of this event, looked to as another peaceful music festival like Woodstock, was shock and horror.

The Woodstock audience was a half-million people and there was no violence. Altamont was attended by about 300,000 people. While we did not details until after the fact, it was a vast roiling clusterfuck, a rock n' roll calamity resulting from the catastrophic folly and deadly naiveté

---

[8]*Altamont*, Joel Selvin, Harper-Collins 2016, p. 162, 223
[9]*Altamont*, Joel Selvin, Harper-Collins 2016, p. 213-221.

of the organizers. It could have been worse. What if the crowd had stampeded? *Jesus!*

MEETING LED ZEPPELIN

My appreciation of Led Zeppelin grew as I listened to their eponymous first album daily, alternating it with *Led Zeppelin II*, the *Whole Lotta Love,* album. At the time I was into doing psychedelic art and decided that I should turn my efforts to doing an album cover for my favorite band.

With that in mind, I took the bus from Anita's apartment to the Winterland auditorium on November 7th, 1969, with my artwork and enough money for bus fare and admission. It was all the cash I had. Getting off the bus I found myself the object of the attention of several gentlemen of color, one of whom had a knife. He wasn't displaying it in a threatening manner, he just wanted to sort of let me know he had it and could cut my honky ass if he wanted to. Naturally, they wanted all my cash.

"Tell you what, my man," said the leader upon relieving me of about a dollar in loose change and taking a five dollar bill out of his pocket and holding it in front of my face, "I bet five dollahs y'all gots anuthuh five dollahs. Ain't that right now, muthafucka? You gots anuthuh five dollahs on you!"

Damn! He must have read my mind! He was dead on accurate, but I wasn't going to tell him. I had a five dollar bill stashed in a small pocket in my Navy surplus pea coat. They didn't find it and they moved on to find some other poor chump to hassle. They got most of my bus fare but I managed to get out of the situation without losing my ticket money or my artwork.

Once at inside Winterland, I headed toward the backstage area. I went over by the dressing rooms and hung out with some British guys. Soon, the band arrived, Page, and Jones carrying their Hi-Watt amp heads. They were much too busy for me to talk to them so I went over near the stage. This was before drumhead tight security. There were a few guards, but none roaming about rousting people about backstage passes. I found myself amongst a bevy of absolutely gorgeous(!) groupies. I got to see the show from a distance of about twenty feet from the stage.

Even as I sit here today, now past 70 with my ears still ringing, I can't help but remember the sensation of being blasted by Jimmy Page's Hi-Watt stacks – four altogether, two on either side of the stage – and to look up and watch him doing his percussive bit with the violin bow and Echoplex, to be at ground zero at the thundering climax of the guitar solo in *Dazed and Confused*, being hammered by *Communication Breakdown*, gut-punched by the *uber* heavy riffing of *Whole Lotta Love* and *Heartbreaker*. It was a smashing, positively superb performance!

When Zeppelin's second set was over I positioned myself where they had to pass to get to the dressing room. When Page went past I said, "Hey, Jimmy, can I talk to you about something?"

He turned and gave me a look, and at that time I was quite skinny, had shoulder length hair and wore John Lennon style glasses, "In a few minutes in the dressing room, man. Got to unwind a bit." He could have said "fuck off, "after all he had just finished an exhausting set. Maybe I looked weird enough that he thought I merited attention!

I hung out at the dressing room door with some British guys for a while and then went to enter. I was stopped by security at that point.

"It's OK," I told him, "I've got some artwork for an album cover that Jimmy wants to see. He told me to come in after the show." A slight exaggeration but, what the hell, it worked! I was admitted into Led Zeppelin's dressing room! I was going to actually meet my rock idols!

Jimmy Page was sitting in an easy chair smoking a cigarette with an oh so *very* sweet groupie on his lap. The bass player, John Paul Jones, was next to him talking to another groupie. I introduced myself to them. "I'm a real Led Zeppelin fan," I added.

"Well, you're one of the few," Page replied.

I really didn't know how to take that, whether he was being facetious or what, so, I ignored it. Hell, he was probably irritated that this long haired jerk was bothering him after a hard gig, especially when his prospects for company for the evening were looking so good. I wouldn't blame him! I gave them my artwork to look over. Robert Plant came over.

"What's this?" he inquired.

"This is Gene," Page said, pointing to me. Plant shook my hand. "These are 'is drawings," Page continued handing the drawings to Plant who perused them in turn. They were interested! *Yes!*

Page referred me to the band's manager, Peter Grant. He looked at the artwork impassively, wrote his name and address on the envelope they were in (I still have the envelope and the drawings) and told me to send finished work to that address. Now, Peter Grant was a imposing individual, a large man with a meticulously groomed beard, looking for all the world like the actor Sebastian Cabot. To be truthful, he looked like a gangster to me.

I took my artwork and left, passing by the drummer, Bonzo, who was in a chair by himself looking at a proof of a promotional fan booklet. He seemed to be a bit drunk and in a rather foul mood. I was going to show him the artwork too, but I thought the better of it and left.

As far as I could tell, I had been successful. I took the bus home, riding with some of the same groupies who struck out trying to score with Led Zeppelin. I was quite satisfied with myself. However, I never did get the artwork done to send to Peter Grant. Why? I got a vibe of untrustworthiness for him. You don't just send finished artwork to a client without a contract. Well, there was also…did you ever hear a song by Shel Silverstein called *I Got Stoned and Missed It*?

At least I got to actually meet and shake hands with three of the members of Led Zeppelin, the band that became the biggest supergroup of the 1970s. That was truly great!

GUITAR PLAYERS I HAVE KNOWN

On one particular acid trip in 1970 I was in the apartment messing with a cheap guitar. While drums were my main instrument at the time, I really wanted to be a rock guitarist. I enjoyed drumming, being the rhythm and drive for a band was exhilarating. But I wanted to be on the top of the music playing screaming psychedelic guitar leads. I had been playing guitar a bit since Lock Haven in the mid 60s. Practically every-guy, even the least talented, learned how to strum a Bob Dylan tune or two on the guitar because the girls dug it!

San Francisco Good Times. 25, 1969 - George worked on a couple of my guitars back in the day.

Source: Archives and Special Collections at the Thomas J. Dodd Research Center, University of Connecticut

As I sat in the kitchen with my beater guitar in my hands, I made up my mind I was going to become an accomplished guitarist. I loved drumming and I loved supporting the music. But I wanted to be *on top* of the music. I wanted to *rock!*

I sold my drums and bought a decent acoustic guitar and commenced to practicing relentlessly. J.C. located a 1961 Gibson SG Special (ser. no. 25625) for $195 in a pawn shop in Mill Valley and put $20 on it to hold it for me. It was the sweetest guitar I have ever played. Unfortunately, hard times forced me to sell it some years back.

Long term plans and goals have not been a part of my life. Guitar playing is one thing I made up my mind to do that I actually accomplished. I think the one-pointedness I developed toward learning the guitar was due to psychedelic imprinting. I have stayed at this for 50 years so far! I practiced five hours a day for five years and then started playing band jobs.

RADIO RAY

Radio Ray was a guy I got to know through the hardware store. I jammed a couple times a week at Radio Ray's house. Radio Ray blew harp and worked as a porn actor/model as well as moving modest weight in grass and coke. . John Cayman was another regular with a black Fender thinline Telecaster. We had a bass player, Jim Burnett, who sucked at playing bass but he always had a pocket full of cocaine to share! We never had a drummer at those sessions. Not even once.

We played anything that was in our technical capabilities, three chords at the most! Sometimes we had people show up who could actually *PLAY*. These jam sessions were held at 123 Day Street, in the Noe Valley section of San Francisco.

We sometimes actually functioned as a band, picking up a drummer and playing for biker parties. We didn't get paid, well not in cash anyway, but, oh boy, we could party in style, all night, and for *free!* And if we ran out of songs, hell, we just played 'em all over again! The second band at these parties was Mothra, some very squared away guys who had a style that alternated between riff-rock and some very jazz stuff. Their drummer sat in with us.

ALBERT SHUFFLE

There was a dude named Albert who jammed with us for a few months. Never knew his last name, he wouldn't tell us. Albert was a white guy with an absolutely fabulous burgundy Gibson ES 345. He could play the most hellacious shuffle I think I ever heard (well, maybe until Stevie Ray Vaughn). We called him "Albert Shuffle." Yeah, we had some badass jams with Albert, slow blues, medium blues, fast blues, always blues.

Albert was one smooth axe man. I learned to "rake" from Albert (raking is an electric blues guitar technique where the pick is stroked downward across the strings which are muted by the palm of the hand at the bridge so the notes are muted giving a percussive sound rather than a clear tone. The last string is played unmuted and rings clear. This is a pretty much universal blues guitar technique. There is also a reverse rake where the pick is stroked upward across the strings. Stevie Ray Vaughn does this on the very beginning of *Texas Flood*).

Albert was into Albert King's style of playing (which makes me think his first name wasn't really "Albert," either). We spent hours jamming together and copping licks from Albert. After a few months, we found out that Albert had a big problem: heroin. Albert wasn't strung out all the time, but he would kind of do binges with it. This problems surfaced after some guitars came up missing (none of them mine). We never saw Albert after that. He wasn't the first talented junkie I ever met and wouldn't be the last. Heroin is a destroyer of souls. Once it gets hold of a person, it rarely lets go and I have seen a number of very talented people destroyed by it.

GUITAR CURTIS

Out in back of the house on Day Street where we jammed was an old cottage that was unoccupied and just generally beat to hell. John and Radio Ray struck a deal with the landlord at Day Street that if they would get the cottage in livable shape, they could get free rent for a while, so they busied themselves at hoeing the place out. There was a huge pile of trash to be hauled away, so they called a guy to come and get it. The guy show up and it turns out to be none other than a black guitarist who has wowed everyone with his appearance at the San Francisco Blues Festival the week before as Guitar Curtis.

"Hey man, aren't you Guitar Curtis?"

"That I am!" came the reply.

One thing led to another and Guitar Curtis started coming by our Day Street jam sessions. it was *enormously* cool! I don't recall Curtis having a style of his own, but, by God, he could play like *anybody* else! Albert King? Sure. B. B. King? Naturally. Chuck Berry? Better than the original! I was in absolute awe of this guy. Curtis taught me Buddy Miles' *Goin' through Them Changes* which was cool because it had this fabulous funk rhythm coupled with a cool riff in the key of E.

Guitar Curtis moved on after a while. He probably had better things to do than jam with some white kids who were blues wannabes. But it was cool having him there, oh *yes!*

VIRGIL

The one guy that really sticks out in my mind is Virgil. I don't know Virgil's last name, never did. Virgil was a burly guy from St. Louis, dark brown hair halfway down his back and a beard. He reminded me of Bob Hite from Canned Heat, only a couple hundred pounds lighter.

Virgil was cool. I don't know what Virgil did besides play blues. He was a nomadic individual. He had a van that he lived in most of the time. In the van were two Gibson Melody Maker guitars, a Vox Super Beatle amp as big as a doorway, the kind with the chrome frame, and a chopped Harley!

Radio Ray ran into Virgil somewhere and invited him to our jams. Virgil was a *hell* of a blues player. He kept one Melody Maker in standard tuning and the other in open D. In standard tuning, he would play a slow blues and it would just smolder. Man, I swear you could see smoke roll off that old Melody Maker. But Virgil played *only* slow blues. No shuffle, and definitely *no* rock n' roll. This seemed strange to me, because I played both and they seemed interchangeable as far as how they were played. Not to Virgil. He was a *blues* player, Goddamnit, and that was *that!* Like Mississippi Fred McDowell who said, "I don't play no rock 'n roll, y'all, just the straight natchrel blues." That was Virgil.

Jamming with Virgil was like going to church, there was a ritual, and Virgil was the high priest. Virgil's big deal was that he knew Canned Heat and would hang and jam with them when he was in L.A. So, every jam session started off with Heat's *Dust my Broom* with Virgil on slide. And we played it *right*, Virgil made sure of that. Everybody knew their part, and Virgil would do the intro. If someone screwed up, we started over. Virgil would get a *little* impatient sometimes.

I can't say if Virgil was a spontaneous player or not. But he was a damned sight better than me, so I was in awe of him. I tried to cop every lick from him I could. Virgil would do a cool lick.

"Oh *yeah!* Hey, Virgil, how'd you do that? Show me, man."

Well, if it was a B. B. King or T-bone Walker lick, he would. but, sometimes, he would turn so you couldn't see his fingers and rip with an outrageous blues lick.

"Oh *wow!* Y'*gotta* show me that one man!"

"Oh no," Virgil would casually reply, "That's mine. I don't show nobody *my* licks." And he didn't, not even once. Virgil's very own licks remained his very own!

We jammed *Stormy Monday* and *Night Life*, any and all 8, 12 and 16 bar blues. And sometime we would get into a rock jam and Virgil would drop out, looking disdainfully at us as we bastardized his precious blues. But he never got on our case about it.

For me, the real revelation of Virgil's blues playing was the night he showed up with ancient looking beat-to-hell guitar case.

"Check this out, you guys," he said, opening it. He pulled out a National Triolian resophonic guitar with a Spanish neck. It was old and funky, the lacquer had oxidized to shades of brown, but you could still see the Hawaiian scene airbrushed on it with a stencil. In the case was an old "How to Play Hawaiian Guitar" book with it copyrighted something like 1935.

Now, I had owned the Columbia *Robert Johnson, King of the Delta Blues Singers* album for a couple years. I had listened to it, but how to play in that Delta style was a complete mystery to me. I listened to that record and was always amazed at the sound. I tuned my $60 Yamaha flattop guitar to open D and messed around, trying to get that…*sound*. I could do some Elmore James type licks, the main *Dust my Boom* lick was within my grasp. But not the Robert Johnson style, not a lick could I play, not a clue did I have. Virgil sat down with this treasure, tuning it, strumming a few rhythm licks.

I asked him "Hey Virgil, can you play any Robert Johnson?"

"Sure. Robert Johnson played in G tuning."

Well, I had read the liner notes to the Columbia LP." Not *Come on in my Kitchen*. That's in D."

"Wanna bet?" He took a slide out of the case and put it on the ring finger of his left hand and proceeded to conjure the spirit of Robert Johnson from the old guitar. *Come on in my Kitchen* just jumped out of that steel box at us. No doubt about it, the album liner notes were incorrect.

I watched Virgil intently, curious about how to *do* this. I had been using a piece of 3/4" copper pipe on my pinky as a slide." Hey Virgil, how come you put your slide on your ring finger. Aren't you supposed to wear it on your pinky?"

"Can't get the *sound* that way. If you want to play like Robert Johnson, you *got* to wear the slide on your ring finger. Trust me." I never used a slide on my pinky after that.

After *Come on in my Kitchen* came *Travelin' Riverside Blues* then *Four Until Late*. And he did Son House's *Poor Boy*. It was part of my blues education. We didn't jam at all that evening, we just sat transfixed, listening to Virgil evoke incredible sounds from that old National.

When I got home, I took my sixty-dollar Yamaha acoustic, tuned it to open G and put my slide on my ring finger. It was awkward at first, but I got used to it fast. I never play slide any other way now, it seems so natural to me. And there is something unique about using a slide on that finger. There is an indescribable quality to feeling the whine and cry of Mississippi Delta Blues form under the ring finger.

After a while Virgil got in a hassle with Radio Ray, punched him out, and moved on. That was the last we saw of him. He left an indelible imprint on my guitar playing. I didn't really cop any standard tuning licks from Virgil, but I owe my ability to play open G Delta slide all to him.

I looked for an old National with a Spanish neck for years, even after I moved back here to Pennsylvania. One evening in 1986 I was jamming at the Northwoods in Coudersport, PA, with Dave Covert and Dave Dorson when Bob and Judy Shunk stopped in. Bob had is fiddle and Judy had her doghouse bass. I played the melody to Bob Wills *Faded Love* while Shunkie wove the most exquisite harmonies around it I had ever heard. Bob and Judy are gone now. He could play just about every stringed instrument known to man.

Later in the evening and I told Bob "if you ever come across a National steel with a Spanish neck, I'm looking for one."

"Just so happens I got one for sale," he replied.

I bought it, a 1932 National Duolian with the gray-green "Frosted Dueco" finished. I spent many hours playing it, enjoying its ringing resonance as I make the strings sing, whine, wail and moan. And every time I picked it up, I thought of Virgil and that one evening he taught me how to play the Delta Blues. Unfortunately, we fell on hard times and I had to sell this treasure. My ROI was in excess of 600% so that took some of the sting out of it!

LEFTY LEWIE

In the mid 1970s I had a relationship with a young woman named Robyn. I mentioned to her that I played guitar and she said, "Oh, you have to meet my brother, Lewis. He plays like Jimi."

Of course I thought *bullshit!* Then I met him, and, by God, Lewis didn't just *play* like Jimi, you could close your eyes and think Lewis was *channeling* Jimi! We became instant friends and jam buddies.

Lew was left handed and played a right-handed Fender Strat upside down like Jimi. In the 70s, we didn't have digital amplifier modeling and the like. If you wanted a big amp sound, you needed a big amp. Jimi played through Marshall amps. Lew managed to get the Marshall sound– and I mean a spot on replication of Jimi's heavy distortion – with a most amazing homebrewed rig. He had a cassette recorder from his days in the Navy which, when he plugged a guitar in to it and cranked it, gave a an amazing crunch. He mounted it in an old portable typewriter case, added a 4"x8" automobile speaker, and powered it with a lantern battery from Radio Shack. He called it the "Mini Marshall." He would do things like show up at demonstrations and play *The Star Spangled Banner* like Jimi, complete with rocket whistles and explosions! Hippie freaks would line up in front of him as he played, saluting him!

Lew and I found we had a natural musical compatibility and would do spontaneous jams for hours.

I lost touch with Lefty Lewie after moving back to Pennsylvania in 1981. About eight years ago I found him on Facebook, living in Virginia. He came up a couple times a year and we jammed even better than back in the day. He retired and moved to Pennsylvania where we enjoy jamming together once again! We are musical soul mates. What a fine thing this is.

HOMECOMING

I came home to Smethport for a visit in 1975 and hooked up with some local musicians, Buz Greenman on bass and his sister Myrna on vocals, Tom Cochran on drums, and Tom Nelson on guitar. This turned out to be one of those times when everything comes together. For about week, we were a fucking monster rock and roll band! We could do nothing wrong. Tom and I traded off guitar solos and just jammed the shit out of everything. The crowd loved it and was chanting our names!

The nights we played at the Fulton House the other bars in town were empty. Norm Hull, owner of Hull's Hotel, called in a phony noise complaint to the police hoping we would get shut down and he could get some customers back in his bar! It is the kind of musical moment every musician live for and experiences too seldom. To this day I treasure that memory and the friendship of those musicians.

JACOB'S LADDER

I hooked up with another guitar player, Richard Cuadra, later that year and played guitar and harmonica with his band, Jacob's Ladder. I don't know what you would call the kind of music we played, some sort of folk-rock I guess. We went through a bunch of personnel, One was a very hot looking Korean-American woman, Yong Moon, who had a voice like Aretha Franklin, but lacked a strong sense of rhythm. She did have nice boobs, though, and used them to hold up the sarongs she frequently wore. It's not like she wanted anyone to notice them or anything! Richard went up to her at a rehearsal and lifted her sarong and she got all bent out of shape! Her masseuse was a friend of the band and told us they were silicone!

She was good eye candy for the band and we did have some excellent gigs with her. I went into the men's room at the Spaghetti Factory one memorable night when we were playing there and someone had written JACOB'S LADDER ROCKS!" on the wall.

In our final lineup we had a bass player, Jorje Pomar and a drummer, Carlos Barreda who were friends originally from Peru. Jorge and I traded off on bass and guitar. This was my first experience playing bass and I found I had a natural knack for it. Carlos also played vibes and I would play drums. Jorge played table as well. Jorge and Carlos – now "Charlie" – are still active in music in San Francisco.

We cut an album titled "If I Had a Wish…" in 1976 on a 16 track that used to belong to the Grateful Dead. It featured six originals by Richard, one by our Grammy winning producer, Robert Hope, one by a friend of Richard's and a reggae versions of "Bye Bye Love," the Everley brothers hit. The piano player for our sessions, Scotty Lawrence, was a fellow I used to do acid with on Shepherd Avenue in Boston in 1968.

After getting my first taste of professional recording I went on to purchase a 4-track reel-to-reel machine and built studio around it, constructing the mixing console and signal processors myself.

For what it's worth, I have received many more offers as from my blues harp playing than my guitar playing. My friend Mike Quirk, a piano player, said to me "It must be that lips and tongue thing!"

W. EUGENE JOHNSON

CHAPTER 21

THE EMERGENCE OF FREAK MEDIA

The freak culture was, of course, at odds with society in general, the basic issue being individual freedom of choice: what are people free to do vs. coercion by the state.

The counterculture developed its own alternative media promoting the values, passions, and aspirations of the counterculture, advocating free speech, civil liberties, draft resistance and antiwar politics, sexual freedom, feminism, gay liberation, black issues, and outright revolution. A chaotic amalgamation of politics, poetry, art, comics, local events, opinions, reviews, advice, personal ads and calls to protest, and the weekly dope reports, counterculture media were a 180-degree alternative to the mainstream corporate media.

Scoop Nisker, ready to take on the day's news!
Source: Author's record collection

Freak culture was about freedom, consciousness and revolution. Now, by revolution I do not mean necessarily the violent kind, but a revolution in the way people think and act towards each other and the earth, thinking outside the box.

Psychedelic drugs played heavily in the consciousness part. Being illegal, these were the main point of contact between freaks and the police generating enormous friction. This was serious shit. The police loved bashing hippie skulls in.

Since the freak community was on the other side of the political fence from the establishment, especially being openly seditious regarding the government's prosecution of the Vietnam War, there was always the *"fuck you, you unpatriotic hippie faggotass atheistic commie peace creep I'm gonna bash your fucking head in!"* factor in police relations with the head munity.

San Francisco had large Italian and Irish populations, largely Catholic.[1] The attitudes of cops and the general mores of the city were heavily influenced by Catholicism so the RCC's high-and-mighty self-righteous moral hypocrisy also entered this cultural confrontation.

List of police undercover cars in San Francisco:

WSJ 346 Olive Green Ford Custom 69
VAP 907 Black Ford Custom 500, 68-9
MFC 550 Olive Ford Custom
XVJ 964 White Ford Custom
NJN 063 Silver Ford
MXB 134 Met. Blue Ford
MFD 572 Lt. Blue Ford Custom 66
TBL 981 Lt. Blue Ford Custom
VAW 624 Tan Ford Custom 500
VGS 817 Black Ford Custom 500
XVG 973 Met. Blue Ford Custom 69
XXW 361 Black Ford Custom ?
NJR 417 Dark Blue Ford Custom 68
MFH 855 Tan Ford Custom 66
XSW 361 Black Ford Custom 69
MFH 898 Tan Ford Custom 66
CYM 641 Met. Blue Ford Custom 67-8
XVG 973 Met. Blue Ford Custom 69
XKJ 341 Black Ford Custom 69
NJE 331 Tan Ford Custom
SWV 953 Blue Ford Custom 68
OWB 436 Black Ford Custom 68
MFC 570 Black Ford Custom 66
SWZ 815 Olive Ford Custom StaWag 68
VNA 464 Black Ford Custom 68
XOJ 512 Black Ford Custom 68
UYE 023 White Chevrolet Impala 68
CZA 133 Lt. Blue ? ?
YHU 563 Black Chev. Station Wagon
WND 096 Black Chev. Station Wagon
XSU 317 Blue ? ?
YIN 770 Tan Ford Custom 69
XVG 973 Turquoise Blue Ford Custom
TLP 607 Tan Ford Custom 68?

San Francisco Good Times Sep. 25, 1969 - always serving their public.

Source: Archives and Special Collections at the Thomas J. Dodd Research Center, University of Connecticut

To the freak community, drugs were a matter of personal freedom as stated in the "…life, liberty and the pursuit of happiness" stated in the Declaration of Independence. If you want to use drugs, it is nobody's business but your own, so long as you are not harming others. An individual's consciousness is not property of the state and not subject to the regulation of the state. Consciousness and spirit are closely related. To use entheogenic substances[2] to expand one's consciousness is a basic human right as well as a religious right.

---

[1] San Francisco's large Latino population was overwhelmingly Catholic took but they did not enter into the ethnic make-up of the police force at the time because they were not white. There was a huge cultural gap with no love lost between Latinos and the SFPD.
[2] The term "entheogen," coined by ethnobotanists in 1979, denotes a class of psychoactive substances that bring about spiritual experiences.

DRAFT HELP: 3684 18th St. near Dolores Park, Free of charge counseling on the draft. Hours 9-5 Mon. thru Fri., Phone 863-0775. No appointments.

EAST BAY DRAFT INFO.: 2320 Dana No. 5, Bkly, 841-7400. Complete draft counseling. This includes extension listing of alternative service work in Calif.

FREE CHURCH: 2200 Parker, 549-0649. Counseling referral service.

AMERICAN DESERTER COMMITTEE: 1227 Rue Wolfe, Montreal 132, Quebec, 521-1143, or American Deserters Committee, Box 3822, Station D, Vancouver, B.C.
CCCO-Western Region- 437 Market St. (near First St.), S.F., call 397-6917.

SOUTHERN ALAMEDA COUNTY DRAFT INFORMATION CENTER: 3137 Castro Valley Blvd, Castro Valley, call 581-4015. Formerly the Hayward Peace Center.

GI HELP: Military counceling "How to Get Out" (psychiatric discharge). 626-2579.

QUAKER DRAFT COUNSELING: Near Walnut and Vine, Tues, Weds, Thurs, from 3-9 pm. 843-9725.

MARIN DRAFT HELP: 406 San Anselmo St. 454-8026.

DRAFT HELP - OAKLAND: Jefferson & 15th, 451-1672.

PALO ALTO RESISTANCE: 424 Lytton 327-3108.

INSTITUTE FOR STUDY OF NON-VIOLENCE: P.O. Box 1001, Palo Alto, 941-5400.

LAWYERS' PANEL - Draft Resistance work - 626-7877.

CHINATOWN DRAFT HELP: 854 Kearny, 781-9622.

SAN JOSE PEACE CENTER: 235 No. 1st St. 297-2299.

A.S.U.C. DRAFT HELP: Rm 209 Eichelman Hall on U.C. Campus. 642-1431.

San Francisco Good Times Nov. 20, 1969

Source: Archives and Special Collections at the Thomas J. Dodd Research Center, University of Connecticut

I truly think there was some police envy over sex. This rebellious younger generation had the advantage of the pill, freeing women from the fear of unwanted pregnancy while freeing men from burdensome child support payments! This was sexual freedom in the truest sense of it. An antiwar aphorism of the day was "girls say yes to boys who say no," so hippie dudes were getting a *lot* of pussy. The cops just couldn't stand that these raggedy-ass longhairs were getting more than they were! Perhaps this is why they enthusiastically beat the women as well as the men, upset that they were spreading their legs for these long-haired bums while leaving the Righteous Forces of Law and Order, God, Country and Everybody Else's Morality to resort to self-abuse or furtive blow jobs coerced from hookers!

The man is on a power trip and has outlawed the right for people to expand their own consciousness, making it illegal for anyone to pursue a state of non-ordinary reality. Why deny anyone that experience[3], that right? This is an egregious violation of the civil right of the individual to their expression and practice of their own personal religious beliefs, a right supposedly protected by the First Amendment. This is why getting high was viewed as an act of revolution.

---

[3] Because people might wake up to the fact that the man has is full of shit.

It's the same old liberal-conservative shit. Liberals are about what everybody is free to do. The conservatives are anti-freedom, always on about what people, other than themselves, their friends and family must be prohibited from doing. Freaks maintained people should be free to take whatever mind-altering substances they wish to take.[4]

Freedom is the ability to live your life as you wish without interference from the state, so long as you are not causing harm to others. The state has no right telling anyone who or how to love, or who to hate. Freedom includes the ability to live one's life without the state insisting you go half way around the world to kill people who pose no threat whatsoever to this nation.

> *If your name is on this list, Switchboard is holding a message for you. You can pick it up at 1830 Fell from 10am to 10pm or by calling 387-3575. Runaways & others who don't wish to be found: our service cannot be used to find you.*
>
> ANTOINE, John
> BAKER, Janet
> CARNES, Cathy
> CRUM, Jack
> CRUMB, R.
> DuBOIS, Mark
> HAUNER, Joe
>
> *This list up-to-date as of August 5, 1969.*

San Francisco Good Times Aug. 5, 1969 - Haight Switchboard message notice

Source: Archives and Special Collections at the Thomas J. Dodd Research Center, University of Connecticut

The draft was seen as anti-freedom, as was the war in Vietnam. Freedom is also the ability to pursue and correct social injustices.

Profanity and obscenity enraged the authorities so, of course, demonstrators freely used the highly offensive pejorative, "motherfucker!" Telling them they fucked their own mothers sent cops into paroxysms of truncheon wielding bloodlust even more than the epithet "pig!" did, especially if that filthy word was directed at them from the mouths of young women.

One hippie remarked to me at the time, "They don't like being called 'motherfuckers.' It's an obscenity so they say, but those motherfuckers have no issues with the U.S. bombing civilians in Vietnam. You tell me which one is fucking obscene."

This was the clearest delineation between the straight culture and the freak culture. Referring to an underarm deodorant commercial, radical and Yippie founder Jerry Rubin said "The American people care more about how their armpits smell than the fact that their government is killing innocent people in Vietnam."

---

[4] All drugs are not created equal. I am referring here to mind drugs: weed and psychedelics, entheogens, not the shit that kills you.

KSAN

We did not have the internet in the 1960s. Mass communication within the freak culture was managed through FM radio stations and underground newspapers who got their news from LNS (Liberation News Service) and, UPS (Underground Press Syndicate), alternative news services sending articles and photographs to underground newspapers and left leaning radio stations across the US and abroad. LNS and UPS enabled people to access news the mainstream and corporate owned media wouldn't touch.

The Metromedia Corporation, no left wing organization, owned San Francisco's KSAN-FM. Smelling money in the weirdness of the counterculture, they put left leaning DJs and newscasters on the air.[5] It worked!

KSAN was an AOR (Album Oriented Rock) format station, no top 40 teenybopper crap at all. I was fortunate to be in San Francisco during the musical renaissance of the era. Every week they would play a new release in its entirety, NO commercials. I heard King Crimson, Blodwyn Pig, Led Zeppelin, and many other new releases. One show was Kris Kristofferson, then a brand-new artist on the scene, interviewed between cuts of his first album. The first tune was "Me and Bobby McGee."

The ads were creative, outrageous and sometimes blindingly hilarious! One firm that advertised daily on KSAN was a dessert shop which carried the owner's name, "Magnolia Thunderpussy."[6] Two of their specialties were "The Montana Banana," a banana with two strategically placed scoops of ice cream shredded coconut and whipped cream, and another erotic dessert specialties such as the "Pineapple Pussy." All the

> "And God said, Behold, I have given you every herb bearing seed, which is upon the face of the earth . . . to you it shall be for meat."
> —Genesis 1:29
>
> US government is attempting to control the grass market by forcing prices up.
> Operation Intercept searched 418,00 people at the border one day and found no grass or hash. It is just a terror. Don't be terrified.
> Some keys, 1-1/2 to 2-1/4, prices ranging from $175 to $275. Hash scarce. Good acid at low prices everywhere. Synthetic mescaline in large caps, $2.50 singles.
> Don't let the rain bring you down.

San Francisco Good Times Sep. 25, 1969

Source: Archives and Special Collections at the Thomas J. Dodd Research Center, University of Connecticut

---

[5] KSAN was the second "underground" FM station, the first being KMPX-FM. After labor struggles, the KMPX staff went to work at KSAN which became the leader in counterculture radio for the bay Area.
[6] (Magnolia Thunderpussy (30 October 1939 – 15 May 1996), born Patricia Donna Mallon was a San Francisco burlesque performer, radio personality, filmmaker and restaurateur. Thunderpussy operated two San Francisco restaurants in the 1960s: the one at 1398 Haight Street (at the corner of Haight and Masonic), which bore her name, featured a late-night delivery service and erotic desserts.)(Source: Wikipedia)

while the voice over is doing the sales spiel there is a stage whisper in the background repeating "mag-*no*-lia-*thun*-der *puss*-ee slowly and deliberately! Simply outstanding!

KSAN's news director was Larry "Scoop" Nisker. Every day he put together amazing sound collages summing up the day's events. He wanted to release an album of these newscasts, but it was impossible to get licenses for all the copyrighted music of which he had used snippets, so he bootlegged himself, releasing a self-titled album in the 70's. I bought my copy at Tower Records. It came in handy years later when I used it as a source for some communications projects while attending the University of Pittsburgh. My daughter's high school social studies teacher also used it as part of the curriculum for his 20th Century American History class. The counterculture was very media savvy. The counterculture was very media savvy, knowing how to draw attention to pertinent issues of the day. Scoop signed off every newscast with "If you don't like the news, go out and make some of your own!"

MORATORIUMS

Anita and I attended several moratoriums, anti-Vietnam War mobilizations. The slogan for the moratoriums was "no business as usual." This was an effort to get people to go to the rallies rather than to work and thus disrupt the nation's business for the day, a sort of general strike. The idea of a general strike was nothing new to San Francisco as one started with the longshoremen on the San Francisco docks in 1934 and spread, crippling the city. The longshoremen were victorious.

These rallies were held in Golden Gate Park. Largely failures in terms of the effect they had on the general community, and they were attended by the usual people you saw at such things.

ARMED BANDS
world news ripoff syndicate

SAIGON—AP photographer Charles Ryan, on patrol south of Da Nang with a platoon from the US Americal Division, said about half of the thirty troops were wearing black arm bands.

"I'm wearing it to show that I sympathize with the anti-war demonstration back home," said the platoon leader, 1st Lt. Jesse Rosen of New York City. "It's just my way of silently protesting.

"Personally, I think the demonstrating should go on until President Nixon gets the idea that every American should be pulled out of here now."

San Francisco Good Times Oct. 16, 1969
Source: Archives and Special Collections at the Thomas J. Dodd Research Center, University of Connecticut

There were always more splinter political groups trying to get the spotlight of media attention. God only knows how many there were in California alone at that time.

Black Panther David Hilliard stepped up to the mic at the October 15, 1969, moratorium and made comments about Richard Nixon that the ever-present feds[7] took to be a call to harm the president and arrested him and several others right then and there.

This same rally was co-opted moments later by a Chicano group calling itself La Raza. They seized the stage and took control of the rally to no effect at all. Not being well organized or articulate, all they did was ramble on at the microphone. People got bored and the crowd dwindled away.

"1-2-3-4, Let's end this fucking war," echoed through lower Sproul Plaza as at least 6,000 people joined Berkeley's Moratorium Day actions.

Throughout the Bay Area and the rest of the country, millions dropped out for the day, dropped back in for the day, or slowed down in some way to tell Nixon that the war is now his, but we don't want it to be ours for one more day.

Berkeley was the liveliest scene, although the heavy rain cut down on protest attendance as it did throughout the Bay Area. The Berkeley crowd got hassled right at the start of the day's program. The rally scheduled for Sproul Plaza was moved to Pauley, then moved back to Sproul where it was chased out by Dean Shotwell, who said UC forbade the meeting and the use of electricity.

Fannie Lou Hamer of the Freedom Democratic Party of Mississippi electrified the crowd. She compared the Berkeley radicals to Mississippi blacks, told of her problems in organizing and announced her candidacy for the Mississippi senate.

Ron Dellums responded to Nixon's proclamation that the Moratorium wouldn't influence him by demanding that he must listen to the people. "And, goddamn it, we are the people. We fired one person and we can fire another."

Speaking to the Berkeley crowd on the resistance among GIs, John Cole of the Fort Johnson Eight said that demonstrations give tremendous encouragement to those organizing and protesting inside. He reported that there is a lot of organizing going on.

Dan Siegal urged the crowd to go into the Berkeley stores that remained open and rap to the owner and ask him why he was open. Sounding prophetic, Siegal said, "We're either going to end this war or end the ability to govern this country."

Almost all the stores on Telly stayed closed . . . only one record store was open. Fewer Shattuck merchants closed, although Hinks honored the Moratorium.

The pigs were generally piggish to the protesters although no busts were made.

San Francisco's Federal Building rally of about 3,000 people was less spirited with a lot of liberals generally uptight about their radical co-protestors, and factional lines were drawn early. Chants varied from "Get out of Vietnam now" to "Give peace a chance" to "Power to the people" to "Off the pigs."

San Francisco Good Times Oct. 16, 1969 Excerpted from "Fall Offensive" article, no byline

Source: Archives and Special Collections at the Thomas J. Dodd Research Center, University of Connecticut

---

Moratoriums were also observed in Vietnam by a military that was becoming increasingly hostile to being fed into an endless meat grinder for no discernable reasons.

---

[7] Demonstrations always had a large percentage of narks and FBI agents in attendance.

Roland Young was a militant black DJ on KSAN who had a show at 6:00 p. m. every day. That evening I tuned in the station and heard him ranting about the arrests at the rally. He was hot! His anger kept building in intensity until he said "I think that everyone in earshot of this broadcast should send a postcard to Nixon at the White House stating 'I want to kill you.'" The following evening when I tuned in the show, the station manager explained how this act was, a federal crime and Roland Young was now in trouble with the FCC and the Secret Service and no longer worked for the station.

We listened to KSAN constantly. It was our pipeline to what was going on in the freak community and kept us informed of the developments of left wing politics and the antiwar movement.

The news director, Scoop Nisker, did the news using these amazing sound collages, snippets of various songs and effects interspersed with his news reading and actualities.[8]

The "Chicago Seven"[9] trial was in the news constantly, and Scoop's report on it might well have started with the chuffing of a steam locomotive starting out from the station, not-so-subtly implying the defendants being railroaded, then a snippet from Al Jolson singing Chicago, then a quote from (political activist) Abbey Hoffman, a few bars of the Rolling Stones "Street Fighting Man," followed by his summary of the days' events at the trial.

These days, sound collages like Scoop's are easily made using a computer. Back in the day this type of editing as done with reel-to-reel audio tape, a razor blade, and splicing tape!

The events reported at that time included Black Panther defendant Bobby Seale, the eighth defendant whose trial was separated from that of the other seven, being gagged and chained to his seat in the courtroom.

EARWITNESS TO THE BIRTH OF TOPLESS RADIO

A San Francisco doctor, Gene Schoenfeld, had a column in several underground papers called "Dr. HIPpocrates." He also had a call-in show on KSAN. One memorable evening, he had a guest by the name of Margo St. James. Margo was a well known San Francisco personality, having

---

[8] On TV it's a "sound bite," on radio it's an "actuality"
[9] The Chicago Seven were seven defendants—Abbie Hoffman, Jerry Rubin, David Dellinger, Tom Hayden, Rennie Davis, John Froines, and Lee Weiner—charged by the federal government with conspiracy, inciting to riot, and other charges related to anti-Vietnam War and countercultural protests that took place in Chicago, Illinois, on the occasion of the 1968 Democratic National Convention. Bobby Seale, the eighth man charged, had his trial severed during the proceedings, lowering the number of defendants from eight to seven. (from Wikipedia)

> Lots of good hash around if you can find it. Hard blond Lebanese at $850/lb., soft black balls from Afghanistan for $75-85/oz. Lebanese pollen hash (kief?) burns fast, costs about the same. Lemon wafers $2.50 on the street. Sunburst microtabs, very pure, very expensive.
>
> Some cocaine around if you dig burning out your brain, $60/spoon, $700/oz., cut once. Some heroin being sold has strychnine in it for that last heavy trip.
>
> Small keys at $150-175, better bricks still going for $225-250. Lids $12-15, $10 for domestic. Don't buy peyote tar available at $45/oz.; it takes about an ounce to get off.
>
> We die every night and are reborn every morning. Stay conscious as you rise to sleep and explore your subconscious/astral plane. See you in your dreams--
>
> *IWW Dope Dealers Local 630*

San Francisco Good Times Aug. 8, 1969

Source: Archives and Special Collections at the Thomas J. Dodd Research Center, University of Connecticut

been a hooker and the founder of an organization advocating legal prostitution called Call Off Your Old Tired Ethics, or COYOTE. On this particular show, they were talking about (what else?!) sex.

At one point, Dr. Hip referred to Margo as an "ex-prostitute," to which she responded, "Honey, there's no such thing as an 'ex' prostitute. I go out and turn a trick once in a while just to keep in practice. I never know when I might have to go back to work!"

"Margo," a female caller asked, "My old man is so big, I have trouble getting him in my mouth. I really dig giving him pleasure in this way. Can you give me any advice?"

"Well, why don't you try practicing on a cucumber of appropriate size? That way you can get used to taking something that size in your mouth!"

The next caller was a male who snorted, "You can't talk about stuff like this on the radio!" to which Dr. Hip replied, "Oh yeah? Just listen!" and went to the next caller.

I like to think that I earwitnessed the birth of what became known as "topless radio!"

THE STRAIGHT DOPE ON STREET DOPE

The counterculture was an outlaw culture that revolved around illegal drugs. There is always risk involved when purchasing and consuming street dope. Underground newspapers did their bit by posting availability and prices of various drugs and issued warnings when warranted. This was no laboratory analysis though, it was just a market summary, and I question its accuracy, The S. F. Good Times reported on numerous occasions on the quality of synthetic mescaline. I highly doubt these was ever any synthetic mescaline for sale on the street, what was sold as synthetic mescaline was LSD or MDA.

In the 1970s, before the advent of pre-employment drug testing, Pharm Chem Laboratories in Menlo Park, just south of San Francisco, instituted a program for testing street drugs. Anyone could get their drugs tested anonymously for strength and purity by calling Pharm Chem and getting a number. A small sample was sent to Pharm Chem with the number, as well the location and price paid. No personal information was collected. A follow-up call to Pharm Chem would get you the test results.

Pharm Chem compiled this information into weekly report that was read over the air on KSAN telling people what was available and the going price, as well as warning about bad acid, adulterated speed and heroin and the like that could prove dangerous.[10]

This was timely as DEA, rather than interdicting drugs at the border, came up with the idea of contaminating the marijuana. Mexico was given $15 million annually in aid that included helicopters to spray marijuana and poppy fields with paraquat.

Tasteless, odorless and invisible, paraquat can be immediately fatal or damage kidneys, liver, lungs, and lead to heart failure for up to thirty days. You couldn't tell if the weed you were smoking had been sprayed with paraquat or not.

Two longhairs, driving around in a 1957 or thereabouts Chevy, have been involved in several busts lately in the Haight area. These phony longhairs (they've got the outward appearance, but not the heart) have been fingering people who smoke grass or take acid—or those who deal. An informant tells me that they are still around, so take note.

Two undercover cops, dressed badly as older hippies, recently approached this writer. Theirs was an incredible story of "being followed by narcs"— then came their pitch. "If you could show us where to turn on, we'd really give you the business." I could imagine, anyway I suggest a better acting school for them (cops are really very bad actors).

San Francisco Good Times Sep. 25, 1969 - always serving their public.

Source: Archives and Special Collections at the Thomas J. Dodd Research Center, University of Connecticut

---

[10] *If You Don't Like the News, Go Out and Make Some of Your Own*, Wes "Scoop" Nisker, Ten Speed Press 1994, P. 54-55.

There was precedent for spraying populations with dangerous chemicals with no regard for the effects on indigenous populations or even on Americans with the U.S. military's indiscriminate use of the herbicide agent orange in Vietnam. In both cases this was chemical warfare prohibited by the Geneva convention.

Marijuana could make the difference to an impoverished Mexican farmer of an annual income of $200 and one of $5,000, so growers harvested and shipped the poisoned pot. Studies showed that 13%–30% of marijuana samples in the southwestern U.S. were contaminated.

It is now generally agreed that marijuana is generally safe. How many Americans were injured or killed by this government policy is unknown. How ironic is it that the same government which had for decades insisted that marijuana was bad for us, devised a way to make it bad for us! [11]

Pharm Chem Laboratories and KSAN provided a needed service to the head community and helped people know about the quality of drugs they bought on the street.

UNDERGROUND NEWSPAPERS

There was no shortage of underground print media. The most notorious Bay Area paper was *The Berkeley Barb*. Berkeley was a hotbed of radical politics and the Barb reflected this in its extreme left articles and editorials. San Francisco had the *San Francisco Express Times*, later becoming the *San Francisco Good Times*. The staff at the Berkeley Barb at one point went on strike against the publisher, Max

---

[11] "Paraquat Pot: The True Story Of How The US Government Tried To Kill Weed Smokers With A Toxic Chemical ". 2018. *Thought Catalog*. Accessed April 22 2019. https://thoughtcatalog.com/jeremy-london/2018/08/paraquat-pot/.

Sherr, then formed the Red Mountain Tribe Commune and published a rival paper, *The Berkeley Tribe*.

Seeing itself under attack from the establishment, the freak community published so-called "underground" newspapers, tabloids sold on street corners by vendors as well in head shops and record stores. These tabloids were a mish-mash of radical politics, poetry, art, and community news. Hundreds of these publications sprang up throughout the country and in the military as well, each serving their own population demographic

The straight press and the underground press mirrored the generation gap. Contents of these papers were scandalous to the older generation, something of which the younger generation took generous advantage. Max Sherr's *Berkeley Barb*, one of the first underground papers, for instance, was notorious for explicit personal ads as well as its radical/revolutionary politics.

These papers were vital to the head community for economic reasons too. Anyone could purchase a stack of newspapers and sell them on the street. I did this several times myself. While I never was harassed by the police, there was an occasional asshole citizen.

These underground newspapers provided some funny shit. One issue, and I can't remember which paper it was, carried a notice saying: IF YOU CALL THIS PHONE NUMBER AND A VOICE TELLS YOU WHAT NUMBER YOU CALLED FROM, YOUR PHONE IS TAPPED! 555-555-5555 (not the number they gave).

And, yes, I called it and heard Anita's number read back to me. I was buzzed and I'm like *holy shit!* Anita, ever more sensible, says "That's gotta be bullshit." She was right. Later KSAN debunked the phone tapping story. It was a phone company number that phone techs used to make certain they were activating or deactivating the right phone line! I can only imagine how many stoners in the city breathed a sigh of relief after having called it!

Recipe of the week: Take a banana and eat it, now take the peel and scrape the inside of it until you have a pile of banana pith. Cure the pith in the oven, like grass, (i.e. heat it until it crumbles easily) roll it into joints and smoke. This recipe has been hinted at in earlier literature, and the high is thought to be something like an opium high. Also smoked together with 50 mg acid swallowed. For those who feel experimental I suggest buying banana oil and soaking grass in it.

Berkeley Barb, March 3 1967. The fallout from this little blurb in a west coast underground newspaper had the establishment shitting bricks.

The power of the press is mighty thing indeed, even if the press is a little left coast underground newspaper in Berkeley. In 1967 the *Berkeley Barb* ran a put-on[12] claiming dried scrapings from the insides of banana peels when smoked produced a high similar to opium. Originally included in a *Berkeley Barb* column on music, it was intended as a social comment on the futility of the prohibition of psychoactive substances it made it on to the wire vices and spread through the mainstream press. In today's internet terms, it "went viral!" The suggestion of smoking banana peels with 50 milligrams (mg) of acid (LSD) is ludicrous. Acid doses are measured in *cro*grams (millionths of a gram) . 50 mg, thousandths of a gram, is about 500 times the necessary dosage.

Light Up a Banana: Students Bake Peels To Kick Up Their Heels

Exhilarating Effect Is Gained By Legal Puffing, Some Say; A Marijuana Farm Lies Idle

By FELIX KESSLER
Staff Reporter of THE WALL STREET JOURNAL
NEW YORK—United Fruit Co. (1966 sales: $440 million) concedes it is a bit concerned. A lot of hippies are tripping on banana peels.

The freak community reinforced this put-on by holding banana skin smoke-ins. The Easter Sunday 1967 New York Times reported crowds of assorted freaks chanting "BANANA, BANANA" and carrying two-foot wooden bananas at a be-in in Central Park. It is thought that smoking banana skins was behind the Donovan song, "Mellow Yellow." The Wall Street Journal reported on the banana skin phenomenon. In Berkeley, California, rumors abounded that police were staking out fruit stands! It was hilarious watching authorities going bananas over bananas

Even the hallowed Halls of Congress were not immune to the banana craze. Here is an address to the House by Congressman Frank Thompson, Jr, (D-NJ) excerpted from the April 19, 1967, Congressional Record:

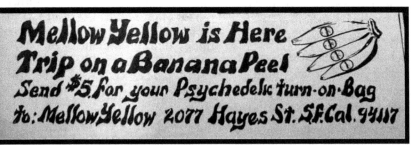

Mellow Yellow ad EVO (East Village Other)April 1-15, 1967
Source: https://www.flickr.com/photos/48457290@N00/6895021925/in/photostream/ [Accessed 22 Oct. 2019].

---

12 "pranking" in today's lingo.

"I have been extremely concerned over the serious increase in the use of hallucinogenics of youngsters. Apparently it was not enough for this generation of thrill-seekers to use illicit LSD, marijuana and airplane glue. They have now invaded the fruit stand...today the cry is 'Burn, Banana, Burn.' Tomorrow we may face strawberry smoking, apricot inhaling or prune puffing...part of the problem is, with bananas at 10 cents a pound, these beatniks can afford to take a hallucinogenic trip each and every day. Not even the New York City subway system, which advertises the longest ride for the cheapest price, can claim pennies a day to send people out of this world. Unfortunately many people have not yet sensed the seriousness of this hallucinogenic trip taking. Bananas may explain the trancelike quality of much of the 90th Congress proceedings. Just yesterday I saw on the luncheon menu of the Capitol dining room a breast of chicken Wakiki entry topped with, of all things, fried bananas."

"An official of the United Fruit Co., daring to treat this banana crisis with levity, recently said: 'the only trip you can take on a banana is when you trip on the peel.' But I am wry of United Fruit and their ilk, because, as the New York Times pointed out, United stands to 'reap large profit if the banana smoking wave catches on.' United has good reason to encourage us to fly high on psychedelic trips."

"We must move quickly to stop the sinister spread...of banana smoking...the banana smoker is a different breed...who cannot get the

The big banana hoax

Banana-peel smoking to get a "psychedelic experience" has been exposed as a hoax. A chemical analysis of the dried scrapings from the inner portion of banana peels shows nothing but inert carboniferous (containing carbon) material.

Subsequent interviews with banana smokers reveal hippies fabricated the story to "bait authorities."

Drs. Louis Bozzetti Jr., Stephen Goldsmith and J. Thomas Ungerleider of the University of California at Los Angeles made the analysis after press reports of a marked increase in the popularity of taking "trips" on bananadine, or "mellow yellow," obtained by baking the inside of banana peels. It was readily prepared in the kitchen or purchased for 20 cents a cigarette.

"There are no known hallucinogens in bananadine," the California specialists report. "Specific tests for arsenic, serotonin, ergot-like compounds and adrenergic compounds were all negative at the level of one part per million."

SOURCE: (2019). Science Digest excerpt. [online] Available at: https://www.flickr.com/photos/48457290@N00/6895057735/in/photostream/ [Accessed 22 Oct. 2019].

banana off his back...he may take to cultivating bananas in his backyard. The character of this country depends on our ability, above all else, to prevent the growing of bananas here."

"I am requesting the Surgeon General to update his landmark report on smoking and health to include bananas...congress has the responsibility to give the public an immediate warning...because of our decisive action with respect to tobacco, cigarette smoking in the United States is almost at a standstill. This is because every pack of cigarettes that is sold now carries a warning message on its side. Therefore I propose the Banana Labeling Act of 1967, a bill to require every banana bear the following stamp, 'Caution: Banana peel smoking may be Injurious to Your Health. Never put Bananas in the Refrigerator.' "

"There is, of course, on practical problem: banana peels turn black with age. At this point the warning sign becomes unreadable. It may be necessary...to provide a peel depository, carefully guarded, to protect the public from aged peels. I am now requesting that the Secretary of the Treasury that, given the imbalance of the gold flow some of the empty room at Fort Knox be given over to such a peel depository."

"I expect the forces of opposition to be quite strong. One only has to look at the total lack of regulation regarding bananas to realize the banana lobby's power. We have regulations on avocados, dates, figs, oranges lemons, peaches, plums and raisins. But bananas have slipped by unscathed. What we need...is a grassroots move to ban the banana, to repeal the peel...I will only breathe easier when this country, the land we love, can declare 'Yes, we have no bananas, we have no bananas today.'"

While obviously humorous, some took it seriously and made editorial comments. Mr. Thompson resigned from the House in 1980 after being caught in the ABSCAM sting involving members of congress taking bribes from Arabs.

The Food and Drug Administration (FDA) investigated and concluded that banana skins were in fact not psychedelic.[13]

This hilarious hoax spread from two column inches in a little hippie newspaper all the way across the nation and ended up involving the FDA and congress *That* is power! It is also a fine illustration of guerilla media anarchy!

---

13 "Berkeley Barb". 2019. En.Wikipedia.Org. Accessed August 24 2019. https://en.wikipedia.org/wiki/Berkeley_Barb.

THE EMPIRE STRIKES BACK

The establishment fought back against this seeming tsunami of political shit-stirring, liberal values and what they viewed as general communist degeneracy by police raids, trashing newspaper offices, arresting publishers on obscenity charges, jailing publishers on various bullshit charges always later dropped. The goal was to cripple the ability of the publication to survive.

While San Francisco is renowned for being liberal, it is also the city that arrested comedian Lenny Bruce for saying "cocksucker" on stage. In San Francisco. Yeah.

Police harassed street vendors. Fuck the First Amendment. Resist and get your skull fractured. A city ordinance stated anyone could sell newspapers in the city without being required to have a license. For the head community this way a person with some money in their pocket could purchase newspapers and sell them on the street, something I did on several occasions. It gave everyone a chance to participate in the economy.

Some papers, notably *The Berkeley Barb,* would accept suitable collateral, a guitar for instance, in exchange for bundles of papers, 50 papers in a bundle. The vendor would sell them and return to the office to redeem their collateral and get more papers to sell. Some people would get their newly printed papers in the evening and spend all night on their favorite street corner to get the best sales of the new issue in the morning rush. This was a boon to numerous longhaired transients. While only pennies were made per sale, the cost of living was relatively low.[14]

In many cases, street corner vendors were about fifty-cents away from starving to death, so the harassment was hitting those who were the poorest and willing to stand on their own two feet and earn some money.

Vendor harassment took various forms. Police would confiscate issues of newspapers they considered obscene from vendors because of erotic poetry or a naked photo or artwork.

Street vendors for blatant horseshit like "It's illegal to sell newspapers on the sidewalk in front of the bus station after 9 pm," and throw the poor unfortunate vendor in jail and confiscated their goods. The powers-that-be wanted longhaired trash to go away. Weird looking people were cluttering up the looks of their pretty city and spoiling it for the tourists.

Not wanting to be left out of this carnival of repression, the FBI's COINTELPRO[15] operation launched phony underground newspapers –

---

[14] "Berkeley Barb". 2019. En.Wikipedia.Org. Accessed August 24 2019. https://en.wikipedia.org/wiki/Berkeley_Barb.

[15] COINTELPRO (**COU**nter**INTEL**ligence**PRO**gram) was a series of covert, and at times illegal, projects conducted by the United States Federal Bureau of Investigation aimed at surveilling, infiltrating, discrediting, and disrupting domestic political organizations. Wikipedia

"fake news" of the day – and even managed to infiltrate the staff of the S.F. Good Times. The FBI would obtain copies of underground publications through phony news services they had set up in San Francisco, Chicago and New York, and send undercover agents to underground press gatherings.[16]

Berkeley Tribe, June 5, 1970.
The eagle and the snake, the struggle of the people against injustices of the state.

Source: University of Michigan

The offices of *The Berkeley Tribe* were firebombed, police would raid it and tear gas the staff just for the fuck of it. Bundles of unsold papers were stacked against windows because snipers were firing through them.

These attacks were not just local. Underground papers around the country were subjected to drive-by shootings, firebombings, break-ins and trashings. Attackers of *Space City* in Houston were suspected of being off-duty military or police personnel, members of the KKK or Minuteman organizations.

San Diego suffered the most violent attacks. In 1976 *The San Diego Union,* a mainstream newspaper, reported that attacks in the early 70s were carried out by a right wing paramilitary group, The Secret Army Organization, which was tied to the local office of the FBI. Fortunately, throughout these violent attacks on the freedom of expression and freedom of the press, no one was killed.[17]

Anthropology tells us that when widely differing cultures come in to contact, violence often results. That is exactly the case here. The head community and the police department were essentially two widely differing cultures at war. While the pen may be mightier than the sword, the cops can kick anybody's ass at will. And they damned well did.

This was a two-way street. In July 1970 *The Berkeley Tribe* published a Weather Underground-provided centerfold exposé of an FBI infiltrator:

---

[16] "Underground Press". 2019. En.Wikipedia.Org. Accessed August 24 2019. https://en.wikipedia.org/wiki/Underground_pre
[17] Ibid.

FLASHING BACK– COMING OF AGE IN THE AMERICAN 1960s

"...all the names mentioned are those you'd expect, with one exception: a 'Weatherman' from Cincinnati named Larry Grathwohl. According to the New York Times, Grathwohl is the same person as Tom Niehman, the undercover pig who was busted with Dionne and Linda in April, and immediately released on his own recognizance. He's a police plant sent out months ago to infiltrate Weatherman collectives in New York, Cincinnati, and New Haven."

The counterculture generation, raised on television, was media savvy and very effective in the use of symbolism. The somewhat awkwardly pasted up pieces of clip-art are as American as it gets, no hammer and sickle, no red stars. The majority of people on the left were not looking for total revolution – although this idea scared the shit out of Nixon and J. Edgar Hoover – as much as they wanted the "liberty, and justice for all" that was in the Pledge of Allegiance they recited in school every goddamned day for 12 years!

The bird and rattlesnake are an interesting choice of symbols. I can be interpreted as the eagle, symbolizing the state[18] and the rattlesnake, as in the Gadsden "Don't Tread On Me" flag, symbolizing those involved in the struggle. The snake is in the talons of the state and, undaunted, about to sink its fangs into the eagle's neck. It is also interesting that, in 2019, the rattlesnake that stood for the people struggling to right wrongs of the state in the Gadsden flag nowadays symbolizes the willful ignorance of the right.

San Francisco Good Times, aka, "Universal Life/Bulletin of the Church of the Times, April 23 1969. The Photo is Bob Dylan from the cover of his just released "Nashville Skyline" album. This particular copy went to the SDS (Students for a Democratic Society) chapter in Ann Arbor, Michigan, a hotbed of left wing/radical politics.

THE SAN FRANCISCO GOOD TIMES

The paper with which I was the most familiar was *The San Francisco Good Times*, a weekly tabloid of 16-24 pages. It had started out as *The San Francisco Express Times* in 1968 and becoming *The San Francisco*

---

[18] I think this graphic was borrowed from the Mexican legend of the snake on a cactus killing a rattlesnake.

Good Times in 1969. Interestingly enough, while it was a for-sure-enough left wing radical paper, it was also the church bulletin for The Church of the Good Times, a Universal Life Church associated organization.[19] There were interviews with many people active on the left as well as musicians and artists, and occasional articles on Rev. Kirby Hensley, the ULC founder.

TO THE PIG POWER STRUCTURE:

The first thing that it is necessary for you to understand is that you don't have us fooled. We know that only a sadist or a lunatic would recognize this madness you perpetrate as "Government." We know. We are hip to you.

Your "Courts" serve as skill centers to train hypocrites and liars. They are trained in sophisticated techniques of suppression of those who would dissent. Your "Bill of Rights" should be printed on a postage stamp, in triplicate. It would still be the greatest hoax and waste of paper in the history of the written word. Your "Constitution" is too stiff to use as toilet paper and your flag is too unsanitary to use as a sanitary napkin. Your alleged "men" are perverts and your "Statue of Liberty" is the greatest rape victim in history. Your "God" is manufactured in the U.S. Mint and your "Justice" is measured in profit. Your "Congress" is a swine pen, and your "Assemblies" resemble county fairs. The only thing you have of value to the people are your lives. Your "Military and Police" are in fact mercenaries, gangsters and hired killers. Their contributions to mankind can only be measured in murder and genocide.

Under your rule the progress of technology has in fact been hampered and has advanced only to the equal extent that it served your class as a tool of oppression and exploitation.

In short, you represent all that is foul, depraved and perverted in the history of society, and we would be less than your lowly equal if we were not *subversive to your bullshit.*

All power to the people!
Masai, Minister of Education
Black Panther Party

San Francisco Good Times Aug. 28, 1969 - The Good Times published Panther articles in solidarity with them.
Source: Archives and Special Collections at the Thomas J. Dodd Research Center, University of Connecticut

Freak culture was about freedom, breaking the chains of convention. "Do your own thing" was the motto. And don't hurt anyone while doing it! Freak communities everywhere were under attack by authorities. Underground newspapers like the *Good Times* were a reaction to that.

---

[19] The Universal Life Church (ULC) is a non-denominational religious organization founded by Kirby J. Hensley under the doctrine: "Do that which is right". The Universal Life Church advocates for religious freedom, offering legal ordination to become a minister free of charge to anyone who wishes to join.

fuck you, sir

ben dover

Persons with obscene tattoos will be found unacceptable for military service and will not be drafted. General Hershey is silent on the question of what is an obscene tattoo when asked for examples but some thoughts do come to mind.

Thought 1: The words FUCK YOU or FUCK YOU, SIR, tattooed on the karate edge of the right hand so as to be visible and legible while saluting.

Thought 2: The words EAT SHIT or EAT SHIT, SIR, if you wish to be polite to murderers, in the same location.

Thought 3: Two large breasts with nipples on the shoulder blades and a belly button in the small of the back.

Thought 4: A wolf chasing a rabbit down your back with tracks for the wolf and rabbit with the rabbit poised on a buttock about to jump into your asshole.

The military is also not about to draft homosexuals but requires evidence of at least two homosexual contacts. One way this evidence can be collected is by hiring a hustler at the bus depot and then having yourself photographed while being blown in the photomatic machine. You will have to crank the stool all the way up and squat on it with your head and face showing as well as your partner's. Do this twice. It should cost under $5 per picture which is cheaper than a passport. Sign and date the pictures and forward them to your draft board to be included in your file.

San Francisco Good Times Oct 16, 1969
Source: Archives and Special Collections at the Thomas J. Dodd Research Center, University of Connecticut

The *Good Times* was, among other things, about community service. This can be seen from the list of undercover police vehicles as well as in the "Cop Watch" column. To the police, the drugs were law enforcement issue. To the head community, drugs were a spiritual and personal freedom issue and none of the state's business.

As a result, almost everything printed in these papers would upset "the man." It was a perfect storm of a diametrically opposed sets of spiritual, political and social values.

Several things stand out when looking at these papers: consciousness, freedom, and community service.

The community service these papers did was enormous. The goal of the head culture was to survive. The Good Times dealt with just that with an "eat-shit-if-you-don't-like-it" attitude. The notice about messages left for people at the switchboard addresses a particular demographic: runaways and others who do not want to be found. Anti-war and anti-draft resources are also listed.

The *Good Times* was radical left publication and held solidarity with the Black Panthers. "To The Pig Power Structure" is the in-your-face militant politics of the period: colorful, passionate and highly unpleasant, the poetry of revolution. The Black Panthers' rhetoric scared the hell out of J. Edgar Hoover and California Governor Ronald Reagan. Police nationwide were kicking in Panthers' doors in the middle of the night and murdering them in their sleep. Another aspect of the Good Times community service was providing helpful hints for draft resisters.

The *Good Times* article about the people's draft cut shows that Phillip at the Boston Draft Resistance Group the previous year was right about draft resistance. As the war consumed thousands more young men, the opposition to it increased. Resisting the draft became an act of civil disobedience. Draftees were simply not showing up for induction. Each man that did this created a new task for the FBI. The figures in this short article show that 50% of draftees were going the "fuck it!" route and not showing up.

> A people's cut in the draft calls was proclaimed before President Nixon announced his cuts last week.
>
> The military was calling young men but more and more of those called just weren't hearing.
>
> On August 27, according to Selective Service, 482 were ordered to appear at the Oakland Induction Center. Only 242 showed up and of these 28 refused induction.
>
> The military was getting similar results at induction centers across the country. California, according to the Associated Press, has been unable to fill its quota since the first of the year.
>
> The Resistance estimates that only about ten per cent of those who refuse induction ever get indicted and end up in courts.
>
> A total of 2472 draft resisters were indicted in 1968. During the first three months of this year 2481 were indicted.
>
> So when Nixon announced his cuts in draft calls last week he was just acknowledging that Selective Service couldn't get the bodies.
>
> But the old tricky Dick really shows through in his draft "reform" proposals.
>
> "A lot of liberals think that drafting only 19-year-olds is a good thing," said one resistance worker. That way all those 20 and over will settle down and forget about the war and become good citizens.
>
> "Most of the resisters have been over 19," he said.
>
> Two years ago a Pentagon report advocated that only 19-year-olds be drafted because at that age a man is easier to shape into a fighting machine than older draftees.
>
> All of the Nixon moves—including the cutbacks of troops in Vietnam—are a carefully constructed cover designed to pacify opponents of the war without really changing anything.
>
> The proof is that there are more American troops in Vietnam today than there were at this same time last year according to an Associated Press report of September 19.

San Francisco Good Times Oct. 16, 1969, "Peoples Draft Cut," no byline

Source: Archives and Special Collections at the Thomas J. Dodd Research Center, University of Connecticut

It also illustrates the desire of the "liberals" in government to get hold of what they thought to be malleable young minds, men who hadn't yet been able to form their own thinking who were still brainwashed enough into the flag-waving bullshit they were taught in schools and by their parents to go kill and die for it.

UNDERGROUND COMIX

Growing up, we were constantly admonished by parents, teachers, preachers and scoutmasters that "no one likes a smartass!" The unintended consequence was that the 60s became the age of smartass. Underground newspapers provided a needed alternative media source for the counterculture. But – my God! – the comix unloosed the beast within us all!

In the 1950s comic books were blamed for juvenile delinquency and the Comics Code Authority was formed to censor this menace and render it harmless. In other words, they fucked up a good thing.

Berkeley Tribe ad for the Rip Off Press, publisher of underground comix, drawn by artist Gilbert Shelton

The emergence of Underground Comix – "comix" was used to differentiate them from "comics", originally they were sold only in head shops. – drawn by such notables as R. Crum, S. Clay Wilson, Gilbert Shelton and many more who didn't give two shits about the Comics Code Authority because the target audience was adults (well…in age if not maturity…).

Underground comix were irreverent and weirdly prophetic in some ways. Themes ran the gamut from antiwar, left politics, revolution, racism, feminism, gay and lesbian issues, social commentary, environmental issues, to copious amounts of gratuitous sex, drugs, violence and horror!

The subconscious of the counterculture, UG Comix were like the "creature from the id" in the movie *Forbidden Planet.* They embodied the secret fears of a generation. Looking at many of these, I think the artists may have drawn in lieu of therapy. UG comix were a canvas upon which anything and everything was painted. I found my experiences with the Catholic Church mirrored in *"Binky Brown Mets the Blessed Virgin Mary,"* a tale of shame, guilt, and frustration at the hands of unrelenting Catholic dogma.

In the countercultural spirit of "fuck the system" *Zap Comics* led the way in fucking with the system and was the subject of obscenity charges.

Even Walt Disney was not immune to underground comics. Artist Dan O'Neil penned satirical *Mickey Mouse and the Air Pirates* comic in which Mickey was going down on Minnie!

The most famous of the UG comix was *Zap Comix*. Zap #4 held the distinction of having been found to be legally obscene. There was court wrangling over this for years as morality squads attempted to stifle freedom of expression.

From *Mickey Mouse Meets the Air Pirates #1*, © Dan O'Neil. From the minds of the generation that grew up watching The Mickey Mouse Club every day after school comes Mickey performing cunnilingus on Minnie! Yes, Disney sued!

Zap Comix #4, the officially "obscene" issue, front and back covers depicting Mr. Peanut metamorphosing into Mr. Penis. Underground comix took great delight in parodying American institutions.

FLASHING BACK– COMING OF AGE IN THE AMERICAN 1960s

S.F. Good Times May 1, 1970 - this rather tame front page illustration by S. Clay Wilson is a combination of underground journalism with underground comix.

With issue #4, released in August 1969, Zap attained infamy because of a story by Crumb called "Joe Blow" that attacked social conventions. "Joe Blow" featured a white-collar executive who enjoyed spending quality time with his family: an incestual orgy, a commentary on societal hypocrisy. Law enforcement attempted to remove it from circulation. There were arrests on the West Coast. As in the cases of obscenity prosecutions of underground newspapers, the charges were dropped.

On the East Coast, *Zap Comix #4* was the subject of a sting operation by the Morals Squad in New York. In court, the prosecution introduced no evidence as to the character or contents of *Zap #4* thinking its examination would reveal the contents as legally obscene. The prosecution simply provided the Court with a copy of *Zap Comix #4* and asked for it to be found obscene.

The Court found *Zap #4* to be obscene. This was upheld on appeal by the New York State Supreme Court. The U.S. Supreme Court dismissed the appeal ruling in 1973 that communities could set their own standards regarding obscenity.[20] This put a bit of a crimp in Comix, but they survived and are the forerunners of today's slick, full color glossy alternative comic magazines.

As true now as it was then. This pair of panels are from the album cover Greg Irons did for Scoop Nisker. No copyright is indicated.

Source: Author's personal record collection.

Greg Irons work was gritty and powerful. These two panels of political comment are from Scoop Nisker's bootleg album cover.

One of the mainstays of the comix was the art of S. Clay Wilson. The illustration on the cover of the S.F. Good Times is an example of underground newspaper meets underground comix. and features some of Wilson's common motifs: demons, a hook-handed pirate, rough trade leatherboy, drugs, Tree Frog Beer, Starry-Eyed Stella (in a rare appearance that does not feature her being gangbanged by demons, deviates, Ruby the Dyke and various drug-twisted mutants), a brilliant nonsequitur dialog balloon, and Wilson's trademark top-notch violence ac-

---

[20] Sergi, Joe. 2013. " Obscenity Case Files: Zap Comix #4 | Comic Book Legal Defense Fund". Cbldf.Org. Accessed August 30 2019. http://cbldf.org/2013/06/obscenity-case-files-zap-comix-4/.

companied by his unmatched onomatopoeia! You can hear leatherboy's guts yielding to the deadly steel of the demon's switchblade! I call it "rather tame" because it does not feature monster penises, gaping female genitalia, and forms of miscegenation hitherto unimagined in any civilized society. Adult comix were not subject to the Comics Code Authority and blazed the way for today's alternative comics.

Wilson suffered brain damage in an incident in 2008, it is not known if he fell or was attacked as he has no memory of it. A special needs trust has been set up for him at http://www.sclaywilsontrust.com/

Mother's Oats Comix 1969 Rip Off Press,
"Doings of Dealer McDope" drawn by Dave Sheridan.
Comix were sometimes downright phiosophical!

Reading "Mother's Oats Comix" like tripping on DMT, interdimensional, mind expanding and a bit philosophical.

SKETCHES FROM MY PAST

Ink sketch July 1970 © W. Eugene Johnson

Recently I stumbled across an old sketch book I had all but forgottenabout. Back in the day, inspired by comix, I decided to try my hand at some comix in that style. I made the sketches included here with no particular purpose in mind, they were more or less stream of consciousness. Well, somewhat *expanded* consciousness! Much of the subject material centered around drugs as did the counterculture. With comix one could express themselves graphically and freely on anything, like a group of freaks sharing some weed. . You could find people looking like this anywhere in the freak scene. Groupings like the hippie chick with flowers in her hair and a "speedfreak braid" and a couple more stoners were everywhere. The other elements were added willy-nilly: dude in the corner with a WTF question mark. A random nark and a curious frog with mushrooms. Perhaps he is contemplating eating one to see what happens!

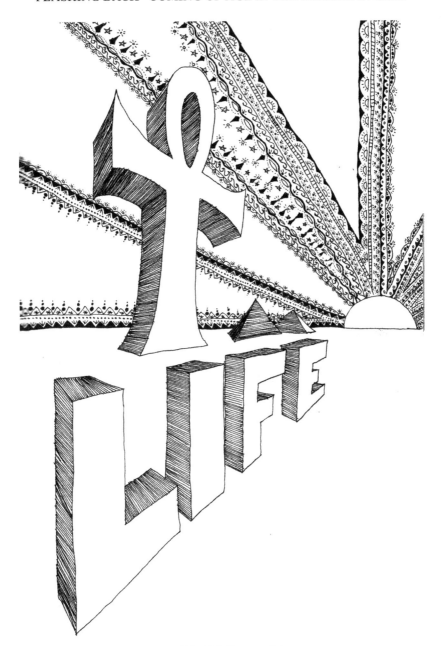

Ink sketch, 1970 © W. Eugene Johnson

This Egyptian themed sketch has the ankh, the ancient Egyptian hieroglyph for life, the pyramids and the sun radiating its energy to all of creation.

Ink sketch, July 1970 © W. Eugene Johnson

"The Weed." Of course! Complete with an annoying Hari Krishna devotee and a hippie bogarting the joint!!

Ink sketch August 1970 © W. Eugene Johnson

A hippie's worst nightmare was opening the door to find this! I had a similar experience in Boston in the Spring of 1969. It goddamned sure gets your adrenaline going!

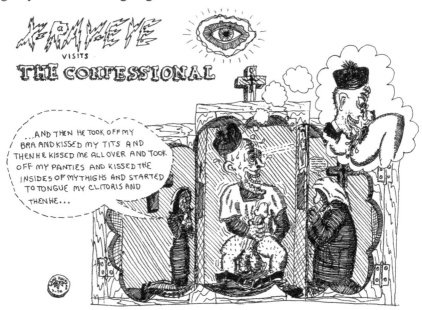

"X-RAY EYE VISITS THE CONFESSIONAL" July 1970, © W. Eugene Johnson. My memory of walking in on our parish priest blowing another priest would not emerge from my subconscious for about another thirty years or I would have likely drawn it! Note the Playboy foldout on the wall of the confessional.

Cartooning was a good outlet for my free-floating hostility toward the institution that completely fucked my head up as a youngster. I found it exhilarating to be able to depict all kind of indecencies projected onto the Catholic Church. In my mind at thd time it was all just a "fuck you!" Decades later it becomes public knowledge that these self-styled purveyors of salvation were carrying out unimaginable acts of pedophilia and general sexual abuse far beyond what I imagined. At the time I made these sketches I hadn't yet recovered the memory of walking in on our parish priest sucking cock. I didn't ever recognize how much anger I was carrying deep inside me regarding the church, I thought I was just being as disrespectful as possible. It would take another thirty years to unfuck myself. Even then I was not fully successful.

Ink sketch, Aug. 1970 © W. Eugene Johnson

Yes, his dick runneth over! In actual fact, it has recently come to light that nuns have been the target of priestly sexual abuse in the Catholic Church although I was not thinking of abuse when I made this sketch, I was just enjoying the freedom to be being generally indecent, fuck the church, fuck the system and all that!

If I drew a clown like the one one on "The Pussy Page" nowadays I would get ripped a new asshole for racism and catch more hell for that than the dripping vulva! It's just a cartoon, folks. No racism intended.

Ink sketch July 1979 © W. Eugene Johnson

Ink sketch July 1970, © W. Eugene Johnson

I had a girlfriend once with tiny labia like that! Pussy is good! No calories, you can eat all you want and never gain weight! And women *love* it. As an acquaintance of mine said, "Show me a guy who doesn't eat his girl and I'll take his girl!"

Pen sketch 1970 © W. Eugene Johnson

A cartoon comment on heroin. While I never did it myself, I knew far too many people who did. That shit is NOT good for you! LSD can ("can," not "does," ok?) make you smarter. Heroin never made anybody smarter. Ditto meth and pharmaceuticals.

Ink sketch 1970 © W. Eugene Johnson

FLASHING BACK– COMING OF AGE IN THE AMERICAN 1960s

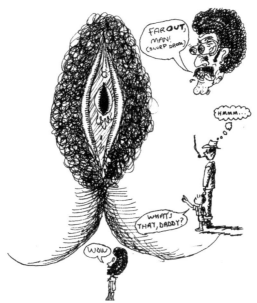

Gratuitous pen and ink filth July 1970 © W. Eugene Johnson

Just some freefloating obscenity. This is the kind of shit that happens when you combine sketching and weed! Hey, it could be the basis for a poster for an X-rated horror movie, "The Attack of the Gaping Vulva!" or "The Vagina That Ate Chicago!" Back in the day, the Mitchell Brothers[1] in San Francisco could have made it!

My homemade hookah constructed from a Drambuie bottle in 1970. I still have it. That thing has incinerated a lot of "toxic vegetation!"

I turned an empty liquer bottle into a useful dope appliance. For a while I was building hookahs (water pipes) out of glass bottles and selling them on the panhandle of Golden Gate Park.

---

[1] Pornographic movie makers, makers of Deep Throat

May 8. 1970 San Francisco Good Times Cartoon on Kent State Massacre
Source: Archives and Special Collections at the Thomas J. Dodd Research Center, University of Connecticut

CHAPTER 22

NIXON'S THEATER OF BLOOD

KENT STATE, JACKSON STATE & SOUTH CAROLINA STATE

Nixon's "incursion" into Cambodia resulted in college campuses erupting in protests. On May 4, 1970, KSAN told us of the fatal shooting of students at Kent State University in Ohio by National Guard troops.[1] Nixon's Theater of Blood[2] was now worldwide, encompassing the U.S. as well as Vietnam, Laos and Cambodia. It was like the whole world was becoming an American free-fire zone.[3]

Was this the final descent of America into fascism predicted by the left? It would seem so. The stated strategy of the hard line revolutionary left was to foment civil disorder to the point that the government would declare martial law. This would bring about massive repression, the condition necessary for people to rise up in revolution and overthrow the government.

The massacre of students by government troops was nothing new on the world scene, the Mexican army had murdered students involved in a protest in Mexico City weeks prior to the Olympics held there in 1968. Was the United States on embarking on a similar course? It seemed like it.

The Kent State Massacre happened on May 4 with National Guard troops gunning students down. At about the same time police shot and killed several students at Jackson State in Mississippi and at South Carolina State in Orangeburg, SC, These events seemed to put the United States on a par with politically repressive nations that had no compunctions about using troops to murder their own civilians.

In the front of this book I cite a quote from Napoleon, "Never attribute to malice that which can be properly ascribed to incompetence." What might seem like a deliberate act can in fact be just a fuck-up.

From the May 8, 1970, edition of the San Francisco Good Times:

Professor Raymond Broaddus of Kent State University described Wednesday what he believes to be the first shot of the Kent State murders on Monday. He told authorities he saw a National Guardsman hit with a returned tear gas canister stumble and, rifle pointed skyward, fire his weapon. Broadus said immediately afterward, the other guardsmen whirled, kneeled and fired into the students. [4]

---

[1] An event captured in two of the greatest protest songs ever: the Beach Boys "Demonstration Song" which stated "America was startled on May 4th 1970. . . four martyrs earned a new degree - a Bachelor of Bullets," and Crosby, Stills, Nash and Young's "Ohio" with lyrics protesting about "tin soldiers and Nixon's coming. . . soldiers are cutting us down. . . four dead in Ohio (Neil Young, a Canadian, penned the best protest songs against the Vietnam War and the Iraq War).
[2] Vietnam was indeed Nixon's Theater of Blood because Nixon helped the U.S. get in to Vietnam when he was Eisenhower's VP.
[3] "Free fire zones were areas in Vietnam designated as such because all in habitants were considered the enemy and could be killed on sight. Gunships routinely expended their leftover munitions in them when returning from a mission.
[4] San Francisco Good Times newspaper, May 8, 1970, page 3, no byline.

S. F. Good Times front page May 8, 1970 - "SHIT HITS FAN" banner headline issue A response to Nixon's expansion of the Vietnam War into Cambodia and the murder of students by the Ohio national Guard at Kent State University. I was a vendor at the time and sold copies of this issue on Fisherman's Wharf.

Source: Archives and Special Collections,Thomas J. Dodd Research Center, Univ. of Connecticut

What has been characterized by the left as deliberate murder may in fact be a fuck-up. A deadly fuck-up, but a fuck-up just the same. Or it may not.[author's comment]

Ohio State Rep. Robert Manning today announced he will file suit calling for the firing of State Adjutant General Sylvester Del Corso, calling him responsible for grossly illegal actions in connection with the shootings on the Kent State Campus. Manning's' declaration followed by a few hours Del Corso's admission that on Sunday night he had ordered guardsmen to shoot anyone cutting fire hoses. Del Corso's latest explanation of the tragedy is, "Guardsmen facing almost certain injury and death were forced to open fire on attacker." [5]

There is an interesting parallel here between the actions of the Ohio National Guard then and Israeli Defense Forces now. The IDF routinely shoots and kills Palestinian youths who throw stones at them. The United States is a big supporter of Israel. The two countries seem to tacitly agree on this type of disproportionate response.

How does one tell if something is intentionally malicious or just a fuck up? If there is significant benefit gained by it, it is intentional. Who had anything to be gained by calling up the guard?

Moderates have accused Republican Governor Rhodes of calling out the Guard–over reported objection by KSU President Robert White who remained in Iowa–as a political stunt because of a tough primary against moderate Robert Taft for a U.S. Senate seat on Tuesday. [6]

Rhodes lost the election. Malice or incompetence? That will be debated as long as people remember this horror.

Cynics viewed the Kent State Massacre as one group of draft dodgers shooting another group of draft dodgers. A fatassed middle aged housewife in a TV report said "I think they should have killed more of them."

Nixon's expansion of the Vietnam War into Cambodia claimed the life of a third young man who graduated from Smethport Area High School. Stephen J. Keesler, a draftee, age 20 years, 5 months, 4 days, was killed on May 12, 1970 becoming yet another young American slaughtered in the endless war. Like all the brave young Americans in Vietnam, he was told the Star Spangled Lie that he was fighting to protect American freedom And he died for it.

---

[5] Ibid.
[6] San Francisco Good Times newspaper, May 8, 1970, page 3, byline "grmi."

W. EUGENE JOHNSON

HELL AND REVOLUTION

The Bank of America, the leading financial institution on the West Coast, offered "scenic checks" for its customers. One of the popular checks was a spectacular west coast sunset: a sky ablaze with shades of reds, yellows and orange as the sun set over the ocean.

The Bank of America became a symbol of corporate involvement in the Vietnam War, because it had huge amounts of money invested in defense related industries. The University of California campus at Isla Vista erupted into protest and rioting. On February 25, and for the first time, a Bank of America branch office was trashed and burned. This was in accordance with the philosophy of the radical left to "bring the war home" so that citizens in the United States proper could see the effects of the war much as the citizens of Vietnam did: as a clear and present danger to life and safety.

The San Francisco Good Times had this to say:

The Isla Vista terrain is ideally suited for street fighting in that there are a thousand ways out of most situations. You can't be trapped.

The people fought back with rocks, and, when the police charged again, they stood and fought, then charged the police! Immensely surprised, the police huddled together, then broke and ran. Back to the buses, three blocks, chased by an angry mob of eight hundred people. All the bus windows were smashed. The police retreated. A police cruiser was abandoned and later destroyed by the crowd. Between 11 p.m. and midnight, the police made short forays, throwing teargas, but teargas security was relatively tight, and the crowds could not be dispersed.

There was partying in the streets, and barricades were thrown up.

The National Guard is currently out of the city during the day and on standby call during the night. Isla Vista looks like an occupied city in a war zone. But for two nights running, the streets really did belong to the people. Right on. [7]

Soon after the trashing and burning of this branch office, a new poster was seen in the head shops. It was a large Bank of America check done in the scenic check style, ablaze with brilliant reds, yellows and orange, only these colors came, not from the sun setting on the ocean, but from the blazing Isla Vista branch of the Bank of America.

---

[7] San Francisco Good times, march 5, 1970, page 5, interview with Steve Jim Gregory of the UC Santa Barbara student newspaper. *El Gaucho*.

FLASHING BACK– COMING OF AGE IN THE AMERICAN 1960s

The war went on. The dying went on. The protests went on. Almost every week another Bank of America was trashed and burned by war protesters. The country was sending its young men to die in Vietnam, a military quagmire with no end in sight, and at the same time murdering students on college campuses. America seemed to be descending straight into hell and revolution.

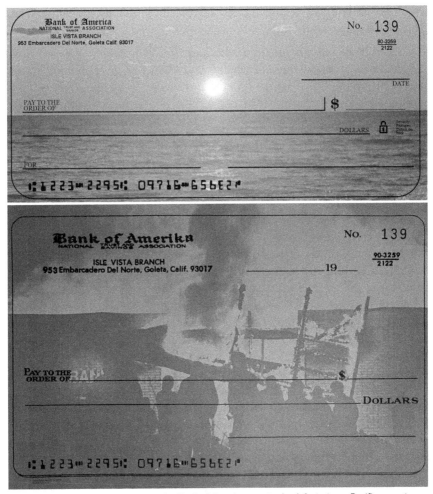

At the top is a mock-up of a popular Bank of America scenic check featuring a Pacific sunset. The bottom picture is a parody of a "Bank of Amerika" scenic check with the same colors showing the Isle Vista Bank of America branch being trashed and burned.

W. EUGENE JOHNSON

THE [BULLSHIT!] WAR ON DRUGS

Nixon was a rotten son-of-a-bitch, we in the freak community all understood that. He was also a paranoid asshole who authorized illegal acts against his political enemies. Nixon was also the originator of the "war on drugs," supposedly to protect the youth of America from this scourge. In 1994, journalist Dan Baum interviewed former Nixon domestic advisor, John Erlichman, regarding the Nixon' administration's actions on drugs. Erlichman said:

"The Nixon campaign in 1968, and the Nixon White House after that, had two enemies: the antiwar left and black people. You understand what I'm saying? We knew we couldn't make it illegal to be either against the war or black, but by getting the public to associate the hippies with marijuana and blacks with heroin, and then criminalizing both heavily, we could disrupt those communities. We could arrest their leaders, raid their homes, break up their meetings, and vilify them night after night on the evening news.

Did we know we were lying about the drugs? Of course we did."[8]

We in the freak community always suspected this. Erlichman confirmed it. Here we are over a half century later and the war on drugs is still going on, still a colossal failure, and turns out to have been implemented as nothing more than an expedient tool for political repression based on lies.

When Nixon founded the DEA and initiated the War on Drugs, the U.S. while having a military presence in a major opium producing region of the world,: Southeast Asia's Golden Triangle, was in the midst of a heroin epidemic

People think "Mafia" when they hear "heroin." Not so true anymore. Back in the day when Turkey was the world's leading opium producer, the Sicilian Mafia smuggled Turkish opium to labs in Marseilles, France, where they processed it into heroin for international distribution.

During the Korean "police action," the CIA helped move opium to gain the co-operation of local war lords.[9] In Vietnam, the CIA had the advantage of their own airline, Air America, to aid them in trafficking the world's purest heroin.[10] That source dried up after the U.S. left Vietnam.

---

[8] Newsmax Media, Inc. 2016. "Richard Nixon Drugs War Quote Rears Its Ugly Head – Again". *Newsmax*. Accessed August 24 2019. https://www.newsmax.com/TheWire/richard-mixon-drugs-war-quote/2016/03/24/id/720681/.

[9] "Opinion | The CIA Drug Connectionis As Old As The Agency". 2019. *Nytimes.Com*. Accessed August 25 2019. https://www.nytimes.com/1993/12/03/opinion/IHT-the-cia-drug-connectionis-as-old-as-the-agency.html.

[10] McCoy, Alfred W.' The CIA and the Politics of Heroin in Southeast Asia 1972

FLASHING BACK– COMING OF AGE IN THE AMERICAN 1960s

Between the Vietnam War and Afghanistan the CIA trafficked cocaine from Central and South America into the US sparking the crack cocaine epidemic in Los Angeles in the 80s, using proceeds to finance right wing paramilitary groups as well as selling missiles to Iran, America's enemy at the time.

Where the U.S. military goes, so does the CIA. In Afghanistan the CIA got there first, supporting the Afghani Muhajadeen resist the Soviet occupation. From an article by Larry Collins in the December 3, 1993, *New York Times:*

"As it had in Laos, the heroin traffic blossomed in the shadows of a CIA-sustained guerrilla war. Soon the trucks that delivered arms to the guerrillas in Afghanistan were coming back down the Khyber Pass full of heroin."

"The conflict and its aftermath have given the world another Golden Triangle: the Golden Crescent, sweeping through Afghanistan, Pakistan and parts of the former Soviet Union. Many of those involved in the drug traffic are men who were once armed, trained and financed by the CIA."

Afghanistan is now the world's leading opium producer with ever increasing annual crops. America is presently asshole deep in cheap and powerful heroin. People are dropping dead on the streets from overdoses.

Yeah. The war on drugs. Political repression. Murder. Smuggling. Greed. Total bullshit. Duplicity.

THE PARK STATION BOMBING

On the evening of February, 16, 1970, Anita's apartment on Stanyan Street was rocked by blast.[11] All hell broke loose outside. We cautiously ventured out the front door and stood on the steps in the foyer.

The scene was surreal. It was an urban combat zone. Police cruisers had the streets sealed off, the scintillating flashes of their strobe lights dazzled in the darkness. Pandemonium reigned. A dozen or so police officers, shotguns at the ready, ran here and there. Ambulances and fire trucks sped past, their sirens rising and falling and overlapping in continuous wails. Radio messages crackled over police radios. Police sirens pulsed, electronic banshees shrieking in the night.

---

[11] The San Francisco Police Department Park Station bombing occurred on February 16, 1970, when a pipe bomb filled with shrapnel detonated on the ledge of a window at the San Francisco Police Department's Upper Haight Park substation at 1899 Waller Street. Brian V. McDonnell, a police sergeant, was fatally wounded in its blast. Robert Fogarty, another police officer, was severely wounded in his face and legs and was partially blinded. In addition, eight other police officers were wounded. (Source: Wikipedia)

From what we could gather, a bomb had gone off at the Park Police Station, about 200 yards away. A shotgun toting officer told us to *"Get the fuck back inside!"* We did.

The San Francisco Chronicle reported the next day that a wall of Park Station had been taken out with ten sticks of dynamite. One officer, a captain with twenty-five years on the force, was killed and several others wounded. The device was described as a "shaped charge" designed to concentrate the force of the blast in one direction. The paper added that this particular method of constructing a charge suggested that it had been made by someone with military demolitions training. Later updates of the story revealed that the device was a pipe bomb placed on a window ledge.

This was consistent with the philosophy of the revolutionary left, to "...bring the war home, to make Americans here at home feel what the Vietnamese were feeling at the hands of the American military. Although I was definitely against the war and more than somewhat sympathetic to the radical left, I could not buy into revolutionary violence.

---

roger lubin

In the aftermath of last week's bombing of the Park police station, paranoia has so deeply struck the police department that they have conspired with the news media to create the impression that each police station has become an impregnable fortress.

When a KGO mobile news unit arrived at the Park station to do a follow-up story on the bombing, an officer with a shotgun was dispatched to parade around the building, much in the manner of guards at Buckingham Palace.

Responding to the theatrical direction of the KGO cameraman, the officer, with much military precision, marched up and back in front of the entrance to the Park station, while the KGO commentator reported that "police security has been intensified in the wake of last week's terrorist attack."

The police officer, who seemed like a fairly decent sort, said, when off the air: "This is bullshit; they're guarding three or four stations that I know of. It doesn't mean anything, though, it's just for publicity."

At this point a couple of things have become apparent. First, the police are now feeling the same paranoia as a result of the bombing that the hip community has felt, as a result of the police, for some time now. Secondly the police are using their paranoia to their own ends, by conveying the image to the hip community that they're going to be even tougher now than ever. This move was heartily seconded, of course, by Mayor Alioto, who may yet be another "law and order" candidate.

Finally, the news media is so intent on maintaining a crisis orientation in the eyes of their reader/viewer/listener public, that when there is a lack of violent news, they go so far as to create it.

Maybe it's all boiling down to the fact that the establishment has finally taken a lesson from Abbie Hoffman, learned the rudiments of street theatre, and is using it in their futile attempts to stop the revolutions. Or maybe a conspiracy of the mayor's office, the police department and the establishment news media is a lot more serious than that.

Feb 27, 1970 San Francisco Good Times - The Park Station Bombing
Source: Archives and Special Collections at the Thomas J. Dodd Research Center, University of Connecticut

FLASHING BACK– COMING OF AGE IN THE AMERICAN 1960s

THE MARIN COUNTY CIVIC CENTER SHOOTOUT

A shootout in the Marin County Civic Center in August, 1970 was brutal and shocking. Three men, George Jackson, Fleeta Drumgo, and John Clutchette, known in activist circles as "The Soledad Brothers," were incarcerated at Soledad State Prison. Jackson's younger brother, John, led an armed attempt to free the brothers. Smuggling three guns into the Marin County Civic Center and taking hostages, Jackson planned to use hostages as leverage to take over a radio station and demand the Soledad Brothers be released. In the resulting firefight, which witnesses say was initiated by the police, Judge Haley was killed by a sawed-off shotgun attached to his neck by adhesive tape. Jackson and two defendants were also killed with a third seriously wounded, Gary Thomas a Deputy DA taken hostage, was left wheelchair bound.

Professor Angela Davis, Communist Party member, affiliated with the Black Panthers and civil rights activist, was connected to the purchase of the shotgun. After going into hiding, capture, and eventual trial, she was found innocent in 1972 by an all-white jury of complicity in the judge's murder.[12]

THE WEATHERMEN

The SDS (Students for s Democratic Society) was a left wing antiwar group that led many protests and campus disturbance in the 60s. The SDS collapsed in 1969 and was replaced by the Weathermen, a revolutionary group taking their name from a in Bob Dylan lyric.[13] While allegedly eschewing violence against people, the Weathermen carried out bombings against institutions up until the mid 80s. Within a year they claimed credit for twenty-five bombings including the U.S. Capitol, the Pentagon, the California Attorney General's office, and a New York City police station.[14] Despite claiming to commit violence against institutions and not people, they managed to kill two police officers and a Brinks driver in a botched holdup.

One of their most famous bombings was unintentional. In 1970 three Weather Underground bomb makers blew themselves up in the bomb factory in the basement of a Greenwich Village townhouse. Oops!

---

[12] Denise, Carletta. 2016. "August 7, 1970: The Marin County Courthouse Shootout Occurs". *Black Then*. Accessed August 27 2019. https://blackthen.com/%E2%80%8Baugust-7-1970-the-marin-county-courthouse-shootout-occurs/.
[13] "You don't need a weatherman to know which way the wind blows," from *"Subterreanean Homesick Blues,"* © Bob Dylan
[14] "Weather Underground Bombings | Federal Bureau Of Investigation". 2019. *Federal Bureau Of Investigation*. Accessed October 15 2019. https://www.fbi.gov/history/famous-cases/weather-underground-bombings.

Over the ensuing decades a Weather Underground fugitive would turn up here and there, arrested and tried for their crimes.

They also aided in LSD guru Timothy Leary's escape from prison at San Luis Obispo, CA, and subsequent flight to Algeria.

THE SYMBIONESE LIBERATION ARMY

It was indicative of the times that bizarre political mutations kept cropping up. A notable one was the Symbionese Liberation Army, a revolutionary organization. Operating in Oakland, San Francisco and Los Angeles. they posted manifestos, robbed banks, assassinated officials, and kidnapped newspaper heiress Patty Hearst. Hearst was with them when they robbed a bank on Noriega Street in San Francisco, a couple miles from where I was living with my wife-to-be. Most of them were killed in a shootout with police in Los Angeles in 1974 when the house they were in caught fire from tear gas police canisters and burned to the ground.

This event was significant for two reasons. First, new TV camera technology allowed live coverage of the shootout as it happened. Second, as a portent of things to come, this was the first time the police deployed military weaponry against citizens.

REVOLUTIONARY VIOLENCE OF THE ERA

Such was the political frustration of the hard left that there were politically motivated bombings all over the country. A senate investigation concluded that from January 1969 to April 1970 there were 4,330 bombings. 43 people were killed. Property damage amounted to $21.8 million.[15]

It is easy to understand social and economic reasons for revolutionary violence. It is not possible to justify the deaths of and injuries to innocents in "the struggle." Motivated by the seeming ineffectiveness of peacefully opposing the war, bombings here in the U.S. that harmed innocent people were no different than bombings by the U.S. military in Southeast Asia that resulted in the deaths of innocent civilians. This was by design. From the point of view of the self-styled "revolutionaries," violence and harm to innocents would "bring the war home" to Americans and was necessary to create a situation where the government would

---

15 Conspiracy Cafe. (2019). Conspiracy Cafe. [online] Available at: https://www.conspiracy-cafe.com/apps/blog/show/44175873-1969-a-year-of-bombings [Accessed 16 Nov. 2019].

suspend the Constitution and Bill of Rights and impose martial law. The reasoning was this would inspire a revolutionary uprising.

Ha! Maybe in their own little self-absorbed bullshit ivory tower world of left wing ideologies (and daddy's credit card!). The world isn't perfect and never will be. That does not mean we must not or cannot try to do what we can to improve it. You can't bomb an ideology out of existence.

I look at the Weathermen as spoiled children of the upper middle class who are upset that they can't get their own way all the time, so they start blowing shit up. Innocent people are harmed.

Yes, there is injustice in the world. No, it is not fair. Killing innocent people does and will not change that.

CHAPTER 23

LIFE IN THE CITY

WHOLE LOTTA SHAKIN' GOIN' ON!

Anita's apartment was a good place for new experiences of many kinds. I was taking a bath on the evening of October 1, 1969. Anita was in the room with me. We were having a pleasant conversation when I felt this curious rocking sensation. The bath brush hanging on a nail on the wall began to sway. The water in the tub was moving, too. And there was this weird creaking sound. What the hell was going on? Then it hit me: a*n earthquake! There's a fucking earthquake! The fucking house is going to collapse and I am stark bareass naked in the bathtub! And all wet! Oh shit oh dear!*

By the time I got out of the tub, it had stopped. Christ, what an eerie sensation that was! About ten minutes later there was another tremor, an aftershock. I heard the mysterious creaking sound again. This time what I knew it was. It was every nail in the whole damned house creaking! That sound is forever etched into my memory.

I grew up in Pennsylvania believing that the ground under my feet stays there, it doesn't move.[1] That is something I took for granted. And the day that it *does* move, well, that brings certain aspects about the impermanence of all things from the realm of the philosophical into the realm of the very real and three-dimensional!

---

[1] In May 2011 this proved to not be true when a 5. 8 earthquake rocked D. C. and shook the ground in PA where I now reside.

The particular quake which had brought this home to me was centered around Santa Rosa, about sixty miles to the north, and knocked down some porches and did some other damage.

PROGRAMMING AND SYSTEMS INSTITUTE

Anita and I were living on her salary of $300 a month supplemented with our casual pot dealing. It was about this time that I responded to an advertisement that I heard several times daily on KSAN. Minimum wage was about $1.50 an hour. Working for minimum wage was not something that appealed to me as you had $60 before taxes at the end of a 40 hour week,.

On the other hand, a skill, such as computer programming, would be in demand, at least according to the radio ad for Programming and Systems Institute. I called the number and got an individual who identified himself as Mr. Moon. He talked very glibly to me about "getting into a field where you can get paid for what you and do and not whether or not you wear a suit and tie and have short hair." This sounded good, and I took him up on his offer to go down to their office and take an aptitude test.

Programming & Systems Institute was on the third floor of the Hearst Building at Third and Market Streets. I took the Haight St. bus downtown and reported to Mr. Moon's office. Just inside the door was a computer. Well, it looked like one. Hell, it was just like one of those things that had spewed out the cards on the old TV quiz show, "The $64,000 Question" when I was a youngster. Yep, a for sure IBM computer! What else could it possibly be?

Mr. Moon was a portly fellow with a crew cut and dark heavy rimmed glasses dressed in a business suit. We talked for a few minutes and he had his secretary take me in to an adjoining room and give me a test. The test took about a half hour. I waited in the reception area, and Mr. Moon called me into his office.

"Well, Gene, you did quite well on our test. I think you will make a fine computer programmer. 90% of our graduates get jobs within a month of finishing our course. You can expect to make $700-$800 a month as an entry level programmer. This is a tremendously expanding field etc., etc." Mr. Moon made me feel that I would be an absolute asshole if I did not take advantage of this opportunity to change my life. It sounded like a damned good deal to me!

I went home and told Anita. She was impressed. There was one thing lacking: money. We didn't have any and the three month PSI course cost $600. Anita called a friend of hers in New York, Barry Epstein, an ACLU lawyer. He agreed to lend us the money for the PSI programming course which I would repay after I got a job as a programmer.

I started the course about a week later. There were about a dozen people in my class, freaks and straights. I was the freakiest, with hair hanging halfway down my back. We got our "official" black vinyl plastic PSI briefcases and logic flowchart stencils the first day. I diligently took notes and studied hard every night. It didn't seem that hard, hell it was easy. Our teacher quit the third week and was replaced by another, Wayne Woodley, who turned out to be a Hari Krishna devotee from Denver. I mean, what the hell, this was San Francisco in the 60's, right?

Wayne was an interesting fellow, tall and thin with dark short hair. He was somewhere between being an Hari Krishna devotee and being an acid head. Wayne came over to out pad one Saturday and he and I dropped acid together. He laid on the floor after he came on to the acid, making slow, sweeping gestures with his hands and arms, becoming Rama and creating and destroying universes. After he came off his peak he went to the Hari Krishna temple a couple blocks away. I don't know if he ever did acid again after that.

We learned how to write Autocoder programs for the older IBM 1401 machines. Then we got into the state of the art IBM machine, the 360. Now, keep in this mind that this was way before microchips. The IBM 360 had a CPU (central processing unit) the size of a chest freezer. The CPU in any modern computer is the size of a fingernail. We were told "The full functionality of the IBM 360 will not be realized until around the year 2000!"

We also learned that the machine in the reception area was a card sorting machine and not a computer. Program code was keypunched into cards, sorted on these machines, then fed into the computer for the program to be compiled and executed. Well, Mr. Moon *did* say there was a computer in the sixth floor.

After a couple of months, things began to unravel. We had written programs in BAL (basic assembler language) and were to run them on a computer. Wayne said he had reserved time on an IBM 360 for us in the IBM center on Market Street. So, what the fuck is this? What about the school's computer on the sixth floor, the one Mr. Moon told us about? *Aha!* There *wasn't* one. Then, stories about previous classes who could not get jobs began filtering in. We were getting the idea PSI was a scam.

About this time, the aerospace industry, a large portion of which was located just south of San Francisco in what is now called Silicon Valley, went through a convulsion because of government spending cutbacks, the result of the tremendous waste of resources on financing the Vietnam War. Thousands of programmers were cut loose and redirected, taking jobs that would otherwise be filled by entry level programmers like myself.

I had time and Anita's money invested into this trip and I was determined to see to through. We took the 26 Valencia bus out to 30th Street to the big Salvation Army second hand store. For about five dollars I got a suit, a pair of used wingtips and a couple white shirts. I even got a (shudder) haircut.

I then spent several weeks walking the corridors of the financial district in search of a computer job. Prospects were not looking good. It felt strange walking in the marbled halls of the high-rise buildings in the financial district, my footsteps making endless echoes that followed me. I felt I was in the belly of the beast the capitalist monster that was sacrificing American youth for profits in Vietnam.

THE MISSION DISTRICT

My first experience of living in San Francisco was living in the Mission District when I found my friend, J.C. Burkhouse, on Valencia St. The topography of San Francisco is such that, due to Twin Peaks blocking clouds and moisture from the ocean, the Mission District is sunny, warm and pleasant much of the time when the rest of the city is overcast and chilly. It is called the Mission District because this is where the Mission Dolores, one of the missions founded by Franciscan priest Fr. Junipero Serra in the 18th century, is located

At the time I was living in San Francisco, the ethnic makeup of the Mission District was transitioning from Irish to Latino. The Mission District was cool for longhairs the cops were too busy getting into shit with Latinos kids to fuck with longhairs. It was brutal and nasty. People died.[2] Hippie-freak longhairs were pretty much left alone. Rents were reasonable and it was not difficult to be cool with the whole neighborhood.

Jack and I shared the apartment for a couple years. He was originally from New York City, about five years older than I and was another lost soul in the middle of the social chaos of the time. He had worked with The Bail Project[3] as part of a VISTA[4] which secured him a draft

---

[2] *Los Siete de la Raza*. (2018). *En. wikipedia. org*. Retrieved 25 April 2018, from https://en. wikipedia.org/wiki/Los_Siete_de_la
[3] https://bailproject. org/
[4] Volunteer in Service to America, a domestic version of the Peace Corp.

deferment. On his 26th birthday when Jack was no long subject to the draft, he quit.

The Bail Project was a program to help poor people arrested for various offenses to secure OR, to be released on their own recognizance rather than having to post bail, which many of them could not afford to do.

"Weekends were really something," Jack would say, "the Indians and the Samoans would get into these tremendous bar fights. They were all large guys and there would be charges of assault, battery, assault with a deadly weapon, destruction of property, attempted murder, all kinds of stuff. We would be up all night working to secure OR for these guys, all bruised and bloodied!"

Jack was Jewish. His mother was from Poland. "My Mom was the oldest of several sisters." He told me. "One of my mother's younger sisters wanted to get married. In Poland, the oldest girl had to marry before any younger sisters could marry. The alternative was that the older sister could go to America, which is what my mother did. Her sister married. They were all killed by the Nazis during the war. My Mom was the only one that survived."

It was stunning to hear this. By knowing Jack I now had a personal connection to the holocaust which, up to that point, been a concept, something from history books, not something that touched me in any way. I thought of my own family, my aunts, uncles and cousins and imagined what it would be to have your family so brutally murdered.

Somehow Jack and I got to know this guy named David Kirst, a short hippie with waist length black hair and a beard. David was a trip! He had a car. Jack had a phone. David would get trashed and forget where he parked his car and come to use Jack's phone to report it stolen. And a little while later he would be back and call the police again and report he had found his car. I remember this happening at least three times! David was a good musician and could play Robert Johnson style Delta Blues slide guitar. He played blues harp (harmonica) too.

David would occasionally show up with peyote buttons and we would brew peyote tea. I have never tasted anything so vile in my life, But the psychedelic buzz is more than worth it.

Delores Park was just two blocks away from where we lived. It was a great place to be when tripping, watching people, checking out their auras, getting all this telepathic stuff…a much fun way to spent a pleasant afternoon

On the west side of the park runs the J-Church streetcar. On the corner was a gold painted fire hydrant. There were a number of them in the city. A gold hydrant denoted a hydrant location that worked during the fires after the 1906 earthquake.

Mission High was next to the northern side of the park, a heavy duty barrio high school. It was always a hoot to see groups of teenage Latinas all done up with makeup like movie stars! All the guys hanging outside the school would be looking as tough as they could. These were serious individuals!

THE R. L. POLK COMPANY

Summer of 1970 found Jack and I working for the R. L. Polk Company as enumerators for the city directory. We reported to the City Directory office which was above the Geary. Each day we given computer printouts and trolley fare and walked around various neighborhoods with the computer printouts knocking on doors to verify and update information. There were fake names and info inserted into the printouts so if an enumerator marked that address as valid and up to date, they were sloughing off and would be caught. We all did it and caught hell from time to time. They would have to send someone else out to do the same area again. I three times and you were fired. I only got nailed once!

It was a minimum wage job, a low pressure gig and interesting as I got to talk to all kinds of people. Every day as we trudged up the stairs to turn in our printouts and clipboards, we would hear the strains of *This is the Dawning of the Age of Aquarius* from the musical, *Hair*, which was playing at the Geary Theater downstairs.

"The Pink Palace" was the euphemistic name for a large housing project on Turk Street. It was nasty! Graffiti, elevators stinking of stale piss, trash was everywhere. It reeked of poverty and misery. It took me the whole day to knock on every door.

Door after door after door was answered by single black women with multiple children and no husband. I remember one woman in particular who had eight children. One of the things we were instructed to do was ask single women if they were divorced and put an "X" by their name if they were. I asked her "Divorced?"

She scowled, spit out "I don't have to tell *you* my troubles!" and slammed the door in my face. I figured she was right and stopped asking the intrusive question.

I am not disrespecting these folks. I am describing how it was for a Pennsylvania hayseed just out in the world to see appalling poverty and hopelessness close up.

When I was ten or eleven years old I became aware of racial inequality, probably from the TV, certainly not from any sort of close-up experience with it. I asked my father why black people had it so bad in this country. "Gener," he replied, "some people are born with two strikes against them." That was as good an explanation as I have heard. It implied nothing racial while acknowledging cultural racial bias, an undeniable fact.

There were also a few elderly white folks living in the Pink Palace too. One old guy was lonely, I guess, so he invited me in for a drink, which I accepted, and then resumed my work. One elderly couple were evidently so glad to see a white face when they opened the door they invited me in and gave me cake and a glass of milk!

Most of the residents had no problem with the city directory, probably thinking that is the phone directory. We never brought that up! The city directory is was a demographic resource for marketers, as well as bill collectors, and bounty hunters looking for deadbeats and bail jumpers. I only mentioned this to hippie types who would then decline to be listed.

I am no multilinguist (unless high school Latin counts!), but it was during this stint as an enumerator that I learned that, when listening to someone speak with broken English, you only need a few words out of a sentence to understand them. Spanish was fairly easy. Filipinos were not too hard to understand. Chinese, much harder.

Senoras who did not speak English were so appreciative of any effort made to speak Spanish and responded with a wide grin, vigorous head nods and "Si! Si!" when I would say "directoria de San Francisco." Then I would ask, "Su hombre es Senor——"(your husband is—) reading the name from the printout.

"Tres ninos?" (three children?)

"Oh, si, si! (yes, yes)

They were just tickled that we could communicate despite us not really knowing the other's language.

It's funny how the mammaries…uh…memories…stick with you over the years. One sunny afternoon I was canvassing near San Francisco General. Hospital. I knocked on the door of one Mrs. Medrano and was greeted by a lovely well-built Latina with light brown skin, probably in her early 30s. She spoke English with a (sexy!) lilting Spanish accent and. As I was verifying her information, she put her hand on my wrist and proceeded to rest her ample bosom with accompanying cleavage on my arm. Yes indeed, it was a *lovely* afternoon!

One afternoon I committed a gaffe that still embarrasses me when I think about it. I was canvassing in the Potrero Hill section. One of the questions we asked was employment. For several dozen houses I asked "Employment?" and received the answer, "unemployed." I was talking to a black lady, probably in her fifties, When I got to the employment question my brain went on autopilot and I said "Unemployed?" to which she responded. "I am employed *and have been for the last twenty-five years!*"

I was mortified. I don't blame her for feeling insulted. My face went red. I turned around and left, too embarrassed to apologize for my unintentional insult.

In this day and age, I cannot imagine knocking on people's doors and expecting them to share personal information in that manner.

WHAT GOES AROUND WILL BITE YOU IN THE ASS

Prior to the city directory gig I was a street corner vendor selling underground newspapers on Fisherman's Wharf. Left-wing capitalist that I was, I would pay 7¢ apiece for them, cross out the 15¢ price and sell them to tourists for 50¢! Screw that "profit is theft" crap. Profit puts food on your table. I sold the *Berkeley Barb*, the *Berkeley Tribe* and the *San Francisco Good Times*. The May 8 issue of the Good Times carried the banner headline "SHIT HITS FAN" relevant to the unrest because of Nixon's invasion of Cambodia and the Kent State slaying of students by the National Guard.

I almost done for the day, I only had a few copies left. This one guy, about 5'7" and well built, probably 45 years old with wavy graying hair and self-righteous off duty cop vibes comes up to me and starts giving me a raft of shit.

"You shouldn't be doing this! What you are doing is bad! You should stop selling this stuff…" and the like. I don't know if it was the "bad word" in the banner headline or the seditious lean of the paper, or what. Articulate this guy was not.

He rattled on with his bullshit on while I sold my last papers. I then turned to him, extended my middle finger, said "go fuck yourself!" and left.

So fourteen months later[5] I am canvassing the neighborhood for the R. L. Polk Company at end of the J-Church streetcar line on 30th street. I go up to a duplex that has steps going up to the upstairs apartment. I knock on the lower door. The upper door opens. A man looks out and says, "Get the fuck out of here!"

As I put a door knob hanger on the downstairs door, he leaned further out the door and repeated, *"I told you to get the fuck out of here!"*

I looked up and flipped him off. Then I recognized him. It was the asshole from Fisherman's Wharf a year earlier! *Holy Shit!* What are the chances? He charged out that door and down the steps with blood in his eye and I hauled ass! I ran a block and got rid of him by jumping over a backyard fence and going through an alley! Lesson learned! Be careful who you flip off![6]

I carefully snuck back to finish the neighborhood canvass. One of the places I stopped at thee was a lovely young Asian-American woman, Quai Ling. I thought her name was like a bell tinkling. I did the city directory thing, and then asked her if she'd like to go to hear a band. She said yes and we went to the Family Dog, a rock dance hall on the beach. Can't remember who was playing, probably the Dead or the Airplane. It was a fun evening. We enjoyed the music, danced, smoked dope, spent the night together, and went our separate ways. She sweet, sexy, uninhibited, and not into permanent relationships. Suited me just fine.

We got about ten weeks of work from the R. L. Polk Company. I met a lot of people with widely varied backgrounds and got a lot of exercise that summer. It was a great way to learn about neighborhoods in the city.

BOEGERSHAUSEN HARDWARE

In November, 1970, I got a job through an employment agency as a clerk in a hardware store, Boegershausen (pron. **Ber**-gerz-how-zen) Hardware, at 2828 California Street near the intersection with Divisadero Street. Jack went to the same agency and got a job as a baggage handler for Greyhound. I worked days, he worked second shift, it was a great arrangement! I could practice guitar without disturbing him. And I practiced constantly, about five hours a day.

I was only making $1.50 an hour minimum wage, but it was steady and I worked six days a week. We were behind by *five months* on the

---

[5] See The Old Curmudgeon's Sage Advice No. 8.
[6] The full text of that is "don't fuck with people you don't know." Period. You never know what they are capable or if they are packing. People get killed by fucking with people they do not know.

rent and had *never* heard a peep from the realty company. I'll bet they fainted when they got the money order for the back rent!

Most important, I bought a stereo! And records!! I quickly developed a 4-record a week habit. I haunted the record stores on payday, particularly the ones that carried used ones. I could now indulge my taste for blues practically without limit: T-Bone Walker, B. B. King, Albert King, Albert Collins, Robert Johnson, Muddy Waters, Freddy King, Blind Lemon Jefferson, Johnny Otis, Aretha Franklin, Lightnin' Hopkins. Of course I bought rock n' roll records too: Led Zeppelin, Rolling Stones, Jefferson Airplane, Cream, Grateful Dead, Dave Mason, Steve Winwood, Jeff Beck, Jethro Tull, Chuck Berry, Jimi Hendrix and on and on and on. I have a modest collection of about a thousand LPs.

John (Johann) Boegershausen with his children Augusta and Charles William (Karl) around 1912. They both look like they just got a swat on the ass! Source: Wiki

The owner of the store was Carl Boegershausen who had turned 65 that year. He was born in 1906 about a month after the San Francisco earthquake! "Must have shaken me loose!" he would say. I earned a survivable income and learned a lot while working there.

Carl's father was from Germany. His grandmother died when his father was 14, so his father, Johann, went to sea as a cabin boy then spent time in the merchant marine ending up in San Francisco and started the store early in the century. Carl would tell stories about his father doing plumbing as well, getting on the streetcars with his pipe and tools to get to a job. Carl's real name was Charles, but his father called him Carl because he didn't want his son called "Charlie," "Charlie's a Chinaman's name!" was his reason. He was *not* going to have his son called by a Chinaman's name! When Carl was a boy, he had a job as a lamplighter, lighting gas street lights at dusk. I wonder if he had to extinguish them at dawn too. I should have asked him!

I found the image of Johann Boegershausen and his children on Wiki. He Americanized his name to "John." The date given is 1907, children are identified as Augusta and William. Carl's middle initial was "W." The face on that boy is unmistakably Carl. The year is incorrect, though Carl was born in 1906 so this picture had to have been taken around 1912. Johann was an inventor as well as hardware man and had a patent for the flue atop the newel post.

Carl taught me everything about hardware. I became so adept at sizing by eye that I could look at a bolt or machine screw and tell the gauge and thread count. He taught me to cut glass, glaze windows, sharpen cutlery on a grinder, repair lamps, and troubleshoot and repair small appliances. I also learned to cut, ream, and thread iron pipe, sizing and cutting window shades, and mixing paint. I sometimes accompanied him as a helper when he went out to install water heaters. Cark taught me some elementary locksmithing skills, how to re-key and master-key lock cylinders, lock installation and the like.

We had music in common as well, Carl was a sax player when he was young. He and his wife had no children. They lived in Kentfield in Marin County, across the Golden Gate Bridge. My sole co-worker was Elliot Hoyer, a WWII vet and as mild mannered a person as I ever met, a wonderful fellow.

Carl was funny. The first thing I did every morning was use a hand truck to put a water heater and a bag of steer manure onto the sidewalk. One day a guy comes in and Carl is at the register.

"How much is your steer manure?" he asks.

"Two-fifty" replies Carl, writing in a receipt book, not looking up.

"Two fifty? Wow! That's kind of expensive, isn't it?"

Looking up Carl said, "Hey, even the bulls don't shit for nothin' y'know," and went back to the receipt book.

Another time a guy comes in and goes to the tool section. Carl asks him if he can help him.

"Yeah, I need a hacksaw. What's your cheapest one?"

Carl picks one off the wall, "Here. Here's one for two seventy-five."

"Two seventy five? Don't you have one for a buck ninety-eight?"

"Nope. Two seventy-five is the cheapest one we got."

"Well, Bowman Hardware on Fillmore has 'em on sale for a buck ninety-eight."

Carl says, "Well, why don't you buy one from Bowman's?"

"He's out of 'em."

Hanging the saw back up, Carl chuckled, "Oh hell, when I'm out of 'em I sell 'em for a buck ninety eight too!"

Carl was as fair and reasonable a man as you would ever meet and gave great Christmas bonuses. The Christmas of 1970 I got a $60 bonus. Every Christmas after that it was $500! THAT was great! I used my $60 bonus to buy a brand new Yamaha FG-80 flattop guitar. I still have it. He floated me a couple interest free loans too.

While I was buying my guitar and thin fellow with longish grey hair, probably in his 60s, came up to me and said, "Would you like some lessons to go with that guitar?"

"Sure," I responded. He introduced himself as Woodie Wedlick. It turns out he gave lessons at the Jewish Community Center just a couple blocks from the hardware. My lessons were Wednesdays after work. My first lesson was the chords to *The Girl from Ipanema*. I learned it and the next week I said, "Woodie, this is a nice tune, but I want to play rock n' roll." So he gave me the chords to *Hey Jude* to learn. At the next lesson I said, "Woodie, I want to play rock and blues lead guitar."

"Well you have to learn chords first," he responded.

"Would you please show me a blues scale?" After some hemming and hawing he showed me a pentatonic minor scale. I paid him his five bucks and never took another lesson.

THE CLIENTELE

The clientele of the store was varied and interesting. California Street ran east-west and was the border between the well-to-do folks up the hill in Pacific heights and the not so well to do folks down the hill in the Western Addition. Working for Carl afforded me the opportunity to interact with people of many different ethnicities and nationalities. There was a small Filipino community on Sacramento St., they were such lovely people to deal with. There was this one very animated fellow who would go off on tirades against the leader of the Philippines at the time, Ferdinand Marcos. He was a property manager and would come in a couple times a week to have keys made.

A character who showed up from time to time was a short, stocky, black fellow named Henry Rampton. Henry was always stewed and talking about the lady who owned the laundromat next door, Mrs. Vance, a good looking, older, and curvaceous black lady.

"Oh, Mrs. Vance, you know, she got that old pussy, you know what I mean…that old pussy, that's some good pussy. You gotta like that old pussy…. you young…maybe you don't have none of that old pussy yet…yeah, that old pussy is mighty good…you get yourself some of that old pussy…you see what I mean!…oooh…I want some of the pussy Mrs. Vance got…yeah…ain't nothing like that old pussy…I'll bet she got that real nice pussy…" and on and on and on. He didn't bother me, he was harmless and amusing. I would unpack, price, and shelve merchandise listening to Henry reciting his "old pussy is good pussy" mantra over and over!

One day when Henry was going on with his "old pussy" routine Carl said, "You know Henry, one of these days you're going to get drunk and fall down and bust your head open on the curb and all that's gonna fall out is a whole bunch of old pussy!"

I had my first experience with adult illiteracy in the hardware store. A black woman, probably around forty, pleasant and very upbeat, bought a box of cleanser. She asked me how to use it. Pointing to the directions on the box I said, "The directions are right here."

"Oh, I'm terrible at following directions like that," she bubbled, "just tell me, please."

And it hit me. *Holy shit. She can't read!* I told her how to use the product. She thanked me and went on her way.

Carl sold kitchen ranges. We didn't stock them but would order them and have them delivered to the customer. Carl would do the installation.

I was dusting the shelves one day, it must have been Elliot's lunch break because Carl and I were in the store by ourselves. Mrs. Tanaka, a middle aged Japanese-American lady and regular customer, came in and started talking to Carl about getting a new range. What she said during the conversation struck me.

"It's time for a new one. We've had this one since we got out of the concentration camp."

They taught us about "internment camps" in school never associating the term "concentration camp" with them, or with America. [7] This statement led me to the realization that she was right. They were U.S. citizens put in concentration camps by the government. That simple statement brought me to a realization about this country and sort of connected me to the Japanese internment. I personally knew someone, an American citizen, who had been rounded up and imprisoned by her own government.

WALTER JOHNSON

My namesake, Walter Johnson, was a crusty old fellow who managed a large apartment building across the street from the hardware. He looked to be in his 70s, white hair, always wore a wife beater shirt, brown trousers with suspenders and sported an old fedora. He smoked a pipe and usually had a 3 day stubble. Walter was thin, almost gaunt. And garrulous! He would keep us posted on what was going on in his building.

One time he mentioned the FBI was asking him about one of the tenants, a woman I knew. After work I went to her apartment and told her about the feds. She thanked me, saying her brother was on the run from the draft and the FBI checked in with her every few months. A lot of people were on the run back in the day. Freaks looked out for each other. It was the *zeitgeist*. It was our brotherhood. It was our conspiracy against the man.

But the funniest thing was…well…here's the story. It involves Walter, of course. And Li Quan, the owner of a Chinese greasy spoon on the first floor of Walter's apartment building. Li Quan was tall and thin and walked slightly swaybacked with his elbows pumping back and forth almost like a cartoon animation. The third party was this absolutely gorgeous young Chinese woman living in Walter's building.

One day Walter came in and said "Ayup, damned near had to shoot that goddamned Chinaman last night." He lit his pipe. "Goddamn Quan. You know that Chinese girl that lives there, you know who I mean?"

---

[7] Now, in 2019, America has concentration camps and rips children from their parents trying to immigrate at the Mexican border. It is definitely a different age.

"Sure, Walter, she's hard to miss."

"Yeah, well she's been fuckin' that Chinaman, Li Quan. You know. Owns the restaurant." Walter went on. "And he was payin' her rent. He stopped payin' it so I told her if she gave me what she gave him I'd take care of her rent. So that's what I been doin'." Lighting his pipe, he looked up and grinned (as well he should!).

"So last night Quan shows up at her place while I'm there. I told him 'she ain't fuckin' you for the rent anymore, she's fuckin' me for it. Now get your chink ass out of here!' He started to squawk in Chinese and come toward me so I got my gun out and told 'im, 'go on! Get your ass out of here. *Now*, goddamnit!' He left."

Walter passed away shortly after that. It made me wonder if the action he was getting from her was just too much for him! I hope the lecherous old bastard died with a smile on his face! We truly missed the color of Walter's daily presence.

CUSTOMER RELATIONS 101

Sacramento Street was on block up the hill from California Street where the hardware was. There was a white stucco apartment building about a block west on the north side of Sacramento Street that had the name "FELICE" in big metal letters over the entrance. I knew a couple who rented there, he was a drunken poet and she was an artist. I also knew their landlord, Mr. Caswell, a large black man in his 50s who always smelled of cheap wine. Easily annoyed, he could be surly beyond belief. We handled him with kid gloves. One day I did not give him that treatment.

The couple I knew who rented from him had some hassle with him and, before they moved out, they had a big party with some friends and trashed the place: marked up the walls, pissed on the carpets, clogged the drains, stole all the light bulbs, the works. Oh, and last but not least, they removed the "FE" from the FELICE sign, so it now read "LICE."

So here comes Mr. Caswell in a foul mood and stinking of wine. He needs some pipe nipples and fittings. We went to the pipe bins in the back. I am picking things he wants out of the bins and he starts this rant about his tenants who just moved out. I had recently talked to them and knew what they had done. I ignored him and he went on at length and "even stole all my light bulbs! Nothing but a bunch of no good goddamned long-haired white trash hippie sonsabitches!" He looks directly at me, "You know, you got that long hair, maybe you should–"

Listening to his shit was one thing, but he was directing the "no good goddamned long-haired white trash hippie sonsabitches" toward me now and I was having none of it. He was the only customer in the store, Elliot was out front at the register. I snapped, "Listen here, motherfucker–"

"Oh…I'm a…*motherfucker*… am I? He tilted his head back and looked down his nose, glaring at me.

"Yeah. You're a motherfucker."

Mr. Caswell raised a piece of pipe in his hand as if to strike me.

"You'd better think real careful about what you're going to do with that pipe because I *will* shove it up your ass!"

He kept the glare and lowered the pipe.

Elliot came running back. "What's going on here?"

"It's all right, Elliot, everything's under control." I turned to Caswell. "If you need pipe fittings, let's get you your pipe fittings. If you want to talk about hair, go somewhere else."

We completed the transaction without any further issues.

I doubt Elliot even told Carl about it. What I said was definitely grounds for termination. Mr. Caswell was such a giant pain-in-the-ass that Elliot probably wished he'd said it! He never brought the subject up.

Mr. Caswell still came in the store regularly and we never had another incident. He was such a pain-in-the-ass that he'd been banned from some neighborhood businesses including Bowman's Hardware on Fillmore Street. I guess he wanted to continue to do business with us. We were respectful of each other after that.

"No good goddamned long-haired white trash hippie sonsabitches!" I have never forgotten that litany of magnificently crafted bit of profanity. Yes, that irascible old bastard could sure cuss! "**No** good **god**damned **long**-haired **white** trash **hip**pie **son**sabitches!" It has meter, it's poetic! It would fit well in a bluegrass lyric!

On occasion some of the nobility from Pacific Heights would visit our humble hardware. These were the moneyed matrons of San Francisco aristocracy occupying the elegant mansions in Pacific Heights and spending their dead husbands' money. There was one lady, can't remember her name, Mrs. Moneybags will do. She was, uh, big, tall and wide. I was waiting on a customer and heard the entry bell ring. Looking up I saw Mrs. Moneybags with diminutive uniformed Filipino chauffer, dwarfed by the imposing dowager head and shoulders taller than he. She looked for all the world like she had a monkey on a leash. Oh God, that is awful, just awful, but it's just one of those things that pops out of your mind on its own…it was funny and awful at the same time.

And dear old Mrs. Munston was another rich old widow, I would guess in her 70s. On her chauffer's day off she would sometimes drive herself down in a big old gray Lincoln Continental and park it with the ass end in traffic. She just couldn't dock that battleship! I would volunteer, "Mrs. Munston, would it be okay if I moved your car just a little bit closer to the curb? "

"Why, yes, dear," she would reply, handing me her keys, "you certainly may do that for me! Thank you," she smiled.

One day I went in the back room and found Carl at the table where we glazed windows replacing the batteries in a vibrator. I had to ask.

"Uh…whatchadoin', Carl?"

"Oh, this belongs to Mrs. Munston. It wasn't working so I'm replacing the batteries for her." He replaced the cap on the base and switched it on. It came to life with a buzzing sound and he rubbed his cheek with it. "There, now she can massage herself! "

"Think about where that's been, Carl, Are you sure you want to be rubbing that on your face?"

He just grinned.

A sign of the times, the SFPD sent a bulletin to all hardware stores in the city to be on the alert for persons purchasing short sections of pipe and pipe caps as they were likely intending to make pipe bombs with them. [8] We were urged to not make the sale and report the incident to police.

RUSSIAN NAVAL OFFICER'S CLUB

I picked up odd jobs here and there that I did after store hours, mostly from store customers who needed some handyman work done. Many jobs Carl referred to me from store customers. One such customer was this Russian lady who managed the Russian Naval Officers Club in

---

[8] I had all but forgotten about this until, while editing the final draft of this book, I saw an article in the October 29, 2019 *Bradford Era* about some local miscreant was apprehended after purchasing short sections of pipe and caps for them who had told his friends he was going to blow up public places in Bradford, PA. He was upset that people didn't like him. Nothing political, just a basic lack of social skills most likely abetted by abusing crystal meth.!

Pacific Heights. Every once in a while she would have a few things for me to do. She was short and stout, almost like a cartoon of an old Russian lady, a Babushka. She was very sweet and gave me a bit of history about the building.

The Russian Naval Officers Club was composed of men who had attended the Czar's Naval College before the 1917 revolution. The walls were lined with portraits of young men – some who were now residents of this building – who graduated from the Czar's Naval academy. After the revolution many went on to serve in other world navies. This was their retirement home. There were few left. The dining hall was done up like an officer's mess, with portholes on the walls. I only saw one in my visits there, and he wasn't ambulatory. We went past his room and his door was open and it was obvious he was in the final stages of dementia. The lady shut his door and said sadly in accented English, "This is so unfortunate. That man was a Naval engineer. He was so brilliant." I thought it must be sad for her to see these men dying off.

There was no end to meeting unique individuals. I was doing some repairs in an apartment where an old Irish woman lived. I mentioned that I had a couple friend who's parent's came to the U.S. just in time for the depression. She in turn told me about how, when she was a small girl, the British Black and Tans[9] would machine gun Catholics coming out of church. I had heard about this, but this was the first time I had ever come into a contact with someone who witnessed it firsthand.

NAKED HIPPIE CHICKS!

I went to an apartment one time to do some maintenance work for a landlord and found the tenant, a lovely blonde hippie chick, completely nude. I did the work in the apartment and she remained in the nude. DAMN! Those were some *good* days!

A lot of hippie chicks loved being naked, and who's to argue the point? Certainly not me! J.C. Burkhouse, was living in Fairfax, Marin County. I went out for a visit one weekend and he and his lady were living in a house that had three other women in it who slept in the nude and never put any clothes on before noon. They all had these large bosoms and lovely, *ample* asses shaped like upside down hearts, and all over tans. And they were, um, *friendly*... I did not sleep alone, I was with

---

[9] "Black and Tans" were members of the Royal Irish Constabulary, the name is taken from their uniforms. They were alleged to have been recruited from British prisons and took part in the murderous reprisals against Irish Catholics for supporting the Republic.

a zaftig hippie hottie with no tan lines named Janie who just loved to fuck. It was a…nice weekend visit. REAL nice.

NORM

Everyone meet someone I the course of their lives who is exceptionally…I don't know what to call it, but Norm was one of them! I lived for a brief time in an apartment a couple blocks from the hardware store that I shared with Norm and his girlfriend Judy, their friend Karen, and a dog with the Tolkien-esque name, Sambo Baggins.

First, there was Norm's appearance. He was about six feet, thin, had long blonde hair that formed loose ringlets that formed a halo around his face, chin whiskers like Uncle Sam, and sharply arched eyebrows giving him the appearance of a gargoyle.

Norm was not into *multiple* drug abuse, he was into *multidimensional* drug abuse!

There was a halfway house for patients recently released from Napa State Hospital around the corner from us on Broderick St. This is before Governor Reagan closed all the mental health facilities in the state and added former mental patients to the ranks of the homeless. Norm would trade some of the residents cheap wine for their psych meds. That is how he started his day. By the time suppertime rolled around, Norm was fucked up beyond description, having ingested whatever drugs he happened to find that day, somehow remaining ambulatory. Usually it would be weed, psych meds, alcohol and of course, and a bottle or two of Robitussin cough syrup. Jesus God!

One evening Ron, our friend Rick, Norm, and I went out for a night of barhopping on Clement Street. We would snort two lines of coke each between bar visit. We were in this one bar where we knew Bill the Bartender. He was a cool dude and would give us a drink on the house. Norm was sloppy drunk and kept falling off his bar stool. Bill came over and said, "hey, you guys got to get your buddy under control. I can't have him in here like that." We took Norm out to Ron's truck and went back in for another drink.

We were enjoying our libation when Bill the Bartender runs up to us and says, "Holy *fuck* you guys! Look what he's doing now!"

We looked toward the door that Norm was standing on of one of the tables waving his dick and pissing! We grabbed Norm up and hustled him out the door. He managed to fall down and split his head open on the curb and was bleeding all over the place. Ron grabbed some bar rags from Bill the Bartender and we took Norm to the ER at San Francisco General. Ron went and got Judy while Rick and I waited. When Ron got back with Judy we went to see Norm. He was gone! Somehow, in his mega-fucked up state he had managed to get out of his bed and leave the hospital. We looked for him and couldn't find him. After a frantic hour we said fuck it and went home. Judy walked in their apartment and there was Norm, passed out on the couch.

Norm is gone, he was found dead under a highway overpass near Portland, Oregon in 1991.

IS IRVING THERE?

Marijuana is now legal for both medicinal and recreational use in many parts of the country. We are just now getting used to the idea of dispensaries where wide selections of various strains of cannabis can be legally purchased. The anti-pot folks are shitting bricks and warning us about the increased potency of modern marijuana. [10]

In the mid 70s, San Francisco had a dispensary located on Oak Street just off Divisadero Street referred to as "The Store." It was, of course, an illegal operation. As in the prohibition days, you had to know somebody. A customer had to give you an introduction to someone connected with The Store. You were then given a code name. When you would knock at the front door, a peep hole would be opened from the other side and someone asked you your code name (mine was "Hardware Dude," my friend, Lewis, who gave me my introduction was "Lefty Lewie"). If your code name was on the list, you were permitted entry.

The entrepreneurs who operated The Store grew their own weed indoors under lights and always had potent flowering tops of a number of varieties from which you made your selection.

These people were not hard core capitalists. If you were broke, out of dope and wanted a to catch a buzz, you could go to the Purple Room where you could freely sample the shake–lower leaves of the plants, not the flowering tops, less potent but still quite buzzworthy– to your head's content. This was one of the last remnants or the love and sharing spirit of the Haight-Ashbury still around.

In addition to weed, The Store also dispensed psychedelic fungi, mushrooms of the psilocybin variety. As with the weed, they grew these themselves and they were not always in stock. If you were looking for

---

[10] The potency of marijuana buds is a moot point now that potency of THC oil in legally obtainable medical vape capsules is around an astounding 87%. Whoo-hoo!

mushrooms you could call the store and ask "Is Irving there?" If the answer was "Yes," you were good to go. If the answer was something like "Irving'll be back in a couple weeks," it meant the current crop would be ready in a couple weeks.

Of course, the inevitable happened. One evening on the evening news there was a picture of a familiar set of steps. Shit! It was the house The Store was in. The cops raided, destroyed all the growing apparatus for the weed and mushrooms and arrested everyone on the premises. Alas, the Store was no more!

THE "OAK STREET SNIPER" & MY '42 DODGE

One day in early 1971 this very cool old pickup truck with "John's Alley Garage" painted on the door parked in front of the store. Out gets a dude with disheveled ratty-looking hair and an equally scraggly beard looking for all the world like a bad guy from Clint Eastwood spaghetti western. He came into the store and bought some nuts and bolts, As I rang him up I said, "That's a cool truck you have,"

"Yeah," he replied, "It's a '42 Dodge. I got another one like it for sale. You interested?"

"How much?"

"Hundred twenty-five dollars."

I glanced at the truck out front. "Yeah, I'm interested." He gave me his address which was on Lily Street – an alley, really – which ran east and west between Oak and Page streets.

My very cool 1942 Dodge

It was a seedy neighborhood of mixed ethnicity. The sellers name was John Mac-Creedy. He lived there with his wife and their two kids. She was dusky, attractive, and pregnant. In contrast to John, his brother Billy was tall and thin with red hair and beard looking like a Celtic warrior!

I looked the truck over. It started just fine, ran ok, not great. It was just cool as hell! Three speed stick, starter button on the floor, air conditioning provided by a dashboard crank that swung the windshield out from the bottom. It was red, had some minor dents in the fenders but nothing I couldn't pound out and fix with Bondo. The motor was an in-line flathead 6. The driver's door and window had a couple round holes in them.

"What's with the holes?"

"Oh, them are bullet holes."

"Really? Uh…how'd they get there?"

He gestured, "Them fuckin' niggers over there on Oak Street."

"Uh…why'd they shoot your truck?"

"'Cause I don't fuckin' like 'em and I don't take their shit. So I was shootin' through their apartment window with a .22. So they fuckin' shot my truck."

"I see," was all I could say. Never having met and individual like this before, I was wondering about the veracity of his story. He must have read my mind.

"Yup. They wrote me up in *The Black Panther Newspaper* as the 'Oak Street Sniper.' " John produced copy of the Panther newspaper and, sure enough, there was an article about the Oak Street Sniper shooting into windows of apartments with black residents on Oak Street.

I am in a state of *holy fuck!* at this Point. John was definitely no hippie, there was no peace and love about him, or his brother, Billy, either for that matter. Their conversations were full of hateful racism.

I bought the truck. It ran and was not over priced and would be a good project. A couple months later I decided to have John rebuild the engine. Dodge was still making that same flathead six for marine use, so getting engine parts was no problem. I was paying for the rebuild in installments and every week would bop on over to Lily Street and give John some money and we would smoke some dope together.

If John liked you, you were all right. If he didn't, you'd better watch your ass as he was a violent man. Sometimes he had a revolver stuffed in his waist. Constantly in scrapes with the cops, John had a space dug out underneath his house where he could hide.

One time he had no shirt on and I saw he had what looked like two bellybuttons and a long vertical scar on his abdomen. "What the hell happened to you?" I asked.

"Oh, I had a .25 automatic stuffed in my waist. I bent over and it fell out of my waistband and went off. The docs had to open me up to patch me, then they had to get the wound to heal from the inside out."

One afternoon I came by and no one answered the door. I turned around to leave and a young woman with long dark hair and liquid brown eyes came up to me and said, "You looking for John?"

"Yeah."

"Well, he and Mary went someplace. Want to come and wait at my place? They should be right back."

I needed no further encouragement. Her name was Joyce and she lived a couple doors down the street with her five year old daughter, Christine, and three year old son, Eric. Joyce liked uppers and talked a lot. We became friends over the next few weeks and then lovers for a time. We made better friends than lovers, so we stuck to that. She filled me in on the action on Lily Street.

Joyce had a razor sharp Ka-Bar knife in her purse. There was a pimp in the neighborhood who wanted to turn her out. She was having none of it. She said to me one time, "If that motherfucker ever touches me I'll cut his fucking throat. That nigger'll be dead before he knows it."

The counterculture and ghetto culture overlapped somewhat and shared an underground economy that revolved around weed and food stamps. It was sort of a barter system with weed, but food stamps functioned as currency.

There was a black guy who wanted to buy a car from John with food stamps. John refused. The guy insisted and there were angry words. One time I showed up at John's and the front of his building was black and scorched. This guy had come in the night and tried to burn the building down with gasoline.

One afternoon Mary went shopping and left John and Billy at the house. They were doing reds. [11] When she came home, John had Billy on the floor holding a kitchen knife to his throat! She was able to pull them apart and nobody died that day.

One day John beat hell out of Joyce. She bought a gun and moved from Lily Street to the Potrero Projects on Missouri Street.[12] A short time later John moved his operation to an old warehouse on Texas Street in a section called Dogpatch. Joyce shit bricks one day when she looked out her front door one day and saw John and his crew downhill several hundred yards off.

---

[11] Seconal, downers in red capsules.
[12] I recently saw her old unit on Missouri Street in an episode of Murder in the First.

When she was speeding she was impossible, hearing voices talking about her coming from her wall heater and the like. I would just stay away when she got like that.

I got to know some of Joyce's neighbors. Hers was he only white household in the projects. They were warm and wonderful people. All the times I visited there I never once got hassled.

I would stop into John's new location from time to time. Frequently Fast Eddie, a solidly built fellow with greased back hair, was there. He had the thickest New York accent I ever heard. He and John liked early 1950s Fords. Fast Eddie sported greased back hair and had a hot rodded flathead V8 '51 Ford. He was a bit crazy, always packing.

Then there was Mac, a beefy guy and a genuine goddamned psycho. One Valentine's day he got in a hassle with his old lady, a petite woman named Mouse. As she was going out the door leaving him, he shot her in the back and killed her. I finally stopped going to John's, his scene was just too fucking weird.

Mary finally left John. She started seeing a cop, so John stayed away. And John never did find out that he was within sight of Joyce's place. He never bothered her again.

My buddy, Ron, from Bradford, PA, hitchhiked to San Francisco in 1972.

We rented the apartment on the third floor of the hardware store building from Carl. There was a small parking lot around the corner on Divisadero Street that went with the apartment. Next to the entrance to the lot was a garage, Ted and Al's. One fine morning Ron was backing out of the parking lot and sideswiped a car that had just been serviced at Ted and Al's. It belonged to City Supervisor Dianne Feinstein, now a U.S. Senator and head of the Senate Intelligence Committee. It didn't take the cops long to scoop Ron up. He got off by saying he had left a note about the accident, it must have gotten blown away by a breeze. And paying for the damage.

CORNER GROCERIES

Corner grocery stores are interesting indicators of changing immigrant demographics. The latest wave of immigrants buy the mom and pop groceries from the previous immigrants. When I arrived in San Francisco in 1969 most of these groceries were owned by Chinese who had immigrated from Hong Kong The latest influx of immigrants were Palestinians from the town of Ramallah on the West Bank, displaced by the aftermath of the 1967 Six Day War in which Israel seized the West Bank. You would see many wearing a crucifix.

The apartment we rented from Carl had once been rented by the writer, Richard Brautigan. When I lived above the hardware store I was in the Diana Market a lot, it was on the northeast corner of California and Divisadero. Brautigan referred to it in some of his writing.

Two Palestinian brothers-in-law, Louie and John, owned it. Another brother-in-law, Eddie, had a gas station out near the beach. Just through small talk and general bullshit over a few years, we were all friends. They were genuinely nice people.

Louie was nobody to fuck with. At six feet, probably mid to late 40s, salt and pepper wavy hair, Louie had a solid build. One evening Louie is at the Diana Market alone – these merchants kept long hours out of necessity – and a black guy comes in a puts a .45 in his face demanding cash. Louie was getting the cash from the drawer and this guy says, "C'mon, *hurry up*, mother*fucker!*" Poor choice of words. Louie came around the counter, grabbed this asshole and pitched him out the door! A piece of the grip from the .45 broke off in the struggle and was left behind. The police used it to ID the perp when they popped him later for another robbery.

Louie said to Ron Lattin and me, "He called me a 'motherfucker'! *Like I FUCK MY OWN MOTHER!*" Yeah. Louie was HOT! You can shove a gun in his face and live, but you better not talk bad about his momma!

Eddie had a tow truck. I had an old Ford van that sat for too long in the salt air near the beach where I lived and the tranny linkage froze. My mechanic was a Russian guy with a garage on Geary Street. I had Eddie tow my van. The boom on his truck was up too high and he managed to damage the Russian mechanic's overhead door! I called this an "international incident," a Palestinian and a Russian yelling at each other in English! It was unfortunate, but, goddamn! It was *funny*. You have to take your humor where you find it! I managed to not laugh out loud!

It's remarkable how you can stay in touch with a group of people over a period of time without even trying. Over the time I was in San Francisco, Louie sold the market and then had a brake shop and then a meat market, both, if I recall, on Ocean Ave. Eddie bought another station. John bought a restaurant out by the beach. When we moved back here in 1981, we had breakfast there before we left on our cross country drive, and I said good bye to John.

You could see differences in the character of the corner groceries as they went from Chinese to Palestinian ownership. The Chinese groceries were invariably family run. Mom and dad would work the counter, the kids would be doing their homework. I rarely saw a family presence in a Palestinian grocery, it was usually one or two guys, very rarely any women.

The Chinese groceries rarely carried liquor. Maybe some beer. And no skin magazines. As soon as the Palestinians took charge, in went liquor, wine – a BIG rack of Ripple, preferred beverage of winos everywhere – beer, and a rack of skin magazines! Except the Diana Market. Louie had no liquor or skin mags.

WATERGATE

I was in my mid 20s and part of the cohesive longhaired left wing pot-smoking freak community in San Francisco during Watergate. We all despised Nixon to begin with. We despised the Democrats as well. The main issues were the Vietnam War, racism and political repression.

The background to Watergate was the 1968 presidential election. There were three candidates, Richard Nixon, Hubert Humphrey, and George Wallace. They all supported the war, so there was no way to support an antiwar candidate. No matter who won Americans were going to continue be shot to hell in Vietnam.

The riots at the 1968 DNC in Chicago sealed the deal for a lot of people as it showed what the Democrats, allegedly a liberal party, were willing to do to Americans who were opposed to the war: let the police beat them bloody in the streets.

The word "radicalization" started appearing in the press, talking about it as if were some arcane process and very difficult to comprehend. It was actually pretty simple. All one had to do was be a member of the generation that had no say about a shitty endless war they were being conscripted to fight, see their friends come home in flag-draped coffins, or get their head bashed by a police truncheon at a peaceful demonstration turned violent because the cops lost their shit. A government commission later determined that the civil disturbances at the 1968 DNC were a *police* riot victimizing Americans citizens exercising their constitutionally protected rights to free speech and assembly. Radicalization. This is how it happened to many people. It's simple, really. If you fuck with anyone long enough and they will get testy about it!

Fatassed J. Edgar Hoover's FBI was in full COINTELPRO mode viewing anyone with views to the left of Hitler as "commanist"[13] and a threat to Western Civilization. Police were murdering black militants in midnight raids in cities throughout the country. During the trial of the Chicago 7 – a federal trial of left wing activists accused of instigating the riots at the '68 DNC –the concept of conspiracy was redefined to mean that conspirators did not have to actually communicate with each other to be part of a conspiracy. The defendants were convicted. These bullshit convictions were later reversed.

Nixon's invasion of Cambodia in May, 1970, was a direct contradiction to his promise of a "secret plan to end the war." This further inflamed antiwar feelings, led to campus unrest, rioting, and the deaths students shot by National Guard troops and police at Kent State University, Jackson State, and South Carolina State.

Watergate was, to us, the best thing that ever happened politically in our lives since JFK's election. I remember reading an, just a few column inches, in the S. F. Chronicle about the break-in. At first it did not get much resonance in the mainstream media. The alternative news services provided news about it for the underground newspapers and left-wing radio stations. As the Watergate investigation flourished, KSAN did a weekly radio show every Wednesday evening called "The Watergate Follies," a sometimes brilliant and always amusing half hour of political satire. Politics for us had been so bleak that Watergate was a breath of fresh air, a crack in the Nixon's monolithic quasi-fascist regime.

Did we think Nixon was a crook? Well, we weren't so certain about him being a crook as we were certain he was a rotten-ass lying piece of shit. Underground papers ran all kinds of stories about Nixon and his henchmen accusing all of them of outrageous shit. History has shown us that those stories were inaccurate, not because they weren't true, but because Nixon *et al* were doing shit that topped the paranoid ravings of even the most strung out leftist meth head.

For instance, no one accused Nixon of drug abuse. What no one knew at that time is that he was freely abusing Dilantin, a powerful anti seizure medication, mixing it with scotch. In his book *The Arrogance of Power*, Anthony Summers revealed that Jack Dreyfus Jr., director of the Dreyfus Fund and close Nixon friend, used to supply Nixon with Dilantin in quantities of a thousand.[14]

Nixon, the originator of the War on Drugs, was not only freely consuming quantities of illegally obtained Dilantin, he also used alcohol and

---

[13] FBI Director J. Edgar Hoover's pronunciation of the word.
[14] *The Arrogance of Power*, Anthony Sutton, Viking, 2000, P 317-318, 455-457.

sleeping pills as well as amphetamines. Columnist Drew Pearson, when learning of the president's drug consumption was distraught enough to wonder if Nixon was the right man to have his finger on the nuclear button. Others wondered the same thing.[15]

An interesting aside to Nixon's alleged "war on drugs" was when, in a brazen display of hypocrisy, Elvis Presley – who was freely abusing prescription drugs – visited the White House and was made an honorary DEA agent by Nixon, who was freely abusing the powerful drug Dilantin. They were *both* fucked up on drugs!

Another instance of underestimating Nixon would be the treason he committed prior to the 1968 election.[16] Nixon urged the North Vietnamese, who were in peace talks with a delegation from the Lyndon Johnson administration, to not make a deal with Johnson because he would give them a better one after he was elected.

Then there were the Mitchells, John and Martha. John Mitchell was Nixon's Attorney General, a Wall St. lawyer who didn't know shit about law enforcement. At one point, Mitchell ordered the roundup of peaceful demonstrators in D.C. and imprisoned them in a stadium, an act the courts later declared unconstitutional. His wife, Martha, was genuinely concerned that her husband was hooked up with a bunch of crooks and was going to end up in jail (she was right!). From time to time she would call up newspapers in an inebriated state and rant about Nixon's gang of thugs. She was such a security risk to the Nixon machine that at one point they drugged and kidnapped her to get her to STFU.

We were delighted as the revelations about Watergate continued to emerge, each one being another nail in Nixon's coffin. Every Wednesday we sat around passing joints and a bottle of Jose Cuervo as we listened to the Watergate Follies.

Agnew resigned as Nixon's vice president. That was a completely unexpected bonus. This asshole had been Nixon's attack dog who often spoke in alliterations such as characterizing those opposed to the war as "nattering nabobs of negativism." He resigned the office over revelations that he had taken bribes from contractors when he was the governor of New Jersey, the most common and lowest and most common form of political corruption.

---

[15] Ibid. p. 319, 457
[16] Dreams, C., Fitrakis, B. and Wasserman, H.
Dreams, Common, Bob Fitrakis, and Harvey Wasserman. 2014. "George Will Confirms Nixon's Vietnam Treason". Common Dreams. Accessed July 22 2019.
https://www.commondreams.org/views/2014/08/12/george-will-confirms-nixons-vietnam-treason.

Rolling Stone ran an article on Agnew's resignation illustrated by a cartoon of a thumb and forefinger holding a nasty, drippy, slimy looking used condom upon which was the unmistakable droopy looking face of Spiro T. Agnew. So long motherfucker! Glory of glories!

The Pentagon Papers were released by Daniel Ellsberg and published in the New York Times informing the public of the lies used by the government to justify the Vietnam War. This drove Nixon even further into paranoia. His solution was to rat-fuck[17] the Democrats. He ordered the "plumbers," the same bunch of clowns who got caught burglarizing the Democrat headquarters in the Watergate complex, to break-in to Ellsberg's psychiatrist's office to get Ellsberg's file in an attempt to find a way to discredit him.

When Nixon's Deputy Assistant, Alexander Butterfield, revealed in the Watergate Hearings that there were recordings of the goings on in the oval office, the shit hit the fan for real! Upon examination, the tapes were discovered to have a mysterious eighteen-minute minute gap that forensic testing determined was repeatedly erased, evidently by Nixon's secretary, Rosemary Woods.

I'll give Nixon credit for this: he stopped the combat role of the US in Vietnam in 1973.

Nixon resigned and was pardoned by his successor, Gerald Ford. Good riddance to bad rubbish. Numerous members of Nixon's staff and cabinet served prison terms. It was glorious!

Reagan was the governor of California at that time. We despised him as well and for much the same reasons. When we would be sitting around, bullshitting and smoking dope, and someone would say something stupid. The comeback would be, "Oh yeah, right. That'll happen when Reagan becomes president," something unimaginable to us at that time. I guess you have to watch what you say.

MATRIMONIAL BLI$$

Along about 1973 my buddy, Ron, who worked in a furniture factory with some older Chicanas, said he was getting paid to marry to a Mexican girl so she could obtain legal status in the US. She would divorce him after a couple years after the paperwork was completed. For this he was paid the sum of $500, half after the ceremony and half after all the DNS requirements were satisfied. They went from San Francisco to Reno one day, got married and the plan proceeded.

---

[17] Rat-fucking is using dirty tricks against an electoral opponent, to interfere with the electoral process.

A while later Ron says, "Hey Gene, you interested in one of these marriages? Elena has another girl who needs to get married for residency."

"Yeah? How much?"

"Well…my deal was for $500. This one is $700. Well now, that was a significant sum in 1973 dollars! My day gig was clerking in a hardware store for minimum wage, about $2. 25 an hour at the time.

"Hell yes, I'm interested,"

He set up a meeting with Elena and the girl. Her name was Magarita Delgado and she was a knockout. She had jet black hair, dark brown eyes, a smile that was just so open and honest. Her skin was the nicest shade of light brown. She was petite, a bit shy, and her English had an intoxicating Spanish lilt, but not Mexican Spanish, she was from El Salvador.

We made our agreement. I would marry her in Reno and do the required paperwork for her to become a legal resident married to an American citizen. For this I would receive $700.00, half after the ceremony and half after she was a legal US resident. She would divorce me three years later.

There were six of us: Genoveva, her friend Mrs. Sanchez, Ron Lattin, his girlfriend, Marty, my girlfriend Anne, and myself. We made the sojourn in Ron's old Orowheat Bread delivery van. These old vans were the ubiquitous hippie vehicles. We brought wine and reefer and made a party out of the trip to Reno and back. Well, my friends and I did! I think Genoveva and Mrs. Delegado were wondering WTF they had gotten themselves into.

Ron didn't fill the gas tank and we ran out of gas in the mountains. He hitchhiked and got enough to get us to a station.

Margarita and I were married that Sunday afternoon at the courthouse in Reno. The official knew the score.

"Well, I have to tell you," he said, with a grin, "I have seen many marriages where the couple cold barely understand each others' language. Last week I had a ceremony for a fellow who didn't speak a word of Spanish and his bride who couldn't speak a word of English!"

He performed the ceremony twice, once in Spanish and once in English. When we got back to the van, Margarita pulled an envelope out of her purse and said, with her delightful Spanish lilt, "And now, my loving husband, I will pay you.

At that time Nixon was strengthening murderous Central American right-wing governments by supplying them with arms and trained their death squads at the School of the Americas at Fort Benning, GA. This was during the cold war and tensions between the US and the USSR were high. Cuba was exporting revolution by sending troops into Africa and promoting communist insurgency in the Western hemisphere. Countries like Guatemala and El Salvador became the pawns in proxy wars between the US and the USSR. There were years of horrible slaughter of indigenous peoples and political opponents by the government death squads in the name of anti-communism. These death squads served Any excess was justifiable as long as it was part of an anti-communist effort.

Without realizing it at the time, I had struck a blow against fascism. El Salvador was descending into terrible political violence. She and her son were spared living in the midst of this horror show.

zWe did get to know each other a bit after we were married, she and her son used to visit my girlfriend and I. Had I known what she went through to pull this off, I would have done it for nothing, but an agreement is an agreement. And the money was already gone! I am so pleased that my action – basically a youthful impulse – had the effect of sparing these two people living in the midst of the political violence that was El

My girlfriend, Anne, myself, and my bride-to-be somewhere on I-80 north of Sacremento. We are waiting for Ron to get back. He hitchhiked to get some gas after running out on the way to Reno for our wedding. We had ample "refreshments" for both legs of the trip.

Salvador in those days.

Now, nearly 50 years later, I see this action as my raised middle finger to Ronald Reagan, governor at the time, Richard Nixon, and now the Orange Idiot. It was not an act of protest. It was not an act of bravery. It was an agreement between my wife and I that would result in gains for each of us. And I look back all these years later and I am glad I did it. Per our agreement, she divorced me several years later and we lost contact.

For those wishing to report me to ICE, the statutes of limitations expired thirty-six years ago. I already checked.

I never thought of it until now, but, I wonder that those two ladies thought of the *pendejos*[18] they were hooked up with: a bunch of pot-smoking, wine tippling hippies partying before noon. We ran out of gas in the middle of I-80 in the mountain.. Ron hitchhiked to get some gas and we goofed until he got back. That was no big deal to us, but I think it might have scared our passengers. They never said anything, though. We made the trip with no further problems

---

[18] Sp., assholes

CHAPTER 24

TRANSCENDENTAL MEDICATION

"To make this trivial world sublime, take half a gramme of phanerothyme."

–Aldous Huxley to Dr. Humphrey Osmond

"To fathom hell or soar angelic, take a pinch of psychedelic."

-Dr. Humphrey Osmond to Aldous Huxley

— *"I see the true importance of LSD in the possibility of providing material aid to meditation aimed at the mystical experience of a deeper, comprehensive reality. Such a use accords entirely with the essence and working character of LSD as a sacred drug"*

—Albert Hofman, creator of LSD

Author's note: Do not misinterpret me. I am not encouraging the use of any of these substances. What I am relating here are things that occurred some fifty years ago, and are germane to the social, political and spiritual mores and upheavals of those times. I most certainly would not and do not encourage anyone to do similar things now.

WHY DRUGS?

I saw a TV Program on "hippies" some years ago where a clueless individual too young to have any direct contact with hippies criticized them for taking bits and pieces of various spiritual traditions instead of adopting one and sticking with its canon and orthodoxy. He was right about bits and pieces. Hippie spirituality was patchwork quilt of astrology, the I Ching, meditation, Native American traditions, Edgar Cayce books, Buddhism, Hinduism and the like. There was a universal belief in karma and reincarnation. And of course, the use of consciousness expanding substances: drugs. What the clueless individual in the TV program did not understand is that spirituality is a path that is different for everyone who follows it. This is where the hippies were coming from.

The counterculture revolved around drugs. Was this because an entire generation just wanted to get high? Or was there some loftier goal? Certainly a lot of people just wanted to get high. I did. Having gotten high, some looked for more than just intoxicated bliss in these states of altered consciousness. I was one of them. What I present here is anecdotal, based on my own experiences and therefore entirely subjective.

The use of mind-expanding – psychedelic – drugs in the counterculture led many on a spiritual quest. Why would this happen in our primarily Judeo-Christian culture with its long religious history and well established churches? Because the churches were not delivering the goods. Now, from Chapter 3 it is obvious I have issues with organized religion particularly the Catholic Church. This goes beyond my experiences and feelings to the core issue of what Christianity is supposed to be vs. what Christianity has become.

Christianity, which should have been a spiritual boon to mankind, has been debased into a toxic mythology of childish tales and medieval superstitions designed to keep an ignorant populace fearful of eternal punishment from a loving(?) God, thereby needful of a mythical "salvation" only available through the church.

The takeaway from Western Christianity is that God is an intolerant vindictive prick who will roast your sorry ass in the flames of hell for all eternity for damned near anything at all, or maybe for doing nothing at all! I attribute this to a basic misunderstanding of Genesis where it says God made mankind in His image. Now, with God being God, and thus having infinite knowledge of everything, and mankind having stunted understanding of *anything*, this has been turned around to "Since I am made in the image of God, and I hate [fill in the ethnicity, religious association, or whatever], then God must hate them too!"

And there is the history of Western Christianity: a mega overload of self-righteousness combined with ignorance, greed, and lust for power.

God is a sadist who created mankind to be an imperfect species and then punishes mankind with eternal damnation for resultant imperfect behavior. This being God's Divine Will, was enforced by His church enforcement being carried out through the force of arms and a willingness to slaughter entire populations over what George Orwell would call "thoughtcrime" (in Jesus' name amen).

In the toxic mythology of Western Christianity, all are born condemned, and must accept Jesus to be *not*-condemned. Original Sin is the default setting upon emergence from the mother's womb. Those who have the misfortune to live in the ages before Jesus are excluded from Heaven, only able to achieve Limbo as an eternal resting place, denied the benefits of heaven for having been born at the wrong time, something over which they had no control whatsoever. So God discriminates, bigoted toward all who do not meet arbitrary standards with which it is impossible to comply. I do not see that as a divine trait so much as I see it as all too human.

Does God create imperfect sentient beings, beings that can experience joy, sorrow, pleasure, love and pain, just so he can punish them for the imperfections that are an intrinsic part of their nature, flaws he created in them? That's just gratuitous cruelty. Asshole behavior. Again, not a divine trait, but an all too human one.

It brings to mind a boy incinerating ants with a magnifying glass, watching each defenseless creature curl up in agony and emit a puff of smoke. Why? Because he can. Asshole behavior. This is excusable in a small boy but highly questionable for anybody's idea of a supreme being.

Is God an asshole? Does God in fact even *have* moral principles? I suppose it depends in whose image – and for whose convenience – God has been created.[1] No, I do not think God is an asshole although many of his self styled representatives are.

To use the oil driller term, Western Christianity is a "dry hole" containing nothing of substance. Nada. Zilch. Zero. Nothing but empty words and pious platitudes accompanied by incense, church bells, the collection plate with absolute belief in and obedience to nonsensical dogma enforced by the threat of eternal torment.

The counterculture disaffection for Christianity is because of the Jesus mythology, a finely spun web of institutionalized ignorance spun by

---

[1] The Old Curmudgeon's Sage Advice No. 6 & 7.

theologians for two millennia. Jesus was not any "divine" being. He was a learned man who traveled extensively in Egypt, India, Kashmir and into Tibet.[2] He was a teacher. His teachings have by and largely been forgotten/ignored, replaced by institutions claiming to have some secret mainline to Almighty God available only to members, and who have committed genocide, murderimg in his name.

The ethical teachings of Christ are basically the same as the ethical teachings of all religions, which I like to paraphrase as "Love each other. Try not to be an asshole. OK?"

It was the failure of Christianity to live up to its own professed ethical teachings that spurred counterculture to abandon it as a source for anything spiritual. We found no use for the centuries of petrified ignorance and dogmatic bullshit over which Christianity has tortured, killed, burned at the stake, committed genocidal slaughter and enslaved populations not meeting its fictitious theological standards.

The counterculture sought *spiritual truth,* not *religious belief.* Religion demands one subscribe to a rigid belief system and submit to an institutionally sanctioned intermediary between the individual and God. Religion is what it is and does not change, it is the same now as hundreds or thousands of years ago.

Spirituality is growth oriented. One is free to explore and, using empirical observations, make conclusion as to what comprises the nature of being. What a seeker believes this evening may differ from what they believed when they awoke this morning because of something learned during the day.

Spirituality, like water, seeks its own level. I care not what anyone else believes, so long as they are not murdering others over it and leave me the hell alone.

Religion requires you consult the rules. Spirituality requires you figure shit out. There is nothing like being faced with a moral choice, that is, a choice involving life and death, particularly being faced with the prospect of having to cause the deaths of others, to encourage you figure shit out. I figured some shit out when I was faced with the choice about whether or not I was going to allow the US government send me halfway across the world to Vietnam to kill people who posed no threat to the US or to me, people who had given no offense, other than a desire for self rule.

Politically, it was a bullshit proxy war between the US and the USSR that conveniently generated mountains of wealth for the US Military-Industrial Complex. It was also encouraged and supported by the Catho-

---

[2] These journeys are described in The unknown life of Jesus Christ, N. Notovich; The Aquarian Gospel of Jesus the Christ, Levi H. Dowling

lic Church because the oppressive authoritarian government in South Vietnam, a Catholic minority oppressing a Buddhist majority, was devised during the French colonization. To the church, it was a "just war;" and one's Christian duty was to kill the atheistic communists in the name of Jesus.

Spiritually, it was "Who, if anyone, should you kill, and why should you kill them?"

I was forced to search within myself and find my own moral compass. It gave me, a single person who disagreed with the status quo regarding the taking of human life, the courage to successfully stand against the Selective Service System and the whole fucking government because I was determined to not participate in their bordering on genocidal slaughter of Asians. It was not Christianity or any belief in a supreme being that brought me to do that, it was my reliance on what I searched for and found within myself. It might be said that God put it there to begin with. I won't argue with that. But I found it entirely without the help of any religion or church.

ENTHEOGENS

Into this spiritual vacuum enters entheogens. The term "entheogen," coined by ethnobotanists in 1979, denotes a class of psychoactive substances that bring about spiritual experiences. Entheogenic substances – mushrooms, cacti, roots, and the like – have played a part in humankind's spiritual search since the first time a cave man ingested some funny mushrooms and got blasted into another dimension.

Being an old acid head, I noticed in the tenth chapter of the Book of Revelation there is a passage that seems to indicate that John may have been tripping his tits off on Patmos.

{10:8} And the voice which I heard from heaven spake unto me again, and said, Go [and] take the little book which is open in the hand of the angel which standeth upon the sea and upon the earth. {10:9} And I went unto the angel, and said unto him, Give me the little book. And he said unto me, Take [it,] and eat it up; and it shall make thy belly bitter, but it shall be in thy mouth sweet as honey. {10:10} And I took the little book out of the angel's hand, and ate it up; and it was in my mouth sweet as honey: and as soon as I had eaten it, my belly was bitter. {10:11} And he said unto me, Thou must prophesy again before many peoples, and nations, and tongues, and kings

Eating the book brings to mind blotter acid, liquid LSD droppered onto blotter paper. The "bitter in the belly" is a reference to puking one's guts out in order to loosen up the solar plexus chakra for energy to flow freely up the spine. This often occurs when mescaline (peyote cactus buttons) are ingested.

Prophesying? When you are that stoned, why not? It doesn't necessarily mean anything, just like if you are tripping with your old lady and she gets all fangy and furry like a werewolf wants to kiss you.

Given by an "angel?" If I was sitting in a cave on Patmos and someone laid some shit on me like that, hell yes, I'd think they were an angel!

The Greek *pharmakeia* from which we get the word "pharmacy" and "pharmaceutical" was translated as "witchcraft" and "sorcery." They had no concept of recreational drug use. Maybe they didn't have a word for "dealer" either!

Religious orthodoxy denies downplays any role entheogens have regarding religion. Of course, religion is not spirituality, and entheogens *do* have a lot to do with spirituality. Religion's opposition to drugs is a way to keep ordinary people from gaining spiritual insights that may enlighten people and help them slip the grip of nonsensical mythologies and childish religious dogma have on them. Religions are hierarchical and those that run them have no clue as to the nature of being and have no use for those who do. They certainly do not want ordinary people gaining their own insights as to the true nature of the universe. It's their "non-competition" clause! Christianity is "revealed religion." But it is not revealed to everyone, just to certain people. By a wild coincidence, these are the same ones who benefit from those revelations! How about that?

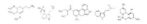

My own personal involvement with drugs in the late '60s and '70s was with mind drugs, substances which affected consciousness, entheogens. I wasn't then, nor have I ever been, into doing what I considered body drugs[3] such as pharmaceuticals, heroin, and the like, although I have retained a lifelong affection for brewed beverages.

There is a difference between getting stoned and getting twisted. While substances such as marijuana and LSD will affect your consciousness, they do not (necessarily) diminish your ability to function effectively in the world on a day to day basis as substances like speed, heroin, cocaine and pharmaceuticals most certainly do. The differentiation I was

---

[3] As I age I do find it necessary to use painkillers from time to time. This is not recreational and I do appreciate the relief I obtain.

making at the time was that I was into substances which enhanced the ability to expand one's awareness, one's consciousness, not substances which tended to diminish ones consciousness.

The 1960s drug subculture was full of rituals related to drug use. It was a closed system. The conspiratorial nature of it all made it appealing to alienated youth. We, the "hip", had our own thing. Dope, i.e., marijuana, was against the law and did not involve "straights." It was an exclusive subculture of youthful lawbreakers bucking the establishment. We did not subscribe to society's values, nor did we subscribe to society's consciousness. We broke the law on a daily basis. We had our own language, codes of behavior, and our own music.

It was a conspiracy, albeit, an open one. In most instances someone could look at you and tell of you were a "head." There were just too damned many of us to put into jail. The cops understood little of head culture, and the politicians and other authorities took turns being scandalized, shocked, and terrified by it.

Many of us of us were long-haired social misfits, refugees from the mainstream American culture, the plastic culture, the culture of death that was sacrificing its children to the seemingly endless war in Vietnam. America, in our view, had lost its spiritual values when it started launching B-52 strikes in Vietnam and Laos that killed thousands of civilians and was no longer "one nation under God." God, as we saw it, had the least to do with it. God was replaced y the Almighty Dollar so America was "one nation under the Almighty Dollar."

The Vietnam generation correctly observed that Christian denominations long ago forsook spirituality for temporal wealth and power. Substituting the hypocrisy of dogma and priestcraft for true Christian spiritual principles, churches supported the war. There were exceptions like the Quakers who really did heed the words of Christ and recognized the moral imperative of the sanctity of life, but most churches went along with the war. The government afforded the churches a climate in which they could swell their membership and their coffers by reinforcing the prevailing cultural and political values. It was consistent, then, that the churches should support the war. The various Christian churches and sects were (are) for the most part heirs to the moneychangers that Christ drove from the Temple in Jerusalem in his fit of rage. Many were heavily invested in defense related industries. I term this type of religion "Churchianity."

Many of us viewed America as a corporate oligarchy.[4] The deities of the American corporatocracy demanded a blood offering to keep the wealth flowing. Executive boards met in their corporate boardroom/temples, reaping windfall profits by supplying materiel for the heinous slaughter in Vietnam. They manufactured the body bags and sold them to the government. Americans' lied to by their own government, willingly sent their sons to fill them. The blood of the young ran to slake the thirst of the gods of commerce, dying dutifully, willingly, bravely, and by the tens of thousands. And this doesn't even begin to account for the millions of civilians slaughtered in a genocidal manner by U.S. munitions. Not for liberty. Not for freedom. Not for principles of American democracy. All for money. All for profit. All for a system of corrupt values.

John Kennedy was assassinated in 1963,followed by the 1964 KKK murders of the civil rights workers in Mississippi, the assassinations of Edgar Evers, Martin Luther King, Jr., Robert Kennedy, and others who dared oppose the monolithic establishment.

Colleges and universities were rocked by protests. American cities were torn apart by racial strife. The government had its paranoia revved to the max and the FBI was working overtime keeping track of students, protesters, radicals, black militants and anyone else whose politics might be construed to be, in J. Edgar Hoover's raging paranoid view, "commanist[5] inspired."

If this insane society was the result of *not* taking drugs, what harm could there be in *taking* drugs? If being straight was the consciousness that led to Vietnam, racism, repression and war profiteering, then to get high was to liberate ourselves from the straight jacket of American material consciousness, to venture into the revolutionary consciousness of spirituality and reject the culture of violence and materialism. Ingesting various substances allowed development of different and radical points of view.

"[In] my era everybody smoked and everybody drank and there was no drug use" — DEA Chief Thomas Constantine, July 1, 1998

---

[4] This concept is now mainstream in American society. At the time is was considered blasphemous, an idea inspired by communists and America haters.
[5] Hoover's pronunciation of the word "communist."

In high school, drug education consisted of the school nurse (who smoked like a chimney) telling us we should not "smoke, snort or inject anything if you don't know what it is." The extended logic of that statement – and I am certain this was not intended – is that if you know what you were smoking, snort or injecting, it was all right. This was in 1963 small town America. There were no drugs to speak of, other than culturally approved alcohol and tobacco. What were the chances we would encounter drugs anyway? We had no idea what was coming our way.

If being "straight" made America in to the culture of death, then being stoned had to be better. So we got stoned.

There were casualties. When young people tried pot and liked it, it became immediately obvious they had been lied to about marijuana. It was not the "killer weed" of the old *"Reefer Madness"* movies from the 1930's. Unfortunately, the logic that we had been deceived about marijuana was extended to other substances which were, in fact, harmful, such as methedrine, heroin and pharmaceuticals. To many, a drug was a drug and one was as good as another. While some in the counterculture saw drugs as a means to an end, others saw them as the end in and of themselves. Some people ingested substances to achieve a particular state of consciousness. Others just got high, and it didn't matter how.

Among drug users there were social stratifications along the lines of drugs being used. Potheads hung out with potheads, and acidheads hung out with acidheads, speedfreaks with speedfreaks, junkies with junkies.

REEFER MADNESS

"I advise any bashful young man to take hashish when he wants to offer his heart to any fair lady, for it will give him the courage of a hero, the eloquence of a poet, and the ardour of an Italian"
– Dr Meredith in Louisa May Alcott's Perilous Play

Marijuana use became for all intent and purposes, universal among young people, at least among those who tended to be even the least bit rebellious. It was the least you could do and be considered hip. Pot smoking tended to be communal and ritualistic to the point of ceremony. The tools and accouterments of pot smoking achieved the status among users that the liturgical items did in churches. The marijuana ritual involved taking out the stash and cigarette papers, rolling the joint and sharing it among a circle of people. In the days before the advent of "double wide" papers, two Zig-Zag papers were glued together, and an even burning joint rolled. The preferred size was 1/4" -3/8" in diameter.

Any larger and the joint would not burn evenly and tended to run down one side with much of the marijuana remaining unburned. Dabbing a bit of saliva on with a finger sometimes checked the uneven burning on a joint rolled by a neophyte who thought that "bigger is better."

In the days before bhongs,[6] shotgun techniques were also used to great effect. A shotgun was constructed using the tube from toilet paper or a roll of paper towels. The simplest shotgun was a hole made toward the end of a tube into which a joint was inserted. The smoker would cover one end of the tube with the palm of their hand while putting the other end to their mouth. The joint was lit and the chamber formed by the tube filled with smoke. The smoker could then let a little air mix in with the pot smoke, getting a "carburetor" effect, or remove their palm from the open end and inhale the smoke all at once, giving a great "rush" effect. Sometimes the shotgun had a bowl fashioned from tinfoil scotch-taped over a hole on the tube.

Another shotgun method was to place the joint with the lit end inside in your mouth and blow the smoke into another's mouth. Lovers would do a shotgun hit by one taking a large hit and then exhaling it directly into the other's mouth, ending up with a highly arousing kiss.

If a pipe was used, the ritual included checking and cleaning the screen. The contents of the bowl had to be stirred occasionally to assure complete burning. Whatever method was used, the joint or pipe was always offered to one of the other participants in the ceremony and lit by the preparer. It was considered gauche to prepare the grass for smoking and then light it yourself, that was mark of a newcomer to the drug culture, or just a plain selfish person.

There were techniques for sharing the "roach." The mythology of the times said the roach was the best part of the joint, as it contained concentrated resins from the rest of the joint. There was a way of passing the roach from hand-to-hand that consisted of holding the roach between the thumb and forefinger, and rolling the roach off the thumb with the forefinger onto the thumb of the next person, who would then grasp it with their forefinger. Clips of various designs were also used to hold the roach until it could be smoked down to practically nothing. The head shops were full of such fancy beaded and feathered clips fashioned by heads in various decorative patterns. Hemostats liberated from doctors offices or clinics were popular. They were also stocked by head shops. In the absence of a pair of "stats" or a roach clip, the cover would be torn from a book of matches and rolled into a tube, the roach inserted in the end and passed among the participants.

---

[6] This is the proper spelling

Another method that was quite popular when I was in Boston was to sandwich the roach between the heads of two paper matches. It was held in the center of the circle of pot smokers. One person would ignite the match heads and, when the sulfur was done burning, blow out the flame. The smoking roach was quickly passed under the noses of the participants while they would inhale the smoke deeply. If it didn't give you a rush, it certainly cleared your sinuses!

Some heads would save roaches in a special roach stash and roll a joint from their contents when there were enough. This would yield a "superjoint."

In the late 60s, marijuana was smuggled in from Mexico in tightly pressed bricks each weighing one kilogram (2.2 pounds) commonly referred to as "keys." In the days before the advent of the murderous Mexican drug cartels, hippie drug lore had it that the grass was grown by peasants and made into bricks using the same molds they used for making adobe bricks with pressure applied by hydraulic automotive jacks, a true "peoples enterprise." Why, by engaging in the marijuana trade, you were helping the poor peasants, liberating the proletariat. Hell, that really made it revolutionary! This of course was pure absolute bullshit, but it is an example of the mythology of the pothead culture.

The resulting bricks were very dense and could be sawed into chunks. A common practice was for the dealer to saw a brick into halves sawing off a slice from each for personal stash and sell the bricks as pounds. Most of the bricks I saw were packaged in what seemed to be heavy bright red or green construction paper. Bricks of Acapulco Gold came in ochre colored paper. Later in the 70s when drug detection techniques became more sophisticated, plastic wrap was used to better conceal the odor.

The more experienced a pothead had in smoking varieties of marijuana originating from different locales, the more the point of origin could be determined by taste. The most common weed was called Michouacan, after the Mexican state of the same name. It was average reefer, greenish brown in color and had a lot of seeds. The legendary Acapulco Gold was from the region around Acapulco and was, as the name says, a very light golden blonde color. The kilo bricks of gold were loosely packed because they were all flowering tops, with few stems to bind them together in contrast with the inferior varieties. Or so people said.[7]

The closer to the equator that grass was grown, the less distance the sunlight traveled through the atmosphere and the less the ultraviolet rays

---

[7] This was before the advent of potent "sensimilla," grass without seeds, was on the market.

were filtered out. This made for the production of more tetrahydrocannabinol (THC) in the plant, making it more potent weed and causing it to have various colors when dried. The grass from Zacatecas had a purple cast to it. Panama Red and Columbian Red were just that, a ruddy brown weed with a distinctive, and very pleasing, earthy aftertaste.

Hashish, made from the Cannabis Indica strains grown high in the mountains near the equator, was a popular commodity and quite plentiful because Boston was a seaport city. Most of the marijuana came from Mexico and was smuggled in cars, trucks and planes over the border. Hashish came from Nepal, Afghanistan and Lebanon and was generally brought into the country by merchant seamen.[8] It was generally purchased in ounce, half ounce and quarter ounce quantities and sold in the street by the gram in chunks wrapped in tinfoil. Small brass pipes imported from Asia and bought in headshops and Chinatown were used to incinerate tiny slivers of the potent cannabinoid.

Lebanese Blonde was made from Indica that was not grown at as high an altitude as in Afghanistan and Nepal and was the least potent of these varieties, but still significantly more potent than marijuana. It came in hard chunks that had to be chipped into pieces with a sharp knife. Kief, a light yellowish brown powder, also came from Lebanon. Made from Indica trichrome crystals that form on the buds, it is about the color as Lebanese Blonde. It is quite potent and priced accordingly.

The Nepalese and Afghani varieties of hashish were dark brown to black in color, soft and very moist. Nepalese Temple Balls from Nepal were round and often imprinted with gold foil characters. The Afghani hashish came in flat patties and sometimes also had similar gold imprinting. Opium was sometimes mixed in with these varieties, giving a high that would transport one to a state of intoxication that bordered on pure bliss.

Are cannabinoid. drugs dangerous?[9] I personally doubt it. To my knowledge there has never been a death attributed to smoking marijuana.[10] The only way it could kill you is if a bale falls on you and crushes you! In truth, I have never heard of this actually happening either. .

---

[8] I had a musician friend in San Francisco who, in the mid 70s, was instrumental in smuggling significant quantities of Hashish in to the U.S. from Europe inside stereo speakers.
[9] With the legalization of marijuana taking place both in states in the USA and in foreign countries, the anti-marijuana faction cautions against the increased potency of sensimilla strains saying the THC levels are dangerous. The fact I that smoking stronger varieties of cannabis will make one pass out sooner from it. However, people can ingest quantities of cannabis edibles that can lead to them going to the emergency room with psychotic symptoms. Edible cannabis products come on slower and people will eat more thinking they are not getting off. While cannabis is not fatal, one has to exercise caution with edibles. Ditto vaping cannabis oil. That shit is 84% THC and WILL put you on the floor!
[10] Now Google "alcohol related deaths."

One of the more dire warnings concerning marijuana is that it causes men's breasts to grow. If that were true, there would be millions of old men with big tits running around today, and I haven't seen any (not that I have been looking for them!).

The most dangerous thing about marijuana is that it is illegal. You can still get into serious trouble with the law for having it. This is a waste of time, money and the American judicial process. It's a hell of a lot less destructive than alcohol and should be legalized. [11]

Almost everyone who smoked grass dealt from time to time. It was a matter of economics. If you wanted a good steady supply of smoke, you bought a brick and sold ounces to friends and acquaintances. This way you had your own private smoking stash for nothing. Well, almost nothing. It was a crime and you were in deep shit if busted!

LSD

The counterculture was really about LSD, the scientific name being *δ-lysergic acid diethylamide-25*. LSD was the common experience among people that gave rise to the head culture. It literally "blew your mind." Marijuana did not. In terms of psychedelics, marijuana was a groove, for sure, but it is tame. LSD is not. It knocks you smack into another dimension of consciousness.

The Central Intelligence Agency was responsible for letting LSD loose in the United States. [12]

"The CIA literally sent over two guys to Sandoz Laboratories where LSD had first been synthesized and bought up the world's supply of LSD and brought it back ...With that supply they began a [secret mind-control] program called MK ULTRA which had all sorts of other drugs involved." [13]

In the never ending quest for weapons to use against the communist aggressors, they tried everything. Much of this was done under the umbrella of the MK-ULTRA program. They were the original source for the

---

[11] Like alcohol and cigarettes. Wake up corporate America!

[12] (1) Szalavitz, M.' & Szalavitz, M. (2018). *The Legacy of the CIA's Secret LSD Experiments on America* | *TIME. com. TIME. com*. Retrieved 5 March 2018, from http://healthland. time. com/2012/03/23/the-legacy-of-the-cias-secret-lsd-experiments-on-america/(2) Liebman, L. (2017). *L. S. D.' Lies, and the C. I. A. : The Incredible True Story Behind Wormwood*. HWD. Retrieved 5 March 2018, from https://www. vanityfair. com/hollywood/2017/12/errol-morris-wormwood-netflix-interview(3) *That Time the CIA Secretly Dosed Americans with LSD*. (2016). OZY. Retrieved 5 March 2018, from http://www. ozy. com/flashback/that-time-the-cia-secretly-dosed-americans-with-lsd/68782

[13] Gillespie, N. (2017). *How the CIA Turned Us onto LSD and Heroin: Secrets of America's War on Drugs. Reason. com*. Retrieved 7 March 2018, from https://reason. com/blog/2017/06/23/anthony-lappe-lsd-heroin

LSD in the United States. Drs. Timothy Leary and Richard Alpert experimented with it at Harvard. The writer Ken Kesey had willingly participated in an experimental government LSD program in California. He liked it and went on to found the Merry Pranksters who went around the country giving people LSD at psychedelic events call acid tests.

I used to read my father's Mechanix Illustrated magazines, which were largely devoted to home construction & improvement projects, along with a automotive and science and technology articles. I remember very well a curious article I read when I was probably about eight or nine. It was about a man who had ingested peculiar substance that did some very strange things to him. One passage from that article has stuck with me for over sixty years:

"...nothing was as it normally seemed. Was that actually a window in the wall I was looking at...or was it just pretending to be a window...until I turned my back?"

When I read that article, I thought what a peculiar – if not terrifying – experience that must be. After I started taking LSD myself in 1968, I remembered the article and recognized that it was about Dr. Albert Hofman, the Swiss chemist who first synthesized LSD, describing what happened to him on his first trip. LSD was legal, that is, there were no laws prohibiting it, until 1966. It had been adopted by college students and the emerging hippie culture. One of the effects of LSD was a feeling of being one with all of creation, which fostered a peace-and-love-brotherhood-of-man attitude in many users.

Acid heads dispensed LSD tablets to each other like a sacrament, the distributor taking on the role of the priest giving the Holy Eucharist to the faithful by placing tablets of the powerful hallucinogen on the tongues of the faithful.

LSD was available in varying quality and types. Each week seemed to bring another "brand" onto the street. These were identified by such names as blue flat (flat tablets), orange domes (rounded on one side), purple double domes (rounded on both sides), white lightning (clear white capsules filled with white powder), swirl acid of various colors (red, green or blue flecks in a white tablet), peace symbol acid (red white and blue tablets each with a peace symbol embossed on them[14]), white Owsley[15](large white tablets with an "O" embossed in them), Sandoz clinical (small capsules with a light yellow powder in them), orange sun-

---

[14] I remember reading an article about street acid in the Boston Globe where the writer described the consternation of police about this."Why would anyone put a peace symbol on an LSD pill?" they asked. This had acid heads rolling on the floor laughing!
[15] Augustus Owsley Stanley was a legendary West Coast acid chemist and sound technician for the Grateful Dead.

shine (large orange tablets that dissolved almost immediately upon being put on your tongue, supposedly cooked by the Brotherhood of Eternal Love and commissioned by Timothy Leary for his 1969 California gubernatorial campaign), purple wedges, orange dots, purple microdots, blotter acid, vitamin C acid (vitamin C tablets with a drop of a green liquid on them). The descriptions and colors seemed numberless.

The rap on the acid, that is, the sales pitch the dealer would use to sell it were things like

"colorful acid, lots of good colors...,"

"a clear light trip, man, you'll hit the clear light...,"

"this stuff is telepathic, man...,"

"500 micrograms, man, put you in orbit...."

The descriptions of the psychedelic qualities of street acid were as colorful and varied as the types of acid available on the street.

There was, of course, a large amount of naiveté involved here. Some acid was tainted with strychnine to give it a heightened hallucinatory effect, or adulterated with amphetamines to give it an added kick.

Other psychedelics were available too, supposedly. Street dealers would hawk their wares to passersby in stage whispers.

"Hey, man, try this mescaline, it's dynamite!"

"Psilocybin, pure psilocybin, man, you'll dig it!"

Mescaline? I doubt there was ever *any* synthesized mescaline on the streets. The chemical synthesis of mescaline available at the time was moderately complex and didn't yield enough product to make it commercially viable. It may have been available as an exotic psychedelic treat for rich hippies (or rich longhairs who fancied themselves hippies!). If you bought capsules with white powder in them thinking it was mescaline, it was most likely LSD. Large clear capsules with a dried brown ground-up vegetable substance may have been shredded and encapsulated peyote buttons. The only sure way to know you are getting natural mescaline is from peyote buttons.

Magic Mushrooms, the source of psilocybin, were rarely available. Most of the "magic mushrooms" were supermarket mushrooms spiked with LSD. The only way you could get real psychedelic mushrooms was to grow them yourself or get them from the person who did grow them. A guy who lived down the street from me in San Francisco who had a small closet stacked floor to ceiling with boxes of mason jars in which he had mushrooms growing. And they were good!

STP was a powerful hallucinogen incorrectly rumored to have been developed by the CIA to use as a means to confuse enemy forces on the battlefield, or with which to dose an unsuspecting head of state. This substance would trip you out for several days. The story was that the government was taken aback when they found that heads were ingesting a chemical weapon for recreational purposes. [16]

Psychedelic drugs were always a pleasant experience for me. Occasional use led to casual use which led to frequent use, not out of any necessity as would be dictated by physical addiction, but because it was a stoned groove. And once a frequent user, this led to dealing.

Casual dealing in psychedelics was participated in by most people who took these substances.

LSD and the heavy psychedelics were frequently dealt by casual users, but this, in many cases involving sales of single hits, was more motivated by and evangelical fervor about psychedelics and the point of view they fostered than by financial profit. Drugs dominated the counterculture and were the general topic of conversation whenever longhairs would gather.

TRIPPING

What happens when taking LSD? That is a question that is extremely difficult to put into objective terms, as an LSD trip is a completely subjective experience. Certain generalities can be made about LSD tripping. The average trip lasts approximately eight hours.

Within fifteen minutes to a half hour of ingestion the flow of psychic energy up the spine increases because the chakras, energy centers, are opening up. There are sensations like bubbles going up the spine cord and popping inside the cranium. This is quite a pleasant experience.

---

[16] 2,5-Dimethoxy-4-methylamphetamine (DOM; known on the street as STP, standing for "Serenity, Tranquility and Peace") is a psychedelic and a substituted amphetamine. It was first synthesized and tested in 1963 by Alexander Shulgin, and later reported in his book *PHIKAL: A Chemical Love Story - Phenethylamines I Have Known and Loved*. DOM is classified as a Schedule I substance in the United States, and is similarly controlled in other parts of the world. Internationally, it is a Schedule 1 drug under the Convention on Psychotropic Substances. It is generally taken orally. DOM was first synthesized and tested in 1963 by Alexander Shulgin, who was investigating the effect of 4-position substitutions on psychedelic amphetamines. In mid-1967, tablets containing 20 mg (later 10 mg) of DOM were widely distributed in the Haight-Ashbury District of San Francisco under the name of STP. This short-lived appearance of DOM on the black market proved disastrous for several reasons. First, the tablets contained an excessively high dose of the chemical. This, combined with DOM's slow onset of action (which encouraged some users, familiar with drugs that have quicker onsets, such as LSD, to re-dose) and its remarkably long duration, caused many users to panic and sent some to the emergency room. Second, treatment of such overdoses was complicated by the fact that no one at the time knew that the tablets called STP were, in fact, DOM. Wikipedia.

The energy aspect of the psychedelic experience is quite important. Eastern traditions teach that psychic energy flows up the spine and passes through seven power centers called "chakras." The word "chakra" means "wheel." To one who can see such phenomena, the flowing psychic energy gives these centers the appearance of revolving wheels. These centers are located at the base of the spine, the genitals, the solar plexus, the heart, the throat, the pineal gland ("third eye") and the crown of the head ("flowering of the lotus" or the "aperture of Brahma"). Energy flow can be restricted if chakras are blocked. This has an effect on the overall health, both physiological and psychological.

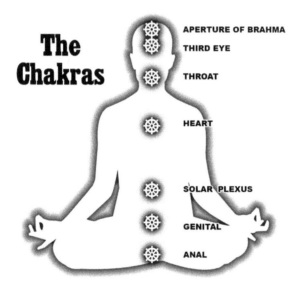

This energy is the feeling in the spine that is felt when coming onto a psychedelic. It is a physical sensation in the spine and, in my experience quite pleasant, as if little switches were being thrown to permit bursts of current to flow in the spine. Sometimes a large burst of energy will come along and makes the spine shiver, shaking off the energy impulse. If it is not shaken off, it shoots up the spine and boosts the psychedelic effect when it hits the brain.

Restrictions in the path of the energy flow can produce physical manifestations. There is no similar concept in our western religion or science. This is no indication that this is not true.

Consider, for example, all of us have experienced a lump in the throat because of some emotional experience. This is the result of a constriction of the energy flow in the throat chakra. There is no physical obstruction, but it can be felt physically.

The heart chakra is opened by love. In the Catholic Church there are many pictures and statues of Jesus showing his heart burning in his chest. There are references to the "Sacred Heart of Jesus on fire with love for me." What is indicated in these artistic representations is his heart chakra opened by love for all. Jesus manifested the Christ consciousness, which is pure love.

In Eastern spiritual traditions, the flow of the energy up from the base of the spine and exiting through the crown of the head is called the "flowering of the lotus." This can be seen in western religious art as the "glory" or halo seen around the heads of Jesus and various saints. Similarly, the visitation of the Holy Spirit on the Apostles in the upper room was accompanied by "tongues of flame" appearing above their heads. This is the raising of energy through all seven chakras, power centers, and exiting through the "Aperture of Brahma." The Holy Spirit does not manifest from without, it comes from within, it is internal.

Freud's classifications of personalities and fixations as anal, genital and oral are references that have directly to do with energy flow being restricted at certain chakras and having definite effects on the personality of the individual.

Now, the buttons of the peyote cactus (*lomphora williamsii,* the natural source of mescaline and the sacrament of certain Southwestern American Indians) are a psychedelic that demand that you be ready for what it is going to do to you. When getting off to peyote, you really should have your solar plexus chakra relaxed and opened. If you don't, the resultant energy released will be constricted at this chakra and you *will* puke your guts out. No big deal, really, because once this is done, the solar plexus chakra opens and the energy flows freely, you experience a psychedelic state.

So while we do not in the our western culture have this concept of energy or the aura, it is still represented in religious art and recognized by psychological effects. It's occurrence in art tells me that there once was a esoteric tradition of this nature in the Christian Church but it has been expurgated in favor of the childish superstitions that presently pass for religion on our spiritually bankrupt culture.

I am going to follow God.

I am never coming back.

I am never coming back.

– Native American peyote song

For the next hour or so consciousness changes radically. One of the first signs of "getting off" to LSD and similar substances is closing your eyes and seeing intricate geometrical patterns. These appear to be of an infinite variety and constantly change like a kaleidoscope. To compare them to something in three dimensional reality, I would say that these patterns are similar to filigree and medieval meander patterns seen in illuminated manuscripts, where vine-like designs are intertwined in an intricate manner. The types of ornate meander type decoration seen in mosques and Islamic art are quite similar, as are the ornate decorations in Gothic cathedrals and the intricately intertwined art of the Celts. The degree of similarity is quite remarkable.

Consciousness continues to change. Time and space are distorted. Conversation is difficult because you are thinking much faster than you can speak. By the time you form the words, your mind is three other ideas ahead. The effect of the psychedelic increases until reaching astute commonly referred to as "peaking." There may be a sense of being outside of one's body, or perhaps having one's consciousness seem to expand to fill an area that goes far beyond one's body. For instance I was tripping in an apartment on 20th Street in San Francisco in 1970 and "felt," that is, had a tactile experience, of someone shutting a car door out on the street.

There may be a feeling of thinking one has died, which frightens some. This is a common occurrence and is called the "ego death." A feeling I associate with this particular stage of an acid trip is not being able to distinguish myself from my environment. It is at this stage where colors, visions, auditory and tactile phenomena may be experienced and where the psychic phenomena can be very pronounced.

After the peak effects of the acid have been experienced, a state of remarkable clarity is reached. At this stage, a person may function fairly normally while in a state of none-ordinary reality. Psychic phenomena can accompany this stage, such as being able to read the inner feelings of other people and experiencing what the Buddhists would call "third eye" phenomena, such as seeing auras.[17] This state will last for several hours and gradually normal consciousness returns.

---

[17] The aura is an electrical field around the body.

Even with the extreme lucidity, the normal, linear, rational process of reasoning doesn't seem relevant in this last stage of psychedelic consciousness. The mind works at an amazing pace, making the causal connections between diverse things. This consciousness results in closures being made in an extraordinary manner. A closure, in this case, means separating an object form the field it occupies, like the classic illustration of two profiles facing each other or a vase, depending on how you make the closure with it. This gave rise to the "psychedelic" art of the mid to late '60s, particularly rock n' roll posters. The stylized lettering seems to flow into the overall design and is sometimes very hard to distinguish from the background. That is because the observer has to make a certain closure with the poster to understand it.

SEEING SOUNDS, HEARING COLORS

A phenomenon called "synesthesia commonly" occurs with psychedelics. Synesthesia is when the stimulation of one sense causes another sense to react to the same stimuli There are many kinds of manifestations of synesthesia. One commonly experienced with psychedelics is experiencing sounds as colors. The Rolling Stones song, "*She Comes in Colors*," is about tripping and a seeing woman have an orgasm.[18]

We talk about "multitasking" these days. I can remember peaking on acid while standing in line to see "Yellow Submarine" in 1968 at the Beacon Hill Theater in Boston, MA. I was able to listen to and follow multiple simultaneous conversations going on around me. It was remarkable to experience being able to divide my attention in this manner.

ACID TELEPATHY

Anita and I did acid together a number of times in the apartment on Stanyan St. Even though the drug culture of the Haight-Ashbury had degenerated into speed and heroin, acid dealers were still common enough in the Haight, and it was easy to score excellent LSD. Stephen's Monday Night Classes were a good place to find good acid.

At that time, there were these little tiny tablets available called "purple microdots." They were potent and melted under your tongue almost instantly. Anita and I tripped together regularly. I never had any problems with acid, but things sometime got fairly weird for Anita. Like

---

[18] I find it highly amusing hearing a song that celebrates sex and drugs on the soundtrack of a TV commercial. Back in the day it was banned from many top 40 stations' playlists. Can't let the teenyboppers hear songs about sex and drugs! The AOR (Album Oriented Rock) stations played it though.

the time she had a vision of a mutual acquaintance of ours all bloody and crucified.

There was one especially memorable trip we took on a pleasant Sunday afternoon in the apartment. It was situated in the rear of the building and was free from street noise, a peaceful environment. Anita had two half grown kittens that provided us with much entertainment. Stubbins was a dark brown tabby with a stumpy tail. Christabel was a sleek feline, shiny black, with a white bikini mark on her tummy.

We dropped purple microdots that afternoon. I was sitting on a chair in the living room, Anita was in a chair to my left on the other side of a cable reel that served as a table. As we were peaking we looked at each other. Her countenance was transfigured in the middle of a psychedelic mélange of colors and undulating shapes. The walls breathed. I became conscious of Anita's breathing, feeling it as if I were her. We realized at that moment that we were completely, totally, and consciously telepathic.

"This is it," she spoke with her mind, "like going off a diving board into the water."

"Let's go together," I thought back to her.

At that moment we both got as stoned as we had ever been in our lives. At that moment we lost any feeling of separateness between us. Our consciousnesses merged. We were tuned in to some cosmic rhythm. It felt like there were waves of energy washing over us, as if we were sitting on the beach and gentle waves were washing up around us. We were completely engulfed by this feeling. When it surged, we merged with the universe, and when it waned, we could actually feel our comingled consciousnesses separate and flow back into the confines of our physical bodies. Out and in, back and forth, yin and yang, to and fro, the tempo of some cosmic rhythm. I do not know how long this went on, time is irrelevant when in this state.

At one point when our consciousnesses were returning to the confines of our bodies, Cristabel was sitting on a table in front of the bay window to my right. She gave a "mrrrp," jumped on that energy wave and ran with it across the room and jumped into Anita's lap. The cat was as stoned as we were, and feeling the same rhythm. I am sure this will sound crazy as hell to someone who has never done psychedelic drugs, but that cat was high right along with us, and telepathic, too, a sentient being.

COMMUNION

There are certain fundamental misconceptions about the substance LSD itself and its role in the psychedelic process. The claims by dealers that "This acid has really good colors," or someone saying "Wow, man, that was some bad acid I took last week," and so on, were really erroneous. If the psychedelics you bought on the street were indeed LSD, the type of trip depended more on environmental factors than anything else. Who you were tripping with and where you were tripping ultimately determined the quality of the trip. So, rather than some "bad acid going around" it is more like there was some bad consciousness going around. Or bad company if you were tripping with assholes! Early LSD researchers quickly discovered the role of environment in acid tripping, referring to it as "set and setting," where you are tripping and with whom you are tripping.

LSD tripping is magical in the purest sense of the word. It is a purely subjective experience that brings you into direct contact with what could be termed astral plane, psychic phenomena, and spirit. One's expectations have a lot to do with the experience. So, if a dealer told someone that his acid "has good colors," that person would likely have that type of experience. The dealer was putting a little of his own magic into his acid. The phenomenon of the quality of a trip being influenced by one's expectations of it is well known to the Southwestern Native Americans Indians who use peyote as a sacrament for their religious ceremonies in the Native American Church for the explicit purpose of seeking a spiritual experience through the expansion of consciousness. .

LSD and other psychedelics have the capability of removing certain barriers that our normal consciousness imposes on us. Aldous Huxley, while experimenting with states of consciousness induced by the ingestion of mescaline, wrote *The Doors of Perception* (from which the 60's musical group The Doors took their name).

In his book, Huxley described the universe at large as being filled with diverse types of information, much of which is not necessary for biological survival. In Huxley's model of the psychedelic process, the mind acts as a reducing valve which permits only the information necessary for biological survival to come through into our consciousness. This information is what is supplied by our senses: taste, touch, smell, hearing and sight, and thought (the Buddhists correctly consider thought to be a sense by which we experience the world).

Certain substances can open up the mind, i.e., the reducing valve, and permit information unnecessary for biological survival to get through to the conscious mind: telepathic and extra-sensory information, information heretofore existing but beyond the perception of our senses. This is, as far as my experiences have shown, quite accurate in terms of describing a mechanism for the psychedelic experience.

Anita and I went to hear a talk by Baba Ram Dass at the Glide memorial Church. Ram Dass was formerly Tim Leary's partner, as Richard Alpert in psychedelic experiments that got them both fired from Harvard. He went to India and studied under a guru in an ashram and a changed his name. He told of giving his guru LSD. "He took the tablet and sat completely motionless for about 6 hours. He then looked at me and said, "God has chosen to come to America in the form of a pill."

THE NATURE OF IT ALL

The psychedelic experience goes farther than this. A more complete explanation requires a digression into Eastern esoteric spiritual principles. These spiritual traditions and teachings form a model through which psychedelic experiences can be integrated.

Certain esoteric aspects of Tibetan Buddhism regarding metaphysical experiences are similar to phenomena experienced on an acid trip. Eastern spiritual traditions claim the world we see is self-manifested illusion.[19] The Buddhists call this illusion, "sangsara," the Hindus call it "maya." This world exists because we collectively agree, on a subconscious (or unconscious or superconscious[20]) level, that it *does* in fact exist. The universe exists by agreement. We create it. We, collectively, are the Creator. We, then, are… God. The road to God is inward. This is central to esoteric spirituality.

Where Western religion concerns itself with a God that is external to man and must be approached by ordinary mortals through special human intermediaries. Esoteric spirituality maintains that within each one of us is a Divine Spark, a part of God. To those who follow the exoteric Western religious tradition, this idea is blasphemy as it equates man with God. Indeed, it does exactly that. Taking the esoteric view of our concealed divinity, it makes perfect sense.

We are told from early on in Sunday school and Catechism classes that "God is omnipresent, He is everywhere; God is omniscient, He knows all things; God is omnipotent, He is all powerful; God created everything in Heaven and on Earth" In the exoteric tradition where God is believed external to man, this is literally held to be true: there is in

---

[19] Physicists are also currently examining this.
[20] The label it is unimportant as long as it is understood that it refers to that which exists in the human mind but is not perceived in a normal, waking conscious state.

Heaven this all powerful being who manifests the world and all that is in it, a big "eye in the sky." Taking the esoteric view, wherein God is internal to man, these concepts of God are still equally and actually true.

"God is omnipresent, God is everywhere" is an actual truth because nothing is or can be external to God. God is part of all that is in creation because nothing can exist without the essence of God *i.e.*, spirit, in it. God is, therefore, internal to all of creation, and therefore mankind.

"God is omniscient, He knows all things" is an actual truth because God, being present in all, would know what is in the minds of all. This is God knowing all things.

"God is omnipotent, He is all powerful..." is an actual truth because everything is manifested by the will of God which is the collective will of sentient beings. The universe exists because of agreement. What we agree and by that agreement manifest all things. This is the all powerful will of God.

"God created everything in Heaven and on Earth..." is an actual truth because the universe is the manifestation of His will channeled through the collective consciousness of all sentient beings.

The main difference between the exoteric approach and the esoteric approach is where one seeks God. The same truths are still accepted, except that the exoteric practitioner requires God to be external to himself and, therefore, he needs an intermediary to go between himself and God. This gives rise to the creation of a priest class and formalized religion. It also, because it does not require consciousness beyond ordinary waking consciousness, allows for corruption. This is seen in Christian denominations and sects by the way they presently concern themselves mainly with power, wealth and control. Many endorse practices and doctrines that have nothing whatsoever to do with the teaching of Jesus. Some of their doctrines are directly in opposition to the teaching of Jesus.

Over the centuries this has resulted in genocidal persecutions, the Inquisition, and soaked the earth in many nations with blood spilled in "religious" wars. Exotericism leads to and "us" and "them" attitude in which "we" are the select, possessing God's truth (or being the "one true church," the "saved," the "elect," the "chosen people," etc.) and because of this being better than "they" who do not posses God's truth and therefore do not receive His favor. Based on this it is all right to persecute, exploit and murder "them," this being permissible because it is done in the name of God.[21]

The esoteric approach, recognizes the innate divinity of all beings and accepts the oneness of all, which is essentially Christ consciousness in its purest and highest form. When Jesus said "None may go to the Father but through me," he was uttering an esoteric truth. Rather than declaring himself a deity, as what has happened in exoteric Christianity where the worship of God has been displaced with the worship of his "divine son," Jesus meant that none may go to the Father but through Christ *consciousness*. Christ consciousness is the realization (in the literal sense of making real) that all people are one and that love among all is not only desirable, but an absolute necessity for spiritual progress and enlightenment. It has become increasingly obvious that it is also necessary for the survival of life in the planet, now that nations possess terrible weapons capable of annihilating all of mankind.

Exoteric religion triumphed in the west after Emperor Constantine made Christianity the state religion. Early esoteric Christian sects, such as the Gnostics, were then systematically murdered by the Church of Rome. The esoteric sects put a great value on personal mystical experience. They did not align themselves with the church of Rome, nor did they ever develop an internal hierarchy to be able to survive the onslaughts of the Church of Rome, well organized in its hierarchical aspects and wielding temporal power with the backing of the state and its armies.

Esoteric traditions, from whatever spiritual tradition they may come, tend toward oneness. Exoteric traditions tend toward divisiveness. The way a single word is divided can show the difference between the exoteric and esoteric approaches to spirituality. Where the exoteric seeker desires *atone*-ment *from* God, the esoteric seeker desires *at-one*-ment *with* God.

Psychedelics enable one to experience this esoteric oneness, albeit for a brief period. I can say it were not for my psychedelic experiences, I could very well be an atheist.

This does not mean that just because one takes a psychedelic substance one will attain this particular point of view. After all I have said about the esoteric path to spirituality and its relationship to psychedelic experiences, why do I now say this? Because consciousness is energy. Attention is consciousness. Wherever you focus your attention is where you are putting your consciousness and is where you are focusing your

---

[21] "Those who can get you to believe absurdities can get you to commit atrocities" – Voltaire

energy.[22] LSD and similar substances expand this consciousness and this energy. Where this energy is focused determines what is manifested. This goes along with the esoteric principle that God is internal to reach one of us, and we manifest the reality of the universe in which we live by agreement. Whatever you pay attention to is going to get "heavy," even if you are not taking a psychedelic.

If you practice playing the guitar, you are putting energy into that so you will manifest yourself as a better guitar player. When you are taking a psychedelic, the "heaviness," the manifestation of this phenomena increases geometrically. If all you want do to is take some LSD and have a honky-tonk circus trip, that's what you will get. If you want a spiritual experience, you will get that. It depends on where you focus your attention.

PSYCHEDELIC DRUGS FAQ

But don't psychedelics cause you to hallucinate, seeing things that aren't there?

Well, yes and no. Psychedelics are classified as hallucinogenic substances. And hallucinations are "things that aren't really there."

Hallucinating on psychedelics, in my experience, is a matter of concentration. Because of the overload on your system due to the increased flow of energy, you may not be able to integrate this increased energy with your senses. When this happens, visual manifestations such as colors, etc., occur. This is also indicative of astral plane phenomena and indicates that the barrier between the conscious and subconscious (which is where astral plane phenomena occur) is open like a gate to another plane of existence.

I found out that, after a while, I could turn the visual phenomena on and off at will. If you make the decision to integrate everything, you achieve a state of consciousness that is astoundingly clear. It is a state unparalleled in your ability to ascertain exactly what is happening around you, not only in terms the physical plane, but on the psychic plane as well. I would have to say that it is, indeed, close to if not identical with Buddha consciousness, enlightenment.

What about bad trips? Don't people have bad trips?

Sure they do. There is a mechanism to tripping. It is only possible to have a bad trip if you are not aware of the mechanics of psychedelic trip-

---

[22] I first heard this from Stephen Gaskin in his Monday Night Classes.

ping. The mechanics of psychedelic tripping are the same as living day to day, only more intense and speeded up because of the increase of energy brought on the by the change in consciousness causing manifestations to happen quicker. The causal relationship between events and their causes are made more evident by the change in consciousness which enables on to recognize this. Stephen Gaskin said "when you are tripping, karma speeds up."

The implication that LSD and similar substances allow one to see beyond what is perceived in an ordinary state of reality is this: reality happens the same way all the time whether or not you are stoned. What is true when you are tripping is true when you are not tripping. What causes things to happen or not to happen when you are tripping causes them to happen or not to happen when you are not tripping. In other words, if we become aware of causing manifestations – manifestations being something that occurs as the result of an event – when we are tripping, then the only difference between being high and not being high is awareness of being the cause of the manifestations. The manifestations continue as we cause them through our actions and consciousness.

That means that we, not some hoary old deity way off in the far distant elsewhere, are responsible for the state of the universe. We are responsible for our own lives because we manifest them.

Eastern spiritual traditions refer to the earth plane as the "causal" plane. This is because everything that occurs is linked together by causes. All that is presently happening is occurring because of every event in the universe that has preceded it, and will, in turn, influence every event in the universe that happens after it. It is cause and effect, hence, the causal plane.

Stephen Gaskin proposed a model of how the universe functions that I have found useful. It is based on Tibetan Buddhism. They believe that the universe is created and destroyed from chronon to chronon (the smallest division of time). How this creation/destruction happens is dependent on everyone's agreement about it. This is all an unconscious process. We don't have to stop every billionth of a second and think, "OK, time to destroy it all and manifest it all again," it just happens. Stephen said the universe functions by agreement.

The Biblical aphorism "as a man sows, sow so shall he reap" is the cycle of karma, the law of compensation. It works because we, through our thoughts and actions, cause things to happen. On that level, life itself is a trip. You *are*. You *do*. Things happen accordingly. You react to them. They get better or worse depending on what kind of a universe you manifest.

A bad trip or "freak out" is an example of a negative feedback loop and lack of awareness of what is occurring on the part of the person having the bad trip.

Let's take an electric guitar as an example of feedback and manifestation. The guitarist stands in front of his amplifier, cranks the volume on it wide open and hits a loud note. The signal from the guitar goes into the amplifier and is boosted and comes out through the speaker. If the vibration in the air from the speaker is strong enough, it will in turn vibrate the string without the string being plucked. So the signal from the guitar string goes back into the amp and out the speaker and vibrates the guitar string more and the signal from the guitar string goes into the amp and out the speaker and so on. The note being produced by the feedback keeps gaining in volume until the player stops the string from vibrating (or the speaker's voice coil overheats and the speaker is fried!).

The same thing can happen when you are tripping. You are high on a psychedelic. You see something happen that is weird. It gets your attention. Because you are now looking at it, it is getting more energy and becoming more of whatever it is. It upsets you. You put more attention into it. It gets weirder. You are scared and you feed that feeling back into it so it gets scarier. You, in turn, get more scared and feed even more energy into it. It becomes monstrous. You become even more terrified and so on. What has happened is that a feedback loop has become established. It will keep feeding on itself until it is revving out of control and you end up in the ER getting pumped full of thorazine. Highly unpleasant. This is exactly how a bad trip happens.

For non-trippers reading this, the closest movie reference I can make to acid hallucinations is the scene in "Fear and Loathing in Las Vegas" where they are tripping in a lounge, and all the people at the tables appear to be dinosaurs, and the patterns in the carpet move fluidly. It is spot on. Whoever was responsible for that was *definitely* an acid head!

How is a bad trip prevented? The Buddhists call it "non-attachment," by not being attached to the phenomena being manifested. Say that you are tripping with a friend and, for some reason, they start turning into a werewolf in front of you: getting hairy, fangs, the whole shot (I once saw this happen). Instead of getting scared, which will only make the situation worse, you just have to say "Hey, Jack, you're turning into a werewolf!" and not get uptight. It will stop. The point is to be non-attached. Non-attachment allows you an awareness that psychedelic phenomena are self-manifested precludes having bad trips because you can break a negative feedback loop before it gets out of control.

Suddenly being thrust into a state of expanded consciousness where the barriers between the conscious and subconscious are eliminated can be quite disconcerting. This brings on an awareness that *everyone is connected on the subconscious level.* Think about that. Once the barrier between your conscious mind and your subconscious mind is eliminated, the barrier to other peoples' minds is also eliminated. And what happens then? You become consciously aware of the contents of someone else's head: extrasensory perception. WHAM! You're telepathic!

The ultimate implication of this is that everyone is telepathic on a subconscious level at all times. It's a matter of being aware of it. Your subconscious is only subconscious to you. Everyone can see it. That's why somebody can be an asshole and be completely unaware that they are an asshole, although it is clearly (and painfully!) obvious to everyone else.

Going beyond the idea of psychedelic tripping, manifesting your life from day-to-day is also feedback loop. If you are not aware of this, you are at a disadvantage, for you have no conscious choice about how events occur in our life. You will forever be an effect of your actions without being aware your actions are the cause of those very effects. If you are aware of your own individual role in manifesting the universe, then you have the choice of being a cause and controlling what happens. In the esoteric aspect, "as a man sows, so shall he reap" is an identical principle to Buddhists saying that knowing the world is self-manifested precludes having a bad life.

How dangerous are psychedelic drugs?

Good question. There are some obvious caveats here. The first one is, do you know what it is you are getting when you buy street drugs? We sure as hell didn't in the 60's. Adulterated acid, whether done on purpose or by poor laboratory procedures, was common enough. As I mentioned earlier, strychnine was added, in some cases, to allegedly enhance the visual effect. Buying street dope is a dumb move. We were naive when we did it in the 60s and it is no smarter an idea today. I was damned lucky that I did not get seriously fucked up by some kind of poison. In at least one incident that I related earlier in the Boston chapter, the red caps alleged to be psilocybin, I did get hooked up with some bad shit. It was bad, but not deadly.

There is the basic "do not operate machinery" warning. Don't drive a car while on a psychedelic. Don't pilot a plane or boat while on a psychedelic. Swimming might be a bad idea too. It is not a good idea to jump out of a ten story window, whether you have taken a psychedelic or not.

Some people are said to have jumped out of windows while on a psychedelic under the impression that they could fly and have died as a result.[23] I am a veteran of dozens of doses of various psychedelic drugs and I have never been tempted to do such a thing, nor have I ever known any other acid head to want to try this. Nevertheless, I would say that it is perhaps inadvisable to do psychedelics near open windows!

Some people who – for whatever reason – do not respond well to psychedelics and simply shouldn't take them.

Are trips "fun?"

Oh hell yes. Listening to music while on a psychedelic is a most amazing experience, whether it is a live band or recordings. Much of my early tripping, before I got into the transcendent aspects of LSD, was at the Boston Tea Party dance hall. The expansion of consciousness and increased flow of psychic energy while tripping can give you a one-pointedness of concentration that is unparalleled. When you "get into" something on LSD, all else ceases to exist. When listening to music, there is not only the aural experience of the sound, but you are joined psychically with the musicians in a telepathic manner. If you are tripped out at a rock concert or dance, you are also joined telepathically with the other members of the audience. This is communion in its truest sense, the common union of everyone in the dance hall on a telepathic level, electric church.

There is also an energy dynamic at work in this rock n' roll situation. As I said before, attention is energy. Where you put your attention is where you put your energy. So, you have a situation where there are a lot of people who are high on a psychedelic listening to a band whose members are also high on a psychedelic, not at all an uncommon situation at that time. All of these people are putting their attention into the band, giving them their energy. The members of the band, with all of this energy focused on them, take this energy and put it into their music, turning the energy around and sending it back out to the people in the audience. The people in the audience like it and are getting off on it. They are transported to an even higher level by the music and they turn this energy around and send it back to the members of the band. The band feels this and gets higher.

At this point, they may, and often do, enter into a state similar to Zen meditation. Each band member has become one with the music. There is no consciousness of producing the music, there is no thought

---

[23] A notable incident like this was the daughter of radio and TV personality, Art Linkletter, who jumped to her death from a window while on acid.

involved in it, it is simply being done. It is a meditative state devoid of ego where the performers' creative energy is channeled directly to their fingers and they play giving no thought whatsoever to what they are playing. A psychic feedback loop is established with the audience and everyone gets off. It seems as if the members of the band lose their own individuality and become a single entity. This is exactly what it happening on a psychic level.

This puts responsibility on the band to properly take care of the energy they are given. It is possible for a band to bum trip an entire dance (or stadium) hall full of people by the kind of feeling they put in their music. The Grateful Dead have always been good custodians of this energy, this is why they have such a dedicated following.

Doesn't LSD give you flashbacks?

I can only speak for myself. It never gave me any, and I took a lot of it, possibly as much as a hundred times. I didn't keep count. Here is what Erowid.org has to say about flashbacks:

Flashbacks are returns of imagery for extended periods after the immediate effect of hallucinogens has worn off. The most symptomatic form is recurrent intrusions of the same frightening image into awareness, without volitional control...these flashbacks are peremptory and recurrent intrusions into awareness long after the ingested drug has worn off...flashbacks (flashes, flashing) may persist for weeks or months after the last drug experience. The most important variety is repeated intrusions of frightening images in spite of volitional efforts to avoid them. [24]

So the short answer is yes, but I never met anyone who had acid flashbacks nor have I had them.

What about the "other dangers" of LSD and psychedelics?

There has been an enormous amount of misinformation circulated about LSD. For instance, in the 1960s there was a widely circulated about LSD causing chromosome damage. The larger implication was that if you took LSD, it might cause birth defects in children you might have later on in life. This is pure absolute bullshit. There never was any proof to support this claim. I have seen literally hundreds of children born to parents who did LSD and never saw any abnormalities. My own child is beautiful, intelligent, and talented. There have never been any abnormalities recorded that are attributable to taking LSD. Still, it would not be a

---

[24] MARDI J. HOROWITZ, MD American Journal of Psychiatry Vol 126, Oct 4, 1969, 565-569

good idea to take any kind of drug while pregnant. This is only common sense.

Also in the mid 60's, there was a widely circulated piece of news about several college students at the University of Pennsylvania who had taken LSD and went blind from staring at the sun. This turned out to be a completely fabricated event, concocted by some university officials, presumably to discourage young people from tripping out. From erowid.org:

Put simply, LSD does not cause death at recreational or therapeutic doses (less than 500 micrograms)... death is not a major risk...LSD has been used by tens of millions of people over the last 50 years and has been administered to tens of thousands of patients in psychotherapeutic settings...because the numbers of fatalities associated with LSD are so low, it is difficult to determine the risk of death associated with LSD. ... "There have been no documented human deaths from an LSD overdose." [25]

A WINDOW ON THE UNIVERSE

It is possible to absolutely discern truth when on a psychedelic. There exists a moral imperative to maintain a commitment to the truth, that's the "bearing false witness" of the Bible. It's in there because it's important. That means don't lie, and don't accept lies. We are responsible for our own psychic condition, our consciousness. That's pretty much a working definition of free will. We are not supposed to let anyone take away our free will. It's ours, individually and collectively, and it doesn't belong to a church, a cult, or the government. [26]

The psychedelic experience is a means to an end and not an end in and of itself. It is a way to "see" [27] the world, the universe, the inner self in a new way, a non linear way.

The most sacramental feature of the psychedelic experience is the window. There is a point at which a window opens on the universe and all of it is laid bare before the observer, a vision of the relationship, structure and function of everything that *is*, in minute detail. Then it is gone. The window slams shut and you are lucky to retain anything at all from it.

---

[25] *Erowid LSD (Acid) Vault : Fatalities / Deaths*. (2018). *Erowid. org*. Retrieved 5 March 2018, from https://erowid. org/chemicals/lsd/lsd_death
[26] The Old Curmudgeon's Sage Advice No. 6.
[27] in the sense of "seeing" that Don Juan relates to Carlos Casteneda in Casteneda's book, *A Separate Reality*

In an early trip I had a vision that showed me the interconnectedness of all that is, a real Buddha flash. I saw all things and all beings as if each one was an island in an ocean. Looking at them form above the surface of the ocean, they were all separate. But looking at them from below the surface of the ocean they were all connected, each island being but a tiny part of that whole that was above the surface of the ocean. From that particular trip, that is all I remember from when the window was open. But now, more than 50 years later, I can still get a flash of intuitive knowledge of the structure of the universe, and the life in it, that has been locked in my unconscious mind all this time.

Like the spirit quest of Native Americans, the psychedelic experience is meaningful only to the person experiencing it. It is first hand. Psychedelics are a means to an end, they are not an end in and of themselves.

CHAPTER 25

AFTERMATH

SAN FRANCISCO

The time I spent in San Francisco from 1969 to 1981 was the defining period in my life. That city turned me into a citizen of the world. I met so many people of differing nationalities and ethnicities. I was exposed to so many aspects of varying cultures. I gained an understanding and tolerance of others from my years there, something I might have missed had I not lived there. The big take away was that most people, despite racial or cultural differences, went to work, paid their bills, paid their mortgage, loved their kids and tried to educate them properly. We all have the same basic needs, concerns, and goals.

There was no planning involved in my going to San Francisco, it just happened. It was serendipitous. The thought of going to San Francisco did not occur to us until we were in Long Beach. When we started our westward journey, we were going to Colorado. Well, we did make a trip into Boulder, but really, we just let it all happen spontaneously. We were wanderers, nomads.

I lived twelve years in San Francisco to the week. My business accountant was also a sidereal astrologer and said it was interesting that I stayed in San Francisco or a complete Zodiacal cycle. Being a country boy and wanting to be near family, my wife and I moved to Pennsylvania in 1981.

While I was fed up with city life, I loved that city. Still do. It was an exciting place to be. Sometimes I dream of being in the various neighborhoods. San Franciscans – while I no longer live there, I still consider myself San Franciscan – can spot a shot of the city in an instant on TV. Sometimes I watch "Bullitt," "Dirty Harry" movies or "Streets of San Francisco" DVDs just to see my beloved city.

In "Dirty Harry," there is a scene involving the shooting of a black child. In the background are the Potrero Hill Projects and I can see the door to Joyce's apartment, 731 Missouri St. It's kind of cool to see a door in a movie and know you got laid behind that door! The interior of that same apartment appears in a TV episode of "Murder in the First."

There is a special reason I watch "The Enforcer." A bad guy being chased by Harry over a roof stumbles through a skylight and lands on a bed in the middle of a porno shoot. Harry follows him through the skylight. A bevy of naked women are all aflutter. One of them is Yong Moon, the young Korean woman who sang in Jacob's Ladder, beaded headband, silicone boobs and naked cooch in full view! Yee hah!

ANITA

I contacted Anita in the 90s while researching for this book to see if she could give me any details on some mutual acquaintances we had back in the day. She was living in Austin, TX and said she had been dealing with severe depression, bipolar issues and panic attacks since the 1980s. I was saddened to hear this. When we were together she was a very intelligent woman with a marvelous sense of humor.

I asked her how she ended up back in Austin. She told me her father was living in Florida and died on a New Year's eve. She was driving back to San Francisco from Florida and he car broke down in Austin, so she stayed there. She had lived there previously with her first husband.

Before we got to the point where it was not good that we remain in contact, we talked about our lives to each other. In one such discussion I talked about searching for a programming job after completing the programming course at Programming and Systems Institute in 1970. I was being interviewed for an IBM 360 Operator at the University of California Medical Center in Parnassus heights where she had worked for Dr. Gold, just above where we lived on Stanyan St.

I recounted to her that before LBJ left office and needing money for the Vietnam War, he gutted the budget for the aerospace industries that were located in what is now called Silicon Valley, just south of San Francisco, and redirected the funds toward the war. Programmers with years of experience were cut loose and taking entry level positions. So I adapted.

There I was, short hair, Salvation Army suit, shirt and wingtips, being interviewed by a hippie hairball. This guy was obviously a head, very laid back and personable. He said to me, "Gene, you are qualified for this job. Of this I have no doubt. I would love to hire you for it. If I don't hire somebody black, they will have my ass. I'm sorry. I can't give you the job" And that was it.

Anita remarked, "There you were, caught between the Civil War and the Vietnam War." I never considered that. It was an interesting observation, and so like Anita.

She filled me in on her life. She had converted to Christianity and was studying Greek and Hebrew biblical literature in Berkeley for a while. She married a friend of hers I met when we were together, Lee MacInerney, something I could never figure out because he was quite gay. She told me he died of AIDS. She also confessed to an inability to maintain sexual fidelity, something I learned when we were together. Eventually her bipolarity turned things ugly and we ceased contact, for the second time.

I was saddened to learn that Anita passed away in November 2014. I don't know if we were actually in love, but in that short period of time we were two souls clinging to each other, while lost in the chaos of the times. Together for about eight months, we experienced incredible passion and a unique psychedelic intimacy. Anita remains unforgettable to me, even fifty years later.

MOCK RIOT RETROSPECTIVE

While my memoir of the riot could be viewed as demeaning the authorities for being incompetent, that is not my intention. There's a difference between incompetence and being blindsided. Everybody was blindsided one way or another in the '60s, it was just their turn.

Some of the aspects of the riot were comical, like the "Student Riot Committee" for instance. The fact that there was a need for a "Student Riot Committee" in a year that is remembered for nationwide civil unrest is... bizarre... to say the least. A committee for a riot? Wasn't the implied organization of a committee the antithesis of the spontaneous chaos of a riot? Oh, that's right, this was only an *exercise!*

Do I recount this story because I take pride in my role in causing the...complications...that attended the crowd control exercise? That's part of it. It was, after all, a *lot* of fun! It *was* an asshole thing to do and I was an *asshole!* Perfect fit! But beyond the recollection of reckless youthful exuberance and humorous situations, hindsight of a half century has made me realize what an utterly unique event it was.

We were requested to stage a mock civil disturbance. We did. A few hundred more people showed up than anyone expected, but everyone abided by the "rules of engagement." Nobody threw a single rock or bottle. What if people on the rooftops had started chucking bricks? That could have resulted in serious injuries or fatalities. Had that been the case, this would be a far different story and not one damned bit funny.

Nobody really got out of line. We made was a mess that was almost beyond description. A lot of people were inconvenienced, to be certain, and some were frightened. No one was arrested and no one was injured. There was zero property damage. No one on either side crossed the lines of acceptable behavior, water balloons and flying foodstuffs notwithstanding! Despite the general disorder there was a marked lack of hostility between the "rioters" and the authorities.

Georg Lindy, a few years my junior, told me a couple years ago, "I was in high school then, I wouldn't have missed it for the world. It's all we talked about that week. I was in the rear of the crowd barricaded inside the square. It wasn't just kids, either. I saw a little old lady tossing eggs at the cops!"

Looking back over fifty years, I think the guard troops, the police, the university officials, my friends, myself, all of us, we were all naive. Innocent. We had not yet been initiated into the national cynicism that was coming.

Bradford was still a sleepy town in the hills of Pennsylvania and in no way subject to the crime and social issues that plagued cities.[1] It was not macrocosm/microcosm. The Guard's request for a mock disturbance for training purposes was an imposition on Bradford and its culture by the outside world, the world at-large, the world of civil disturbances and social and political issues, attempting to hijack the social structure of a small town that was unprepared for any of it. In 1968 Bradford had no racial strife or tensions over social and political issues.

The mock riot was a perfect storm of unlikely circumstances. Plans went awry. Authorities were unprepared. No one panicked. No one was hurt. While blood ran in the streets of America, pancake batter flowed in the streets of Bradford! The situation really *was* out of control and it could have turned tragic. Everyone involved was just too good natured to

---

[1] Unlike the present day 2019 when Bradford is ravaged by rampant opioid abuse, overdose deaths, and meth labs.

let that happen. A remarkable level of trust was displayed was by all. People by and large liked each other!

We all had friends in the guard unit. We knew policemen and firemen personally. No one was out to harm any of them. Throwing eggs, water balloons and flour at them? Well...that's *different*, as they say!

The "riot" caused quite a stir and even made the Buffalo, N. Y., evening TV newscasts. Life in America in 1968 was extraordinary under any circumstance. Even in Bradford life was surreal at times.

REFLECTING ON MARISSA

Looking back I would have to say Marissa, my lovely, passionate teenage lover, was hypersexual, what we called a "nympho" in those days. In the decades that have passed since I was with her I have learned hypersexuality can result from sexual abuse.

Marissa introduced me to her parents one evening. About a week later she said "My father asked me if I was having sex with you."

This got my attention! "What did you tell him?"

"I told him 'yes.' "

I went into panic mode because I was open for a corruption of a minor/statutory rape charge. "What the fuck did you do *that* for?"

"Don't worry," she replied, "it's ok with him."

Evidently it was because no complaint was ever made to the police. In retrospect, I think that Marissa was sexually abused by her father. Most fathers would have someone who was banging their underage daughter thrown in jail. He evidently had a reason to not do this. I think that reason was that it might have come out that he was abusing her.

I mentioned this to Ron. "Yeah, I worked with him at the box factory. He was a kind of creepy, pervy little dude.

I do not know whatever became of that lovely and passionate young woman, but my loins have never forgotten her.

FAMILY

My grandmother, the sweet long suffering woman who loved me so dearly and who made sure I was thoroughly indoctrinated into Catholicism, died in 1970 at the age of seventy-two. She was lying in the hospital literally dying by inches as they cut pieces off her because of diabetes.

Not one time did fat-assed Monsignor Geddes, from St. Elizabeth's parish, visit her. Here was a woman who was widowed ten months before the depression started in 1929 and left with 4 small children to raise, who went to church every Sunday and all the Holy Days of Obligation, who literally gave the "widow's mite" to the regular collection and donated to the weekly "special collection" as well every goddamned Sunday of her life. And Monsignor Geddes – now deceased – couldn't go see her in the hospital 20 miles away. He was too busy with his hunting dogs. The Episcopal priest from Smethport did visit her, he knew my grandmother was from the same town. That's what her faith got her. For sure the church isn't worth much, but the least she should have gotten some solace in her last days as she lay in terrible pain dying from diabetes. She got none. I know where Monsignor Geddes is buried and have considered pissing on his grave, but he wouldn't be worth the effort.

In 2008 I had bronchitis that was just hanging on and on and on. I was on the phone one day with Martha Brooks, a woman who was a good mutual friend of my wife and I. She was an agnostic and not given to general irrational weirdness or religiosity. Not at all. At the same time, she is sensitive in the meaning of being somewhat psychic. The dichotomy of this was not lost on her and she is both puzzled and fascinated by it. She was in her mid sixties and has had this kind of stuff happen to her all her life. It took her most of that time before she could accept it as what it is: real and unexplainable.

In the Bible, there are many stories of messages being received in dreams. Like when Joseph had the dream to take Mary and Yeshua (that is his name in Hebrew or Aramaic, "Jesus" is Greek) into Egypt. These types of dreams are known as "lucid dreams" among people who are into investigating such phenomena. They are dreams that are so real that you can describe the tiniest detail. I have had one in my lifetime involving a friend who was killed in Vietnam in 1968.

So I am on the phone in early 2008 with Martha says to me "I had a dream last night and I don't know whether or not I ought to tell you about it."

You can't just brush something like that off!

"Well, you have to tell me now," I responded, "you can't *not* tell me now that you gave me that teaser!"

"I had one of those dreams. I saw a woman, an older woman. She was wearing a dark blue cotton dress that had white polka dots about the size of nickels. She was wearing an apron, a washed out white with little green flowers printed on it. Her hair was up on her head. She was wearing oxford shoes and had on those stockings that old ladies wear, the ones that no matter how the pulled them up they would still sag at the ankles. She was wearing rimless glasses. I couldn't see her face all that clearly, but her expression seemed careworn. She had a dish towel, white with blue stripes on the ends, in her hands and was worrying it."

Wow! That's as good a description as I have ever heard of my grandmother, Alwilda Wright, who died in 1970.

Martha continued,. "We were on a walk, sort of like a sidewalk, but more like slate. There was shrubbery on either side of us. She said to me, 'Tell Gener that if he wants to get better, he needs to find the special rosary.'

"Well, Gener's not a Catholic anymore. I don't think he has a rosary," Martha replied in the dream.

The woman said, "He has it, he needs to find it." And then she added – this is the kicker – "tell Gener that his Andy Panda isn't lost, he's behind his bed up against the wall."

Tears immediately came to my eyes. Andy Panda was a stuffed bear I had as a small child and he slept with me every night. He was so old I couldn't remember when he was new. His eye were buttons my mother sewed on when the old ones - whatever they were - fell off. There is NO way that Martha or any other living being on earth knew about Andy Panda. None. Absolutely.

I emailed Martha a picture of my grandmother, the one shown here. She confirmed what I already knew, my grandmother was definitely the woman she saw. She said, "When I looked at the picture of your grandmother, I realized that in the dream I had seen her from the point of view of a child, which is why most of what I could remember was her hands, dress, apron, shoes and so on. She was speaking to me as if I were a small girl and she wanted me to give you - also a small child - this message."

The location Martha described is familiar. I believe it is in the garden area in back of what was the Robert A. Digel house at the intersection of U.S. Route 6 and Main Street in Smethport where my grandmother worked as a cook. When I was small I would spend time there in the summers when the Digels were at their summer residence. I remember the hedge and a walk along side it and on the other side of the walk was lush foliage of some sort.

I took this mysterious message under advisement and searched through boxes of family stuff until I found three rosaries. There was an old one that may have been my grandmothers when she was a child. I have her crucifix too. And there were two rosaries that came from Rome in the 1960s. Father Grode, our parish priest at St. Elizabeth's in Smethport, gave them to altar boys, of which I was one. One of them had been blessed by Pope John XXIII when Father Grode, had an audience with him.

I took the rosary and for the first time in over forty years said a couple, minus the Apostle's Creed because I am just not going to profess something in which I do not believe.

I figured, hey, if there is an entity, a spiritual being, a thought form, or whatever, out there that can do some good, any kind of good, from having some of my energy – when you pray, that's what you are doing, directing energy to achieve an end – directed towards it, why not?

Some people have asked me why I have not gone back to being a practicing Catholic. I don't see that as the point of this incident. It is not the rosary. It is not Catholicism. It is my Grandmother reaching out and communicating with me, giving me a message, trying to help me heal. She didn't tell me to go back to church. She told me to find the rosary. She didn't even tell me to say it. I found it. I even said it a couple of times. I got better. Was the rosary the cause? Was the Catholic church the cause? Was Yeshua beth David ben Joseph the cause? Not from where I sit. It was the love of this woman, my grandmother, Alwilda Wright, reaching out to me beyond time and space to heal me.

This odd - but completely true - story is undeniable proof to me of the enduring quality of love that goes beyond any physical existence. It shows that the familial love with which we grace each other transcends all else.

My father was an alcoholic, probably from the time he got out of the Navy. While my mother was alive he was a controlled alcoholic. Dad seemed to always have a beer in his hand. When I was a small child, there were many evenings he never came home, or came home very late and very drunk. He and my mother would argue loudly. I was terrified and would flee to my grandmother's side of the house.

After parents adopted my sister, sometimes my father would go onto town to get milk and baby food for her and stop at the Legion and forget to come home. More than once my mother called my aunt who brought milk and baby food out to the house. My grandfather took him aside one day and threatened to have him committed to the state hospital in North Warren, PA., if he did not cease the drinking and start paying attention to his family. I don't know what effect that actually had on my father, but things did start going a bit smoother then. My parents in their later years were inseparable.

Nobody's perfect. An honest and decent man, my father worked harder than any man I knew, always working two, sometimes three, jobs to support us. He was not so closed minded and set in his ways that he couldn't process new information and change his opinion on something. He did this over the war in Vietnam, something I found rather remarkable.

Many, if not most, WWII vets had a hard time with that. Their generation trusted the government implicitly. My generation figured out the government was buttfucking us. Those are difficult positions to reconcile, and reconciliation never did happen with some families.

My mother died suddenly in 1979. Carol and I were married by the local JP in a civil ceremony at my father's house on the spot where she died later that year.

My father lost his zest for life after my mother's death and started drinking more. After his retirement for the Post Office in 1985, that was all he did. This caused my sister and I no end of concern, but there was no reaching him on the subject. In his words, "It's none of your goddamned business!" We talked to counselors and discussed an intervention. My father, stubborn individual that he was, would never deviate from his established ways.

My wife and I moved back to Pennsylvania in 1981. I returned to college at the University of Pittsburgh in Bradford in 1987, the same place where I had pulled .69 out of 4.0. I graduated Cum Laude in 1989 having qualified for it by .026 of a quality point.

I received a call from the family doctor one day in the spring of 1989, my father was at his office and was severely ill from the effects of his drinking. I took him to the hospital wherein was told he had only 10% of his liver function left. My sister came up from Greensburg with her two children. My father almost died twice in the hospital from the liver damage, then he almost died from kidney failure.

I was torn. He was my father, and I loved him for that. I wanted him to live. He had given me so much, he had sacrificed for us. That ran so very deeply through the core of my being. However, I felt I was never an adequate son to him, a most common feeling between a son and a father. I felt wracked with guilt over my inadequacies as a son. I was never the athlete he was, I was not the outdoorsman and hunter he was. He had friends who were my age of whom I was jealous because I felt they were getting some of his love for a son I should have gotten.

I found myself in a whirlwind of loss, anger, and guilt. I hated him for getting so sick, for deliberately poisoning himself and being so selfish as to cause us all this anguish. I wanted him to live. I wanted him to die. I loved him for being my father. I cursed his alcoholism. I adored the strength that he showed when I was growing up, often working two and three jobs to support us. I loved him because I was a part of him, I was his progeny. I felt myself wishing that he had died in 1979 instead of my mother. I cherished and desperately wanted his approval. I bitterly detested his rages that had ruled our family for as long as I could remember. These things are still not resolved.

My father made a recovery, sold the house he and my mother had built and spent several good years enjoying his grandchildren before his death in 1993, the day after Veteran's Day.

My sister died from cancer in 1998 at the age of forty-two leaving behind a loving husband and two wonderful sons.

BECOMING A RECOVERING CATHOLIC

Nothing can be completely bad, not even the time I spent associated with the RCC. I did get one thing out of my association with the Catholic Church that I value highly, friends that I have known since first grade catechism in 1953, people who will always remain dear to me.

I can now look back and see that church indoctrination had manipulated me to where I could be blackmailed by my basic human nature. It was/is psychological abuse of the worst sort.

The church's take on free will was pure absolute bullshit. The free will of which the church speaks is the free will to do and believe exactly as they tell you. You are free to accept it, or burn. It made me fucking crazy.

I used to think the Catholic Church gave me a moral compass that has proved to be steadfast and unfailing. Now, in my 70s, I have come to see that good people are good people no matter what their faith or lack of same. Perhaps the church gave me a moral compass. Perhaps I was born with it and just *thought* the church gave it to me. I don't know. In any case, I am pleased that I have one.

While the the ethical teachings of the church were fine, implementation of those teachings was pure, unmitigated hypocrisy backed by lies and psychological manipulation. It was this that led to me separating myself from the church and to my opposition to the war in Vietnam, a Catholic war if there ever was one. Catholic dogma is medieval superstition devised to exploit an ignorant, credulous, unwashed, and illiterate population.[2] When it was obvious the church was not practicing what it was preaching regarding the Vietnam War, I severed my ties with them. That was 1968, the year I took LSD for the first time.

I discarded everything I had been taught thus far as lies. I would conduct my own inquiry into the nature of the universe. Some years later in the midst of my spiritual meandering I stumbled across Buddah's "Believe Nothing" statement:

Believe nothing because it is written.

Believe nothing because a wise man said it.

Believe nothing because it is generally true.

Believe only that which you, yourself, have determined to be true.

This is an encouragement for a rational and empirical inquiry into the nature of the universe. It requires no church membership, no prayers, no belief in mystical beings, just the six senses[3] with which we are equipped.

I have had some difficulty coming to terms with the church for their brutal and thorough mindfucking that put me in a place (as I have detailed in Chapter 3) of where I was actually considering self-mutilation.

When I started doing acid, it was fairly easy to let go of the brainwashing and dogma that they etched into my consciousness. Acid gave me a completely different perspective on life and was somewhat therapeutic. It did nothing for the inner rage I harbored that was concealed so deep within me I had no idea it was there.

In the 90s I became aware of the anger I carried toward the church. The church had destroyed my self-esteem, causing me no end of emotional pain in my youth. It is an organization that exists only to propagate itself, using brainwashing, guilt, and shame to psychologically dominate its members, infecting the minds of millions, its dogma a rancid mélange of medieval ignorance passed off as holy truth, even now in twenty-first century.

---

[2] and to extort riches from the rulers of Christian lands, another contributing factor to the reformation
[3] Buddhists believe thought is also a sense with which we perceive the universe. I agree.

It took forty years to release the astonishing and emotionally crippling rage I was harboring. Ten of them were spent raging, ranting, and flaming in an online recovery newsgroup,[4] alt. recovery. Catholicism.

Since my separation from the church, I have been able to establish to myself that I am, in fact, a worthwhile human being, and worthy of absolutely everything I can attain. Fuck that "Oh Lord I am not worthy" shit. I am just fine the way I am.[5]

I was thoroughly indoctrinated into the RCC doctrine because I trusted my grandmother and, because of that, trusted The Nunz. I believed all of it because I was afraid not to. I bear my grandmother no ill will, she was as much a victim as I was, as anyone who has ever been brainwashed by the RCC. In the end she was betrayed by the church as she lay dying painfully.

No person or organization *ever* has the right to destroy the self-esteem of a young person–or *any* person for that matter. That is a deed that goes far beyond insidious. That is what the church has done for so many. It's been a long, difficult and painful process reclaiming pieces of my self-esteem.

I have come to regard the Roman Catholic Church as a virus of the mind, an idea, once implanted into a psyche, acts upon it in a negative manner like an infection does on the body. Implanted into societies, it acts the same way as does a deadly epidemic. I am not even sure where the RCC mind virus got into our family, but it damned well stops with me.

My wife and I now have a lovely and talented daughter, a professional artist, who has never been taught to believe that she is unworthy of anything. I vowed when she was born to never let RCC or any other peddlers of religious claptrap near my precious child. I never gave those rotten bastards an opportunity to contaminate her innocence and unblemished spirit with their toxic mythology and medieval superstitions. They never have. She is moral, intelligent and mega-talented. And she our friend. We are *so* happy with her. After seeing what religion has done for some of her friends, she has thanked my wife and me several times for never forcing religion on her.

Anger is not productive. It does not affect those against whom it is directed, but it does affect the one who holds it. I vented mine in alt.recovery.catholicism for about a decade. There was so much of it in

---

[4] USENET, coined from the words USE(rs) and NET(work) is a branch of the internet consisting of a vast network of severs. NNTP (Network News Transfer Protocol) is the protocol used to connect to Usenet servers and transfer newsgroup articles between systems over the Internet. (from Wikipedia)
[5] The Old Curmudgeon's Sage Advice No. 8.

me, in all of us on in the newsgroup. One day I woke up and my anger toward the church was gone. I didn't hate them, I didn't love them. I just didn't give a shit about them. I won...or so I thought.

When the Pennsylvania Attorney general released the report on sexual abuse by Roman Catholic priests in Pennsylvania in August, 2018, there were internet discussions on it. I related my experience of walking in on Father Grode engaged in oral sex with another priest. Several people remarked that, since the investigation is ongoing, I should report it. I thought "what the hell" and called the Clergy Abuse Hotline. This was the day after the report was released. The woman who took my call said they had four lines busy taking the hotline calls, they were deluged. She took my information and said they would contact me.

So I got to thinking about the extra, super-deluxe Catholic mindfucking I had received that was so very destructive. I called the following day and asked if institutional psychological abuse was part of the investigation and was informed it was. I explained that they had my info and they said we could discuss it when they contacted me.

As soon as I hung the phone up. I was hit with a real by golly genuine flashback. Not a psychedelic acid flashback, but one that took me back to being that little boy, fearful of the church, fearful of this terrible, terrible God who wouldn't answer his prayers, fearful of the eternal torments of hell. I lost it completely, completely immersed in the fear, horror, and hopelessness in which I had dwelt in my Catholic childhood. My wife comforted me in her arms as I broke down into deep, heaving sobs. My therapist told me I had experienced a form of PTSD. Guess I the church ain't done fucking with me yet!

The Nunz told us that God puts an indelible mark on your soul when you are baptized. I don't know about my soul, but they goddamned certain put an indelible scar on my psyche.

Reporting it to the Pennsylvania Attorney General isn't going to instigate any action because of it, it is more of an indictment of an institution than of individuals behaving badly. It will at least put this kind of cruel indoctrination on the list of shit that the church does to gratuitously fuck over the weak and defenseless.

BILL WASSAM

In 1980, I came back from San Francisco to attend my fifteen year high school reunion. There were a hundred thirty-four kids in my graduation class (the largest class to ever graduate from Smethport). We had all known each other for many years, some of us had gone together since first grade.

Jerry Fay brought a fellow over to me who had a drooping mustache, heavy, dark-rimmed glasses and shoulder-length blonde hair that hung over his face.

"Hey Gener," he said, "do you know who this guy is?"

Well, like I said, as you get older, it gets harder to recognize people. I certainly knew this guy, hell, that's why he was here! I damned sure couldn't recognize him, though.

"Hey, man, it's Bill Wassam!"

I hadn't seen him since our chance meeting in front of Nick's Red Hots in Bradford in August, 1968. I was elated to see my old friend. We caught up on the twelve years that had passed. He now had a PhD as well as several post-doctorate degrees and was currently working as a theoretical biophysicist at Cornell University.

"Man!" he said with enthusiasm, "They pay me for *thinking!* I don't even have to *look* at a test tube!"

We conversed for a while, and then I asked him if he remembered when we had last seen each other. He didn't. I reminded him of our conversation in front of Nick's in 1968. Then I asked, "Bill, whatever happened to you after that? Did you go into the army?"

"Yes," he said. The smile left his face. He spoke in a deliberate manner, looking me in the eye, "I went. They drafted me and made me a grunt. I went to Vietnam…and came back an armed revolutionary. I figured I was shooting the wrong people over there."

I was astounded. The boy genius from rural northwest PA had come back from Vietnam ready to wage war on America. I fully understood how he could arrive in such a place.

There is a certain irony in the twists and turns that lead a person to adopt revolutionary politics. One could be resentful of being forced into military service, shipped halfway around the world and forced to kill, and at the same time be willing to carry out the same actions in one's own country for entirely different reasons.

In the late 90s, at the time an expatriate professor of physics in Mexico City, Bill wrote me:

"…I supported the war in Vietnam…I felt that I could…serve in a noble cause. Vietnam devastated me. I could not and cannot deal with it. At times, I feel completely overwhelmed by it. If I talk or write about

FLASHING BACK– COMING OF AGE IN THE AMERICAN 1960s

Vietnam, it would tear me apart. It is better for me to keep it buried deep in the dark corners of my mind...science allowed me to hide from the war and the advocacy of revolution served as a mechanism for venting my rage and expressing my disgust over the status quo..."

Many feelings about that period of time still linger with those of us who lived through it. Bill and I experienced the turbulence of the 1960's from two different perspectives. Bill's was certainly fraught with more risk and danger. He passed away in 2001.

DRAFT DODGING SON-OF-A-BITCH

It is common knowledge where I live that I never served in the military. Small towns being what they are, when someone farts in the bank, by the time it gets across the street to the grocery store, it's become a wheelbarrow full of shit. This has turned into the story that I and several of my high school classmates went to Canada to evade the draft.

In small town culture, you cannot live down anything you have ever done. That is also true about the thing you haven't done. I occasionally get "You went to Canada and you're a draft dodging son-of-a-bitch!" flung at me. I deny going to Canada, to no avail. My absence from my home town between 1968 and 1981 is all the proof needed to support the canard. What the hell. One man's draft-dodger is another man's war resister.

I have said to several individuals: "While I don't owe you – or any other asshole – any explanations about anything I may or may not have done in my life, it so happens I was in California from 1969 until 1981. 'Canada' and 'California' begin with the same two letters, but are nonetheless easily distinguished from each other. Now that you have been correctly informed, you are no longer ignorant asshole. However, if you repeat this falsehood, you will be a lying sack of shit."

I am certain they consider me an asshole. A lot of people do. I will not argue with them, I have given a lot of people damned good reasons for it. They avoid me after that. Mission accomplished! It makes my life better!

I think it is easier for a lot of people to simply remain in denial about Vietnam than admit that the government fucked America over in an unconscionable manner. I don't blame them. Everyone lost someone in Vietnam: father, husband, son, cousin, brother, uncle, someone. It is most reasonable to expect that they do not want to see this as the vain sacrifice it in fact was.

In the late 80s I was taking classes at the Pitt campus in Bradford, PA. One day I was riding to class with aforementioned Terry Tessena, who graduated a year ahead of me, and spent 14 years in the Marines. He was a recovering alcoholic pursuing a degree. "Gener," he said, "everyone got fucked in the 60s. I got fucked, you got fucked. It is a matter of degree. It took as much courage for you to do what you did as took for me to do what I did. That's just the way it is."

Over the years and decades since the end of the U.S. military involvement in Vietnam, many vets from my high school have suffered with severe PTSD. Others died too young from a myriad of conditions resulting from agent orange exposure. Some are in their 70s and still suffering. Some children of Vietnam Veterans have died from fatal congenital effects of the Agent Orange with which their fathers were showered with in Vietnam. How terribly the innocent suffer for the crimes of the brutal and the ignorant.

MACNAMARA

Vietnam and its attendant death and suffering were entirely avoidable. As Lyndon Johnson's Secretary of Defense, Robert S. McNamara was its chief architect. In 1995, he published *In Retrospect*, part confession, part apology, but mostly rationalization for his part in engineering this monumental and bloody clusterfuck.

The Vietnam war drove a wedge into my generation between those who went and those who didn't. That split often occurred along economic lines: those who could afford college, the accompanying 2-S draft deferment – and I admit I benefited from that privilege – didn't have to go to war. When married men were still exempt from the draft, there were many young men suddenly getting married, or going to divinity schools as clergy were exempted as well. Vietnam tore families asunder, not only with the deaths of thousands of America's sons, but with the generational rift that occurred over the war. Such was my own experience.

I did not suffer the horror and brutality of war as did so many others. My own personal loss is Buddy. Those most affected are those who served and loved ones left behind. What must they feel now when the man who sent them to Vietnam now says it was a mistake? It is incomprehensible to me that McNamara could be such a perfidious prick.

The demons of Vietnam have possessed America's soul for decades and no amount of exorcism seems to help. The flames die, but the still coals smolder, and then McNamara throws gasoline on them with his book. Once again we can feel the rage. And still the unanswered question: how could McNamara do this? How could he, when he admits he knew *before the end of 1965* it was futile, how could he go ahead with this folly which would consume so very many lives, Asian as well as American?

Only by understanding that Vietnam was doomed from its inception, administered by liars and incompetents who wasted over 58,000 American lives, could this slaughter have served some useful purpose, for then the American people would form the resolve that this would never happen again.

Instead we have had the first Gulf War, the Invasion of Iraq, and the war in Afghanistan which are, like Vietnam, wars of choice and not wars of necessity. Nobody's freedom has been secured. America is not more safe. The only thing learned from Vietnam was to keep the press from having free access to the front lines and reporting the truth to the American people. No purpose can be assigned to the forced sacrifice that was Vietnam. All those dead soldiers are no more than names chiseled on a wall, ghostly memories that haunt those left behind. If they died for anything, it was for each other. It sure as hell wasn't for anybody's freedom.

It was all for naught, except to the arms industries and their congressional lickspittles. They are reptiles, black-hearted soulless sons-of-bitches in expensive suits, driving BMWs, snorting cocaine through hundred-dollar bills in corporate boardrooms, thousands of miles away from the stench of profitable putrefaction they create. They have garnered unimaginable wealth turning living human beings into maggot infested corpses. All that dead Americans soldiers represent to them is the cost of doing business. They turn a profit on body bags they sell to Uncle Sam. And you know goddamned well their kids are *never* counted among the KIA. It was this way for Vietnam, it hasn't changed one goddamned bit.

THE MYOPIA OF THE PEACE MOVEMENT

The arrogance inherent in the upper middle class makeup of the peace movement made them pass up a great opportunity for getting a lot of Americans to stand up against the war by the way they treated the returning vets. The manner in which these men were greeted upon returning to the U.S. was unconscionable and turned many Americans off to the antiwar movement who might have otherwise supported it. But then, the people who did these things generally didn't know anyone who served in Vietnam. And since they didn't know anyone who served in

Vietnam, they could not comprehend that good men could still end up fighting in a bad war. The warrior does not choose the war.

When I was living on the West Coast I was struck by the fact that, while I knew scores of men who went to Vietnam, no one out there seemed to know *anyone* who went to Vietnam. They did not understand that there were no choices for many of the men who served in the war. If you grew up where I did, there was certainly no choice. There was no choice unless you were aware there *was* a choice. Had I been drafted a year or even six months earlier, there would have been no choice for me.

Those who served in Vietnam were victims of the system. I managed to not be one of those victims. I stated previously that those who survived the sixties did so because they had it figured out or were lucky. I sure as hell didn't have it figured out. I was lucky and managed to avoid being cannon fodder for the green machine. Friends with whom I grew up, some highly decorated Vietnam veterans, have told me I was smart to not go. Smart didn't have a hell of a lot to do with it. I survived mainly through plain, dumb luck. I have never taken another human life. I refused to blindly submit to the whim of a government[6] that wanted to have me do just that for reasons that were not morally justifiable. But that does not make me superior to those who did go.

GRAY AREAS

When one is young, the answers are easy because everything is black and white. As one gets older and experiences life, gray areas begin to emerge.

If a man can't be true to himself, he is no good to anyone. People, for whatever reasons, can make diametrically opposed choices and still be right. You could go to war and be right. You could not go to war and be right. The individual's conscience and principles were the determining factors. Karma follows accordingly.

I could not go to war and be right because I was convinced it was fundamentally wrong politically and morally. But if you *truly* believed in it, it couldn't be wrong… for you. It was a matter of how you saw your duty to your country. You make your choice and deal with the karma that comes as the result of that choice.

There are those who will disagree with me on this point, and that's OK. Opinions are like assholes, everyone's got one.

---

[6] The Old Curmudgeon's Sage Advice No. 8.

In 1975 I told my father in detail about my successful effort in resisting the draft. By then he had changed his mind on the war and he told me then, as well as several other times before he died in 1993, that I did the right thing and that he, in retrospect, supported my actions.

"Even World War Two was a bunch of shit," he once remarked to me. He never elaborated. I found that to be a remarkable statement coming from a WWII Navy veteran and Past Commander of American Legion Bucktail Post 138.

He told me that my uncle, who had three sons, had made a deal with the draft board. If one of his sons served in the military, the others would not be drafted. This is a sweetheart deal that could only have been worked out with Milt Hodges. Interesting. There were twin brothers, members of the Class of 1965 who were both drafted and sent to Vietnam. There was no "...if one goes the other will not be drafted..." deal to be had there.

I related this to my cousin, who said that his father was not one to game the system. I have no doubt of that. Things change when life and death are involved. My father had no reason to speak an untruth and my uncle had every reason to protect his sons the best he could. This was 1967. People that were paying attention saw the direction the war was going in but did not speak out about it. The general public still supported the war. My uncle was a business owner. Opposing the Vietnam War would hurt his business. He had a wife and four kids to take care of. I make no judgment here. This is just another example of the unfair circumstances that faced many Americans at the time.

HONORING THE DEAD

Memorial Day is about honoring those who served and those who died, so they told us. Honor isn't just flags, bunting and parades. Honor is understanding the sacrifices made. Of course we are inundated asshole deep in red-white-and-blue patriotic claptrap, maudlin poems and songs.

What is never discussed is that no American soldier has died fighting for anybody's freedom since WWII, the last conflict in which the US actually achieved a military victory. The American people have become timorous, a nation of sheep blindly following leaders who send troops off to fight in bullshit wars that do not have one fucking thing to do with defending American principles.

Korea was a bullshit war. Vietnam was a bullshit war. Both Gulf Wars were bullshit wars. The war in Afghanistan became a bullshit war after troops were ordered by the Bush II administration to stand down after cornering Bin Laden at Tora Bora in 2001, thus aiding in his escape. We have been there so fucking long that the kids of soldiers who fought there in 2001 are old enough to go and spill their blood in Afghanistan too. This is not honor. This is not patriotism. This is intergenerational manipulation that exploits Americans' innate love of their country for the benefit of the arms industries. America used to manufacture weapons to fight wars. Now America manufactures wars to sell weapons.

The US Military is composed of people willing to die defending this country. We dishonor them by lying to them about defending America while whoring them out as muscle to for brutal authoritarian regimes like the Saudi royal family and send them to third world shitholes to kill indigenous foreign people – usually non-Christian and people of color – so corporations can freely loot foreign natural resources (oil!). This is so obvious and so egregious that other countries now view the US as the greatest threat to world peace.

To those who wish to honor the war dead and our veterans, I say oppose these wars of choice and stop voting for the politicians who do support these wasteful, destructive and ignorant foreign policies

We Americans need to collectively pull our heads out of our asses and recognize things for what they are. Politicians will polish a turd, paint it red-white-and-blue, salute it and hold a parade for it. In the end, a piece of shit is still a piece of shit.

TOO TALL PAUL

The same Paul Maynard who wanted to "go outside and throw a few" at the acid blast Christmas party in 1968 did two tours in Vietnam with the Marines earning three purple hearts, two of them on consecutive days. When Paul passed in 2014 he was the most highly decorated Vietnam vet in the county. After leaving the Marines he appeared to be in complete denial of his role in the war, looking like a hippie freak from the '60's with shoulder length hair and a handlebar mustache. The VA gave him just enough disability that he could afford drugs and alcohol, which he freely consumed. A Marine veteran schoolmate of mine said, "Paul's entitled to any goddamned thing he wants after the shit he went through."

A year younger than myself, I knew Paul since he started riding the school bus in 1954. When I was visiting Smethport in December of 1977, I ran into Paul one evening at the Corner Restaurant, Smethport's head hangout. He was somewhat the worse for 'ludes and whisky. It was cold and snowing like a damned blizzard outside.

He finished his drink and put the empty glass on the bar. "Well, Pard," he said to nobody in particular, "gotta get on home…," and started toward the door.

Paul, at that time, had lost every license a man could lose: drivers license, fishing license, hunting license, the works. He was living with his mother a couple miles out of town. I was afraid he would freeze to death.

Vietnam Veteran Paul Maynard, USMC, at the dedication of the Vietnam Memorial in Smethport, PA, May 31 2014. He was a LCPL in the U.S. Marine Corps, serving in Vietnam from 1966 to 1969 receiving the National Defense Service Medal, Vietnamese Service Medal with two stars, Vietnamese Campaign Medal, and Purple Heart Medal with three stars. Paul passed away in 2015.
Photo: W. Eugene Johnson

"Paul," I called. He turned from the door. "I'll give you a ride."

"Wow…I'd…really appreciate that…pard…"

We got in the car. Paul was so trashed he could barely sit up. I headed the car out of town. He was silent. and lit a cigarette, struggling with the lighter. Finally he spoke, his speech slowed by the drugs and alcohol, his thin voice quavering.

"You guys…were right, man."

"What guys?"

He hesitated. "You guys that…didn't go, man. You… you were right." He took a drag on his cigarette. "I didn't…know it was…wrong."

I had never discussed the war on this level with a Vietnam vet. "You did what you had to do. That's all any man can do, Paul."

He was weaving. "I never killed…a man…who wasn't trying to…kill me."

"You'd have been a damned fool not to kill a man who was trying to kill you, Paul." He was being chased by the ghosts from his tour in Vietnam.

As he got out of the car and stumbled up the steps to his mother's house, I could hear him mumbling.

"I…didn't know…it was wrong…I…just didn't know…I just…didn't…know…"

After his second tour, Paul told a younger brother "If they ever try to send you over there, Pard, we'll both go to Canada." Paul passed away in 2014.

Paul's highly decorated service in the Marine Corps did not insulate him from the hypocrisy of Smethport's mayor, Russell C. Dickhead, a bigot and general all around politically connected Republican asshole. Russell C. Dickhead was a "good ol' boy" who would indoctrinate youngsters into his racist views by occasionally riding the team bus to a football game and talking about "them goddamned niggers" and telling racist jokes all the while.

Mayor Dickhead owned a clothing store. I went in one time, probably 1967, to get some things. Paul was in the back part of the store at a small table with a couple of the Dickhead's redneck cronies, who were pretty much cut from the same cloth as was Russell. They were asking Paul about the war, killing gooks, and so on. He was their hero.

Flash forward to the 1980s. I was back in Smethport and operating a plumbing service. Russell C. Dickhead calls me up, there is a clogged drain in apartment above his store. Paul was living there with his mother. I took care of the problem and gave Russell the bill. As he was writing out the check he said, "Probably got clogged up by that goddamned long-haired kid!"

Well, fuck me! What blatant hypocrisy. What a fucking scumbag! This was unconscionable. Paul was a fucking hero to Mayor Dickhead when he was getting all shot all to hell in Vietnam, doing everything he could for his country except dying for it. Now that Paul is home and trying to get on with his life with what was left of him that the war hadn't taken, he's just a "goddamned long-haired kid." I held my tongue.

I am convinced Russell C. Dickhead was a fucking Nazi, if not in membership to the party, certainly in world view. I did some work in the upstairs bath at his house. Hanging on the wall of the staircase was an oil painting of Adolph Hitler, probably two by three feet. He told me it was a war souvenir. We talked about WWII and he also said that he had an SS uniform, another war souvenir. When I read his obit after he died, there was mention of Korea service but not WWII. Interesting. A Korean War vet with an oil painting of Hitler who owns an SS uniform. Did Russell C. Dickhead get a stiffy while wearing his SS uniform and admiring himself in a mirror?

WORLD VIEW

My world view and politics are forever colored by the events of the 1960's. I see the same kind of evil sons-of-bitches fucking America over in the same way. The result is that I am a chronic political malcontent who sees America as a corporate oligarchy verging on becoming a corporate-fascist state. We may already be there. The government in Washington D. C. does what the corporate interests want, to hell with the rest of us.

I am not an atheist. I believe in spirit. I do not subscribe to the idea of an all-powerful-God-who-gives-a-shit-about-everything-you-do-from-birth-til-death. I have arrived at the place I am in because of my experiences with psychedelics. I do not regret them. However, I want to make it very clear, that I do not recommend that anyone follow my example in that respect. I was a very lucky individual, buying drugs of questionable substance and quality from complete strangers on the street and freely ingesting them. It was purely stupid.

Nevertheless, the experiences I had were invaluable in terms of my own spiritual and philosophical development. I consider LSD, peyote and mushrooms to be truly sacramental because they can put you directly in touch with spirit. While I don't believe in a god who takes a personal interest in *anything* that happens – let alone *everything* that happens – I still believe in the innate sanctity of life. The spark of consciousness that exists in each sentient being is a divine spark from the fire that would constitute God, the sutratman, the thread self that runs through and binds together all creation, the spiritual part the we all have in common with each other, the thing that truly makes us all brothers and sisters. I think this was the message Jesus wanted us to learn. And if we don't, we still have the capability of turning the world into a charred cinder spinning through space.

John Lennon said "God is the concept by which we measure our pain." I would amend that to "God is the concept by which we justify our bigotry." All too often in the history of the world we have see this manifested in many ways. Too often I have seen those who like to spout that "man is created the image and likeness of God" turn around and show their God to be created in the image and likeness of man, complete with prejudices and intellectual shortcomings. God needs better PR than what he gets from organized religion.

God gets a lot of things shoved off on him that aren't his responsibility. As I stated previously, each one of us has a divine spark that is our consciousness, our life, our outlook on the world. And having that, it is our responsibility to make the world a decent place. We don't need to *pray* for peace, we need to *make* some peace!

In my younger acid-head days, I desperately wanted enlightenment. I wanted to hit the white light. I wanted to become Buddha. In order to do that, one has to extinguish desires and attachments. That I have not done. Guess I won't be enlightened this time around! Oh, I'm still some kind of a half-assed electric Buddhist/Agnostic. I take each day as it comes and try to keep my karma clean.

FINIS

The Henry Wright House still stands on Route 6 outside Smethport, third house on the right heading west past the McKean County Jail. I have driven past it countless times, and each time I think of the years when the five of us lived under that roof. I am the only one left. My last living aunt, my mother's sister, passed away in 2017 at the age of 92.

At 72 and counting, I can still get my ass behind me on a more or less daily basis. My wife and I have been married for 40 years and have a grown daughter who is a mega-talented artist who has thanked us for the way we raised her.

As it is, I am satisfied with my life. We have a familial love that binds us so very tightly. What more is necessary?

ABOUT THE AUTHOR

Born in Kane, Pa, in 1947, Walter Eugene Johnson graduated from Smethport Area High School in 1965. He attended Lock haven State College 1965-1967, majoring in secondary education with a chemistry emphasis. He attended the University of Pittsburgh, Bradford PA., campus for the winter trimester of 1968 before moving to Boston, MA., where he played drums with a band and became immersed in the counterculture. In 1969 Mr. Johnson headed west with a van full of longhairs ending up in San Francisco. After working as a hardware store clerk for three and a half years, he became a state licensed contractor in 1976. He met his wife, Carol, originally from Minnesota, in San Francisco. They were married in 1979.

He plays guitar, harmonica, fiddle, bass and drums. After recording with a band in a 16 track studio, Mr. Johnson built his own 4 track reel-to-reel studio, constructing the mixing console and signal processors himself. He used this setup do produce recording for himself and local bans up into the late 90s when affordable digital recording became practical.

Moving back to his home town of Smethport, PA., in 1981 he operated a plumbing business. He and his wife had a daughter in 1983. Returning to the University of Pittsburgh, Bradford, PA., Campus in 1987, he earned a bachelor's degree in Broadcast Communications with a Creative Writing minor, graduating cum laude in 1989. While attending UPB, Mr. Johnson took on students for guitar, bass and drums. He then worked as a newspaper reporter, an account executive for several radio stations and for cable TV ads for local businesses. In the mid 90s he did editing and layout for a local advertising magazine. Joining Adelphia Communications in Coudersport, PA in 1998, he worked there as a customer service representative and Access database programmer until the company's demise.

He runs an online business, Gene's Weird Stuff, and is a prize winning leather craftsman. Mr. Johnson lives in Hazel Hurst, PA., with his wife.

Email genejhsn@gmail.com

CPSIA information can be obtained
at www.ICGtesting.com
Printed in the USA
FSHW022138241219
65457FS